Tafsīr al-Qurṭubī

Vol. 6

Sūrat al-Mā'idah – The Table

Tafsīr al-Qurṭubī

The General Judgments of the Qur'ān
and Clarification of what it contains
of the *Sunnah* and *Āyah*s of Discrimination

Abū 'Abdullāh Muḥammad ibn Aḥmad ibn Abī Bakr
ibn Farḥ al-Anṣārī al-Khazrajī al-Andalusī al-Qurṭubī

Vol. 6

Sūrat al-Mā'idah – The Table

translated by
Aisha Bewley

DIWAN PRESS
Classical and Contemporary Books on Islam and Sufism

Published by: Diwan Press Ltd.

Website: www.diwanpress.com

E-mail: info@diwanpress.com

By: Abu 'Abdullah Muhammad ibn Ahmad al-Qurtubi

Translated by: Aisha Abdarrahman Bewley

Edited by: Abdalhaqq Bewley

A catalogue record of this book is available from the British Library.

ISBN13: 978-1-914397-00-4 (Paperback)
978-1-914397-01-1 (Casebound)
978-1-914397-02-8 (ePub & Kindle)

Contents

Table of Transliterations

ء	’	ض	ḍ
ا	a	ط	ṭ
ب	b	ظ	ẓ
ت	t	ع	‘
ث	th	غ	gh
ج	j	ف	f
ح	ḥ	ق	q
خ	kh	ك	k
د	d	ل	l
ذ	dh	م	m
ر	r	ن	n
ز	z	ه	h
س	s	و	w
ش	sh	ي	y
ص	ṣ		

Long vowel		Short vowel	
ا	ā	ـَ	a [*fatḥah*]
و	ū	ـُ	u [*ḍammah*]
ي	ī	ـِ	i [*kasrah*]
أَوْ	aw		
أَيْ	ay		

Translator's note

The Arabic for the *āyat*s is from the Algerian State edition of the *riwāyah* of Imam Warsh from the *qirā'ah* of Imam Nāfi' of Madina, whose recitation is one of the ten *mutawātir* recitations that are mass-transmitted from the time of the Prophet ﷺ.

There are minor omissions in the text. Some poems have been omitted which the author quotes to illustrate a point of grammatical usage or as an example of orthography or the usage of a word, often a derivative of the root of the word used in the *āyah*, but not the actual word used. Often it is difficult to convey the sense in English. Occasionally the author explores a grammatical matter or a tangential issue, and some of these may have been shortened. English grammatical terms used to translate Arabic grammatical terms do not have exactly the same meaning, sometimes rendering a precise translation of them problematic and often obscure.

The end of a *juz'* may vary by an *āyah* or two in order to preserve relevant passages.

Sūrat al-Mā'idah – The Table

It is Madinan by consensus. It is related that it was revealed when the Messenger of Allah ﷺ left al-Ḥudaybīyah. An-Naqqāsh mentioned that Abū Salamah said, 'When the Messenger of Allah ﷺ returned from Ḥudaybīyah, he said, "Alī, are you aware that *Sūrat al-Mā'idah* has been revealed to me? There is great benefit in it."' Ibn al-'Arabī says, 'This *ḥadīth* is forged and it is not lawful for a Muslim to believe it is sound. But we do say that *Sūrat al-Mā'idah* is of great benefit and we do not prefer it to any other.' Ibn 'Aṭiyyah said, 'I do not think that it resembles the language of the Prophet ﷺ.'[1] It is related that the Prophet ﷺ said, "*Sūrat al-Mā'idah* calls out in the dominions of Allah: "The one who has it will be delivered from the angels of punishment.""

Part of this *sūrah* was revealed during the Farewell Ḥajj and part in the year of the conquest of Makkah, which is its second *āyah*. All of the Qur'ān that was revealed after the Hijrah is Madinan, whether it was revealed in Madīnah or on a journey, and all that was revealed before the Hijrah is called Makkan. Abū Maysarah says, '*Al-Mā'idah* is part of the last of what was revealed. There is nothing abrogated in it. It contained eighteen obligations. These are found in *āyah*s 3, 4, 5, 6, 38, 95, 103 and 106.' There is a nineteenth obligation in *āyah* 58, which is the only mention of the *adhān* in the Qur'ān. What is mentioned in *Sūrat al-Jumu'ah* is particular to the *Jumu'ah* prayer, whereas here it is about all the prayers.

It is reported that the Messenger of Allah ﷺ recited *Sūrat al-Mā'idah* during the Farewell *Ḥajj* and said, 'People! *Sūrat al-Mā'idah* is one of the last parts of the Qur'ān to be revealed. Consider its *ḥalāl* to be *ḥalāl* and its *ḥarām* to be *ḥarām*.' Something similar is reported from 'Ā'ishah in a *mawqūf* transmission. Jubayr ibn Nufayr said, 'I visited 'Ā'ishah and she asked, "Do you recite Sūrat al-Mā'idah?" "Yes," I replied. She said, "It was one of the last parts of the Qur'ān to be revealed by Allah. Whatever you find is *ḥalāl* in it, consider that to be *ḥalāl*. Whatever you find is *ḥarām* in it, consider that to be *ḥarām*."' Ash-Sha'bī said that nothing of this *sūrah* was abrogated except for: '*...or the sacred months or the sacrificial animals*' (5:2). Some have said that 5:106 was also abrogated.

1 it uses rhyme.

يَٰٓأَيُّهَا ٱلَّذِينَ ءَامَنُوٓاْ أَوۡفُواْ بِٱلۡعُقُودِۚ أُحِلَّتۡ لَكُم بَهِيمَةُ ٱلۡأَنۡعَٰمِ إِلَّا مَا يُتۡلَىٰ عَلَيۡكُمۡ
غَيۡرَ مُحِلِّي ٱلصَّيۡدِ وَأَنتُمۡ حُرُمٌۗ إِنَّ ٱللَّهَ يَحۡكُمُ مَا يُرِيدُ ١

1 You who believe, fulfil your contracts. All livestock animals are lawful for you, except those that are recited to you now; but it is still not lawful to hunt while you are in *iḥrām*. Allah makes whatever judgments He wills.

You who believe, fulfil your contracts.

'Alqamah said, 'Everything in the Qur'ān which has *"You who believe"* in it is Madinan whereas *"O mankind"* is Makkan.' This is usually true and has already been mentioned. This *āyah* is one of those whose eloquence is evident to someone who has insight into language: it contains many meanings in few words. It contains five rulings.

The first is the command to fulfil contracts. The second is that livestock is lawful. The third is that there is an exception in what is mentioned after it. The fourth is that the state of *iḥrām* is an exception for game which is hunted. The fifth is that it is permitted for someone who is not in *iḥrām* to hunt.

An-Naqqāsh related that the companions of al-Kindī said to him, 'Wise one, produce for us the like of this Qur'ān.' He said that he would and retreated for several days and then came out and said, 'By Allah, I cannot, and no one can! I opened the copy of the Qur'ān to *Sūrat al-Mā'idah*, and I looked at it. It speaks of fulfilling and forbidding the breaking of contracts, makes a general ruling of lawfulness and then excepts one exception after another, and then speaks of Allah's Power and Wisdom, all in two lines. No one can do the like of that except in several volumes.'

There are two dialectical possibilities of 'fulfilling': *wafā* and *awfā*. Fulfilling is also referred to in the words: *'Who is truer to his contract than Allah?'* (9:11) and: *'Ibrāhīm, who paid his dues in full.'* (53:37) A poet said, using both:

Ibn Ṭawq fulfilled (*awfā*) his responsibility
as he fulfilled (*wafā*) when he called her at Qilāṣ an-Najm.

'Uqūd means ties. The singular is *'aqd*. The verb is used in reference to making a pledge and tying a rope. The verb is also used for thickening honey. So it is used both for ideas and physical bodies. Al-Ḥuṭay'ah said:

When a people make a contract (*'aqd*)with their neighbour,
tie a rope tight on it and above it tie an upper rope.

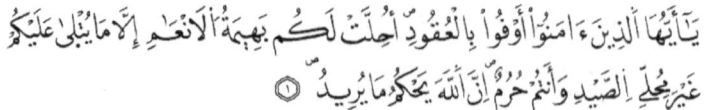

Allah commanded that contracts be fulfilled. Al-Ḥasan said that by contracts He means those which involve debts – which is what a person agrees for himself in respect of buying and selling – hire and renting, marriage and divorce, sharecropping, reconciliation ownership, options, freeing and other matters which are not outside the *Sharī'ah*. It also includes whatever obedience he contracts for himself with Allah, such as *ḥajj*, fasting, *i'tikāf*, prayer, vows and the like which are part of the worship of Islam. As for vows which are not part of worship, they are not included by the consensus of the community. Ibn 'Arabī stated that.

Then it is said that it was revealed about the People of Book since Allah says: *'When Allah made a covenant with those given the Book: "You must make it clear to people and not conceal it."* (3:187)' Ibn Jurayj said that it was particular to the People of the Book and revealed about them. It is said that it is general, and that is sound. The term 'believers' can include the believers of the People of the Book because there was a contract between them and Allah in their Books to fulfil the trust concerning Muḥammad ﷺ and they are commanded to do that here and elsewhere. Ibn 'Abbās said that the meaning covers what Allah made lawful and made unlawful and what is obligatory and the limits He set regarding all things. That is what Mujāhid and others said.

Ibn Shihāb said, 'I read the letter of the Messenger of Allah ﷺ which he wrote to 'Amr ibn Ḥazm when he sent him to Najrān. It began: "This is clarification to people from Allah and His Messenger: *'O you who believe, fulfil your contracts'* and it includes the *āyah*s until the end of *āyah* 4: *"Allah is swift at reckoning."*"'

Az-Zajjāj said, 'The meaning is: "Fulfil Allah's contract with you and your contracts with one another."' All of this refers to the general meaning, which is sound. The Prophet ﷺ said, 'Believers abide by their agreed conditions.' He ﷺ said, 'Every agreed condition which is not in the Book of Allah is void, even if there are a hundred of them.' He was explaining that the contracts which must be fulfilled is those which are in harmony with the Book of Allah, in other words Allah's *Dīn*. If it is contrary to it, then it is void as the Prophet ﷺ confirmed by his words: 'If anyone does something which is not part this affair of ours, it will be rejected.'

Ibn Isḥāq said, 'The tribes of Quraysh met in the house of 'Abdullāh ibn Jud'ān because of his honour and lineage, and they made a contract that there would not be anyone in Makkah who had been wronged – of their people or others – but that they would stand with him until his wrong was righted. Quraysh called that alliance "The Fuḍūl Alliance". It is that about which the Messenger ﷺ said, "I was present at an alliance in the house of 'Abdullāh ibn Jud'ān, that I would not exchange for red camels. If I were invited to it in Islam, I would respond.'" This alliance is what is meant by his words ﷺ, 'Any alliance there was in the Jāhiliyyah is only strengthened by Islam' because it was in harmony with the *Sharī'ah* since it commands anyone who wrongs another to act justly. As for false treaties and invalid contracts for the sake of wrongdoing and aggression, Islam has destroyed them. Praise belongs to Allah.

Ibn Isḥāq said, 'Al-Walīd ibn 'Uqbah wronged al-Ḥusayn ibn 'Alī regarding some property of his on the strength of al-Walīd's authority since he was the governor of Madīnah. Al-Ḥusayn said to him, "I swear by Allah that you will give me my fair share or I will take my sword and stand in the Mosque of the Messenger of Allah ﷺ and invoke the Alliance of Fuḍūl!" 'Abdullāh ibn az-Zubayr said, "I swear by Allah that if he calls me I will take my sword and stand with him until he has his due or we die together!" When that reached al-Miswar ibn Makhramah, he said the same, and it reached 'Abd ar-Raḥmān ibn 'Uthmān ibn 'Ubaydullāh at-Taymī and he also said the same. When al-Walīd heard about that, he gave him satisfaction.'

All livestock animals are lawful for you

This is addressed to all those who believe. The Arabs had superstitious customs about livestock – *baḥīrah, sā'ibah, waṣīlah* and *ḥām* – which will be explained in the appropriate place (5:103). This *āyah* was revealed to remove those illusions and false opinions. There is disagreement about the meaning of '*bahīmatu-l-an'ām*' (*livestock animals*). The noun '*bahīmah*' means all animals with four legs. They are called that because they are unable to speak or understand, cannot discriminate, and lack intelligence. A door which is '*mubham*' is locked, '*bahīm*' describes a black night, and '*buhmah*' describes a hero who does not know from which direction he will be attacked.

The noun '*an'ām*' includes camels, cattle and sheep and goats. They are called this because the gentleness of their gait. Allah says: *'And He created livestock. There is warmth for you in them, and various uses…'* (16:5-7) Allah also says: *'And also animals for riding and for haulage'* (6:142). This means both large and small. Then He explains what they are and says: '*…eight kinds in pairs*' (39:6). He says: *'He has made houses for you out of cattle hides which are light for you to carry both when you are travelling and when you are staying in one place. And from their wool,'* referring to sheep, *'and fur'*, referring to camels, *'and hair'* (16:80), referring to goats. These are three proofs that tell us that the term *an'ām* includes these species: camels, cattle and sheep and goats, and this is the position of Ibn 'Abbās and al-Ḥasan. Al-Harawī said that *na'am* means camels.

Aṭ-Ṭabarī said that some people say that it also includes wild animals like antelopes, wildebeests, asses and others. That was mentioned by other than aṭ-Ṭabarī, ar-Rabī', Qatādah and ad-Ḍaḥḥāk. It is as if Allah were saying, 'Livestock are lawful for you,' and then ascribing the genus to that making it more specific. Ibn 'Aṭiyyah said, 'This is a good view because livestock falls into eight kinds. Other animals that are added to them are called "livestock" because they are joined with them. It is as if beasts of prey like lions and fanged animals are outside of the definition of livestock. So "*livestock animals*" are those with four legs that graze.'

According to this, it would include all animals with hooves because they graze and do not kill prey. That is not the case because Allah says: *'And He created livestock. There is warmth for you in them, and various uses.'* (16:5) Then He added to that: *'And horses, mules and donkeys.'* (16:8) When He mentioned those, and added them to livestock, it indicates that they are not part of them. Allah knows best.

It is said that '*livestock animals*' are those that are not game because game is called 'wild' (*waḥshī*), not *bahīmah.* This goes back to the first statement. It is related that 'Abdullāh ibn 'Umar said that '*bahīmatu-l-an'ām*' are foetuses that emerge when the mother is slaughtered. They are eaten without being slaughtered. Ibn 'Abbās said that. It is unlikely because Allah says: '*...except those that are recited to you now.*' There is no exception about the foetuses. Mālik said that slaughtering an animal also slaughters its foetus, if it is not born alive and its hair has begun to grow and its form is complete. If the form is not complete and hair has not begun to grow, it may not be eaten unless it is born alive and then slaughtered. If they rush to slaughter it and it dies on its own, some say that that constitutes slaughter and some say that it does not.

except those that are recited to you now;

This means except what is recited to you in the Qur'ān and the *Sunnah.* That includes carrion (5:3) and the words of the Prophet ﷺ, 'Every wild beast with fangs is unlawful.' If it is said that the words: *'what is recited to you now'* do not include the *Sunnah*, we reply that the *sunnah* of the Messenger of Allah ﷺ is part of the Book. There are two corroborations which support that. One is the *ḥadīth* of al-'Asīf which contains the words: 'I will decide between you by the Book of Allah,' and stoning is not a text in the Book of Allah. The second is the *ḥadīth* of Ibn Mas'ūd: 'Why should I not curse the one who curses the Messenger of Allah ﷺ when it is in the Book of Allah?' This will be further discussed in *al-Ḥashr.* It is possible that *'except those that are recited to you'* is now or 'what is recited to you' is in the future on the tongue of the Messenger of Allah ﷺ. So it is evidence that it is permitted to delay clarification, when it is not necessary at a particular time, until the time when it is needed.

but it is still not lawful to hunt while you are in *iḥrām*.

Hunting is not allowed to those in *iḥrām,* but others may hunt. That which is not game is allowed for both, whether they are in *iḥrām* or not. Grammarians disagree about whether it is an exception or not. The Basrans say that it is another exception to '*livestock animals*'. So both exceptions are to '*livestock animals*' and it is an exception to them as well. It implies: except those that are recited to you except for game while you are in *iḥrām'* which differs from the form of the exception in 15:57-58 as will be explained there.

It is also said to be an exception to the exception and so it is in the position of Allah's words: '*We have been sent to a people who are evildoers.'* (15:57) If it had been like that, it would be obliged to permit hunting while in *iḥrām* because it is an exception to what is forbidden since the words: '*except those that are recited to you'* is an exception with respect to their permissibility. This approach is discarded. It then means: 'Athough hunting game is not lawful when you are in *iḥrām,* livestock animals are lawful for you except for what has been recited to you concerning things other than game.' It is also permitted for it to mean: 'Fulfil your contracts without thinking it lawful to hunt, but livestock is lawful for you except what is recited to you.'

Al-Farrā' said that the words '*except those that are recited to you*' could be in the nominative as an appositive, on the basis that they are added by '*illā'* as it is added by '*lā*'. The Basrans only permit it to be in the indefinite and what is close to it of generic nouns, as in 'The people came except for Zayd.' He considers the accusative in '*ghayra*' to be in the accusative in the *ḥāl* which is in 'fulfil.' Al-Akhfash said it means, '"You who believe, fulfill your contracts except to those who consider game lawful."' Others said that it is a *ḥāl* modifying *kum* in '*lakum*'. It implies: Livestock animals are lawful for you without that making game lawful.

Then it is said that it is possible that that *iḥlāl* refers to people, meaning: 'do not make game lawful while in a state of *iḥrām.'* It is also permitted for it to refer to Allah Almighty, meaning: 'I have made lawful for you livestock animals except for game during the time you are in *iḥrām.'* It is as you say, 'I have made this lawful for you except for allowing it to you on Friday.' If you say that it refers to people, then it means 'not making game lawful' and the *nūn* is elided for lightening.

while you are in *iḥrām*.

This is being in *iḥrām* for the *ḥajj* or *'umrah*. *Ḥurum* is the plural of *ḥirām* which is the one in *iḥrām* on the *ḥajj*. A poet said:

I told her, 'Return to yourself.
I am in *iḥrām (ḥirām)*, and furthermore have said the *talbīyah*.

Someone is called this because the one who enters this state is forbidden women, perfume and the like. The verb *aḥrama* is also used for entering the *Ḥaram*, and so the game of the *Ḥaram* is also unlawful. Al-Ḥasan, Ibrāhīm and Yaḥyā ibn Waththāb recited *'ḥurm'* (instead of *'ḥurum'*) which is the dialect of Tamīm. They say *'rusl'* for *'rusul'*, *'kutb'* for *'kutub'* and the like.

Allah makes whatever judgments He wills.

This strengthens these legal rulings which differed from Arab customs. It means: 'You, Muḥammad, hear the abrogation of their rulings to which Allah calls attention. He is the King of all. He makes whatever judgments He wills.' *'There is no reversing His judgment.'* (13:41) He legislates whatever He wishes however He wishes.

يَٰٓأَيُّهَا ٱلَّذِينَ ءَامَنُوا۟ لَا تُحِلُّوا۟ شَعَٰٓئِرَ ٱللَّهِ وَلَا ٱلشَّهْرَ ٱلْحَرَامَ وَلَا ٱلْهَدْىَ وَلَا ٱلْقَلَٰٓئِدَ
وَلَآ ءَآمِّينَ ٱلْبَيْتَ ٱلْحَرَامَ يَبْتَغُونَ فَضْلًا مِّن رَّبِّهِمْ وَرِضْوَٰنًا ۚ وَإِذَا حَلَلْتُمْ فَٱصْطَادُوا۟
وَلَا يَجْرِمَنَّكُمْ شَنَـَٔانُ قَوْمٍ أَن صَدُّوكُمْ عَنِ ٱلْمَسْجِدِ ٱلْحَرَامِ أَن تَعْتَدُوا۟ ۘ وَتَعَاوَنُوا۟ عَلَى
ٱلْبِرِّ وَٱلتَّقْوَىٰ ۖ وَلَا تَعَاوَنُوا۟ عَلَى ٱلْإِثْمِ وَٱلْعُدْوَٰنِ ۚ وَٱتَّقُوا۟ ٱللَّهَ ۖ إِنَّ ٱللَّهَ شَدِيدُ
ٱلْعِقَابِ ﴿٢﴾

2 You who believe! do not profane the sacred rites of Allah or the sacred months, or the sacrificial animals, or the ritual garlands, or those heading for the Sacred House, desiring profit and good pleasure from their Lord. When you have come out of *iḥrām*, then hunt for game. Do not let hatred for a people who debar you from the Masjid al-Haram incite you into going beyond the limits. Help each other to goodness and *taqwā*. Do not help each other to wrongdoing and enmity. Have *taqwā* of Allah. Allah is Severe in Retribution.

do not profane the sacred rites of Allah

This is addressed to those who are truly believers. 'Do not transgress the limits of Allah in any matter.' *Sha'ā'ir* is the plural of *sha'īrah.* Ibn Fāris said that the singular is *shi'ārah.* It is better. A *sha'īrah* is a camel which is sacrificed. *Ish'ār* means to cut its hump so that it bleeds and so that it is known that it is a sacrifice. *Ish'ār* is to make known by physical means. The verb *ash'ara* is to make a mark by which it is known that the animal is a sacrificial camel. From the same root comes *mashā'ir,* the singular of which is *mash'ar,* which are the places which are known by signs. From the same root comes *shi'r* (poetry) produced by a poet (*shu'ūr* and *shā'ir*). That is because by his poetry he makes understood what is not understood by another. There is also *sha'īr* (barley) because of the hair on its head. *Sha'ā'ir* denotes either the sacrificial animals or all the sacred rites of the *ḥajj,* as Ibn 'Abbās said. Mujāhid said that it comprises Ṣafā and Marwah, the sacrifices, and the camels. A poet said:

> We kill them generation after generation, and you see them
> with the sacrificial (*sha'ā'ir*) animals approaching.

The idolaters used to make *ḥajj* and *'umra* and brought sacrifices with them. The Muslims wanted to attack them and Allah revealed this. 'Aṭā' ibn Abī Rabāḥ said that it is all that Prophet ﷺ commanded and forbade. Al-Ḥasan said, 'It is all the *dīn* of Allah,' as when He says: *'That is it. As for those who honour Allah's sacred rites, that comes from the taqwā in their hearts.'* (22:32) It means the *dīn* of Allah. This is the preferred position because it is general.

Scholars disagree about the marking of the sacrifices. The majority permit it. Then they disagree about which side of the animal should be marked. Ash-Shāfi'ī, Aḥmad and Abū Thawr say that it is the right side, and that is related from Ibn 'Umar. It is confirmed that Ibn 'Abbās stated that the Prophet ﷺ marked his camel on the right side of its hump. Muslim and others transmitted that, and it is sound. It is also related that he marked his camels on the left side. Abū 'Umar ibn 'Abd al-Barr says, 'I consider this *ḥadīth* to be *munkar.*' The sound transmission is that which Muslim has from Ibn 'Abbās.' He said that it is not sound from anyone else.

One group say that the marking should be on the left side, and that is the position of Mālik. He said, 'There is no harm in doing it on the right side.' Mujāhid said that it can be done on either side, and that is one of the two positions of Aḥmad. Abu Ḥanīfah forbids all of that, saying that it is torturing animals, but the *ḥadīth* rejects that. Furthermore, that is like branding by which ownership is known. It is as if he had not heard of this in the *Sharī'ah*! It is very famous among scholars.

What I have seen written in the books of Ḥanafī scholars is that the position of Abu Ḥanīfah is that marking is disliked. Abū Yūsuf and ash-Shaybānī, however, say that it not disliked and not *sunnah*, but permissible. That is since marking is notification, it is a *sunnah* like garlanding. The unlawful aspect of it is that it is a wound and mutilation. So it contains both *sunnah* and innovation and is made allowable. Abu Ḥanīfah holds that marking is mutilation and is unlawful since it entails torturing an animal which is disliked, and what is related from the Messenger of Allah ﷺ was at the beginning when the desert Arabs used to loot all property unless it was a marked sacrificial animal. They only recognised sacrificial camels by marking. Then that was removed when the excuse was removed. That is how it is related from Ibn 'Abbās.

It is related that the Imam, Shaykh Abū Manṣūr al-Māturīdī, said, 'It is possible that Abu Ḥanīfah disliked the marking done by the people of his time because it was taken to excess by marking on the face. As for that which is not excessive, as was done in the time of the Messenger of Allah ﷺ, it is good.' Abū Ja'far aṭ-Ṭaḥāwī mentioned something like that. This is the excuse offered for Abu Ḥanīfah by the Ḥanafī scholars regarding the *ḥadīth* related about marking. They heard it, it reached them and they knew it. They said, 'According to the view that it is disliked, no one goes into *iḥrām* by it because doing something disliked is not counted as one of the practices.'

or the sacred months,

This (*shahr*) is a singular noun which is used generically for all sacred months. They are four, three in a row and one on its own, and will be mentioned in *Sūrat at-Tawbah*. The meaning is: 'Do not profane them by fighting or raiding in them nor change them around to make them lawful.' They used to do that by delaying the month.

or the sacrificial animals, or the ritual garlands,

This means: 'Do not profane sacrificial animals in general.' The garlands mark them out as being sacrifices. *Qalā'id* (garlands) is the plural of *qilādah*. So Allah forbade profaning sacrificial animals altogether and then mentioned garlanded animals to stress their sanctity. A *hady* is what is given (*uhdā*) to the House of Allah, be it a camel, cow or sheep. The singular is *hadyah, hadiyah, hady*. Those who say that *sha'ā'ir* means rites say that 'sacrificial animals' clarifies them in particular. Those who say that it means the sacrificial animals, say that a *mash'ar* is marked by blood on its hump and a *hady* is not marked but it is enough that they be garlanded. It is said that the difference is that *sha'ā'ir* are camels and *hady*s are cattle, sheep, garments and all that is offered.

The majority say that *hady* is general and includes all that one uses to draw near to Allah with respect to sacrifices and *sadaqāt*. Confirming that are the words of the Prophet ﷺ: 'Someone who goes early to Jumu'ah is like someone who sacrifices (*muhdī*) a camel,' and it goes on to 'sacrifices (*muhdī*) an egg.' So he ﷺ called it a *hady*. Calling an egg a sacrifice can only be because *ṣadaqah* is meant by it. That is like scholars saying that when someone says, 'I have made this garment of mine a sacrifice (*hady*),' he must give it away as *ṣadaqah*. However, it is usually applied to one of the three categories of camels, cattle and sheep and driving them to the *Ḥaram* and slaughtering them there. This is taken as the custom of the *Sharī'ah* from His words: *'If you are forcibly prevented, make whatever sacrifice (hady) is feasible'* (2:196) which means sheep, and: *...the reprisal for it is a livestock animal (hady) equivalent to what he killed, as judged by two just men among you'* (5:95), and: *'Anyone who comes out of* iḥrām *between 'umrah and ḥajj should make whatever sacrifice (hady) is feasible'* (2:196), the minimum of which is a sheep according to the *fuqahā'*. Mālik said, 'When someone says, "My garment is a *hady*," then he must use its price to buy a *hady*.'

'Garlands (qalā'id)' are what people garland them with to protect them. There is some elision here, meaning: 'nor those with garlands.' Then this was abrogated. Ibn 'Abbās said, 'Two *āyah*s are abrogated in *al-Mā'idah*: the *āyah* of garlands and the words: *"If they come to you, you can either judge between them or turn away from them."* (5:43) The *āyah* about the garlands was abrogated by the command to kill the idolaters wherever they were and in any month. (9:5) The other *āyah* was abrogated by the words of Allah: *"Judge between them by what Allah has sent down."* (5:49)' It is also said that what is meant are the garlands themselves and it forbids taking the bark of the trees of the Haram to use as garlands to seek security, as Mujāhid and Muṭarrif ibn ash-Shikhkhīr stated. Allah knows best.

The true meaning of *hady* is that it is anything that is given for which no recompense is given. The *fuqahā'* agree that if someone says, 'I owe a *hady* to Allah,' he must send its price to Makkah. As for the garlands, they are what are hung from the humps and necks of sacrificial animals as a sign that they are for Allah: be it sandals or anything else. That was an Abrahamic custom which existed in the Jāhiliyyah and Islam affirmed it. It is the *sunnah* for cattle and sheep. 'Ā'ishah said, 'The Messenger of Allah ﷺ once brought sacrifices to the House in the form of sheep and he garlanded them.' Al-Bukhārī and Muslim transmitted it. A group of scholars believe this, namely ash-Shāfi'ī, Aḥmad,

Isḥāq, Abū Thawr and Ibn Ḥabīb. Mālik and the people of opinion negate it. It is as if they had not heard of this *ḥadīth* about garlanding sheep, or it reached them, but they refuted it since only al-Aswad has it from 'Ā'ishah. Allah knows best. As for cattle, if they have humps, they are marked like camels. Ibn 'Umar said that. Mālik said that. Ash-Shāfi'ī said, 'They are garlanded and marked and there is no distinction.' Sa'īd ibn Jubayr said, 'They are garlanded and not marked.' This is the soundest position when they do not have humps. Then they are more like sheep than camels. Allah knows best. They agree that when someone garlands a camel with the intention of *iḥrām* and drives it, it becomes sanctified as Allah says here. He did not mention *iḥrām* because when garlanding is mentioned, it is known that that is the same as *iḥrām*.

Someone can send sacrificial animals without driving them himself and then he is not in *iḥrām* based on the *ḥadīth* of 'Ā'ishah. She said, 'I plaited the garlands of the sacrificial camels of the Messenger of Allah ﷺ with my own hands and then he garlanded them with his own hands. Then he sent them with my father – and nothing was unlawful for the Messenger of Allah ﷺ that Allah has made lawful for him – until the sacrifice was slaughtered.' Al-Bukhārī transmitted it. This is the position of the school of Mālik and of ash-Shāfi'ī, Aḥmad, Isḥāq and most scholars.

It is related from Ibn 'Abbās that someone who does that becomes like someone in *iḥrām*. Ibn 'Abbās said, 'If someone offers a *hady*, he is forbidden what is unlawful for someone on *ḥajj* until the *hady* is slaughtered.' Al-Bukhārī related it. This is the position of Ibn 'Umar, 'Aṭā', Mujāhid and Sa'īd ibn Jubayr. Al-Khaṭṭābī related it from the People of Opinion and they use as evidence the *ḥadīth* of Jābir ibn 'Abdullāh who said, 'I was sitting with the Prophet ﷺ when he cut his shirt open at the neck and then took it off over his feet. The people looked at the Prophet ﷺ and he said, "I commanded my camels, which I sent, to be garlanded and marked at such-and-such place. Then I put on my shirt and forgot. I would not remove my shirt from over my head." He had sent his camels on while he remained in Madīnah.' Its *isnād* contains 'Abd ar-Raḥmān ibn 'Aṭā' ibn Abī Labībah who is weak.

If someone garlands a sheep and sends it with them (the people going on *ḥajj*), the Kufans say that he is not in *iḥrām* because garlanding a sheep is neither *sunnah* nor one of the rites. The reason for this is that it is feared that a wolf might seize it and it will not reach the *Ḥaram* which is not the case with camels. It is left until it reaches water, grazes in the trees and reaches the *Ḥaram*. We find in *Ṣaḥīḥ Bukhārī* that 'Ā'ishah, the *Umm al-Mu'minīn*, said, 'I plaited their garlands from some dyed wool that I had.' Allah says: *'On the day that the mountains will be like tufts of coloured wool.'* (101:5)

Once a sacrificial animal (*hady*) is garlanded or marked, it is not permitted to sell it or give it away a because sacrificing it has become an obligation. If the person then dies, the animal is not inherited from him and the sacrifice is carried out. This is not the case with other sacrificial animals (*dhabīḥah*) which only become obligatory when they have been slaughtered, especially in the view of Mālik, unless someome has verbally made it mandatory. If he has done so verbally, then the sacrifice is accepted. This is as when he says, 'I have made this specific sheep a sacrifice.' He must do that. If it is lost and then he finds it in the days of sacrifice or afterwards, he sacrifices it and is not permitted to sell it. If he has purchased another sacrifice, then he slaughters both of them according to Aḥmad and Isḥāq. Ash-Shāfi'ī said, 'There is no replacement for it if it is lost or stolen. Replacement only applies to an obligation.' It is related that Ibn 'Abbās said, 'If it is lost, the requirement is met.'

If someone dies on the Day of Sacrifice before the sacrifice, his sacrificial animal is inherited from him like the rest of his property. This is not the case with a *hady*. Aḥmad and Abū Thawr said that it is sacrificed in any case. Al-Awzā'ī said, 'It is sacrificed unless he has a debt that cannot be settled except by that sacrifice in which case it is sold to cover the debt.' If he dies after it has been sacrificed, his heirs do not inherit it from him, but prepare it for eating and *ṣadaqah* as he would have done. Its meat is not distributed according to the rules of inheritance. If the sacrificial animal develops defects before slaughter, then its owner must replace it, which is not the case with the *hady*. This is a summary of the position of Mālik. It is also said that the owner must replace the *hady*. The first is more correct and Allah knows best.

or those heading for the Sacred House.

This comes from *ammama*, to aim for something. Al-A'mash recited *'walā āmmiyy'* with *iḍāfah*. This means: 'Do not stop the unbelievers making for the Sacred House for the sake of worship and devotion.' It is said that what is in these *āyah*s is about forbidding idolaters or recognising their sanctity through garlanding or heading for the House. It was, of course, abrogated by the *Āyah* of the Sword where Allah says: '*...kill the idolaters wherever you find them*' (9:5) and: '*...after this year they should not come near the Masjid al-Ḥarām.*' (9:28) After that it was no longer possible for an idolater to perform *ḥajj* or to be safe in the Sacred Months, even if he had garlanded *hady*s and was making *ḥajj*. That is related from Ibn 'Abbās and was stated by Ibn Zayd as will be mentioned.

Some people say that it is not abrogated and that it is about the Muslims, and Allah forbade alarming the Muslims heading for His House and the prohibition is general to the Sacred Months and other times. However, the Sacred Months are singled out out of respect. This follows the position of 'Aṭā'. It means that the sacred hallmarks must not be profaned. That is on account of Allah's commands and prohibitions and what He has told people must not be profaned and it is why Abū Maysarah said that it is an *āyah* of judgment. Mujāhid said that only the part of about garlands is abrogated. A man would use some of the bark of the *Ḥaram* as a garland and not be approached and then that was abrogated. Ibn Jurayj said, 'This *āyah* forbade al-Ḥajjāj from cutting off their routes.'

Ibn Zayd said, 'The *āyah* was revealed in the year of the Conquest when the Messenger of Allah ﷺ was in Makkah. Some of the idolaters came to perform *ḥajj* and *'umrah* and the Muslims said, "Messenger of Allah, these are idolaters. We must attack them!" and the *āyah* was revealed: *"...or those heading for the Sacred House."*' It is said that this was Shurayḥ ibn Ḍubay'ah al-Ḥuṭam al-Bakrī. He was captured by the army of the Messenger of Allah ﷺ while on *'umrah* and the *āyah* was revealed. Then it was later abrogated. This al-Ḥuṭam was involved in the Riddah in Yamāmah and was killed as an apostate. It is related that he was brought to the Prophet ﷺ in Madīnah while his horses were outside of Madīnah and asked, 'What do you call people to?' He ﷺ answered, 'To testify that there is no god but Allah and Muḥammad is the Messenger of Allah, to establish the prayer and to pay the *zakāt*.' He said, 'Good. However, I have commanders and I never do anything without them. Perhaps I will become Muslim and bring them.' The Prophet ﷺ said to his Companions, 'A man has come to you who speaks with the tongue of shayṭān.' When he left, the Prophet ﷺ said, 'He entered with the face of an unbeliever and left with the back of someone treacherous. The man is not a Muslim.' He passed by some of the grazing animals of the Madinans and drove them with him. They pursued him but did not catch him. He left, saying:

'The night enveloped them when Ḥuṭam drove them off.
  The camels and sheep had no herdsman
And no butcher in an abattoir.
  They spent the night asleep when the son of Hind does not sleep.
A boy spent the night dividing them like arrows,
  large in the flanks, light of foot.'

When the Prophet ﷺ set out in the year of the Fulfilled Hajj, he heard the *talbīyah*s of those from Yamāmah performing *ḥajj* and remarked, 'This is al-

Ḥuṭam and his people.' He had garlanded the animals of Madīnah that he had looted and given them to the people of Makkah. They went out to look for him and this was revealed. It means: 'Do not profane what has been marked for Allah, even if they are idolaters.' Ibn 'Abbās mentioned it.

If the *āyah* is one of judgment, then the words *'do not profane the sacred rites of Allah'* obliges completion of the rites. This is why scholars say that if a man begins the *ḥajj* and then invalidates it, he must perform all the actions of the *ḥajj* and is not permitted to omit any of them, even if his *ḥajj* is invalid, and then he must make it up the following year. Abū al-Layth as-Samarqandī said that *'Sacred Months'* is abrogated by Allah's words: *'Fight the idolaters totally'* (9:36), and that the words: *'the sacrificial animals or the ritual garlands'* are a judgment and not abrogated. So anyone who garlands a sacrificial animals and makes the intention of *iḥrām* becomes someone in *iḥrām* and, by the evidence of this *āyah*, is not permitted to be considered profane. These judgments are added together and some are abrogated and some are not abrogated.

desiring profit and good pleasure from their Lord.

The majority of commentators say that they may seek bounty and profit in trade and also seek Allah's pleasure in their opinion and desire. It is said that some of them seek trade and some seek to perform *ḥajj* for the pleasure of Allah, even if they do not obtain it. Some Arabs used to believe that the repayment was after their death and resurrection. It is not unlikely that they would have some sort of alleviation in the Fire. Ibn 'Aṭiyyah said, 'This *āyah* is one by which Allah is gentle and kind to the Arabs to relieve them so that they could mix with the people and go to the festival and listen to the Qur'ān. Faith entered their hearts and they had the evidence.' This was revealed in the year of the conquest of Makkah and abrogated later in 9 AH by *Sūrat at-Tawbah.*

When you have come out of ihrām, then hunt for game.

The consensus of the people is that it is a command that is permission for what was forbidden on account of being in *iḥrām* for the *ḥajj.* That [being a command] is related from many scholars, but it is not sound. It is rather in that linguistic form in which a matter reverts to its previous basic state before the prohibition occurred. That is the position of the school of Qāḍī Abū aṭ-Ṭayyib and others, because that which demands the obligation exists and did so before the prohibition which is no longer effective. The evidence is found in Allah's words: *'When the Sacred Months are over, kill the idolaters'* (9:5) where the verbal form indicates the obligation because what is meant is *jihād*. But here permissibility is understood as is the case elsewhere as in: *'Then when the prayer is finished spread through the earth.'* (62:10) There are other examples where the consensus is that a command is not intended. Allah knows best.

Do not let hatred for a people who debar you from the Masjid al-Ḥarām incite you into going beyond the limits.

'Do not be moved by that,' as Ibn 'Abbās and Qatādah said, and it is the view of al-Kisā'ī and Abū al-'Abbās. It is transitive with two objects. You say, 'That moved me to hate you.' A poet said:

You thrust Abū 'Uyaynah with a thrust
which made (*jaramat*) Fazārah hate [you] afterwards.

Al-Akhfash said, 'Do not let it make you full of malice. Do not be moved to abandon the right for the wrong and justice for injustice.' The Prophet ﷺ said, 'Return the trust to the one who entrusted it to you and do not betray the one who betrayed you.' This has already been discussed. It is like the *āyah*: *'If anyone oversteps the limits against you, overstep against him the same as he did to you.'* (2:194)

It is said that a person is the '*jarīmah*' of his family, meaning 'their earner'. '*Jarīmah*' and '*jārim*' mean 'earner'. *Ajrama-l-ithm* means 'earning sin'. A poet said:

The earner (*jarīmah*) of the chicks is the one that rises at the top of the mountain.
You see the fat (*ṣalīb*) remaining on the bones of what it has collected,

It means that it is the one who collects the food and *ṣalīb* is fat. 'Earning' is the basis of the root *j-r-m*.

Ibn Fāris said that one says *jarama* and *ajrama*, and the expression '*lā jarama*' means 'there is no avoiding it'. Its root is from *jarama*, to earn, as we mentioned in the above poem about Fazarah. Another said:

You who complain of 'Ukl and what they have brought on (*jaramat*)
the tribes of killing and misfortunes.

The verb *jarama, yajrima, jarm* also means 'to cut'. 'Alī ibn 'Īsā ar-Rammānī said that that is the root meaning. *Jarama* is also to incite someone to do something in order to cut it off from someone else, since acquiring is earning by attaching it through earning. *Jaram* is also a right because the right is definite. Al-Khalīl said that Allah's words: *'There is no doubt at all (lā jarama) that they will receive the Fire…'* (16:62) mean that it is right that they receive the Fire. Al-Kisā'ī said that *jarama* and *ajrama* are two dialects with the same meaning: earn. Ibn Mas'ūd recited *'yujrimmannakum'* which also means 'bring you about to'. The Basrans do not know it with a *ḍammah*. They only say *'jaram'*.

Shanān is hatred. It is recited both with a *fatḥah* and *sukūn* on the *nūn*. The verb is *shana'a, yashna'u* which means to hate. The verbal nouns are *shan'a, shan'ah, shanān* and *shana'ān*. So it means: hatred for some people who have barred you should not result in you overstepping. It means your hatred of a people and the verbal noun is ascribed to the object.

Ibn Zayd said, 'When the Muslims were barred from the House in the year of al-Ḥudaybīyah, some of the idolaters passed them intending to perform *'umrah* and the Muslims said, "We will bar them as their friends barred us!" and this *āyah* was revealed, meaning, "Do not attack them and do not debar them in the way that their companions debarred you."'

Abū 'Amr and Ibn Kathīr recite *'in* [rather than *'an'*] *ṣaddakum'*. That is what Abu 'Ubayd preferred. Ibn 'Aṭiyyah said, 'It is for repayment', meaning if the like of that action occurs in the future. The first reading is the more probable meaning. An-Naḥḥās said, 'As for the reading with "*in*", most scholars of grammar, *ḥadīth* and investigation forbid it for various reasons. One is that the *āyah* was revealed in the year of the Conquest in 8 AH and the idolaters stopped the Muslims at Ḥudaybīyah in 6 AH. So the barring took place before the *āyah* was revealed. If it is read as "*in*", then it would have had to have been after it. If it is read as "*an*" then it is about the past. That is why the "*an*" is obliged. Furthermore, even if this *ḥadīth* were not sound, the *fatḥah* would have been necessary because His words: *"Do not profane the sacred rites of Allah..."* indicate that Makkah was in their possession and they were only forbidden this because they were able to hunt from the Sacred House. Therefore "*an*" is obliged because it is in the past.' *'Going beyond'* is in the accusative as the object, in other words do not let hatred for a people incite you to transgression. Abū Ḥātim and Abū 'Ubayd did not acknowledge *'shanān'* with a *sukūn* on the *nūn* because the verbal nouns come vowelled in such cases. Others disagree with them and say that it is not a verbal noun, but a noun which is an active participle on the measure of *kaslān* and *ghaḍbān*.

Help each other to goodness and *taqwā*.

Al-Akhfash said that this is separate from the words before it. This is a command to all people to help one another to goodness and *taqwā*, to encourage what Allah has commanded and to act by it, and to leave what Allah has forbidden and refrain from it. This agrees with the words of the Prophet ﷺ: 'The one who guides to good is like the one who does it.' People also say, 'The one who guides to evil is like the one who does it.'

It is said that *birr* and *taqwā* are synonyms and they are both used here for emphasis since every goodness is *taqwā* and every *taqwā* is goodness. Ibn 'Aṭiyyah says, 'There is a degree of lack of particularity here. The custom about these two expressions is that *birr* includes both the obligatory and the recommended, and *taqwā* is concern for the obligatory alone. It is permissible to replace one word with the other.' Ibn al-Māwardī said, 'Allah recommended mutual help to goodness and joined *taqwā* to it because *taqwā* contains Allah's pleasure and *birr* contains people's pleasure. Whoever combines the two has perfect happiness and complete blessing.'

Ibn Khuwayzimandād said, 'Mutual help to goodness and *taqwā* has various aspects. It is obligatory for a scholar to help people with his knowledge and teach them. A wealthy person helps with his wealth and a brave person helps with his courage in the Way of Allah. So by mutual support the Muslims are like one hand. "The blood of the believers is the same. Their protection extends to the lowest of them, and they are like one hand against others."'

Do not help each other to wrongdoing and enmity.

This is a prohibition. It is obliged to turn away from a transgressor and not abet him and to turn him away from what he is doing. This ruling is connected to crimes and transgression which wrong people. So Allah commands *taqwā* and then gives a comprehensive threat.

حُرِّمَتْ عَلَيْكُمُ الْمَيْتَةُ وَالدَّمُ وَلَحْمُ الْخِنزِيرِ وَمَا أُهِلَّ لِغَيْرِ اللَّهِ بِهِ وَالْمُنْخَنِقَةُ
وَالْمَوْقُوذَةُ وَالْمُتَرَدِّيَةُ وَالنَّطِيحَةُ وَمَا أَكَلَ السَّبُعُ إِلَّا مَا ذَكَّيْتُمْ
وَمَا ذُبِحَ عَلَى النُّصُبِ وَأَن تَسْتَقْسِمُوا بِالْأَزْلَامِ ذَٰلِكُمْ فِسْقٌ الْيَوْمَ يَئِسَ
الَّذِينَ كَفَرُوا مِن دِينِكُمْ فَلَا تَخْشَوْهُمْ وَاخْشَوْنِ الْيَوْمَ أَكْمَلْتُ لَكُمْ دِينَكُمْ
وَأَتْمَمْتُ عَلَيْكُمْ نِعْمَتِي وَرَضِيتُ لَكُمُ الْإِسْلَامَ دِينًا فَمَنِ اضْطُرَّ فِي مَخْمَصَةٍ غَيْرَ
مُتَجَانِفٍ لِّإِثْمٍ فَإِنَّ اللَّهَ غَفُورٌ رَّحِيمٌ ۝

3 Unlawful for you are carrion, blood and pork, and what has been consecrated to other than Allah, and animals which have been strangled, and animals which have been killed by a blow, and animals which have fallen to their death, and animals which have been gored, and animals which wild beasts have eaten – except those you are able to slaughter properly – and animals which have been sacrificed on altars, and deciding things by means of divining arrows – that is deviance. Today the unbelievers have despaired of overcoming your *dīn*. So do not be afraid of them but be afraid of Me. Today I have perfected your *dīn* for you and completed My blessing upon you and I am pleased with Islam as a *dīn* for you. But if anyone is forced by hunger, not intending any wrongdoing, Allah is Ever-Forgiving, Most Merciful.

The first four categories were already discussed in *al-Baqarah*.

animals which have been strangled,

These are those which are choked to death either by a person or by a rope or branches or the like. Qatādah mentioned that the people of the Jāhiliyyah used to strangle sheep and other animals which they then ate. Ibn 'Abbās said something similar.

animals which have been killed by a blow,

Those which have been shot at or hit with a stone or stick which kills them without proper slaughtering. Ibn 'Abbās, al-Ḥasan, Qatādah, aḍ-Ḍaḥḥāk and as-Suddī said that. The verb *waqadha* is to strike a strong blow. *Waqīdh* is struck down and *waqdh* is a strong blow. Qatādah said that the people in the Jāhiliyyah used to do that and then eat the animals. Aḍ-Ḍaḥḥak said, 'They hit camels with wood for their gods until they had beaten them to death. Then they would eat them. Also included are animals killed by a cross-bow. [POEM] Muslim reported that 'Adī ibn Ḥātim said, 'I said, "Messenger of Allah, I shoot featherless arrows at game and hit them." He said, "When you shoot featherless arrows and they pierce, eat it. If the side [of the arrow] hits it, do not eat it."' One version adds, 'It has been killed by a blow.'

Abū 'Umar mentioned that scholars, old and new, disagree about hunting with pebbles, stones and featherless arrows. Some believe that an animal felled by a blow [which does not pierce] is only lawful if it is then properly slaughtered, based on what is related from Ibn 'Abbās, which is the position of Mālik, Abū Ḥanīfah, ath-Thawrī and ash-Shāfi'ī. The Syrians disagree with them about that. Al-Awza'ī said that you may eat what is killed by a featherless arrow, whether it pierces the animal or does not. Abū ad-Dardā', Faḍālah ibn 'Ubayd, 'Abdullāh ibn 'Umar and Makḥūl saw nothing wrong in it.

Abū 'Umar said, 'That is what is related by al-Awza'ī from 'Abdullāh ibn 'Umar. What is known from Ibn 'Umar is what Mālik mentioned that Nāfi' transmitted from him.' The foundational principle in the question is the earlier *ḥadīth* mentioned. It is what the normative practice is based on and it contains evidence for what is found in the *ḥadīth* of 'Adī ibn Ḥātim: 'Do not eat what has been hit by a featherless arrow. It has been struck down by a blow.'

animals which have fallen to their death,

This is an animal that falls down from a height and dies. That can be from mountain, or into a pit, or something similar. *Mutaraddiyah* comes from Form V of *radā* which implies destruction. It is the same whether it has fallen by itself or someone or something else has caused it to fall. When an animal is hit by the arrow of a hunter and then falls, it is unlawful since it might have died from the fall rather than the arrow. That is upheld by the *ḥadīth*: 'If you find it drowned in water, do not eat it. You do not know whether it was the water or your arrow that killed it.' Muslim transmitted it.

In the Jāhiliyyah, they used to eat animals killed by a fall, and did not consider it to be carrion unless it had died on account of illness or without a known cause. If the cause of death was known, they considered that to be the same as slaughter. The *Sharī'ah* restricts slaughter to a specific description as will be explained. All of these other cases remain as carrion. All of this is an agreed-upon ruling. The same is true of animals that have been gored or eaten by wild beasts.

animals which have been gored,

Naṭīḥah is the form *fa'īlah* with a passive meaning. It is a sheep or other animal which has been gored by another, or by something else, and then dies before being slaughtered. Some people take the word to have an active meaning because two sheep can gore each other and both die.

Allah says *naṭīḥah* and not *naṭīḥ*. The measure *fa'īl* is not mentioned with a *hā'*, as is said '*kaff khaḍīb*' and '*liḥyah dahīn*', but here He mentioned a *hā'* because the *hā'* is elided from *fa'īlah* when it is an adjective of something described which is spoken. One says '*shāh naṭīḥ*' and '*imratan qatīl*'. If the described is not mentioned, then the *hā'* is kept and you say, 'I saw the one of the Banū so-and-so killed (*qatīlah*)' and 'this is the gored sheep (*naṭīḥatu-l-ghanam*).' If you had not mentioned the *hā'*, you would say *qatīl*, and it would not have been known if it was a man or woman.

Abū Maysarah recited '*wa-l-manṭūḥah*'.

animals which wild beasts have eaten

This refers to beasts of prey with fangs and claws such as lions, leopards, foxes, wolves, hyenas and the like. These are all wild beasts (*sabu'*). The verb *saba'a* is to bite something with teeth, to mar it and attack it. There is some elision in the words: '*...which wild beasts have eaten*' because what they eat is dead. The Arabs used to use the term to mean lions. When beasts of prey took a sheep and killed it and then left it, the Arabs used to eat it, even when some of it had been eaten. Qatādah and others said that.

Al-Ḥasan and Abū Ḥaywah used to recite '*as-sab'*' which is the dialect of the people of Najd. Ḥassān said about 'Utaybah ibn Abī Lahab:

Whoever returns in the year to his family
is not someone eaten by a lion (*sab'*) on return.

Ibn Mas'ūd recited '*akīlatu-s-sabu'*' and 'Abdullāh ibn 'Abbās recited '*akīlu-s-sabu'*'.

except those you are able to slaughter properly

This is in the accusative as a connected exception according to scholars and *fuqahā'*. This means, 'If you reach any of the categories before they die and then slaughter them'. If they are alive, they can be slaughtered because the exception refers to what was previously mentioned, and it is only made separate by evidence which must be accepted.

Ibn 'Uyaynah, Sharīk, and Jarīr related from ar-Rukayn ibn ar-Rabī' that Abū Ṭalḥah al-Asadī said, 'I asked Ibn 'Abbās about when a wolf attacks a sheep and rips its belly open so that its insides spill out and which I then manage to slaughter (before it dies). He said, "Eat it, but do not eat what has spilled out of its insides."'

Isḥāq ibn Rāhawayh said, 'The *sunnah* in respect of a sheep is what Ibn 'Abbās described, as long as it is still alive and the place on the animal where it is slaughtered is sound. What one considers is whether the animal is alive or dead, not whether it might or might not survive. The same is true of a sick animal.' Isḥāq added, 'Whoever differs from this differs from the *Sunnah* of the majority of Companions and most scholars.' This is what Ibn Ḥabīb believed and this position is mentioned from the Mālikīs, and is the position of Ibn Wahb and the best known position of ash-Shāfi'ī. Al-Muzanī said, 'I have another position from ash-Shāfi'ī that it is not eaten when wild beasts have reached it or it falls in a manner that cannot be survived. That is the position of the Madinans and the well known position of Mālik. It was mentioned by 'Abd al-Wahhāb in *at-Talqīn*. It is related from Zayd ibn Thābit. Mālik mentioned it in the *Muwaṭṭā'*. It was the position of Qāḍī Ismā'īl and a group of Baghdadī Mālikīs. According to this position, it is a separate exception. It means: 'I have forbidden you these things, but what you slaughter is not unlawful.'

Ibn al-'Arabī said, 'The position of Mālik about these things varies. It is related that you should only eat what is slaughtered by sound slaughter. The *Muwaṭṭā'* states that if it is slaughtered while breathing and shaking, it may be eaten. That is sound and it is his position which he wrote with his own hand and read to the people of every land throughout his life. That is more appropriate than rare readings.' Our scholars say that it is permitted to slaughter a sick animal, even if it is about to die, provided it is still alive. I wish I knew the nature of the difference between a sick animal still alive and an animal still alive after being attacked by a wild beast: a balanced view and one free from any doubt! Abū 'Umar said, 'They agree that a sick animal for which there is no hope of survival may be slaughtered when there is still life in it when it is slaughtered. According to what they mentioned, that is known by the movement of a leg, tail or the like of that. They agree what when it has died and there is no movement of any limb, then it may not be slaughtered. The same analogy applies to the ruling of an animal which falls as well as what else is mentioned in the *āyah*. Allah knows best.'

Dhakā is slaughter as Quṭrub said. Ibn Sayyidihi said in *al-Muḥkam* that the Arabs say, 'The slaughter of the foetus is achieved by the slaughter of its mother.' Ibn 'Aṭiyyah said that this is a *ḥadīth*. The verbs *dhakā* and *dhabaḥa* are both used for slaughtering. The *ḥadīth* which indicates that was transmitted by ad-Dāraquṭnī from the *ḥadīths* of Abū Sa'īd, Abū Hurayrah, 'Alī and 'Abdullāh who said that the Prophet ﷺ said, 'The slaughter of the foetus is achieved by the slaughter of its mother.' That is the position of a group of the people of knowledge except for what is related from Abū Ḥanīfah who disagreed and said, 'When the foetus emerges from its mother's womb dead, it is not lawful to eat it because the slaughter of one life is not the slaughter of two lives.'

Ibn al-Mundhir said, 'The words of the Prophet ﷺ, "The slaughter of the foetus is achieved by the slaughter of its mother," is evidence that the foetus is separate from the mother.' He says that if a pregnant slavegirl is emancipated, the emancipation of the child goes along with that of his mother. This necessitates considering the slaughter of the mother to also include the slaughter of the foetus. If the emancipation of the one is considered to be the emancipation of both, it follows that the slaughter of the one should also be considered the slaughter of both. That is based on the report from the Prophet ﷺ and what has come from his Companions, and the position of most people is enough in face of any other statement.

The people of knowledge agree that if the foetus emerges alive, then the slaughter of its mother does not entail its slaughter. They disagree about when the mother is slaughtered while pregnant. Mālik and all his people say that the slaughter of the mother also includes the slaughter of the foetus if its form is complete and its hair has begun to grow. That is when it emerges alive or barely alive, although it is recommended that it be slaughtered separately if it emerges moving. If it has already died, it may be eaten. Ibn al-Qāsim said, 'I slaughtered a ewe, and when I had slaughtered it, its lamb began to kick inside the womb. I ordered that they leave it until it died in the womb. Then I ordered them to split open its belly and that it be removed and I slaughtered it and its blood flowed. I told my wife to roast it.'

'Abdullāh ibn Ka'b ibn Mālik said, 'The Companions of the Messenger of Allah ﷺ said, "When the foetus has hair, its slaughter is its mother's slaughter."' Ibn al-Mundhir said, 'Among those who said that its slaughter is its mother's slaughter, without mentioning hair or lack of it, were 'Alī ibn Abī Ṭālib, Sa'īd ibn al-Musayyab, ash-Shāfi'ī, Aḥmad and Isḥāq.' Qāḍī Abu-l-Walīd al-Bājī said, 'It is related that the Prophet ﷺ said, "The slaughter of the foetus is that of its mother, whether or not it has hair." However, it is a weak *ḥadīth*. The position of the school of Mālik is the sound one and it is the position of most of the *fuqahā'* of the different regions. Success is by Allah.'

Dhakā linguistically means 'completion' and an ancillary meaning is 'of full age'. A horse which is *mudhakkī* is a year older than when it has all its teeth. That is the completion of strength. The verb is *dhakkā, yudhakkī*. The Arabs say, 'The running of horses of full age (*mudhakkīyāt*) is a race for superiority.' *Dhakā'* is sharpness of spirit. A poet said:

He was given preference over him when they strove against him
with full age and sharpness.

It also means quickness of perception and the verb in that case is *dhakā, yadhkā*. *Dhukwah* is that which makes a fire blaze. Form IV is used for inciting war and kindling a fire. *Dhukā'* is the sun. That is because it blazes like fire does. *Ṣubḥ* (dawn) is called '*ibn dhukā*' (son of the sun)' because it comes from its light.

So '*dhakkaytum*' means 'you achieved its full slaughter' and slaughtered it in a complete manner. The verb for slaughtering is also derived from having a strong fragrance. One calls a scent '*dhakīyah*', meaning 'strong'. When the blood flows from the animal, it has a strong scent since it is quick to dry. We find in the *ḥadīth* of Muḥammad ibn 'Alī: 'The *dhakāh* of land is its dryness,' by which he meant its purification from impurity. So the term is used in respect of a slaughtered animal and the permission to eat it. The dryness of the ground after there has been impurity on it purifies it and allows one to pray on it, which is the position that slaughtering has to the slaughtered animal. That is the view of the people of Iraq.

When this is confirmed, then know that in the *Sharī'ah* it denotes shedding blood and cutting the veins of the animal ['veins' here includes the carotid artery], stabbing the throat in the case of camels, or fatally wounding them (*'aqr*) when proper slaughter is not possible accompanied by an intention aimed at Allah and mentioning Him over it. Scholars disagree about what achieves slaughter. The majority of scholars say that everything that cuts the veins and lets blood flow can be an implement of slaughter except for teeth and claws, based on many transmissions. That is the position of the fuqahā' of the different regions.

Teeth and nails/claws are forbidden for use in slaughtering except for those which are removed [from their source] because that would constitute strangling. If they have been removed from their source and they can make the blood flow from the veins, then it is considered permissible to slaughter using them. Some people disliked using teeth, nails and bones in any case, whether are not they have been removed. They include Ibrāhīm, al-Ḥasan, and al-Layth ibn Sa'd. The same is also related from ash-Shāfi'ī. Their argument is the apparent meaning of the *ḥadīth* of Rāfi' ibn Khadīj who said, 'I said, "Messenger of Allah, we will meet the enemy tomorrow and have no knives with us. Can we slaughter with reeds?"' We find in the *Muwaṭṭā'* of Mālik from Nāfi' from a man of the Anṣār from Mu'ādh ibn Sa'd or Sa'd ibn Mu'ādh that a slavegirl of Ka'b ibn Mālik was herding some sheep at Sal'. One of the sheep was injured and was about to die, so she went to it and slaughtered it with a stone. The Messenger of Allah ﷺ was asked about that and said, 'There is no harm in it, so eat it.'

We find in the *Muṣannaf* of Abū Dāwūd: '"Can we slaughter at Marwah using a sharp stick?" He said, "Make haste and look to what makes the blood flow. Mention the Name of Allah over it and then eat what is not slaughtered with a tooth or nail. I will tell you [why]. The tooth is a bone and 'nail' is the knife of the Abyssinians.' Muslim transmitted it. It is related that Sa'īd ibn al-Musayyab said, 'Whatever is slaughtered with a split reed, split stick, or cracked stone is a lawful slaughter.' *Līṭah* is what is split from a reed and with which it is possible to slaughter. *Shaṭīr* is a split stick and it is possible to slaughter with it because it has a fine edge. *Ẓurar* is a split stone with which is possible to slaughter but not to slaughter camels in the throat.

Mālik and a group said that slaughter is only made valid by cutting the throat and veins. Ash-Shāfi'ī said that it is sound by cutting the throat and gullet because they are the place of the passage of food and drink without which there is no life. So the goal of death is achieved by that. Mālik and others take into consideration death in a manner by which the meat will be made good. He distinguishes between what is lawful, namely meat, and what is unlawful, which is [the blood] that emerges by cutting the jugular veins. That is also the position of the school of Abū Ḥanīfah. That is what is indicated by the *ḥadīth* of Rāfi' ibn Khadīj when he said, 'What makes the blood flow.' The Baghdadīs related from Mālik that there is a fourth precondition: that slaughter must include the gullet, two jugular veins and esophagus. That is the position of Abū Thawr. What is well known is what was already mentioned, which is the position of al-Layth. Then our people disagree about severing one of the veins and the gullet and whether that amounts to slaughter.

The consensus of scholars is that slaughtering is done by cutting through the throat under the epiglottis. That is complete slaughter. They disagree about when slaughtering is done above it and passes through it to the body. There are two views about it. It is related from Mālik that in that case it may not be eaten. The same is true if it is slaughtered from the back of the neck, even if it goes through, the blood flows, and the throat and veins are cut: it may not be eaten. Ash-Shāfi'ī said that it may be eaten because the aim has been achieved. This is based on a principle, which is that even though the aim of slaughtering is to make the blood flow, it is a form of worship. The Prophet ﷺ slaughtered in the throat and slaughtered camels in the upper chest. He said, 'Slaughter is done in the throat and upper chest'. So he made the site clear and specific. He clarified that: 'Eat that which has had its blood flow and the Name of Allah is mentioned for it.' When that is ignored and happens without an intention, precondition or specific quality, then the portion of worship is removed and that is why it may not be eaten. Allah knows best.

They disagree about when the slaughterer lifts his hand before finishing and immediately puts it back and completes the slaughter. There are two views about whether it is sufficient or not. The first is sounder because he injured it and then slaughtered it while it was still alive. It is recommended that someone should only have someone he is pleased with do the slaughter and who does it according to his custom, be he Muslim or Kitābī, male or female, adult or not. A slaughter done by a Muslim is better than one done by a Kitābī. The *ḥajj* sacrifices may only be done by a Muslim. There is disagreement about the position when a Kitābī does it. The final position of the School is that it is not permitted, but Ashhab allows it.

Domestic animals which have become wild should only be slaughtered by the same means as domestic animals according to Mālik and his people, Rabī'ah, and al-Layth ibn Sa'd. The same is true about an animal that falls down a well. It should only be slaughtered in the throat or upper chest according to the *sunnah* of slaughtering. Some of the people of Madīnah and others differ about these two cases. The area is dealt with in the *ḥadīth* of Rāfi' ibn Khadīj which ends after his words, '...knife in Abyssinian'. He said, 'We took some booty consisting of camels and sheep and one of the camels ran away. A man shot an arrow at it and stopped it. The Messenger of Allah ﷺ said, "Some camels are wild beasts, or as wild as wild beasts. If one of them overpowers you, then do what this man did."' One variant says, 'They ate it.' That is the position of Abū Ḥanifah and ash-Shāfi'ī. Ash-Shāfi'ī said, 'The fact that the Prophet ﷺ endorsed this action is evidence that it is proper slaughter.' He used as an argument what Abū Dāwūd and at-Tirmidhī related from Abū al-'Usharā' that his father said, 'I asked, "Messenger of Allah, is slaughter only in the upper chest (*naḥr*) or throat?" He answered, "If you had pierced its thigh, it would be enough."' Yazīd ibn Hārūn said that this is a sound *ḥadīth* which Aḥmad ibn Ḥanbal liked and related from Abū Dāwūd. He indicated that the recorders who had entered should write it down. Abū Dāwūd said, 'This is only proper for an animal that has fallen or one that has gone wild.' Ibn Ḥabīb applied this *ḥadīth* to an animal that has fallen into a pit and that it is only possible to slaughter by stabbing it in a place other than a place where slaughtering is normally done. It is a position which only he has from Mālik and his people.

Abū 'Umar said, 'The position of ash-Shāfi'ī is more evident among the people of knowledge. It is that such an animal may be eaten on the basis that a wild animal is eaten based on the *ḥadīth* of Rāfi' ibn Khadīj. That is the position of Ibn 'Abbās and Ibn Mas'ūd. By way of analogy, when someone is able to get control of a wild animal, it is only made lawful in the same way that a domestic animal is made lawful because he has power over it. That is by analogy with the fact that when it becomes wild, or is like a wild animal, one is only able to slaughter it as one would a wild animal.'

Our scholars answered the *ḥadīth* of Rāfi' ibn Khadīj by saying, 'The Prophet ﷺ endorsed stopping it, not slaughtering it. That is demanded by the literal wording of the *ḥadīth* since he said, "Stopped it." He did not say that the arrow killed it. Furthermore, one usually has power over such an animal in most cases, so one does not pay attention to the rare case. That is in hunting. The *ḥadīth* clearly states that the arrowed stopped it, and after it was stopped, he had power over it. It is only eaten by proper slaughter. Allah knows best.'

As for the *ḥadīth* of Abū al-'Usharā', at-Tirmidhī said that it is a *gharīb ḥadīth* that we only know from the *ḥadīth* of Ḥammād ibn Salamah and we only know this *ḥadīth* from Abū al-'Usharā' from his father. They disagree about the name of Abū al-'Usharā'. Some of them said that his name was Usāmah ibn Qihṭim. It is also said that it was Yasār ibn Barz or Balz. It is also said that his name was 'Uṭārid who is ascribed to his father. This is an unknown *isnād* which is not authoritative. Even if it is assumed to be sound, as Yazīd ibn Hārūn says, there is nothing authoritative in it because it would necessitate the permission to slaughter the animal via any of its limbs, and does not differentiate between someone who has power to properly slaughter it and someone who does not. This is not just said about someone who has the power to properly slaughter it. So the literal meaning is not definitive. The interpretation of Abū Dāwūd and Ibn Ḥabīb is not agreed upon and so there is no authority in it. Allah knows best.

Abū 'Umar said, 'The evidence of Mālik is that they agree that if a domestic animal does not bolt away, then it may only only be slaughtered in the manner in which an animal over which one has power is slaughtered. Then they disagree. So the basic principle remains until they agree. There is no authoritative argument in this because the consensus is about an animal under control, and this animal is not under control. Also connected with this matter are the words of the Prophet ﷺ: 'Allah has prescribed excellence in everything. So when you kill, kill well. When you sacrifice, sacrifice well. Each of you should sharpen the edge of his knife and should calm down his sacrificial animal.' Muslim related it from Shaddād ibn

Aws. He said, 'I memorised two from the Messenger of Allah ﷺ. He said, "Allah has prescribed..."'

Our scholars say, 'Slaughtering animals well is being gentle with them. Do not throw them down with violence or drag them from one place to another. Sharpen the knife, and have the intention of permission and devotion and turn it towards *qiblah.* Kill it by cutting the veins and the throat. Let the blood flow out and leave the animal until it is cool. Acknowledge Allah's favour and thank Him for His blessing since He subjected this animal to us and allowed us what He could have forbidden us.' Rabī'ah said, 'Part of good slaughtering is not to slaughter an animal while another is looking at it, although the permission to do that is related from Mālik. The first is better.'

As for excellent killing, it is general and encompasses all things: slaughter, retaliation, *ḥudūd* and other things. Abū Dāwūd related that Ibn 'Abbās and Abū Hurayrah said, 'The Messenger of Allah ﷺ forbade the *sharīṭah* of Shayṭān.' Ibn 'Īsā added in his *ḥadīth* that a *sharīṭah* is an animal which is slaughtered and its veins are not cut and then is left until it dies.

animals which have been sacrificed on altars

The word for 'altars' is *nuṣub.* Ibn Fāris says that they are stones which were set up and worshipped and on which the blood of sacrifices was poured. *Naṣb* means the same. *Naṣā'ib* are stones set up on the edge of a well. Dust that is '*muntaṣab*' is elevated. It is said that the plural is *nuṣub* and the singular *niṣāb.* It is also said that it is a singular noun and the plural is *anṣāb.* There were 360 stones. Ṭalḥah recited '*an-nuṣbi*'. '*An-naṣbi*' is recited from Abū 'Amr. Al-Jaḥdarī has '*an-naṣabi*' which he makes as a singular noun like *jabal* and *jamal.* The plural is *anṣāb*, like *ajmāl* and *ajbāl.*

Mujāhid said that there were stones set up around Makkah on which slaughtering was done. Ibn Jurayj said, 'The Arabs used to slaughter at Makkah and pour the blood out before the House and they would cut the meat in strips and place it on the stones. When Islam came, the Muslims told the Prophet ﷺ, "We are more entitled to esteem this House with these actions." So the Prophet ﷺ did not dislike that and Allah revealed: "*...neither their flesh nor blood reaches Allah*" (22:37) and: "*...animals which have been sacrificed on altars*".' So the intention to esteem the altars rather than merely slaughtering on them is not permitted. Al-A'shā said:

With altars set up, not devoting it to well being.
Worship Allah, your Lord.

It is said that in this *āyah* the preposition *"alā'* means *'li'*, meaning 'for the sake of' as Quṭrub said. Ibn Zayd said that what is slaughtered on altars and consecrated to other than Allah are the same thing. Ibn 'Aṭiyyah says that it is a part of what is consecrated to other than Allah, but it is singled out because of its fame, the honour of the site and how people esteemed it.

deciding things by means of divining arrows

This is added to what was before it. *'An'* is in the accusative, meaning: 'deciding things by casting lots is forbidden'. *Azlām* are gambling arrows, the singular being *zalam* or *zulam*.

A lad spent the night dividing them like arrows (*zalam*).

Another said:

If the chiefs of Jadhīmah are killed,
its women are divided by lots.

Muḥammad ibn Jarīr related from Ibn Wakī' from his father from Sharīk from Abū Ḥuṣayn that Sa'īd ibn Jubayr said that they are white pebbles with which they used to play. Muḥammad ibn Jarīr said, 'Sufyān ibn Wakī' told us that it refers to chess.' As for the words of Labīd, 'It removes its *azlām* from the ground,' they say that it means the hooves of wild cows.

The Arabs had three ways of using divining arrows. The first method consisted of three arrows: written on one was: 'Do it', on the second 'Do not do it' and the third was blank. When a man wanted to do something, he would put them in a bag and then put in his hand and remove one. If he got the one which said 'Do it,' he did what he wanted. If he brought out, 'Do not do it,' he left it. If he drew the blank, he did it again. This is what was done by Surāqah ibn Mālik ibn Ju'shum when he pursued the Prophet ﷺ and Abū Bakr during their Hijrah. This action is called divination (*istiqsām*) because they used to divide (*taqassama*) provision and whatever they wished using them. It is as *istisqā'* is asking for rain. This is like Allah [in a *ḥadīth* qudsi] forbidding an astrologer to say: 'Do not set out because of such-and-such a star, or go out because of such-and-such a star.' Allah says: *'No self knows what it will earn tomorrow.'* (31:34). This will be explained later.

The second way entailed the use of seven arrows which were kept with the idol of Hubal inside the Ka'bah. Written on them were the disasters which befall people. Each arrow had something different written on it. On one of them was written 'blood money (*'aql*)', on another 'from you', on another 'from other than you', on another 'attached', and the others had rulings about water and other things. They are those which were drawn for the sons of 'Abd al-Muṭṭalib when he vowed to sacrifice one of them if he had ten sons. There is a long and well-known account of it mentioned by Ibn Isḥāq. The soothsayers and arbiters of the Arabs also had seven such arrows with them, like those that were with Hubal inside the Ka'bah.

The third way used ten arrows, seven with lines and three blanks. They used to gamble with them. Any game which becomes a form of gambling is unlawful. Intelligent people used them to feed the poor and destitute in winter, severe cold, and when it was impossible to earn. Mujāhid said that the arrows are the dice of the Persians and Greeks with which they gamble. Sufyān ibn Wakī' said that it refers to chess. Drawing arrows in that way to determine a share and a portion is an aspect of false consumption of wealth which is unlawful. Every form of gambling with doves, backgammon, chess or any of those games is similar to drawing lots with arrows and all of it is unlawful. It is a sort of divination and claiming to have knowledge of the Unseen.

Ibn Khuwayzimandād said, 'This is why our companions forbade the things which astrologers do in their charts and foretelling good omens and the like.' Aṭ-Ṭabarī said, 'Allah forbade them to engage in anything connected to matters of the Unseen. A soul does not know what his portion will be tomorrow and so the divining arrows have absolutely no effect in defining matters which are unseen. Someone who was ignorant of this used it to refute ash-Shāfi'ī's statement regarding drawing lots between slaves in cases of emancipation. This ignorant person did not know that what ash-Shāfi'ī said was based on sound reports and was not part of what is subject to the prohibition of using diving arrows. Emancipation is a legal ruling. It is permitted in the *Sharī'ah* to use lots to confirm the ruling of emancipation, to remove dispute or for a benefit which can be openly ascertained. That is not the same as someone saying, "If you do or say this, that will direct you to a certain matter in the future." It is not permitted to use lots to indicate something in the future, but it is permitted to use lots as a clear indication of emancipation. The difference is clear.'

Seeing good omens is not part of this. The Prophet ﷺ liked to hear, "O Rāshid (Guide)! O Najīḥ (Successful)!" At-Tirmidhī transmitted that and said that it is a sound *gharīb ḥadīth*. He liked good signs because they delight a person and give hope and give one a good opinion of Allah. Allah says [in the *ḥadīth qudsi*], 'I am in My slave's opinion of Me.' But he ﷺ disliked looking for omens in a bird's flight because it is something the idolaters do and because it entails having a bad opinion of Allah.

Al-Khaṭṭābī said, 'The difference between good omens (*fa'l*) and bad omens (*ṭīrah*) is that the latter entail reliance on something (other than Allah).' Al-Aṣma'ī said, 'I asked Ibn 'Awn about good omens and he said, "It is like when someone is ill and hears someone say, 'O Sālim (healthy)!' or is seeking something and hears, 'O Wājid (Finder)!'" This is the meaning of the *ḥadīth* of at-Tirmidhī.' We find in *Ṣaḥīḥ Muslim* that Abū Hurayrah said, "I heard the Messenger of Allah ﷺ say, 'There are no bad omens. The best of that is a good omen.' He was asked, 'Messenger of Allah, what is a good omen?' He said, 'A good word which one of you hears.'"'

The meaning of *ṭīrah* (seeking omens) will be explained later, Allah willing. It is related that Abū ad-Dardā' said, 'Knowledge comes through learning. Forbearance comes through affecting forbearance. Whoever seeks good will be given it. Whoever protects himself from evil will be protected from it. There are three who will not obtain the high degrees: those who soothsay, those who practise divination, and those who abort a journey because of an evil omen.'

That is deviance.

This indicates using divining arrows. The meaning of the word for deviance, *fisq*, is going outside something. It is said that here it is resorting to deeming any of these mentioned forbidden things as lawful. All of them are deviance and leaving the lawful for the unlawful. Refraining from these forbidden things is an aspect of fulfilling contracts given that Allah ordered that at the beginning of the *sūrah*.

Today the unbelievers have despaired of overcoming your *dīn*.

They despair of your reverting to their *dīn* and becoming unbelievers again. Aḍ-Ḍaḥḥāk said, 'This *āyah* was revealed when Makkah was conquered. That was when the Messenger of Allah ﷺ conquered Makkah in 22 Ramaḍān 9 AH or 8 AH. The Messenger of Allah ﷺ called out, "Whoever says 'There is no god but Allah' is safe. Whoever lays down his weapons is safe. Whoever locks his door is safe."'

So do not be afraid of them but be afraid of Me.

This means: 'Fear Me rather than them. I have the power to help you.'

Today I have perfected your *dīn* for you

That is because when the Prophet ﷺ was in Makkah, only the prayer was obligatory. When he went to Madīnah, Allah continued to reveal the lawful and unlawful until he ﷺ performed the *ḥajj*. Once he had performed the *ḥajj* and thus completed the *dīn*, this *āyah* was revealed.

The Imāms report that Ṭāriq ibn Shihāb said, 'A Jewish man came to 'Umar and said, "Amīr al-Mu'minīn, there is an *āyah* in your Book which, had it been sent down to us, the Jewish community, we would have made that day a holiday." He asked, "What is the *āyah*?" He answered, *"Today I have perfected your dīn for you…"* 'Umar said, "We know the day and the place when it was revealed to the Messenger of Allah ﷺ: while he was standing at 'Arafah on Friday after *'Aṣr*."' Muslim has it like this. In the variant of an-Nasā'ī it says Friday night. It is related that when it was revealed during the *ḥajj*, and the Messenger of Allah ﷺ recited it, 'Umar wept. The Messenger of Allah ﷺ asked him, 'Why are you weeping?' He replied, 'I weep because we were in increase in our *dīn*, and now it is complete. When something is complete, it can only decrease.' The Prophet ﷺ said to him, 'You have spoken the truth.' Mujāhid said that it was revealed on the day of the conquest of Makkah. The first opinion is the sounder: that it was revealed in 10 AH on Friday, the day of 'Arafah after *'Aṣr* during the Farewell Ḥajj while the Messenger of Allah ﷺ was stopped at 'Arafat on his she-camel, al-'Aḍbā'. The weight of the revelation made the camel kneel.

The word '*day*', although designating the whole of it, can be used when only a part of it is intended. The same is true of 'month'. You say, 'I did it in such-and-such a month or year' when it is known that you were not occupied for the entire month or year in doing it. That is a usage common both among the Arabs and non-Arabs. The word *dīn* designates the laws which were prescribed for us which were revealed in instalments. The last of them to be revealed is this *āyah* and no judgment was revealed after it. Ibn 'Abbās and as-Suddī said that.

Most, however, say that what is meant is the bulk of obligations and the lawful and unlawful, and they say that a lot of the Qur'ān was revealed after this, including the *āyah* of usury, the *āyah* about a person who dies without an heir and other judgments. The bulk of the *dīn* and the *ḥajj*, however, was complete. In that year no idolater performed *ṭawāf* with them nor did anyone do *ṭawāf* naked. All the people stood at 'Arafah. The phrase *'perfected your dīn'* is said to mean: 'I have destroyed your enemies for you and made your *dīn* victorious over all other *dīns*.'

and completed My blessing upon you

This is by completing the laws and rulings and making the *dīn* of Islam victorious as I promised you. The words: *'I will complete My blessing to you'* (2:150) refer to entering Makkah secure and safe and other things which are part of the Ḥanīfiyyah religion up until entering the Garden in Allah's mercy.

It may be said that the words: *'Today I have perfected your dīn for you...'* indicate that the *dīn* was not complete before that, and that that would mean that all of the Muhājirūn and Anṣār who died having been at Badr and al-Ḥudaybīyah and given their allegiance to the Messenger of Allah ﷺ twice and expended themselves for Allah in the immense trials which befell them, died when the *dīn* was incomplete and that the Messenger of Allah ﷺ called people to an incomplete *dīn*. They say that it is known that incompleteness is a fault, but the *dīn* of Allah is straight, as He says: *'a straight dīn.'* (6:161). The answer to this is: Why would one say that every incompleteness is a fault? What is the proof? Is the incompleteness of a month a fault or the shortening of the travelling prayer a fault? It cannot be said that the incompleteness of the parts of the *dīn* in the *Sharī'ah* before the rest of the parts were added in Allah's knowledge constitutes a fault or defect.

The meaning of Allah's words here is understood in two ways. One is: 'I have made it reach the furthest limit of the power I have judged and determined for it.' That does not mean that what was before was imperfect but that it was a limited incompletion. It is said that it is incomplete in respect of what Allah knew would be attached and added to it. It is like a man whom Allah will make reach the age of a hundred at which it will be said, 'Allah has completed his life.' That does not necessitate that when he was sixty, he was incomplete in the sense of having imperfections and faults. The Prophet ﷺ said, 'If Allah lets someone live to the age of sixty, he has not given him an excuse in his life.' But it is permitted that he be described with a limited incompletion. He has not completed the age to which Allah will let him live. Allah made *Ẓuhr*, *'Aṣr* and *'Ishā'* extend to four *rak'ahs*. If it were to be said, they are complete, that would be true, yet that does not oblige saying that when they were two *rak'ahs*, they were imperfect with shortcoming and defects. If it were to be said that they were incomplete with regard to what Allah later added to them, that would be a valid statement. That also applies to the laws of Islam and what was legislated by progressive stages until Allah made the *dīn* reach the end He intended for it. Allah knows best.

The other way of understanding it is that Allah's words mean that He stopped at the Hajj since there does not remain any other pillars of the *dīn* after Hajj. Once you have made Hajj, you have performed all the pillars of the *dīn* and undertaken its obligations as the Prophet ﷺ said, 'Islam is based on five.' So they had given the *shahādah*, prayed, paid *zakāh*, fasted, done *jihād* and made *'umrah*, but not performed Hajj. When they performed Hajj on that day with the Prophet ﷺ, Allah revealed this when they were standing at 'Arafah. It indicates that all the acts of obedience in the *dīn* are complete.

and I am pleased with Islam as a *dīn* for you.

'I have informed you of My pleasure in it as a *dīn* for you.' Allah is still pleased with Islam as a *dīn* for us. Therefore, specifying pleasure for that day is not taken literally. The word '*dīn*' is in the accusative for distinction and, if you wish, as a second object. It is said that it means, 'I am pleased with you when you carry out the *dīn* which has been prescribed for you, or I am pleased with the Islam you have today as a *dīn* which is complete to the last *āyah* and none of it will be abrogated.' Allah knows best. The word '*Islam*' in this *āyah* means the same as that which He states in His words: '*The dīn in the sight of Allah is Islam.*' (3:19) It is that which was explained by what Jibrīl asked the Prophet ﷺ: it is faith, actions and behaviour.

But if anyone is forced by hunger,

It means if he is forced by necessity to eat carrion and any of the things forbidden in this *āyah*. The word *makhmaṣah* denotes the kind of hunger experienced when the stomach is completely empty of food. *Khamṣ* is the emaciation of the stomach due to its being empty of food. A man is described as *khamīṣ* and *khumṣān*, and a woman is *khamīṣah* and *khumṣānah*. *Akhmaṣ* is the hollow of the sole of the foot. It is frequently used for hunger. Al-A'shā said:

They spent the night with full bellies
while their neighbours were hungry
and spent the night empty-bellied (*khamā'iṣ*).

An-Nābighah said about the emaciation (*khamṣ*) of the belly in respect of its leanness:

The belly has folds, empty (*khamīṣ*), soft,
The throat makes it inflate with an unmoving breast.

We find in a *ḥadīth*: 'lank-bellied (*khimāṣ*), with light backs.' *Khimāṣ* is the plural of *khamīṣ* and means with a lank belly. He is saying that they abstain from other people's possessions. Another *ḥadīth* says, 'The birds go out in the morning with empty stomachs (*khamā'iṣ*) and return in the evening full.' *Khamīṣah* is also a garment. Al-Aṣmā'ī said, '*Khamā'iṣ* are black garments of wool/silk or wool with borders. They are part of people's clothing.' The meaning of the verb '*forced*' was already discussed in *al-Baqarah* (2:173)

not intending any wrongdoing

This means not inclining towards the *ḥarām*. It has the same meaning as the words: '*...without desiring it or going to excess in it.*' (2:173) *Janāf* is inclination.

'*Wrongdoing*' is doing something unlawful. An illustration of that is the words of 'Umar: 'We do not incline to wrongdoing in it nor intend it knowingly.' A person who inclines is described as *mutajānif* or *janif.* An-Nakha'ī, Yaḥyā ibn Waththāb and as-Sulamī recited '*mutajannif*' without an *alif.* It is broader in meaning because the doubled *nūn* intensifies, going deeper in the meaning and confirming its ruling. The form *tafā'al* is imitation of something and approaching it. Do you not see that when you describe branches as *tamāyala*, swaying, that demands twisting and the appearance of bending. If you use *tamayyala*, the idea of actual bending is confirmed. It is like that with *taṣāwana* and *taṣawwana*, and *ta'āqala* and *ta'aqqala*. It means not intending disobedience as Qatādah and ash-Shāfi'ī said.

Allah is Ever-Forgiving, Most Merciful.

He is Ever-Forgiving, Most Merciful to him, and 'him' is elided.

يَسْـَٔلُونَكَ مَاذَآ أُحِلَّ لَهُمْ قُلْ أُحِلَّ لَكُمُ ٱلطَّيِّبَٰتُ وَمَا عَلَّمْتُم مِّنَ ٱلْجَوَارِحِ
مُكَلِّبِينَ تُعَلِّمُونَهُنَّ مِمَّا عَلَّمَكُمُ ٱللَّهُ فَكُلُوا۟ مِمَّآ أَمْسَكْنَ عَلَيْكُمْ وَٱذْكُرُوا۟
ٱسْمَ ٱللَّهِ عَلَيْهِ وَٱتَّقُوا۟ ٱللَّهَ إِنَّ ٱللَّهَ سَرِيعُ ٱلْحِسَابِ ④

4 They will ask you what is lawful for them. Say: 'All good things are lawful for you, and also what is caught for you by hunting animals which you have trained as Allah has taught you. Eat what they catch for you, mentioning Allah's name over it.' And have *taqwā* of Allah. Allah is swift at reckoning.

They will ask you

The *āyah* was revealed because of 'Adī ibn Ḥātim and Zayd ibn Muhalhal. He was Zayd al-Khayl (Increase in horses) whom the Messenger of Allah ﷺ named Zayd al-Khayr (increase of good). They said, 'Messenger of Allah, we are people who hunt with dogs and falcons. The dogs take cattle, donkeys and antelopes. Some we slaughter and some they do not kill but we do not manage to slaughter. Allah has forbidden carrion. What is lawful for us?' The *āyah* was revealed.

Say: 'All good things are lawful for you,

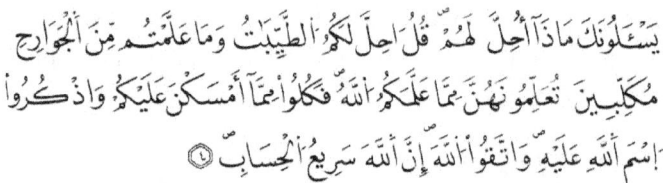

In *mādhā*, the suffix *dhā* is either redundant or it means 'which'. '*Good things*' are what is lawful, and what is unlawful is not good. It is said that it is what is enjoyable in respect of food and drink and what there is no harm in in this world or the Next. It is said that *'good things'* means slaughtered animals because they become good by slaughter.

what is caught for you by hunting animals

There is an elision here in the Arabic which implies 'Game which is caught by what you have trained.' That is a necessary implication. Otherwise, the meaning would demand that the lawful which is asked about is the eating of trained hunting animals. That is not the position of anyone. The meat obtained by a dog is made permissible by virtue of its training. We will mention what scholars say about eating dogs in *al-An'ām*.

One of those who wrote about the judgments of the Qur'ān said that the *āyah* indicates that the permission includes animals that we train, which are hunting dogs and birds of prey. That demands that all aspects of its use are permitted and so it indicates the permission to sell dogs and hunting birds and to use them in beneficial ways unless there is evidence to the contrary. That is consuming what is caught by trained dogs and birds of prey. 'Adī had five dogs with names. Their names were Salhab, Ghallāb, al-Mukhtilis and al-Mutanā'is. As-Suhaylī says that he is unsure about the fifth and whether it was Akhṭab or Waththāb.

The Community agree that when the dog is not black and is trained by a Muslim so that it comes when called, stops when told to and stops after catching the game, not eating any of the game it catches, and a Muslim hunts with it, mentioning the name of Allah when he releases it, what it catches can be eaten. This is undisputed. The dispute arises when any of these conditions is lacking. Most of the community agree that when someone hunts with something other than dogs, such as lynxes and the like, and falcons, hawks and similar birds, what they catch after training is something that has been caught by a trained animal. The verb *jaraḥa* and *ijtiraḥa* mean 'to earn'. From it comes *jāriḥah* (hunting animal) because it catches prey. *Ijtirāḥ* in respect of bad actions is to commit them. Al-A'shā said:

> Without consequences, suppurating, the branding iron
> reminds the committer of what he wrought.

And we see in Revelation: *'...knowing the things you perpetrate* (jaraḥtum) *in the day'* (6:60) and: *'Or do those who perpetrate* (ijtaraḥū) *evil deeds suppose...'* (45:21)

The word *'hunting animals' (mukallibīn)* refers to those with dogs which they train or 'those forced to hunt as a dog is forced to hunt'. Both are possible: the owners of the dogs or the dogs themselves. The term does not indicate that it is only permitted to hunt with dogs. If it is taken to apply only to dogs, it is reported by Ibn al-Mundhir that Ibn 'Umar said, 'When you slaughter what falcons and other birds catch for you, it is lawful for you. Otherwise do not eat it.' Ibn al-Mundhir said, 'Abū Ja'far was asked about whether it was lawful to hunt with a falcon and said, "No, not unless you manage to slaughter it (what it catches)."' Aḍ-Ḍaḥḥāk and as-Suddī said that it applies only to dogs.

If the dog is jet black, al-Ḥasan, Qatādah and an-Nakha'ī disliked hunting with it. Aḥmad said, 'I do not know anyone who allows it if the dog is jet-black.' Isḥāq ibn Rāhawayh said, 'The common people of knowledge in Madīnah and Kufa think that it is permitted to hunt with any trained dog. The prohibition against hunting with a black dog is based on the words of the Prophet ﷺ: 'A black dog is a shayṭān.' Muslim transmitted it.'

Most take the *āyah* to be general. They also find evidence for allowing hunting with a falcon in what was mentioned in the course of the revelation and what at-Tirmidhī transmitted from 'Adī ibn Ḥātim who said, 'I asked the Messenger of Allah ﷺ about hunting with a falcon and he said, "Eat what gets for you."' The *isnād* contains Mujālid and is only known through him. He is weak.' What is said about eating what a dog brings also applies to eating what a lynx brings. There is no difference except regarding something which is of no consequence. This is an analogy based on the root meaning. It is as a sword is analogous to a knife and a slave-girl to a slave.

Having confirmed this, know that a hunter must intend slaughtering and to make the catch permitted when he releases the animal. There is no disagreement about that since the Prophet ﷺ said, 'When you release your dog and mention the Name of Allah over it, then eat.' This necessitates an intention and saying the Name. If someone simply intends amusement in doing that, Mālik dislikes it while Ibn 'Abd al-Ḥakam allows it. It is the literal meaning of the position of al-Layth. He said, 'I have not seen anything true that more resembles the false.' He meant hunting. If someone does it without the intention of slaughter, it is unlawful because it is part of corruption and taking a life without any benefit. The Messenger of Allah ﷺ forbade killing animals unless it is to eat them.

The majority of scholars believe that it is necessary to say the Name when releasing the animal since the Prophet ﷺ said, 'Mention the Name of Allah over it.' If that does not exist in any manner, then the game should not eaten. That is the position of the literalists and the group of the people of *ḥadīth*. One group of our people and others believe that it is permitted to eat what a Muslim hunts and slaughters, even if he deliberately fails to mention the Name. They take the command to say the Name to be a recommendation. In his well known position, Mālik distinguished between omitting it deliberately and out of forgetfulness. He said that if it is deliberate, it should not be eaten, but it may be eaten if it is out of forgetfulness. That is the position of the *fuqahā'* of the different regions and one of the two positions of ash-Shāfi'ī. This question will be further discussed in *al-An'ām*.

Then the dog must be released from the hand of the hunter when he has its lead in his hand. He releases it and encourages it, and so it is sent, or the hunting animal is still when it sees the game and does not move unless the hunter tells it to. This is like having a lead in his hand. According to one of two positions, his encouraging it amounts to releasing it. If the dog goes off on its own without being released or encouraged, the game it catches is not permitted and it is not lawful to eat it according to most – Mālik, ash-Shāfi'ī, Abū Thawr and the People of Opinion – because unless it is actively released it is just hunting for itself. The hunter has done nothing and he is not considered to have released it because it does not conform to the words of the Prophet ﷺ, 'When you have released your trained dog.' 'Aṭā' ibn Abī Rabāḥ and al-Awzā'ī said, 'Someone may eat what it catches when they release it in order for it to hunt.'

Most recite '*'allamtum*'. Ibn 'Abbās and Muḥammad ibn al-Ḥanafiyyah recited '*'ullimtum*', meaning the business of dogs and hunting with them. The word *jawāriḥ* here indicates dogs and similar animals used for hunting. The same word is also used for the limbs because they bring acquisitions. It is said that they are called that because they wound (*jaraḥa*) and make blood flow, taken from *jirāḥ* (wound), but this is weak. Linguists differ from that. Ibn al-Mundhir related it from some people.

The majority recite '*mukallibīna*'. A *mukallib* is a trainer of dogs and it is said that it can used for someone who trains other animals besides dogs, because that is like training a dog. Some of them related that. The hunter is called that and it can be said that they are hunters. It is also said that it is the owner of the dog. The verb is *kallaba*, and the noun is *mukallib* or *kallāb*. Al-Ḥasan recited '*muklibīna*' which means 'those who own dogs'. One says of a man who has many livestock (*māshiyah*): '*amshā'r-rajul*' and so '*aklab*' is having many dogs. [POEM -AMSHA]

which you have trained as Allah has taught you.

The feminine pronoun is used because *jawāriḥ* is the plural of *jāriḥah*. Scholars do not disagree that there are two conditions attached to training: that the animals obey when ordered and stop when told to stop. There is no disagreement about these two conditions where dogs and similar animals are concerned. There is disagreement about hunting birds. The well-known position among most is that that the conditions also apply to them. Ibn Ḥabīb mentioned that it is not a condition for them to stop when told to. It is enough that they obey when commanded. Rabī'ah said that it is enough that the bird obeys when called: then it is a trained hunter because it is the nature of most animals to leave.

Ash-Shāfi'ī and a group of scholars stipulated that its being trained entails it staying with its owner. In his well known position, Mālik does not stipulate that. Ash-Shāfi'ī said, 'A trained animal is one that goes when its owner releases it and returns to him when he calls on it to return, and keeps the game for its owner and does not eat it. When it does that several times, the people of custom say that it is trained like a trained dog.' Ash-Shāfi'ī and the Kufans also said, 'It goes when released and stays when stopped and does that time after time. The game may be eaten after the third time.' Some scholars said that it does that three times and the game may be eaten on the fourth. Some say that when it does that once, it is trained and its game may be eaten the second time.

Eat what they catch for you,

This is what they keep for you. Scholars disagree regarding its interpretation. Ibn 'Abbās, Abū Hurayrah, an-Nakha'ī, Qatādah, Ibn Jubayr, 'Aṭā' ibn Abī Rabāḥ, 'Ikrimah, ash-Shāfi'ī, Aḥmad, Isḥāq, Abū Thawr, an-Nu'mān and his people say that it means, '...provided they have not eaten any of it. If the animal eats from it, the rest of it should not be eaten because it caught it for itself and not for its master.' Abū Ḥanīfah and his people consider a lynx or leopard to be like a dog in that respect. They did not stipulate that for birds and eat (what has been caught) even if they have eaten some of it. Sa'd ibn Abī Waqqāṣ, 'Abdullāh ibn 'Umar, Salmān al-Fārisī, and Abū Hurayrah said that the meaning is that if the hunting animal – be it a dog, lynx or bird – eats, then the rest of the catch may be eaten, even if only a morsel of it remains. This is the position of Mālik and all his people and the second verdict of ash-Shafi'i. It is based on analogy.

There are two *ḥadīth*s which deal with this topic. One is the *ḥadīth* of 'Adī about the dog, 'If they eat of it, do not eat it for they caught for themselves.' Muslim transmitted it. The second is the *ḥadīth* of Abū Tha'labah al-Khashānī who said that the Messenger of Allah ﷺ said about game caught by a dog, 'When you release your dog and mention the Name of Allah over it, then eat, even if it eats. Eat what is returned to your hand.' Abū Dāwūd transmitted it. It is related from 'Adī and is not sound. What is sound is the *ḥadīth* of Muslim.

Although the two transmissions conflict, some of our people and others want to join them together, and go by the prohibition out of scrupulousness and the *ḥadīth* of the permissibility as limited permission. They said, "Adī did it a lot and so the Prophet ﷺ gave him a *fatwā* to refrain and be scrupulous. Abū Tha'labah was in need and so he gave him a *fatwā* that it was permitted, and Allah knows best. The soundness of this interpretation is indicated by the words of the Prophet ﷺ in the *ḥadīth* of 'Adī: 'I fear that it may have caught it for itself.' This is our scholars' interpretation. Abū 'Umar said in *al-Istidhkār*: 'This *ḥadīth* of 'Adī contradicts the *ḥadīth* of Abū Tha'labah. It is clear that the *ḥadīth* of Abū Tha'labah abrogates it. He said, "Even if it eats, Messenger of Allah?" He replied, "Even if it eats."'

I say that this is debatable because the respective dates are not known. It is more appropriate to combine both *ḥadīths* when the dates are not known. Allah knows best. The people of ash-Shāfi'ī said, 'If the eating was due to excessive hunger on the part of the dog, it may be eaten. Otherwise it should not be eaten. That comes from poor training.' It is related that some of the early generations made a distinction between what is eaten by a dog or lynx, which they forbade, and that eaten by a falcon, which they allow. That was stated by an-Nakha'ī, ath-Thawrī, the People of Opinion, and Ḥammād ibn Abī Sulaymān. It is related from Ibn 'Abbās. They said, 'Dogs and lynxes can be beaten and restrained. That is not possible with birds. The extent of their training is to call them and they come and release them and they go. More than that is not possible as beating would harm them.'

Most scholars believe that if a dog drinks some of the blood of the game, the game may still be eaten. 'Aṭā' said that drinking blood was not eating. Ash-Sha'bī and Sufyān ath-Thawrī disliked it. They do not disagree that the reason that game is permitted is its wounding by the hunting animal, which must be real and undoubted. If there is doubt, then it is not permitted to eat it.

An example is when another dog is found with the hunting dog which might not have been released by another hunter, but has hunted out of its own nature and instinct. There is no disagreement about this case because the Prophet ﷺ said, 'If other dogs are mixed with it, do not eat it.' Another variant has, 'You said the Name over your dog, but not any other.' If another hunter has released it and both dogs share in it, then the two hunters share in it. If one of the dogs kills the game and then the other dog comes, it belongs to the one that killed it. Similarly, what is shot with arrow and then falls from a cliff or drowns in water should not be eaten, because the Prophet ﷺ told 'Adī, 'When you shoot your arrow, mention the Name of Allah. If you fail to find it for a day and only find the mark of your arrows on it, then eat it. If you find it drowned, do not eat it. You do not know whether it was the water or your arrow that killed it.'

If the game dies in the dog's mouth without being cut, it should not be eaten because it died of strangulation. So it is like slaughtering using the knife as a throttling instrument so that the animal dies during the slaughter before its throat has been cut. If someone is able to take the game from the hunting animal and slaughter it, but does not do so before it dies, it should not be eaten. He fell short with respect to slaughter because he was actually able to slaughter the animal properly. Slaughter by someone able to do it differs from that of someone who was unable to do it. If he takes it but it dies before he gets out his knife, then it is permitted to eat it. If he does not have a knife with him and is busy looking for it, then the animal should not be eaten.

Ash-Shāfi'ī said, 'There are two views in the case of game taken by hunting animals which does not bleed. One is that it may not eaten until it is wounded because Allah says "*jawāriḥ*", which is the position of Ibn al-Qāsim, and the other, which is the view of Ashhab, is that it is lawful. Ashhab said that if it dies by being hit by the dog, it may be eaten.'

His words ﷺ, 'If you fail to find it for a day and only find the mark of your arrow on it, then eat it,' and the similar statement in the *ḥadīth* of Abū Tha'labah that Abū Dāwūd transmitted, although he adds, 'Eat from it after three days, as long as it has not gone putrid,' contradict the other words of the Prophet ﷺ, 'Eat what you kill straightaway and leave what dies out of sight.' Killing straightaway means what is killed quickly while you can see it, and dying out of sight means you shoot it and loose track of it and it dies somewhere where you cannot see it. The verb here, *anmā*, means you loose sight of it and it dies. Imru al-Qays said:

What he shot is not lost sight of (*tanmī*).
It was unable to run away.

Scholars have three different views about eating game that dies out of sight. It is said that it may be eaten whether it is killed by an arrow or by a dog. The second view is that none of it may be eaten when sight of it is lost, based on the *ḥadīth* above. It is not eaten out of the fear that other creatures may have assisted in its death. The third view makes a distinction between game shot with an arrow, which may be eaten, and game killed by a dog, which may not be eaten. The reason behind this is that the arrow kills in one manner and so there is no confusion. A dog may kill in various manners and so there is confusion. Our scholars express all three positions.

Mālik said outside of the *Muwaṭṭā'*: 'If the prey is found dead after a night has passed and was not killed by a bird, dog or arrow, it may not be eaten.' Abū

'Umar said, 'This will indicate to you that when it is a fatal hit, then it is lawful to eat it, even if it is missed overnight. Otherwise it is disliked if there is failure to find it overnight, based on what has come from Ibn 'Abbās, 'If you fail to find it overnight then do not eat it.' The same is reported from ath-Thawrī who said, 'When you do not find it for a day, then it is disliked to eat it.' Ash-Shāfi'ī said, 'By analogy it should not be eaten when its fall is not seen.' Al-Awzā'ī said, 'If you find it dead on the following day and find an arrow in it or the mark of your dog on it, then eat it.' Ashhab, 'Abd al-Malik and Aṣbagh said the same: it is permitted to eat game, even if it is not found overnight if the hit was fatal.

The words in the *ḥadīth*, 'as long as it has not gone putrid', are causal because when it is putrid, that indicates that impure things have infected it and so it is disliked to eat it, although it is permitted to eat such meat as the Prophet ﷺ ate foetid fat. It is said the reason is that one fears harm on account of eating it. According to this reasoning, eating it is unlawful if the fear is actual. Allah knows best.

Scholars disagree, under this heading, about hunting with a dog owned by a Jew or Christian, even if it is trained. Al-Ḥasan al-Baṣrī disliked it. Jābir ibn 'Abdullāh, al-Ḥasan, 'Aṭā', Mujāhid, an-Nakha'ī, ath-Thawrī and Isḥāq disliked hunting with a dog or falcon owned by a Magian. Mālik, ash-Shāfi'ī and Abū Ḥanīfah allowed hunting with their dogs provided the hunter is Muslim and said that it is like using their knives. If the hunter is one of the People of the Book, most commentators, with the exception of Mālik, hold that it is permitted. He distinguished between that and their slaughtering, reciting: *'You who believe! Allah will test you with game animals which come within the reach of your hands and spears.'* (5:94) He said, 'Allah did not mention Jews or Christians in this.' Ibn Wahb and Ashhab said, 'Game caught by Jews and Christians is lawful like their slaughtered animals.' We find in the book of Muḥammad: 'Neither the game nor slaughtered animals of Sabaeans are permitted. They are a people between the Jews and Christians and have no *dīn*.'

If the hunter is a Magian, Mālik, ash-Shāfi'ī, Abū Ḥanīfah and their people and most other people forbid eating his game. Abū Thawr said that there are two views about this. One is the same view as the others, and the other view is that a Magian is one of the People of the Book and their game is, therefore, permitted. If someone who is drunk hunts or slaughters, neither their game nor slaughtered animals may be eaten because slaughter requires an intention and a drunk has no intention.

Grammarians disagree about the use of *'min'* in Allah's words *'what (mimmā) they catch for you'*. Al-Akhfash said that it is extra as in 6:141. The Basrans say that that is an error and say that '*min*' is not extra in the positive, but is in the negative and interrogative. Here and in 2:271 and 71:4 it can be partitive. The answer is that in 61:12 the *mīn* is omitted, and that indicates that it is extra in the positive. The answer then to that is that it is partitive here because since the flesh is lawful, but not the blood or faeces. I say that this is neither meant nor customary in respect of eating so that there could be any confusion. It is possible that what is meant is what the hunting animals leave for you, according to the position that there is no harm if the animal eats some of it. The reason for this possibility is the scholars disagreement about eating game if the hunting dog has eaten some of it, as we already mentioned.

So the *āyah* indicates that it is permitted to use dogs for hunting. That is confirmed in the sound *Sunnah*. They can also be used for guarding crops and livestock. At the beginning of Islam, it was commanded to kill dogs. Muslim reports from Ibn 'Umar that the Prophet ﷺ said, 'If anyone acquires a dog – except one used for hunting or herding – his reward is decreased by two *qirāṭ*s every day.' Abū Hurayrah reported that the Messenger of Allah ﷺ said, 'Someone who keeps a dog loses a *qirāṭ* of his actions every day – unless it is a farm or cattle dog.' Az-Zuhrī said, 'What Abū Hurayah said was mentioned to Ibn 'Umar and he said, "May Allah have mercy on Abū Hurayrah. He had crops."' The *Sunnah* indicates what we have mentioned and the decrease applies to someone who acquires a dog without there being any use in that, because dogs alarm the Muslims and disturb them by their barking, as one of the poets of Basra said when he stayed with 'Ammār and heard his dogs barking. He composed:

We stayed with 'Ammār and he called his dogs on us
and so we were almost eaten between his houses.
I said to my companions, confiding in them,
'Which is longer: today or the Day of Rising?'

Or it is because the angels refuse to enter a house when there is a dog or because they are impure, as ash-Shāfi'ī thinks, or it is because of the prohibition of acquiring them without any benefit in doing so. Allah knows best.

One variant has two *qirāṭ*s and one has one *qirāṭ*. That can be because of two types of dogs, one of which is worse than the other, like black ones which the Prophet ﷺ commanded be killed. He did not include them in the exception when he said, 'Kill the jet-black one with two spots. It is a shayṭān.' Muslim transmitted it. It is also possible that it refers to different places. It could, for instance, be that in Madīnah and Makkah it is two *qirāṭ*s and one *qirāṭ* elsewhere. Allah knows best.

As for those it is permitted to have, the reward is not then decreased; they are like horses and cats. It is permitted to buy and sell them so that Saḥnūn said that it is permitted to perform *ḥajj* from their price. According to Mālik, it is permitted to have dogs for herding cattle which go with them, not those that protect a house from thieves. A farm dog is one that protects crops from wild animals by day and night, not from thieves. Those other than Mālik permitted using them against cattle, crop and house thieves in the wild.

This *āyah* indicates that a person with knowledge has a superiority which the ignorant does not possess, because when a dog is trained it is superior to untrained dogs. When a human being has knowledge, it is more fitting for him to possess excellence over other people, especially when he acts on what he knows. This is as it is related from 'Alī ibn Abī Ṭālib who said, 'Everything has a worth, and the worth of a person is what beautifies him.'

mentioning Allah's name over it.

This is saying the *basmalah*. It is said that it should be said when the animal is released to catch the prey. The position in *fiqh* regarding mentioning the Name when hunting and slaughtering is the same as will be explained in *al-An'ām*. It is also said that what is meant is saying the *basmalah* when eating it. That is more apparent. We find in *Ṣaḥīḥ Muslim* that the Prophet ﷺ said to 'Amr ibn Abī Salamah: 'Boy, say the Name of Allah, eat with your right hand and eat from what is in front of you.' Ḥudhayfah reported that the Prophet ﷺ said: 'Food is lawful to Shayṭān except for that over which the name of Allah has been mentioned.' If someone forgets to say it at the beginning, they should say it at the end. An-Nasā'ī related from Umayyah ibn Makhshiyy, one of the Companions of the Messenger of Allah ﷺ, that the Messenger of Allah ﷺ saw a man eating without mentioning the Name of Allah. When he took the last morsel, he said, 'In the Name of Allah, at its beginning and its end.' The Messenger of Allah ﷺ said, 'Shayṭān continued to eat with him and when he said the Name, he vomited all that he had eaten.'

and have *taqwā* of Allah.

This is a general command which is in keeping with the commands contained in the *āyah*. Allah is swift at reckoning because He encompasses all things in knowledge and numbers everything so that He already knows it without any need to count as a reckoner does. This is why He says: *'We are sufficient as a Reckoner.'* (21:47) The Almighty will reckon all creatures all at once. It is possible that it is a threat about the Day of Rising. It is as if He were saying, 'Allah's reckoning of you is quick since the Day of Rising is near.' It is also possible that reckoning means requital and it is as if Allah were promising rapid requital in this world if they do not fear Him.

ٱلْيَوْمَ أُحِلَّ لَكُمُ ٱلطَّيِّبَٰتُ وَطَعَامُ ٱلَّذِينَ أُوتُوا۟ ٱلْكِتَٰبَ حِلٌّ لَّكُمْ وَطَعَامُكُمْ
حِلٌّ لَّهُمْ وَٱلْمُحْصَنَٰتُ مِنَ ٱلْمُؤْمِنَٰتِ وَٱلْمُحْصَنَٰتُ مِنَ ٱلَّذِينَ أُوتُوا۟ ٱلْكِتَٰبَ
مِن قَبْلِكُمْ إِذَآ ءَاتَيْتُمُوهُنَّ أُجُورَهُنَّ مُحْصِنِينَ غَيْرَ مُسَٰفِحِينَ
وَلَا مُتَّخِذِىٓ أَخْدَانٍ وَمَن يَكْفُرْ بِٱلْإِيمَٰنِ فَقَدْ حَبِطَ عَمَلُهُۥ وَهُوَ فِى
ٱلْءَاخِرَةِ مِنَ ٱلْخَٰسِرِينَ ۝

5 Today all good things have been made lawful for you. And the food of those given the Book is also lawful for you and your food is lawful for them. So are chaste women from among the believers and chaste women of those given the Book before you, once you have given them their dowries in marriage, not in fornication or taking them as lovers. But as for anyone who rejects belief, his actions will come to nothing and in the Next World he will be among the losers.

Today all good things have been made lawful for you.

This bears the same meaning as: *'Today I have perfected your dīn for you.'* It is repeated for emphasis: 'I have made lawful for you the good things which you asked about.' Good things were allowed to the Muslims before this *āyah* and this answers their question: 'What is lawful for us?' It is said that '*Today*' refers to the time of Muḥammad ﷺ, so this is the time of the appearance and spread of Islam and so Allah is saying, 'I have completed your *dīn* for you made good things lawful for you.' The meaning of '*good things*' has already been discussed.

And the food of those given the Book is also lawful for you

Food includes what is eaten and includes slaughtered animals. Here many scholars say that it is particular to slaughtered animals. What is forbidden to us of their food is not included under the generality. Ibn 'Abbās said, 'Allah says: *"Do not eat anything over which the name of Allah has not been mentioned"* (6:121), and then He makes an exception: *"And the food of those given the Book is also lawful for you,"* meaning animals slaughtered by Jews and Christians; even if a Christian says when slaughtering, "In the Name of the Messiah" and a Jew says, "In the Name of 'Uzayr". That is because they are then slaughtering according to their religion.'

'Aṭā' says, 'Eat any animal slaughtered by a Christian, even if he says, "In the name of the Messiah", because Allah has allowed their slaughtered animals and He knows what they say.' Al-Qāsim ibn Mukhaymarah said, 'Any animal they slaughter, even if they say, "In the name of the church of Sarjis," and that is the position of az-Zuhrī, Rabī'ah, ash-Sha'bī and Makḥūl, and it is related from the Companions, Abū ad-Dardā' and 'Ubādah ibn as-Sāmit.' One group say that if a *Kitābī* says something other than the name of Allah, it may not be eaten. That was stated by 'Alī, 'Ā'ishah and Ibn 'Umar among the Companions, and was the position of Ṭāwūs and al-Ḥasan, holding to the words of Allah: *'Do not eat anything over which the name of Allah has not been mentioned. To do so is sheer deviance.'* (6:121) Mālik said, 'I dislike it,' but he did not forbid it.

There is an extraordinary position from aṭ-Ṭabarī in which he cites the consensus that slaughtered animals of the People of the Book are permitted and then uses that as evidence for the fact that saying the Name of Allah over the animal is not a necessary condition. He stated, 'There is no doubt that they do not only name over what they slaughter a "god" that is not truly worshipped – such as the Messiah and 'Uzayr – but that even if they were to name the true God, it would still not be a recognised form of worship. It does not matter whether an unbeliever says the Name of Allah or not, because correct worship is inconceivable in his case anyway, and because Christians slaughter in the name of the Messiah. Allah judges that their slaughtered animals are generally lawful and that indicates that the Name of Allah is not a basic precondition as ash-Shāfi'ī says.' The positions of scholars regarding this matter will be discussed in *al-An'ām*.

There is no disagreement among scholars that the food of People of the Book, which does not require slaughter, such as wheat and fruit, is permitted, since no one's right of possession is harmed by having it. Food which requires effort (on the part of the producer) is of two sorts. One is the sort that requires effort in manufacture which has no connection to the *dīn*, like grinding flour, pressing oil and other such things. Keeping away from anything of this kind produced by a *dhimmī* would be simply in order to avoid any possible impurity. The second sort is what involves slaughtering, which, as we mentioned, is dependent on intention and has religious implications. If you make an analogy that their slaughtered animals are not permitted on the basis of the assertion that such people have no prayer, fasting or accepted worship, Allah has given this community a dispensation regarding their slaughtered animals and, by a text, removed it from such an analogy as Ibn 'Abbās mentioned. Allah knows best.

There is also disagreement about whether those parts of slaughtered animals which are unlawful for them are lawful for us. Most say that all that has been slaughtered, both what is lawful and unlawful for them, is considered properly slaughtered. A group of scholars have said, however, that only those parts of their slaughtered animals that are lawful for them are lawful for us, because their slaughtering is not operative on what is not lawful for them. This odd group forbid the fat of the animals slaughtered by the People of the Book and confine the term '*food*' in the *āyah* to only part of it, whereas the first group apply the term to generally to everything that is eaten. This disagreement exists within the Mālikī school. Abū 'Umar stated that Mālik disliked the fat of animals sacrificed by Jews and camels which they slaughtered but most scholars see no harm in it. This will also be discussed in *al-An'ām*. Mālik disliked eating their meat when meat slaughtered by a Muslim is available. He disliked them having meat markets. This is just a matter of fastidiousness on his part.

In the case of the Magians, scholars agree that their slaughtered animals should not be eaten, nor should they be married, because, in the best known position, they are not considered People of the Book. There is no harm in eating food other than meat of those who have no Book, like idolaters and pagans – except for cheese when there is carrion rennet in it. If the father of a child is Magian and his mother a Kitābī, Mālik believes that his ruling is that of his father. Others say that the animal slaughtered by a child may not be eaten if one of his parents is someone whose slaughtered animals may not be eaten.

As for the animals slaughtered by the Christians of the Banū Taghlib and those of any of those who falsely claim to be Christians or Jews, 'Alī forbade the animals slaughtered by the Banū Taghlib because they are Arabs. He said, 'They do not hold to anything in Christianity other than drinking wine.' That is the position of ash-Shāfi'ī. According to this, animals slaughtered by true Christians are not forbidden. The majority of the community say that an animal slaughtered by any Christian is lawful, whether Banū Taghlib or others. The same is true of Jews. Ibn 'Abbās argued by Allah's words: *'Any of you who take them as friends is one of them.'* (5:51) If the Banū Taghlib had been Christians, taking them as friends would entail eating their slaughtered animals.

There is no harm in eating, drinking and cooking in a vessel of an unbeliever, as long as they are not made of gold or silver or pigskin, after they have been washed and boiled. This is because they do not guard against impurities and eat carrion. When their vessels such as clay pots are used for cooking, there may be bits of impurity left in them. Any food cooked in them may then mix with what was previously cooked in them. So scrupulousness involves refraining from it. Ibn 'Abbās said, 'If the vessel is made of copper or iron, it should merely be washed. If it is made of clay, water should be boiled in it in it and then it should be washed when it is needed.' Mālik said that. As for using them for other than cooking, there is then nothing wrong in using them without washing them. This is known by from a report by ad-Dāraquṭnī that 'Umar did *wuḍū'* in the house of a Christian with a jug belonging to the Christian. That is sound and will be mentioned in full in *al-Furqān*.

In *Ṣaḥīḥ Muslim* Abū Tha'labah al-Khashanī said, 'I went to the Messenger of Allah ﷺ and said, "Messenger of Allah, I live in a land of People of the Book and we eat from their vessels, and it is a land where we hunt. I hunt with my bow and with my trained dog and with my untrained dog. Tell me what is lawful for me of that." He said, "As for what you mentioned about being in the land of People of the Book, eat from their vessels. If you find other vessels than theirs, then do not eat from them. If you do not find any, then wash them and eat from them."'

and your food lawful for them.

This is evidence that they are addressed by our *Sharī'ah*. It means: when they buy meat from us, the meat is lawful for them and it is lawful for us to take the price from them.

So are chaste women from among the believers and chaste women of those given the Book before you,

This was already discussed in *al-Baqarah* and *an-Nisā'*. It is related from Ibn 'Abbās that this refers to the People of the Book with whom there is a treaty and not the people of war. Others say that it is permitted to marry a woman who is a *dhimmī* or a *ḥarbī* since the *āyah* is general. It is related that Ibn 'Abbās said that '*muḥṣanāt*' are chaste, intelligent women. Ash-Sha'bī says that 'a chaste woman' is one who guards her private parts and does not commit fornication and washes when she is in *janābah*. Ash-Sha'bī recites '*muḥṣināt*' as does al-Kisā'ī. Mujāhid says that it means 'free women.' Abū 'Ubayd said [of Mujāhid], 'He believed that it is not lawful to marry slavegirls of the People of the Book taking as evidence Allah's words: '*...you may marry slavegirls who are believers*'. (4:25) This is the position of most scholars.

But as for anyone who rejects belief, his actions will come to nothing

It is said that when Allah revealed: *'chaste women of those given the Book'*, the women of the People of the Book said, 'Were it not that Allah was pleased with our *dīn*, He would not have allowed marriage with us.' So this was revealed. The word '*belief*' here means belief in what was revealed to Muḥammad ﷺ. Abū al-Haytham said, 'The *bā'* (in *bi-l-īmān*) is connective, implying, "whoever rejects belief".' Ibn as-Samayfa' recited: '*ḥabaṭa*'.

It is said that when obligations and rulings which must be carried out are mentioned, the threat for those who disobey them is also mentioned. That increases the rebuke for failing to implement them. It is related from Ibn 'Abbās and Mujāhid that the meaning is 'Whoever disbelieves in Allah.' Al-Ḥasan ibn al-Faḍl added, 'If this is true, then the meaning is "The Lord of Belief."' Abū al-Ḥasan al-Ash'arī said, 'It is not permitted to call Allah "belief", which differs from what was held by the Ḥashwiyyah and Sālimiyyah sects because "*belief*" (īmān) is a verbal noun. The active particle is *mu'min*. Belief is also affirmation and affirmation is a matter of words and it is not possible for the Creator to be words.'

يَـٰٓأَيُّهَا ٱلَّذِينَ ءَامَنُوٓا۟ إِذَا قُمْتُمْ إِلَى ٱلصَّلَوٰةِ فَٱغْسِلُوا۟ وُجُوهَكُمْ
وَأَيْدِيَكُمْ إِلَى ٱلْمَرَافِقِ وَٱمْسَحُوا۟ بِرُءُوسِكُمْ
وَأَرْجُلَكُمْ إِلَى ٱلْكَعْبَيْنِ ۚ وَإِن كُنتُمْ جُنُبًا فَٱطَّهَّرُوا۟ ۚ وَإِن كُنتُم
مَّرْضَىٰٓ أَوْ عَلَىٰ سَفَرٍ أَوْ جَآءَ أَحَدٌ مِّنكُم مِّنَ ٱلْغَآئِطِ أَوْ لَـٰمَسْتُمُ ٱلنِّسَآءَ
فَلَمْ تَجِدُوا۟ مَآءً فَتَيَمَّمُوا۟ صَعِيدًا طَيِّبًا فَٱمْسَحُوا۟ بِوُجُوهِكُمْ
وَأَيْدِيكُم مِّنْهُ ۚ مَا يُرِيدُ ٱللَّهُ لِيَجْعَلَ عَلَيْكُم مِّنْ حَرَجٍ وَلَـٰكِن
يُرِيدُ لِيُطَهِّرَكُمْ وَلِيُتِمَّ نِعْمَتَهُۥ عَلَيْكُمْ لَعَلَّكُمْ
تَشْكُرُونَ ﴿٦﴾

6 You who believe, when you get up to pray, wash your faces and your hands and your arms to the elbows, and wipe over your heads, and wash your feet to the ankles. If you are in a state of major impurity, then purify yourselves. But if you are ill or on a journey, or have come from the lavatory, or have touched women, and cannot find any water, then do tayammum with pure earth, and wipe your faces and your hands. Allah does not want

to make things difficult for you, but He does want to purify you and to perfect His blessing upon you so that hopefully you will be thankful.

Al-Qushayrī and Ibn 'Aṭiyyah mentioned that this *āyah* was revealed in connection with the story of 'Ā'ishah when she lost the necklace in the al-Muraysī' expedition. It is the *Āyah* of *Wuḍū'*. Ibn 'Atiyyah said, 'But since *wuḍū'* was already confirmed with them as a practice, it is as if the recitation of the *āyah* only confirmed them in it. It gave them the added benefit and dispensation of *tayammum*. We mentioned the disagreement concerning this in *an-Nisā'*, and Allah knows best. The *āyah* contains the command to fulfil contracts and the perfection of the blessing. This dispensation (for *tayammum*) is part of the perfection of the blessing.

You who believe, when you get up to pray,

Scholars disagree about what is meant by these words. One group said that it is general to every getting up to perform the prayer, whether one is purified or not. When someone gets up for the prayer, they must perform *wuḍū'*. 'Alī used to do it and recited this *āyah*. Abū Muḥammad ad-Dārimī mentioned it in his *Musnad*. Something similar is related from 'Ikrimah. Ibn Sīrīn said that the caliphs used to perform *wuḍū'* for every prayer. According to this, the *āyah* is one of judgment which is not abrogated.

Another group say that it is specific to the Prophet ﷺ. 'Abdullāh ibn Ḥanẓalah ibn Abī 'Āmir al-Ghasīl said that the Prophet ﷺ was commanded to perform *wuḍū'* for every prayer. That was hard on him and he was commanded to use the *siwāk* and the obligation to do *wuḍū'* was removed from those who had not broken it. 'Alqamah ibn al-Faghwā' related from his father, one of the Companions, who was the guide of the Messenger of Allah ﷺ to Tabūk, that this *āyah* was revealed as a dispensation for the Messenger of Allah ﷺ because he used not to do anything without being in *wuḍū'* nor would he speak to anyone nor return a greeting. So Allah informed him in this *āyah* that *wuḍū'* is for rising for the prayer alone rather than other actions.

Yet another group said that what is meant is *wuḍū'* for every prayer out of the desire for excellence, and so the command is just a recommendation. Many of the Companions, including Ibn 'Umar, used to do that. The Prophet ﷺ did that up until the Conquest of Makkah when he did five prayers with one *wuḍū'* to make things clear for his Community. So it would appear from the literal meaning of these words that *wuḍū'* for every prayer was recommended and not obligatory before it was abrogated. That is not the case. When a command comes, it means that it is an obligation, especially among the Companions, as is known from their biographies.

Others say that *wuḍū'* was originally obligatory for every prayer and then that was abrogated at the Conquest of Makkah. This an error because of the *ḥadīth* of Anas which says: 'The Prophet ﷺ used to perform *wuḍū'* for every prayer while his community differed from that,' and also because of the *ḥadīth* of Suwayd ibn an-Nu'mān who said that the Prophet ﷺ prayed *'Aṣr* and *Maghrib* at aṣ-Ṣahbā' with one *wuḍū'* in the expedition to Khaybar in 6 AH or 7 AH. Makkah was conquered in 8 AH. It is a sound *ḥadīth* that Mālik related in the *Muwaṭṭā'* and was transmitted by al-Bukhārī and Muslim. These two *ḥadīth*s make it clear that it was not, in fact, an obligation for every prayer before the Conquest of Makkah.

If it is said that Muslim related from Buraydah ibn al-Ḥuṣayb that the Messenger of Allah ﷺ used to do *wuḍū'* for every prayer and then, on the day of the Conquest, he prayed all the prayers with one *wuḍū'* and wiped over his leather socks. 'Umar said, 'Today you have done something that you did not do before.' He answered ﷺ, 'I did it on purpose, 'Umar.' Why did 'Umar question him? It is said that he questioned him because he ﷺ differed from what he did when he prayed at Khaybar. Allah knows best. At-Tirmidhī related from Anas that the Prophet ﷺ used to perform *wuḍū'* for every prayer whether in purity or not. Humayd said, 'I asked Anas, "And what did you do?" He said, "We used to do *wuḍū'* once."' It is a *ḥasan* sound *ḥadīth*. It is related that Prophet ﷺ said, '*Wuḍū'* on top of *wuḍū'* is a light.' So the Prophet ﷺ used to renew *wuḍū'* for every prayer. If a man greeted him when he had urinated, he would not return the greeting until he had done *tayammum*. Then he would return it. He said, 'I dislike to mention Allah when I am not in a state of purity.' Ad-Dāraquṭnī related it.

As-Suddī and Zayd ibn Aslam said that the *āyah* means: 'when you get up from your beds to pray,' in other words from sleep. The aim of this interpretation is that breaking purity is general. This is especially the case with sleep. There is a disagreement about whether sleep breaks *wuḍū'* by itself or not. According to this interpretation, there is a change in the normal order of words in this *āyah*. It implies: 'O you who believe! When you get up from sleep to pray, or one of you comes from the lavatory, or you have touched women (meaning lesser touching), then wash,' and the rules for lesser purification are given.

If you are in a state of major impurity, then purify yourselves.

This is another ruling. And Allah says about both types: '*If you are ill or on a journey, or have come from the lavatory...*' (4:43) This is the interpretation of Muḥammad ibn Maslamah among Mālik's people as well as others. The majority of scholars say: the *āyah* means: 'When you rise for the prayer and are not in purity,' and there is no change in order of the sentence. The order in the *āyah* gives the ruling governing those who have water. Then Allah adds touching of women and then mentions the ruling governing those who do not have water in both cases. Touching here means sexual intercourse and it is necessary for Allah to mention those who are in *janābah* and lack water, as He mentioned the first category. This is the interpretation of ash-Shāfi'ī and others, and it is the basis of the positions of the Companions like Sa'd ibn Abī Waqqāṣ, Ibn 'Abbās, Abū Mūsā al-Ash'arī and others. These are two interpretations which are the best of what is said about the *āyah*. Allah knows best.

The meaning of 'when you get up' is 'when you have got up' because *wuḍū'* in the state of actual rising to the prayer is not possible.

wash your faces

Allah mentions four body parts: the face, which one is obliged to wash, the hands, which must be washed, the head, which is wiped, and there is disagreement about the feet. Only mentioning these points indicates that other elements are a matter of *adab* and *sunnah*s, and Allah knows best.

The face must be washed by bringing water to it and running the hand over it. This is the reality of washing as we explained in *an-Nisā'* (4:43). Others say that it is just making water flow on it, and the hand is not part of that. There is no doubt that if a man is immersed in water and his face or hand is immersed without rubbing, it is called 'washing' the face and hand. That is considering the word alone. If that is achieved, it is sufficient. Linguistically the noun *wajh* (face) is taken from *muwājahah* (direct encounter). The face is a part of the body which includes other parts and has length and width. It begins at the flat of the brow and reaches the end of the beard and extends from ear to ear for a beardless person. If someone has a beard, water must touch the beard whether it is thick or thin. If the skin can be seen through the beard, then water must penetrate it. If it is thick, then the obligation is like that of the hair of the head. If there is a lot of hair on the chin and the beard hangs down, Saḥnūn said that Ibn al-Qāsim said, 'I heard Mālik being asked whether he had heard any of the people of knowledge saying that the beard was part of the face and so water must be passed over it. He answered that he had and said, "Penetrating it in *wuḍū'* is not part of what people do." He censured those who do that.'

Ibn al-Qāsim also mentioned that Mālik said, 'Someone who performs *wuḍū'* moves the outside of the beard without inserting his fingers into it.' He said that it is like a person's toes. Ibn 'Abd al-Ḥakam said that it is mandatory to penetrate the beard in both *wuḍū'* and *ghusl.* Abū 'Umar said, 'It is related that the Prophet ﷺ penetrated his beard in *wuḍū'* but all the paths of the transmission which say that are weak.' Ibn Khuwayzimandād mentioned that *fuqahā'* agree that it is not mandatory to penetrate the beard in *wuḍū'* with the one exception of something that is related from Sa'īd ibn Jubayr who said, 'Why would a man wash his beard before it grows and not wash it after it has grown? Why would a beardless man wash his chin and a man with a beard not wash it?'

Aṭ-Ṭaḥāwī said, 'In *tayammum* it is mandatory to wipe the skin before the beard grows but all of them drop that afterwards. That is also the case in *wuḍū'*.' Abū 'Umar said, 'If someone makes washing all of the beard mandatory, he makes it part of the face because *wajh* (face) is taken from *muwājahah* and Allah commanded washing the face in general and did not distinguish someone with a beard from someone who is beardless. So, based on the literal text of the Qur'ān, it is obligatory to wash it because it replaces the skin.' Ibn al-'Arabī preferred this position and I also take that view based on the fact that it is related that the Prophet ﷺ used to wash his beard. At-Tirmidhī and others transmitted it. What is probable is made specific by the action being done. Ibn al-Mundhir related from Isḥāq that someone who deliberately omits to make the water penetrate his beard should repeat *wuḍū'*. At-Tirmidhī related from 'Uthmān ibn 'Affān that the Prophet ﷺ used to make water penetrate his beard. He said that it is a sound *ḥasan ḥadīth.*

Abū 'Umar said, 'Those who do not believe that it is mandatory to wash the part of the beard which hangs down believe that the basic principle, which is commanded, is that of washing the skin and so it is mandatory to wash any of the skin that is visible. On that basis, since it is not skin, the hanging part of the beard is not part of what one is obliged to wash.' There is also disagreement about washing what grows on the cheeks up to the ears. Ibn Wahb related that Mālik said, 'What is below the temples, which is what is beyond the hair of the beard to the jaw, is not part of the face.' Abū 'Umar said, 'I do not know of any of the *fuqahā'* of the land who says what Ibn Wahb related from Mālik.'

Abū Ḥanīfah and his people said, 'The whiteness between the cheek and ear is part of the face, and washing it is mandatory.' Ash-Shāfi'ī and Aḥmad said something similar. It is said that it is recommended to wash the white part. Ibn al-

'Arabī said, 'What I consider sound is that anyone other than a beardless person must wash it, not one with down on the cheeks.' That is what Qāḍī 'Abd al-Wahhāb preferred. The reason for the disagreement is whether the term facing directly (*muwājahah*) applies to it or not. Allah knows best.

There is disagreement about whether the command to wash the face includes the inside of the mouth and nose. Aḥmad ibn Ḥanbal, Isḥāq and others believed that it is mandatory to wash the inside of the nose and mouth, except for Aḥmad who said, 'Someone who fails to inhale water up the nose in his *wuḍū'* should repeat it, but need not repeat it if he fails to rinse his mouth.' Most scholars say that they constitute two *sunnah*s in both *wuḍū'* and *ghusl* because the command deals with the outside, not the inside. The Arabs only use the term 'face' for what is directly visible. Furthermore, Allah did not mention them in His Book nor did the Muslims oblige them. There is not unanimous agreement about it. Obligatory elements are only established in these ways and this was discussed in *an-Nisā'*.

As for the eyes, all people agree that it is not obliged to wash the inside of the eyes except for what is related about 'Abdullāh ibn 'Umar splashing water onto his eyes. Washing them is omitted because that can cause harm. Ibn al-'Arabī said, 'That is why 'Abdullāh ibn 'Umar used to wash his eyes when he had gone blind since there would then be no harm in doing so.' While this is confirmed regarding the ruling of the face, an undefined part of the head must also be washed together with the face. Similarly part of the head must be wiped in the position of those who say that the entire head must be wiped. This is based on one of the fundamental principles of *fiqh*: 'If something mandatory can only be achieved in a particular way, then that too becomes mandatory.' Allah knows best.

Most scholars agree that there must be an intention for *wuḍū'* since the Prophet ﷺ said, 'Actions are according to their intentions.' Al-Bukhārī said, 'That includes belief, *wuḍū'*, the prayer, *zakāt*, *ḥajj*, fasting and other rulings. Allah says: *"Each man acts according to his nature."* (17:84) This means "according to his intention".' The Prophet ﷺ said, '...*jihād* and intention.' Most Shāfi'īs say that there is no need for an intention, which is also the position of the Ḥanafīs who say, 'An intention is only mandatory in obligations which are intended for themselves and nothing else. In the case of something that is a condition for the validity of another action, an intention is not obligatory, because the command indicates that it only needs to accompany it. Purity is a condition. There is no prayer for someone for whom the obligation of purity is not possible, like a woman menstruating or in lochia.'

Our scholars and some Shāfi'īs argue by Allah's words here. Since washing is mandatory before the prayer, the validity of the action is conditional on an intention because the obligation to do it comes from Allah Almighty and so it is an obligation commanded by Allah. If you were to say that if the intention [for *wuḍū'*] is not mandatory, then aiming to do what Allah has commanded is not mandatory either. If that were the case, then someone who washes simply to cool himself or for some other reason, would also be fulfilling the obligation.

There are sound *ḥadīth*s that say that *wuḍū'* expiates wrong actions. If it was valid without an intention, it would not expiate wrong actions. Allah says: *'They were only ordered to worship Allah, making their dīn sincerely His.'* (98:5) Ibn al-'Arabī said, 'Some of our scholars say, "If someone goes to a river with the intention of washing, that satisfies the obligation, even if he forgets his intention on the way. But if he goes to a bath-house and forgets on the way, then the intention is void."'

Qāḍī Abū Bakr ibn al-'Arabī said, 'Some inferior *muftī*s use this as a basis for saying that there are two positions about the intention for the prayer. They produce a text on it from someone who does not distinguish between opinion and certainty and says that it is permitted to put the intention [for *wuḍū'*] in it just before the *takbīr.* O Allah, what a dire state the world is in when we are a community that desires to strive and give *fatwā* but Allah does not give us success or let us be correct! May Allah have mercy on us! So know that scholars disagree about the obligatory nature of the intention in respect of *wuḍū'*. Mālik's position also varies regarding it. When something is less than agreed upon, it is allowed to advance it in certain situations. None of the imams disagree about the prayer. It is the basic premise of the intention, so how can an intended basic premise, about which there is agreement, be dependent on a subsidiary element about which there is disagreement? Is this anything but utter stupidity? As for fasting, the *Sharī'ah* has removed difficulty from it [by not having to renew the intention every day] when there is already a prior intention [at the beginning of the month] since the fast begins at a time when one lacks focus.'

and your arms to the elbows

People disagree about whether the elbows are included. Some say that they are included because when what follows the preposition '*ilā*' (to) is of the same genus it is included in it. Sībawayh and others said that. This was already explained in *al-Baqarah* (2:187). It is also said that that they are not included. Both views are related from Mālik. The second is from Ashhab while the first is the sound position of most based on what ad-Dāraquṭnī related from Jābir that when the Prophet ﷺ did *wuḍū'*, he brought the water over his elbows. Some say that '*ilā*' here means 'with'. This is not a valid argument as we explained in *an-Nisā'* (4:43).

It is also because the Arabs apply the term *'yad'* to what is between the tips of the fingers right up to the shoulder. Similarly the term *'rijl'* (foot) is applied to what is between the toes and the beginning of the thighs. On this basis 'elbows' are included in *'yad'*. Therefore, the meaning 'with' is not applicable. When Allah uses 'to', it defines the limit of the elbows in washing and so the elbows are washed [and the arms and hands] down to the nails. These are sound words based on fundamental principles in language and meaning. Ibn al-'Arabī said, 'No one properly understood the definitive point in the question except for Qāḍī Abū Muḥammad who said that "to the elbows" defines the limit of what is left of "arms" that are not washed. That is why the elbows are included in being washed.'

Since the terms *'yad'* and *'rijl'* are used linguistically in the way we have mentioned, Abū Hurayrah used to wash right up to his armpits and thighs. He said, 'I heard my friend ﷺ say, "The adornment of a believer will reach where his *wuḍū'* reaches.' Qāḍī 'Iyāḍ said, 'What people are agreed on differs from this. One should not exceed the limits in *wuḍū'* since the Prophet ﷺ said, "Whoever does more has transgressed and acted wrongly."' Someone else said, 'This action was his position and he alone did it. He did not relate it from the Prophet ﷺ and took it from his words about having a white blaze and white feet and his words about the extent of adornment.'

and wipe over your heads

It was already mentioned in *an-Nisā'* (4:43) that *masḥ* is a word with multiple meanings. The word 'head' (*ra's*) designates the whole head which people know by necessity. It includes the face. When Allah mentioned it in *wuḍū'* and specified the face for washing, it is clear that the rest should be wiped. If washing had not been mentioned, the obligation would be to wipe all of it: the hair on the head, the eyes, the nose and the mouth. Mālik indicated the obligation to wipe the head as far as we mentioned. He was asked about someone who omitted part of the head in *wuḍū'* and said, 'Do you think that if washing part of the face were omitted, it would be sufficient?' By what we mentioned he made it clear that the ears are part of the head and that they have the same ruling as the head. This differs from az-Zuhrī who said, 'They are part of the face and are washed with it.' It also differs from ash-Sha'bī who said, 'The front part of them is part of the face and the behind part is part of the head.' That is the view of al-Ḥasan and Isḥāq. Ibn Abī Hurayah related it from ash-Shāfi'ī. Their argument will be mentioned.

The 'head' (*ra's*) is called that because of its height and the growth of hair on it. Another use of it is in the expression the 'head of the mountain'. It is said that 'head' is a name for all of the limbs as a poet said:

When they carry my head – and my head contains most of me –
and it is betrayed in the encounter, the same is true of the rest of me.

Scholars disagree about the extent of the wiping. There are eleven positions among scholars for the extent of the wiping: three from Abū Ḥanīfah, two from ash-Shāfi'ī and six from the Mālikīs. The sound version is that it should be inclusive, and scholars agree that it is good to wipe all of the head and that then one has done what is obliged. The *bā'* can be for emphasis and not partitive (i.e. meaning part of the head), so it means 'wipe over your heads'. It is said that including it here is like its inclusion in *tayammum* when He says, '*wipe your faces*'. If it had been partitive, it could convey that in that place as well. This is definite.

It is said that it is included as an expression of excellent style. It is that linguistically washing necessitates the existence of what is washed whereas wiping does not linguistically necessitate the existence of what is wiped. If Allah had said, 'Wipe your head', it would be enough to wipe the hand over once without actually properly wiping the head. So the *bā'* conveys what it should be wiped with: water. Therefore, it is as if Allah is saying, 'Wipe your heads with water.' That is eloquent in language for two reasons: either for reversal or for inclusion. [POEMS] This is what our scholars say about the meaning of the preposition *bā'* here.

Ash-Shāfi'ī said that it is possible that the use of the *bā'* means both that it can indicate wiping part of the head and wiping the entire head. The *Sunnah* indicates that wiping part of it satisfies the requirement. It is said that the Prophet ﷺ wiped his forelock. Elsewhere ash-Shāfi'ī said, 'If it is asked in respect of Allah's words "*wipe your faces*" whether part of the face suffices in *tayammum*, the answer is that in *tayammum* wiping the face is a substitute for washing it. So the wiping must cover every part of it that is washed. Wiping the head is the basis, and this is the difference between them.'

Our scholars answer the *ḥadīth* by saying that it may be that the Prophet ﷺ did that with an excuse for it, and that is very likely because he ﷺ did it on a journey where excuses are likely to be valid. Journeys entail haste and shortening things. Many obligations are omitted because of difficulty and danger. Then he was not content with just the forelock and wiped over his turban. Muslim transmitted it from al-Mughīrah ibn Shu'bah. If wiping the entire head had not been mandatory he would not have wiped over his turban. Allah knows best.

The majority of scholars agree that one full wiping is adequate. Ash-Shāfi'ī said that the head should be wiped over three times. That was related from Anas, Sa'īd ibn Jubayr and 'Aṭā'. Ibn Sīrīn used to wipe twice. Abū Dāwūd said, 'All the sound *ḥadīth*s of 'Uthmān indicate wiping the head once. They mentioned doing *wuḍū'* three times and said, 'He wiped his head,' but they did not mention the number.

They disagree about where to start the wiping. Mālik said that you start at the front of the head, go to the back of it and return to the front based on the *ḥadīth* of 'Abdullāh ibn Zayd in Muslim. It is the position of ash-Shāfi'ī and Aḥmad. Al-Ḥasan ibn Ḥayy said that you should begin at the back of the head based on the *ḥadīth* of ar-Rubayyi' bint Mu'awwidh ibn 'Afrā'. That is a *ḥadīth* in which the wording varies. It centres on 'Abdullāh ibn Muḥammad ibn 'Aqīl who is not considered to be a *ḥāfiẓ* in *ḥadīth*. Abū Dāwūd transmitted it from Bishr ibn al-Mufaḍḍal from 'Abdullāh from ar-Rubayyi'. Ibn 'Ajlān related from him from ar-Rubayyi': 'The Messenger of Allah ﷺ did *wuḍū'* in our presence and wiped all of his head from the top of his hair on both sides with the fall of the hair. He did not move his hair from its position.' This manner is related from Ibn 'Umar who began from the middle of the head. The soundest thing about this matter is the *ḥadīth* of 'Abdullāh ibn Zayd. All allow wiping part of the head. That 'part' is said to be at the front of the head. It is related that Ibrāhīm and ash-Sha'bī said, 'Any parts of the head that are wiped satisfy the requirement.' 'Umar wiped just the top of his head.

The consensus is that it is recommended to wipe with both hands and over all parts of the head if the wiping is done with one hand. There is disagreement about wiping with just a finger, even if that covers what is related to satisfy the required part of the head. The well-known position is that it satisfies the requirement and that is the position of Sufyān ath-Thawrī. Sufyān said, 'It is enough if someone wipes his head with one finger.' It is also said that it is not satisfactory because it is outside the *sunnah* for wiping: it is playing. If, however, that is due to necessity arising from illness, there is no disagreement that it satisfies it. Abū Ḥanīfah, Abū Yūsuf and Muḥammad said that wiping the head with less than three fingers is not sufficient. There is disagreement about bringing back the hands over the hair and whether that is obligatory or *sunnah*. There is a consensus that the first wiping is obligatory based on the Qur'ān. Most say that the former is *sunnah* although some say that it is obligatory.

If someone doing *wuḍū'* washes his head instead of wiping it, Ibn al-'Arabī said about that, 'We do not know of any disagreement that it satisfies the requirement although Imam Fakhr ad-*dīn* ash-Shāsī reported to us in a lesson from Abū al-'Abbās ibn al-Qāṣṣ from their people that it does not satisfy it.' This is due to an interpolation from the unsound Dāwūdiyyah school which arises from following the literal text which invalidates the *Sharī'ah*. Allah censured it in His words: '*They know an outward aspect of the life this world*' (30:7) and: '...*or are they words that are simply guesswork on your part.*' (13:33) This washer does what he is commanded to do and then adds more to it. If it is said that this addition derives from the words by which worship occurs, we say that it is not derived from its meaning in connecting the action to its proper place. That is the case if he wipes his head and then shaves it, he does not have to wipe it again.

According to Mālik, Aḥmad, ath-Thawrī, Abū Ḥanīfah and others the ears are part of the head. They disagree about renewing water [to wipe the ears]. Mālik and Aḥmad said that water should be renewed for them rather than using the water left on the hands after wiping the head, according to what was done by Ibn 'Umar. That is what ash-Shāfi'ī said about renewing water and they said that they [the ears] constitute a *sunnah* on their own and are not part of the face or the head. Scholars agree that any hair on them should not be shaved during the *ḥajj*. The position of Abū Thawr regarding this is the same as that of ash-Shāfi'ī. Ath-Thawrī and Abū Ḥanīfah said that they should be wiped together with the head using the same water. A similar position is related from a group of the early generations of the Companions and *Tābi'ūn*. Dāwūd said that it is good to wipe the ears, but if it is not done, the person owes nothing since they are not mentioned in the Qur'ān. He needs to be told that the term 'head' includes them as we made clear.

There are sound *ḥadīth*s in the books of an-Nasā'ī, Abū Dāwūd and others that the Prophet ﷺ wiped the back and front of the ears and put his fingers inside them. The fact that they are not mentioned in the Book indicates that they are not an obligation like washing and face and hands. The *Sunnah* confirms that it is *sunnah* to wipe them. The people of knowledge dislike anyone performing *wuḍū'* to abandon wiping their ears and say that if they do they are abandoning one of the *sunnah*s of the Prophet ﷺ, but only Isḥāq obliges them to repeat *wuḍū'*. He said, 'It is not sufficient if someone omits wiping his ears.' Aḥmad said, 'If someone omits them deliberately, I prefer them to repeat *wuḍū'*.'

It is related from 'Alī ibn Ziyād from the people of Mālik that Mālik said, 'If someone deliberately abandons one of the *sunnah*s of *wuḍū'* or the prayer, they should repeat it.' This is weak in the view of the *fuqahā'*. None of the early generations said that and it has no place in logic. If that were the case, there would be no way of distinguishing between the obligations and any other actions. Allah knows best.

The argument of those who say that the ears are part of the face is the fact that is confirmed that the Prophet ﷺ said in his prostration: 'My face has prostrated to the One Who created it fashioned it, and divided its hearing and sight.' So he ascribed hearing to the face and confirmed that they have the same ruling as the face. We find in the *Muṣannaf* of Abū Dāwūd from the *ḥadīth* of 'Uthmān that he washed the front and back of the ears once and then washed his feet. Then he said, 'Where are those who asked about *wuḍū'*? This is how I saw the Messenger of Allah ﷺ do *wuḍū'*.' The argument of those who say that their fronts should be washed with the face and their backs wiped with head is that Allah Almighty commanded washing the face and commanded wiping the head, so the front part of the ears must be washed because they are part of the face and it is mandatory to wipe their backs because they are part of the head. This is refuted by traditions which state that the Prophet ﷺ used to wipe both the back and front of his ears, as reported by 'Alī, 'Uthmān, Ibn 'Abbās, ar-Rabī' and others. Those who say that they are part of the head argue by the words of the Prophet ﷺ in the *ḥadīth* of aṣ-Ṣunābiḥī: 'When he wipes his head, the sins leave his head until they emerge from his ears.' Mālik transmitted it.

your feet

Nāfi', Ibn 'Āmir and al-Kisā'ī recited *'arjulakum'* in the accusative and al-Walīd ibn Muslim related that Nāfi' recited *'arjulukum'* in the nominative which is the reading of al-Ḥasan and al-A'mash. Ibn Kathīr, Abū 'Amr and Ḥamzah recited *'arjulikum'* in the genitive. The Companions and *Tābi'ūn* disagree according to these readings. If it is read as *arjulakum* in the accusative, it is the object of 'wash' and so the feet must be washed and not wiped. This is the school of the majority of most scholars and it is confirmed as the action of the Prophet ﷺ and necessary. He saw some people doing *wuḍū'* and missing out their heels. He said in his loudest voice, 'Woe to the heels from the Fire! Do full *wuḍū'*.'

to the ankles.

Allah then defines its extent as when He says about the arms 'to the elbows' and this indicates that it is mandatory to wash them, and Allah knows best. If it is read *arjulikum* in the genitive, the regent is the *bā'*. Ibn al-'Arabī said, 'Scholars agree that it is mandatory to wash them. I do not know of anyone among Muslim *fuqahā'* who rejects that other than aṭ-Ṭabarī and the Rāfiḍite Shi'ah. Aṭ-Ṭabarī based that on the reading in the genitive. It is related that Ibn 'Abbās said, '*Wuḍū'* consists of two washings and two wipings.'

It is related that al-Ḥajjāj gave a *khuṭbah* in al-Ahwāz in which he said, 'Wash your faces and hands and wipe your heads and [do your] feet. There is nothing in a human being closer to foulness than his feet. Wash the top and bottom of them as well as the heels.' Anas ibn Mālik heard that and said, 'Allah spoke the truth and al-Ḥajjāj lied. Allah says: *"Wipe over your heads, and your feet."*' He said that when he wiped his feet, he moistened them. It is also related that he said, 'The Qur'ān revealed wiping and the *sunnah* is washing.' 'Ikrimah used to wipe his feet and said, 'There is no washing of the feet. Wiping was revealed about them.' 'Āmir ash-Sha'bī said, 'Jibrīl brought down washing. Do you not see that *tayammum* wipes what is washed and sets aside what is wiped?' Qatādah said, 'Allah imposed two washings and two wipings.' Ibn Jarīr aṭ-Ṭabarī believed that the obligation about them consists of a choice between washing and wiping, and he made both readings like two transmissions. An-Naḥḥās said, 'The best of what is said about it is that wiping and washing are both obligations. Wiping is obligatory according to the reading in the genitive, and washing is obligatory according to the reading in the accusative. The two readings are in the position of two *āyah*s.'

Ibn 'Aṭiyyah said that some of those who recite it in the genitive believe that wiping the feet is actually washing. This is sound. *Masḥ* is a word with several meanings. It can mean wiping or washing. Al-Harawī said that al-Azharī reported from Abū Bakr Muḥammad ibn 'Uthmān ibn Sa'īd ad-Dārī from Abū Ḥātim that Abū Zayd al-Anṣārī said, 'In Arabic, wiping can mean washing or wiping. When a man does *wuḍū'* and washes his limbs, it is said that "he has wiped (*tamassaḥa*)." It is said that Allah has "wiped" away what you have when He washes you and purifies you of sins.' Since it is confirmed from the Arabs that 'wiping' can mean washing, one prefers the statement of those who say that what is meant by the genitive reading is washing, going by the reading in the accusative where there is no ambiguity. There are also many *ḥadīth*s that affirm washing. The threat issued against those who fail to wash them is found in countless sound reports transmitted by the Imams.

In that case wiping the head comes between what is washed to clarify the order since that is done before the feet. It implies: 'Wash your faces and arms to the elbows and your feet to the ankles and wipe your heads,' but since the head is wiped before the feet, it is put before them in the recitation. Allah knows best. It is not because they share with the head but because it precedes them in the description of purification. 'Āṣim ibn Kulayb related from Abū 'Abd ar-Raḥmān as-Sulamī that al-Ḥasan and al-Ḥusayn recited '*arjulikum*' and 'Alī heard them when giving judgment between people. He said, '*Arjulakum*. This is a change in word order.'

Abū Isḥāq related from al-Ḥārith that 'Alī said, 'Wash your feet to the ankles.' Similarly it is related that Ibn Mas'ūd and Ibn 'Abbās recited it in the accusative.

It is said that the genitive in the context of the feet makes their wiping specific, but it refers to when people are wearing leather socks and we learn this specification from the Messenger of Allah ﷺ because it is only soundly reported from him that he wiped his feet when he was wearing leather socks, and so through his action the Prophet ﷺ made it clear when the feet are washed and when they are wiped. This is good. If it is said that wiping over leather socks was abrogated by *Sūrat al-Mā'idah,* that 'Abbās said that, that Abū Hurayrah and 'Ā'ishah rejected wiping, and that Mālik objected to it in one transmission, the answer is that negating one thing while affirming another is not an authoritative proof for the negator. Wiping over leather socks was confirmed many times from the Companions and others. Al-Ḥasan said, 'Seventy men of the Companions of the Prophet ﷺ wiped over leather socks.'

It is confirmed by sound transmission that Hammām said, 'Jarīr urinated and then did *wuḍū'* and wiped over his leather socks.' Ibrāhīm an-Nakha'ī said, 'They liked this *ḥadīth* because Jarīr became Muslim after the revelation of *al-Mā'idah.* This is a text that refutes what they mentioned as an argument from al-Wāqidī from 'Abd al-Ḥamīd ibn Ja'far from his father that Jarīr became Muslim in Ramadan 10 AH. *Al-Mā'idah* was revealed in Dhū'l-Ḥijjah on the day of 'Arafāt. This *ḥadīth* is not confirmed because it is weak. That part which was revealed on the Day of 'Arafah was: '*Today I have completed your dīn for you.*' Aḥmad ibn Ḥanbal said, 'I prefer the *ḥadīth* of Jarīr about wiping over leather socks because he became Muslim after the revelation of *al-Mā'idah.* As for what was related from Abū Hurayrah and 'Ā'ishah, that is not sound. We do not think that 'Ā'ishah had knowledge of that. That is why she referred the questioner to 'Alī ﷺ. She said, 'Ask him. He used to travel with the Messenger of Allah ﷺ.'

As for Mālik, nothing *munkar* is related from him and so it is not sound that something *munkar* should be attributed to him. What is sound is what he said when he was dying to Ibn Nāfi': '[Wiping over leather socks while resident and on a journey is absolutely sound.] I used to adopt full purification in respect of myself but I do not think that someone who wipes fall short in what is obliged for him.' This is the interpretation that Aḥmad ibn Ḥanbal made about the words related by Ibn Wahb: 'I do not wipe either while resident or on a journey.' Aḥmad said, 'It is related that Ibn 'Umar commanded them to wipe over their leather socks, but he himself removed them and did *wuḍū'*, saying, "I love *wuḍū'*." The like of that is reported from Abū Ayyūb.' Aḥmad said, 'If someone abandons that in the way it was abandoned by Ibn 'Umar, Abū Ayyūb and Mālik, I do not object to it. We pray behind such a man and do not censure him even though he abandons that. He is not seen as one of the people of innovation so that one would not pray behind him. Allah knows best.'

It is said that *'your feet'* is added to the words but not the meaning. This also indicates washing and one observes the meaning, not the word. It is in the genitive due to proximity which is something the Arabs do, and this usage is found in the Qur'ān and elsewhere as we see in 55:35 where *naḥḥās* is in the genitive because it is smoke. Another instance is in 85:11-12 where the genitive is used. [POEMS+ POEM DISCUSSION]

The definitive position where this matter is concerned is that it is an obligation to wash the feet as we already mentioned, supported by what is confirmed that the Prophet ﷺ said, 'Woe to the heels and the bottom of the feet from the Fire!' He alarmed us by mentioning the Fire so that we do not oppose what Allah Almighty desires. It is known that only those who abandon what is an obligation will be punished by the Fire and it is known that wiping is not a comprehensive action. There is no disagreement among those who say that when the feet are wiped that it is the top of them and not the bottoms that are wiped. So this *ḥadīth* makes it clear that the position that they should be wiped is false since they believe that it does not include wiping the bottoms of the feet. That can only be achieved by washing, not wiping. Another proof comes from the consensus. There is agreement that washing the feet fulfils the obligation. There is disagreement about those who wipe their feet. Certainty consists in that on which there is agreement, not in that about which there is disagreement.

The majority transmit, all from all, that the Prophet ﷺ used to wash his feet when performing *wuḍū'* once, twice or three times until he cleaned them. That is enough for you as an argument for washing, along with the rest of what we have explained. It is clear and apparent that the genitive reading means washing rather than wiping as we have mentioned and that the regent which affects *'your feet'* is *'wash'*. The Arabs add one thing to another with a verb that only actually affects one of them as when you say, 'I ate bread and milk' when you, in fact, drank the milk. Supporting that are the words in the poem:

Their fodder was straw and cold water.

Another said:

I saw your husband in the battle, girded with a sword and spear.

Another said:

Its gazelles and ostriches have their young on the slopes.

Yet another said:

A drink of milk, and dates and curds.

The first means that their fodder was straw and drink was cold water and the second that he was girded with a sword while carrying a spear. The gazelles have their young fawns on the slopes and the ostriches hatched their eggs. Ostriches do not have fawns, but eggs. 'Slopes' are the sides of the *wādī*. One drinks milk and eats dates. Thus the words: '*wipe over your heads, and your feet*' is adding washing to wiping, based on the meaning. What is meant is washing. Allah knows best.

Concerning ankles, al-Bukhārī related from Mūsā from Wuhayb from 'Amr ibn Yaḥyā that his father said, 'I saw 'Amr ibn Abī Ḥasan ask 'Abdullāh ibn Zayd about the *wuḍū'* of the Prophet ﷺ. He called for a pot with water in it and did *wuḍū'* for them in the way that the Prophet ﷺ did it. He poured water from the pot over his hand and washed both hands three times. Then he put his hand in the pot and then rinsed out his mouth and then sniffed water up his nose and blew it out using three handfuls of water. Then he put his hand in [the water-pot] and washed his face three times. Then he washed his arms three times to the elbows. Then he put his hand in [the water-pot] and wiped his head, bringing his hands from the forehead to the nape of the neck and then bringing them back again once. [Then he washed his feet to the ankles.]'

This *ḥadīth* contains evidence that the *bā'* in '*wipe your heads*' is extra and does not actually mean '*bi-ra'sihi*'. The head is wiped over once. This is clarified in the book of Muslim from the *ḥadīth* of 'Abdullāh ibn Zayd in explaining his words: 'bringing them forward and back' that he began with the front of his head and then took them to the nape of the neck and then back to the place where he began.

Scholars disagree about the ankles and the majority say that they are the bones at the sides of the feet. Al-Aṣma'ī did not accept people's statement that *ka'b* means the top of the foot. He said that in *aṣ-Ṣiḥāḥ*. It is related from Ibn al-Qāsim and it was stated by Muḥammad ibn al-Ḥasan. Ibn 'Aṭiyyah said, 'I do not know of anyone who says that this is the extent of *wuḍū'*, but in at-*Talqīn* 'Abd al-Wahhāb uses an expression about that which is confused and unclear.' Ash-Shāfi'ī said, 'I do not know of anyone who disagrees that the *ka'b* refers to the bones at the joints.' Aṭ-Ṭabarī said, 'The *ka'bān* which one must wash in *wuḍū'* are the bones connecting the legs to the heels. It is not the top of the feet.'

This is sound in language and in the *Sunnah*. Linguistically, *ka'b* is derived from height, and the Ka'bah takes its name from that. The verb *ka'aba* is used of breasts swelling and becoming round. The *ka'b* of a bamboo cane is its internode. The internode is what is between two nodes. It is used as a metaphor for nobility and glory. An example of its use is found in a *ḥadīth*: 'May Allah continue to make elevation (*ka'b*) rise.' The *Sunnah* is found in the words of the Prophet ﷺ related by Abū Dāwūd from an-Nu'mān ibn Bashīr: 'By Allah, make your rows straight or Allah will cause disagreement between your hearts.' He said, 'I saw men with their shoulder stuck to that of another man, and his knee to his knee or his ankle bone (*ka'b*) to his ankle bone.' The heel (*'aqib*) is the end of the bottom of the foot under the Achilles' tendon, and the Achilles' tendon is where the leg joins the foot. Illustrating that are the words of the *ḥadīth*: 'Woe to the heels from the Fire' when they are not washed.

Ibn Wahb said that Mālik said that no one has to make the water penetrate between the toes in *wuḍū'* or *ghusl*. There is no good in harshness and excess. Ibn Wahb said that it is desirable, but that water must penetrate between the fingers. Ibn al-Qāsim said that Mālik said, 'There is nothing owed for not making the water penetrate between the toes.' Muḥammad ibn Khālid related from Ibn al-Qāsim from Mālik about someone who does *wuḍū'* by a river and shakes his feet in the water that it is not sufficient unless he washes them with his hands. Ibn al-Qāsim said, 'If he can wash one of them with the other, it is sufficient.'

What is sound in both cases that it is only sufficient when he washes what is between them like the rest of the foot since they are part of the foot as the fingers are part of the hand and must be washed. There is no consideration for opening or closing the toes. A man is commanded to wash all of the feet as he is commanded to wash all of the hands. It is related that when the Prophet ﷺ did *wuḍū'*, he rubbed his toes with his little finger, and it is confirmed that he ﷺ used to wash his feet. This demands doing all of them. At the end of his life, Mālik used to rub his toes with his little finger or part of his fingers, based on the *ḥadīth* that Ibn Wahb related from Ibn Lahī'ah and al-Layth ibn Sa'd from Yazīd ibn 'Amr al-Ghifārī from Abū 'Abd ar-Raḥmān al-Ḥubulī that al-Mustawrid ibn Shaddād al-Qurashī said, 'I saw the Messenger of Allah ﷺ doing *wuḍū'* and he put his little finger between his toes.' Ibn Wahb said, 'Mālik told me, "This is good. I only heard it just now."' Ibn Wahb said, 'After that I heard him being asked about going between the toes in *wuḍū'* and he commanded it.' Ḥudhayfah related that the Prophet ﷺ said, 'Penetrate between the toes and the Fire will not penetrate between them.' This is a text which is a threat about abandoning penetration. It is confirmed as we said, it is Allah Who grants success.

The wording requires that there be continuity in washing the limbs. That means that you should wash each limb one after the other without any gap between them or any action that is not part of it. Scholars disagree about this matter. Ibn Abī Salamah and Ibn Wahb said, 'That is one of the obligations of *wuḍū'*, both when remembered and forgotten. Someone who separates the limbs washed in *wuḍū'* deliberately or forgetfully has not satisfied the requirement.' Ibn 'Abd al-Ḥakam said that it is satisfied whether it is done forgetfully or deliberately. Mālik said in the *Mudawwanah* and the book of Muḥammad that continuity is not necessary and that is the position of ash-Shāfi'ī. Mālik and Ibn al-Qāsim said, 'If someone deliberately does *wuḍū'* discontinuously, it does not satisfy the requirement, but if they do so out of forgetfulness it does.' According to Ibn Wahb, Mālik said that it satisfies it in respect of what is washed, but not of what is wiped.

These are five positions based on two principles. The first is that Allah made a general command, to do *wuḍū'* whether continuously or discontinuously. What is desired is the fact of washing all of the limbs when getting up for the prayer. The second is that these are acts of worship with different pillars and so continuity in them is obliged, as is the case with the prayer. This is sounder, and Allah knows best.

The words of the *āyah* imply that there is an order in performing *wuḍū'*. There is disagreement about it. Al-Abharī said that to do it in that order is *sunnah*. The literal position is that in the case of a reversal due to forgetfulness, the requirement is still satisfied. There is disagreement about someone who does this deliberately. It is said that it satisfies the requirement, but they should follow the correct order in the future. Qāḍī Abū Bakr and others said that when there is violation of the order, the requirement is not satisfied. This is what is believed by ash-Shāfi'ī and the rest of his people, and it is the position of Aḥmad ibn Ḥanbal, Abū 'Ubayd al-Qāsim ibn Salām, Isḥāq and Abū Thawr. It is also held by Abū Muṣ'ab, Mālik's companion, and he mentioned it in his *Mukhtaṣar.*

It is related from the people of Madīnah and Mālik that someone who washes his hands before his face in *wuḍū'* has not performed *wuḍū'* according to the order in the *āyah* and must repeat what he has prayed with that *wuḍū'*. In most of his transmissions, and the most famous, Mālik said that the '*wāw*' here does not oblige succession and does not denote order. That is what his people say and it is the position of Abū Ḥanīfah and his people, ath-Thawrī, al-Awzā'ī, al-Layth ibn Sa'd, al-Muzanī, and Dāwūd ibn 'Alī.

Aṭ-Ṭabarī said that the literal meaning of the *āyah* demands satisfying the requirement, whether separate or together, or continuous, according to what is sound in the school of ash-Shāfi'ī. It is the position of most scholars. Abū 'Umar said, 'Mālik preferred to people start *wuḍū'* anew in the proper order if there is still time before the prayer. He did not think that it was mandatory for the person concerned. This is the final position of his school.' 'Alī ibn Ziyād related that Mālik said, 'If someone washes his arms and then his face and realises what has happened, he should repeat the washing of his arms. If he does not realise until after he has prayed, he should repeat *wuḍū'* and the prayer.' 'Alī said after that, 'He does not have to repeat the prayer, but should repeat *wuḍū'* for any future prayer.'

The cause of the dispute is the fact that some of them said the use of the conjunction *fā'* when Allah says '*wash*' necessitates the order. If it is an apodosis of a precondition, then it is connected to what is stipulated. Therefore, the order is necessitated in all of it. The answer to this is that it would be necessary to begin with the face if it is the sole result of the condition. So the order is demanded in all if the apodosis has just one object. If the entire sentence is an apodosis, however, it does not matter if one begins with it since the aim is to achieve it. It is said that the order is demanded by the *wāw*. That is not the case because you say, 'Zayd and 'Amr fought, and Bakr and Khālid argued.' So that is an aspect of reciprocity, not order.

The correct position is that the prescribed order comes in four ways. The first is that one begins with what Allah begins with, as the Prophet ﷺ said when he performed *ḥajj*, 'We began with what Allah began with.' The second is that it is something about which there was consensus among the *Salaf*. They followed that order. The third is that *wuḍū'* resembles the prayer. The fourth is that the Prophet ﷺ continued to do it like that. Those who allow the order to be broken argue by the consensus that there is no order in washing the limbs for *janābah*. So they say that it is the same when washing the limbs in *wuḍū'* because the aim in it is washing, not beginning. It is related that 'Alī said, 'When I finish my *wuḍū'*, I do not care with which limb I began.' 'Abdullāh ibn Mas'ūd said, 'There is nothing wrong in beginning with your feet before your hands.' Ad-Dāraquṭnī said, 'This is *mursal* and not confirmed. The obligation of the order is more fitting, and Allah knows best.'

If doing *wuḍū'* will cause someone to miss the time [of the prayer], most scholars say that he should not do *tayammum* instead. Mālik permits *tayammum* in that situation because the fundamental reason that *tayammum* came about was in order to preserve the time of the prayer. If that had not been the case, then it would have been obliged to delay the prayer until water became available. Most cite as evidence Allah's words: '*...if you cannot find any water, then do tayammum.*' For this person, water is available, so the condition that would allow him to do *tayammum* is lacking.

Some scholars use this *āyah* as evidence that it is not an obligation to remove impurity because Allah says: *'When you get up to do the prayer...'* not mentioning the removal of impurity, and then mentions *wuḍū'*. If removal of impurity had been mandatory, it would have been the first thing mentioned. That is the position of the people of Abū Ḥanīfah, and Ashhab transmitted it from Mālik. Ibn Wahb related that Mālik said that it is mandatory to remove impurity when it is remembered and when forgotten. That is the position of ash-Shāfi'ī. Ibn al-Qāsim said that it is mandatory to remove it when it is remembered but ignored when it is forgotten. Abū Ḥanīfah said that it is mandatory to remove any impurity that is greater in size than a Baghlī dirham. He meant the large coin which is like a *mithqāl*. That is based on analogy with the normal size of an orifice which is ignored.

The mandatory nature of its removal is taken from the sound transmission of Ibn Wahb that the Prophet ﷺ said about the two people in the grave, 'They are being punished, and they are not being punished for anything very great. One of them used to carry tales and the others did not protect himself from his urine.' One is only punished for abandoning something that is mandatory. There is no argument in the literal text of the Qur'ān because in the *Āyah* of *Wuḍū'* Allah is only giving the description of *wuḍū'* and does not deal with removing impurity or anything else.

The *āyah* is also evidence for wiping over leather socks as we will make clear. Mālik has three transmissions about that. One is that there is no acknowledgement of it at all, as the Khārijites said. This is not sound. The second is that they may be wiped over on journeys but not while resident because most of the *ḥadīth*s which deal with the matter take place on journeys. The permission to do it while resident, however, is indicated by the *ḥadīth* of the rubbish dump as well as other *ḥadīth*s. Muslim related that Ḥudhayfah said, 'I remember when the Messenger of Allah ﷺ and I were walking and he came to the rubbish dump of a people which was behind a wall. He stood as one of you does and urinated. I went away and he indicated to me to come back and I stood behind him until he had finished.' One variant adds: 'He performed *wuḍū'* and wiped over his leather socks.'

There is a similar *ḥadīth* from Shurayḥ ibn Hāni' who said, 'I went to 'Ā'ishah to ask her about wiping over leather socks and she said, "You must ask the son of Abū Ṭālib ['Alī]. He used to travel with the Messenger of Allah ﷺ." We asked him and he said, "The Messenger of Allah ﷺ allowed it for three days and nights for a traveller, and a day and a night for someone resident."' This is the third transmission: he can wipe over them while resident and on a journey. According to Mālik, there is no time-limit for a traveller in wiping over leather socks. That is the position of al-Layth ibn Sa'd. Ibn Wahb said, 'I heard Mālik say that the people of our town set no time-limit on that.'

Abū Dāwūd related that Ubayy ibn 'Umārah asked, 'Messenger of Allah, can I wipe over leather socks?' 'Yes,' he replied. He asked, 'For a day?' 'For a day,' he answered. 'For two days?' he asked. The reply was 'For two days.' Then he asked, 'And for three days?' He said, 'Yes, and whatever you wish.' One variant has, 'Yes, and what seems proper to you.' Abū Dāwūd said that there is disagreement about its *isnād* and it is not strong. Ash-Shāfi'ī, Aḥmad ibn Ḥanbal, an-Nu'mān and aṭ-Ṭabarī said that someone resident may wipe for one day and night and a traveller for three days according to the *ḥadīth* of Shurayḥ and its like. It is related from Mālik in his letter to Hārūn [ar-Rashīd] or one of the caliphs. His people did not acknowledge it.

All agree that wiping can only be done by someone who put on his leather socks while in *wuḍū'* based on the *ḥadīth* of al-Mughīrah ibn Shu'bah who said, 'I was with the Messenger of Allah ﷺ one night on a journey ... I bent down to remove his leather socks and he said, "Leave them. I put them on while pure." He wiped over them.' Aṣbagh thought that this purification was *tayammum*, based on the fact that *tayammum* removes minor impurity. Dāwūd takes an aberrant view and said that what is meant here is only being pure of impurity, and when the feet are clear of impurity, then it is permitted to wipe over leather socks. The reason for the disagreement is the usage of the term 'purity'.

Mālik permits wiping over leather socks that have small tears in them. Ibn Khuwayzimandād said that it means when the tears do not affect their use and wearing them. One can walk in such socks. A similar view to that of Mālik is taken by al-Layth, ath-Thawrī, ash-Shāfi'ī and aṭ-Ṭabarī. It is related from ath-Thawrī and aṭ-Ṭabarī related that it is permitted to wipe over leather socks with tears. Al-Awzā'ī said, 'One then wipes over leather socks and what shows of the feet.' That is the position of aṭ-Ṭabarī. Abū Ḥanīfah said, 'Someone can wipe if less than three toes of the foot show. If three show, then they may not wipe over them.' Such a definition requires a source of instruction. It is known that the leather socks of the Companions ﷺ and others among the *Tābi'ūn* were not free of small tears. Most of them overlooked that.

It is related from ash-Shāfi'ī that when the tear is at the front of the foot, it is not permitted to wipe. Al-Ḥasan ibn Ḥayy said, 'One may wipe over leather socks when what shows is covered by normal socks. If any of the foot shows, they may not be wiped over.' Abū 'Umar said, 'This is based on the position in his school about the permissibility of wiping over normal socks when they are thick. That is the position of ath-Thawrī, Abū Yūsuf and Muḥammad. According to Abū Ḥanīfah and ash-Shāfi'ī, it is not permitted to wipe over normal socks unless they are bound with leather. That is one of the two views of Mālik. In the other view it is not permitted to wipe over normal socks, even if they are bound with leather.

We find in the book of Abū Dāwūd from al-Mughīrah ibn Shu'bah that the Messenger of Allah ﷺ did *wuḍū'* and wiped over normal socks and sandals. Abū Dāwūd said that 'Abd ar-Raḥmān ibn Mahdī did not relate this *ḥadīth* because it is known from al-Mughīrah that the Prophet ﷺ wiped over leather socks. This *ḥadīth* is related from Abū Muṣā al-Ash'arī from the Prophet ﷺ, but it is not strong or connected. Abū Dāwūd said that 'Alī ibn Abī Ṭālib, Abū Mas'ūd, al-Barā' ibn 'Āzib, Anas ibn Mālik, Abū Umāmah, Sahl ibn Sa'd, and 'Amr ibn Ḥurayth wiped over normal socks. That is also related from 'Umar ibn al-Khaṭṭāb and Ibn 'Abbās.

As for wiping over sandals, Abū Muḥammad ad-Dārimī related in his *Musnad* from Abū Nu'aym from Yūnus from Abū Isḥāq that 'Abd Khayr said, 'I saw 'Alī do *wuḍū'* and he wiped over his sandals. He expanded on this and said, "If it had not been that I saw the Messenger of Allah ﷺ do as you saw me do, I would have thought that the bottom of the feet are more entitled to be wiped than the top."' Abū Muḥammad ad-Dārimī said that this *ḥadīth* is abrogated by this *āyah*.

What 'Alī said about it being preferable to wipe the bottom of the feet than the top is like what he said about wiping over leather socks. Abū Dāwūd transmitted it. He said, 'If the *dīn* had been based on opinion, it would be more appropriate to wipe the bottom of the leather socks rather than the tops.' Mālik and ash-Shāfi'ī said that it is sufficient for someone to wipe the top of the leather socks and not the bottoms. Mālik, however, said, 'If someone does that, he should repeat it within the time.' If someone wipes the bottom of the leather socks and not the top, it is not sufficient and they must repeat it both within the time and after it. That is what all the people of Mālik have said, except for something related from Ashhab who said, 'The bottom and top of leather socks are the same. So if someone wipes the bottom rather than the top, he need only repeat it when it is still within the time.' It is related that ash-Shāfi'ī said that it is sufficient to wipe the bottoms rather than the tops. What is well known in his school, however, is that if someone wipes the bottoms and only them, it is not sufficient and he is not carrying out the wiping. Abū Ḥanīfah and ath-Thawrī said that you should wipe the tops rather than the bottoms of leather socks. That is what is stated by Aḥmad ibn Ḥanbal, Isḥāq and a group. Mālik, ash-Shāfi'ī and their people preferred to wipe both the tops and bottoms. That is the position of Ibn 'Umar and Ibn Shihāb, based on what Abū Dāwūd and ad-Dāraquṭnī related that al-Mughīrah ibn Shu'bah said: 'I was assisting the Messenger of Allah ﷺ with *wuḍū'* in the Tabūk expedition and he wiped the top and bottom of his leather socks.' Abū Dāwūd said, 'It is related that Thawr did not hear this *ḥadīth* from Rajā' ibn Ḥaywah.'

There is disagreement about when someone removes their leather socks having wiped over them. There are three positions. One is that they should wash their feet straight away, even if they delay renewing *wuḍū'*. Mālik and al-Layth said that. That is also what ash-Shāfi'ī, Abū Ḥanīfah and their people said. It is related from al-Awzā'ī and an-Nakha'ī, but they did not mention the time and place. The second is that they should renew *wuḍū'*, and al-Ḥasan ibn Ḥayy said that and it is related from al-Awzā'ī and an-Nakha'ī. The third is that they need do nothing and may pray as they are. Ibn Abī Laylā and al-Ḥasan al-Baṣrī said that. It is transmitted from Ibrāhīm an-Nakha'ī.

If you are in a state of major impurity, then purify yourselves.

Janābah was discussed in *an-Nisā'* (4:43). The imperative *'purify'* is a command to wash with water. That was the view of 'Umar and Ibn Mas'ūd – that the one in *janābah* never does *tayammum*. He does not do the prayer until he finds water. The position of most people is that this ruling is for someone who finds water. The ruling of someone who lacks water comes in Allah's words: *'...or have touched women.'* The verb 'touching' here means sexual intercourse. Then 'Umar and Ibn Mas'ūd reverted to the position of the people about allowing the person in *janābah* to do *tayammum*. There is a *ḥadīth* of 'Imrān ibn Ḥuṣayn which is a text referring to that. The Messenger of Allah ﷺ saw a man who was standing to one side and not praying with the people. He said, 'You! What keeps you from praying with the people?' He answered, 'Messenger of Allah, I am in *janābah* and there is no water.' He said, 'Use earth. It is enough for you.' Al-Bukhārī related it.

But if you are ill or on a journey, or have come from the lavatory

This was also already discussed in full in *an-Nisā'* (4:43). We will add another point here, which is defining the undefined by the prevailing custom. Going to the lavatory (*ghā'iṭ*) indicates the impurities which emerge from both passages as we explained in an-*Nisā'*, and so it is general although our scholars make it specific to the normal impurities which emerge in a normal way. If something abnormal emerges, such as worms and pebbles, or is constant like what happens in incontinence and illness, that does not break it.

They refer to the word because the word confirms what is indicated by the prevailing custom in usage. That prevalence was preceded by the understanding of the listener in a general way and the mind finds it unlikely that the expression would mean something else and so it is not indicated. It is a little like the use of the word 'animal'. When it is used, the mind imagines something with four legs and the idea of an ant does not occur to the mind of the listener. So it is not what is meant nor indicated by that expression literally. The one who argues against that says that the prior nature of the prevalent understanding does not necessarily exclude the rarer meaning. The expression for them is one and the same. That indicates the intended feelings of the one who speaks them. The first is sounder. It is in the book of fundamental principles.

or have touched women,

Abū 'Ubaydah related that 'Abdullāh ibn Mas'ūd said, 'A kiss is part of touching and all that is less than sexual intercourse is still touching.' That is what Ibn 'Umar said and it is the preferred position of Muhammad ibn Yazīd because the beginning of the *āyah* indicates what is obliged for someone who has had intercourse: *'If you are in a state of major impurity.'* 'Abdullāh ibn 'Abbās said, 'Touching (*lams*, *mass*, and *ghashayān*) all refer to sexual intercourse, but it is an allusion.' Mujāhid said about Allah's words: *'...when they pass by worthless talk, pass by with dignity'* (25:72) that they mean, 'When they mention sexual intercourse and make allusion to it.' We also dealt with this fully in *an-Nisā'* (4:43).

and cannot find any water,

This was also discussed in *an-Nisā'* (4:43). There is the case where a healthy resident person has no water because he is imprisoned or restrained. He may be someone who has access to neither water nor earth and fears to miss the time of the prayer. Scholars disagree about him, taking four positions. The first is, as stated by Ibn Khuwayzimandād, considered to be the sound position of the school of Mālik – that such a person does not pray and does not owe anything. He said that the Madinans related that from Mālik. It is sound in the School. Ibn al-Qāsim said that he should pray and then repeat the prayer. That is the view of ash-Shāfi'ī. Ashhab says that he should pray and does not have to repeat it. Asbagh said that he does not pray and does not make it up. That is what Abū Ḥanīfah said.

Abū 'Umar ibn 'Abd al-Barr said, 'I do not know how Ibn Khuwayzimandād made out what he mentioned to be the sound position of the School. It is contrary to the majority of the *Salaf* and most *fuqahā'* and the bulk of the Mālikīs. I think he relies on the literal meaning of the words of Mālik: "they did not have water" and he did not then mention that they prayed. This is not an authoritative argument.' Hishām ibn 'Urwah mentioned from his father from 'Ā'ishah in this *ḥadīth* that they prayed without *wuḍū'* and there was no mention of repeating it. A group of *fuqahā'* believed this. Abū Thawr said that it is analogy.

Al-Muzanī argued by what aṭ-Ṭabarī mentioned in the story about when the necklace of 'Ā'ishah was lost and the Companions of the Prophet ﷺ, who were sent to look for it, prayed without *tayammum* or *wuḍū'* and told him about that. Then the *Āyah* of *Tayammum* was revealed and he ﷺ did not object to what they had done without *wuḍū'* or *tayammum*. Since *tayammum* had not yet been prescribed, they prayed without any purification at all. Al-Muzanī said, 'The prayer was not repeated.' It is a general text permitting the prayer without purification when it is impossible to achieve it.

Abū 'Umar said, 'It is not appropriate to make this situation analogous to someone unconscious because someone who is unconscious has had his consciousness removed, while the person without water still has his consciousness.' Ibn al-Qāsim and other scholars said, 'The prayer is obligatory for him if he is conscious. When the impediment is removed from him, he does *wuḍū'* or *tayammum* and prays.' There are two transmissions from ash-Shāfi'ī. What is well known from him is that the person prays as he is and then repeats it. Al-Muzanī said, 'If he is imprisoned and cannot reach clean earth, he prays and then repeats it.' That is the position of Abū Yūsuf, Muḥammad, ath-Thawrī and aṭ-Ṭabarī. Zafar ibn Hudhayl said, 'Someone imprisoned in a town does not pray, even if he finds clean earth.' This is remaining on the principle that one does not do *tayammum* in a town.

Abū 'Umar said, 'Those who say that he prays as he is, and repeats it if he is able to purify himself, preserve the prayer without purification. They say that the words of the Prophet ﷺ, "Allah does not accept a prayer without purification," only apply to someone who can purify himself. That is not the case with someone who is unable to do that. Praying within the time, however, is obligatory and he is able to do that. Therefore, he should pray within the time and then repeat it, thus guarding both the time and the need for purification. Those who say that such a person should not pray take the literal meaning of this *ḥadīth*. That is the position of Mālik, Ibn Nāfi', and Aṣbagh who said that anyone who lacks both water and earth should not pray and does not have to make it up if the time the prayer passes because the fact that it is not accepted without its preconditions indicates that he is not called on to perform it when its preconditions are lacking. Therefore, this does not entail any responsibility, so he does not make it up.' That was also stated by other than Abū 'Umar. According to this, purity is one of the preconditions of the prayer.

then do *tayammum* with pure earth, and wipe your faces and your hands.

The disagreement about what the term *'earth'* entails was already mentioned in *an-Nisā'* (4:43). The *ḥadīth* of 'Imrān ibn Ḥuṣayn is a text in support of what Mālik says since if *ṣa'īd* had meant 'dust', he ﷺ would have told the man covered with dust that it was enough for him. When he said, 'you must use earth,' it refers to what is on the surface of the earth Allah knows best.

As the discussion of the *āyahs* have led us here, you should know that scholars have discussed the excellence of *wuḍū'* and purification. It is the conclusion of the topic. The Prophet ﷺ said, 'Purity is half of faith.' Muslim transmitted it from Abū Mālik al-Ash'arī. It was already discussed in *al-Baqarah* (2:187). Ibn al-'Arabī said, '*Wuḍū'* is a fundamental of the *dīn* and is the purity of the Muslims and a special gift to this community.' It is related that the Prophet ﷺ performed *wuḍū'* and said, 'This is my *wuḍū'* and the *wuḍū'* of the Prophets before me and the *wuḍū'* of my father Ibrāhīm.' That is not sound, but another said that this does not contradict his words, 'You have a special mark which others do not have.' This was referring to *wuḍū'* and what is specific to this community are the blazes of light it leaves, not the *wuḍū'* itself. This is one of the special virtues of this community to honour it and its Prophet ﷺ like the other favours bestowed on other nations. It is also as He singled our its Prophet ﷺ for the Praiseworthy Station and other things rather than other Prophets. Allah knows best.

Abū 'Umar said, 'It is possible that the other Prophets did *wuḍū'* and by that obtained blazes of light while their followers did not. It is reported that Mūsā said, "Lord, I find a community all of whom are like Prophets. Make it my community." He told him, "That is the community of Muḥammad." It is a long *ḥadīth*.' It is related from Sālim ibn 'Abdullāh that Ka'b al-Aḥbar said that he heard a man relate that he had a dream in which people were gathered for the Reckoning, and then the Prophets were summoned, each Prophet with his community. He saw that each Prophet had two lights between which he walked while those of his community who followed him only had a single light. Then Muḥammad ﷺ was summoned and the hair of his head and his face were entirely light which was seen by all who looked at him. Those who followed him had two lights like the light of the Prophets. Ka'b, who was unaware that it was a dream, said to him, 'Who related this *ḥadīth* to you and who taught it to you?' He told him that it was a dream and Ka'b entreated him, 'By Allah – there is no god but Him! – did you truly see what you said in a dream?' He answered, 'Yes, by Allah, I saw that.' Ka'b said, 'By the One Who has my soul in his hand (or 'by the One Who sent Muḥammad with the truth'), this describes Aḥmad and his community and the description of the Prophets in the Book of Allah. It is as if you were quoting from the Torah!' Its *isnād* is in *at-Tamhīd.*

Abū 'Umar said, 'It is said that all the other nations used to do *wuḍū'*. Allah knows best.' I do not know this from any sound path of transmission. Muslim transmitted from Abū Hurayrah that the Messenger of Allah ﷺ said, 'When the Muslim - or believing – slave does *wuḍū'* and washes his face, every wrong thing at which his eyes have looked leaves with the water – or with the last drop of water. When he washes his hands, every wrong thing which his hands have touched leaves with the water – or with the last drop of water. When he washes his feet, every wrong thing to which his feet have walked leaves with the water – or with the last drop of water, until he emerges cleansed of wrong actions.' The *ḥadīth* of Mālik from 'Abdullāh aṣ-Ṣunābiḥī is more complete.

What is correct is Abū 'Abdullāh and not 'Abdullāh. That is part of what Mālik erred in. His name was 'Abd ar-Raḥmān ibn 'Usaylah, a great Syrian Tābi'ī who was alive in the beginning of the caliphate of Abū Bakr. Abū 'Abdullāh aṣ-Ṣunābiḥī said, 'I came as an emigrant to the Prophet ﷺ from Yemen. When we reached al-Juḥfah, we saw a rider and asked him for news. He said, "We buried the Messenger of Allah ﷺ three days ago."' These *ḥadīth*s as well as similar ones from 'Amr ibn 'Abasah and others tell you that what is meant is that *wuḍū'* is prescribed as a form of worship to expiate sins. That requires the need for a legal intention because it was prescribed to obliterate sin and elevate degrees with Allah.

Allah does not want to make things difficult for you but He does want to purify you

He does not want to constrict you in the *dīn*. The proof is found in His words: *'He has not placed any constraint on you in the dīn.'* (22:78) The preposition *'min'* is connective here, meaning 'impose constriction on you.' He wants to purify you of wrong actions, as we mentioned in the *ḥadīth*s of Abū Hurayrah and aṣ-Ṣunābiḥī. It is also said it means to purify them of both minor and major legal impurity. It is said that it is so that you may achieve the description of purity just as the people of obedience are described by it. Sa'īd ibn al-Musayyab recited *'li-yuṭhirakum'*. The meaning is the same. It is as you say *najjā* and *anjā*.

The words: *'to perfect His blessing upon you'* refer to the dispensation of doing *tayammum* when ill and on a journey. It is said it means 'by the clarification of the

Sharī'ah' or 'by the forgiveness of wrong actions,' as in the report: 'The completion of blessing is to enter the Garden and be saved from the Fire.' *'So that hopefully you will be thankful'* for His blessing and obey Him.

وَاذْكُرُوا نِعْمَةَ اللَّهِ عَلَيْكُمْ وَمِيثَاقَهُ الَّذِي وَاثَقَكُم بِهِ إِذْ قُلْتُمْ
سَمِعْنَا وَأَطَعْنَا وَاتَّقُوا اللَّهَ إِنَّ اللَّهَ عَلِيمٌ بِذَاتِ الصُّدُورِ ۝٧

7 Remember Allah's blessing to you and the covenant He made with you when you said, 'We hear and we obey.' Have *taqwā* of Allah. Allah knows what the heart contains.

It is said that this is the covenant which is found in the words of Allah: *'When your Lord took from the sons of* Ādam...' (7:172) Mujāhid and others said, 'Even if we do not remember it, the Truthful one told us about it and so we are commanded to fulfil it.' It is said that it is addressed to the Jews to instruct them to preserve their covenant in the Torah. What the majority of commentators like Ibn 'Abbās and as-Suddī said is that it is a reference to the covenant the Companions made with the Prophet ﷺ to obey him in respect of both what they liked and disliked, as happened at 'Aqabah and under the Tree at al-Ḥudaybīyah. Allah ascribes it to Himself when He says: '*...they pledge allegiance to Allah.*' (48:10) At 'Aqabah they gave allegiance to the Prophet ﷺ that they would defend him as they defended themselves, their women and children, and that he and his Companions would emigrate to them. The first to give him allegiance was al-Bara' ibn Ma'rūr. That night he gained the Praiseworthy Station by making a covenant with the Messenger of Allah ﷺ and concluding the pledge. He said, 'By The One Who sent you with the truth, we will defend you from everything we defend our women from. Messenger of Allah, we give you our allegiance. By Allah, we are people of war from father to son.' The report is well known in the *Sīrah* of Ibn Isḥāq. The Pledge of Riḍwān will be mentioned in its proper place. This matter is connected to Allah's words: *'Fulfil your contracts'* (5:1). They fulfilled what they pledged to do. May Allah reward them well because of their allegiance to their Prophet and Islam. May Allah be pleased with them and please them!

'Have taqwā of Allah' and do not oppose him. Allah knows all things.

يَٰٓأَيُّهَا ٱلَّذِينَ ءَامَنُوا۟ كُونُوا۟ قَوَّٰمِينَ لِلَّهِ شُهَدَآءَ بِٱلْقِسْطِ ۖ وَلَا
يَجْرِمَنَّكُمْ شَنَـَٔانُ قَوْمٍ عَلَىٰٓ أَلَّا تَعْدِلُوا۟ ۚ ٱعْدِلُوا۟ هُوَ أَقْرَبُ لِلتَّقْوَىٰ ۖ
وَٱتَّقُوا۟ ٱللَّهَ ۚ إِنَّ ٱللَّهَ خَبِيرٌۢ بِمَا تَعْمَلُونَ ﴿٨﴾ وَعَدَ ٱللَّهُ ٱلَّذِينَ ءَامَنُوا۟
وَعَمِلُوا۟ ٱلصَّٰلِحَٰتِ ۙ لَهُم مَّغْفِرَةٌ وَأَجْرٌ عَظِيمٌ ﴿٩﴾ وَٱلَّذِينَ
كَفَرُوا۟ وَكَذَّبُوا۟ بِـَٔايَٰتِنَآ أُو۟لَٰٓئِكَ أَصْحَٰبُ ٱلْجَحِيمِ ﴿١٠﴾

8-10 You who believe, show integrity for the sake of Allah, bearing witness with justice. Do not let hatred for a people incite you into not being just. Be just. That is closer to *taqwā*. Have *taqwā* of Allah. Allah is aware of what you do. Allah has promised those who believe and do right actions forgiveness and an immense reward. But those who reject and deny Our Signs, are the Companions of the Blazing Fire.

You who believe, show integrity for the sake of Allah, bearing witness with justice.

This was discussed in *an-Nisā'* (4:135). It means: 'I have completed My blessing to you, so show integrity for the sake of the reward of Allah. Establish what is true and testify to the truth without favouring your relatives and being biased against your enemies.'

Do not let hatred for a people incite you into not being just.

So that you abandon justice and prefer aggression and exceed the truth. This is evidence for someone passing judgment on his enemy for the sake of Allah and testifying against him, because he is commanded to be fair even if he hates him. If he were not permitted to judge or testify against him when he hates him, there would be no point in commanding him to be fair. It also indicates that one is not permitted to unjust to unbelievers nor to limit them to being people who should be fought or enslaved. It is not permitted to mutilate them. Even if they kill our women and children and distress us by doing that, we are not permitted to kill them by mutilation to distress them. 'Abdullāh ibn Rawāḥah indicated that in his famous story: ['My love and my hatred for you does not prevent me from being fair to you.] This is the meaning of the *āyah* and was already mentioned at the beginning of this *sūrah*.

It is also recited as *'walā yujrimannakum'*. Al-Kisā'ī said that they are two dialectical forms. Az-Zajjāj said that *'lā yujrimannakum'* means 'It should not cause you to commit a crime'.

That is closer to *taqwā*.

It is closer because you have *taqwā* of Allah or because you fear the Fire.

forgiveness and an immense reward

This is for the believers. The understanding of creatures cannot truly encompass its nature, as Allah says: *'No self knows the delight that is hidden away for it.'* (32:17) He says here: *'an immense reward'* and elsewhere: *'a generous reward'* (36:11) and: *'a great reward'* (11:11), so who can possibly estimate its worth?

When the promise comes from good words, the *lām* is added, as in *lakum*. It is in the accusative because it is in the position of what is promised. It means: 'He has promised them that they will have forgiveness,' but the sentence is in the position of the singular as we see in the words of the poet:

We found that the righteous have a reward,
    and gardens and a spring of Salsabīl.

The sentence is in the position of the accusative, which is why it (a spring of Salsabīl) is added to it in the accusative. It is said that it is in the nominative on the basis that what is promised is elided. It implies: 'They will have forgiveness and an immense reward in what they were promised.' Al-Ḥasan said that this is the meaning.

But those who reject and deny Our Signs, are the Companions of the Blazing Fire.

This refers specifically to the Banū an-Naḍīr but it is said that it applies to all unbelievers.

يَٰٓأَيُّهَا ٱلَّذِينَ ءَامَنُوا۟ ٱذْكُرُوا۟ نِعْمَتَ ٱللَّهِ عَلَيْكُمْ إِذْ هَمَّ قَوْمٌ أَن
يَبْسُطُوٓا۟ إِلَيْكُمْ أَيْدِيَهُمْ فَكَفَّ أَيْدِيَهُمْ عَنكُمْ ۖ وَٱتَّقُوا۟ ٱللَّهَ ۚ وَعَلَى
ٱللَّهِ فَلْيَتَوَكَّلِ ٱلْمُؤْمِنُونَ ۝١١

11 You who believe! remember Allah's blessing to you when certain people were on the verge of raising their hands against you and He held their hands back from you. Have *taqwā* of Allah. The believers should put their trust in Allah.

A group said that this was revealed because of what the bedouin man did in the Dhāt ar-Riqā' expedition when he took the sword of the Messenger of Allah ﷺ and asked, 'Who will protect you from me, Muḥammad?" This was mentioned earlier in *an-Nisā'* (4:102). We find in al-Bukhārī that the Prophet ﷺ summoned the people and they gathered while the man was sitting with the Messenger of Allah ﷺ and did not punish him. Al-Wāqidī and Ibn Abī Ḥātim mentioned that he became Muslim. Some people said that he hit his head against a tree trunk until he died. We find in al-Bukhārī about the Dhāt ar-Riqā' expedition that the man's name was Ghawrath ibn al-Hārith. Some say that it was Ghūrath, but the first is sounder. Abū Ḥātim Muḥammad ibn Idrīs ar-Rāzī and Abū 'Abdullāh Muḥammad ibn 'Umar al-Wāqidī mentioned that his name was Du'thūr ibn al-Hārith and said that he became Muslim. Muḥammad ibn Isḥāq said that his name was 'Amr ibn Jiḥāsh, one of the Banū an-Naḍīr. One of them said that the story of 'Amr ibn Jiḥāsh is a different one. Allah knows best.

Qatādah, Mujāhid and others said that it was revealed about some of the Jews to whom the Prophet ﷺ went to ask for their help in paying some blood money. They intended to assassinate him, but Allah protected him from them. Al-Qushayrī said, 'The *āyah* was revealed about one event and then mentioned another time as a reminder of what had happened.

وَلَقَدْ أَخَذَ اللَّهُ مِيثَاقَ بَنِي إِسْرَائِيلَ وَبَعَثْنَا مِنْهُمُ اثْنَيْ عَشَرَ
نَقِيبًا وَقَالَ اللَّهُ إِنِّي مَعَكُمْ لَئِنْ أَقَمْتُمُ الصَّلَاةَ وَآتَيْتُمُ الزَّكَاةَ
وَآمَنتُم بِرُسُلِي وَعَزَّرْتُمُوهُمْ وَأَقْرَضْتُمُ اللَّهَ قَرْضًا حَسَنًا
لَّأُكَفِّرَنَّ عَنكُمْ سَيِّئَاتِكُمْ وَلَأُدْخِلَنَّكُمْ جَنَّاتٍ تَجْرِي مِن
تَحْتِهَا الْأَنْهَارُ فَمَن كَفَرَ بَعْدَ ذَٰلِكَ مِنكُمْ فَقَدْ ضَلَّ سَوَاءَ
السَّبِيلِ ﴿١٢﴾

12 Allah made a covenant with the tribe of Israel and We raised up twelve leaders from among them. Allah said, 'I am with you. If you establish the prayer and pay *zakāt*, and believe in My Messengers and respect and support them, and make a generous loan to Allah, I will erase your wrong actions from you and admit you into Gardens with rivers flowing under them. Any of you who reject after that have gone astray from the right way.'

Allah made a covenant with the tribe of Israel and We raised up twelve leaders from among them.

Ibn 'Aṭiyyah said that this *āyah* speaks about the Jews breaking their covenant with Allah. This strengthens the probability that the previous *āyah* is about the Banū an-Naḍīr. The people of interpretation disagree about how those leaders were raised while agreeing that the *naqīb* (leader) is the chief of a people who deals with their affairs which he examines (*naqaba*) and acts in their best interests, and that a *naqqāb* is the great man who looks into his people in this way. 'Umar was called a *naqqāb*. They are the ones who are responsible.

The singular of *nuqabā'* is *naqīb*, the witness and guarantor of the people. It is said that he is charge of them and has good character (*naqībah*). *Naqb* and *nuqb* are both used to designate a path in the mountain. It is said that someone is called *naqīb* because he knows the inside (literally pierces, *naqaba*) the inside of the people and knows their virtues (*manāqib*). It is the path of recognition of their affairs. Some people say that the leaders are the trustees of the people. A *naqīb* has a greater standing than an *'arīf*. 'Aṭā' ibn Yasār said, 'Those who bear the Qur'ān are the *'arīf*s of the people of the Garden.' Ad-Dārimī mentioned it in his *Musnad*. Qatādah and others said, 'They are the great men of every tribe who are answerable for their tribes believing and being fearful of Allah.' The same is true of the leaders who gave allegiance at 'Aqabah: seventy men and two women. The Prophet ﷺ chose twelve of them and called them *nuqabā'*, imitating Mūsā.

Ar-Rabī', as-Suddī and others said that Allah raised up leaders from the tribe of Israel, trusted people, to investigate the gigantic people and examine them and their defences. They reported about their state and told them what they knew about them so that they could decide about how to attack them. They saw that the giants had great strength and thought that they had no way against them and they agreed between them that they would conceal that from the tribe of Israel and that they would only tell Mūsā about it. When they went to the tribe of Israel, ten of them were treacherous and informed their relatives and those they trusted about their secret and the word spread until the business of the tribe of Israel was set awry and they said, *'Go, you and your Lord and fight. We are waiting here.'* (5:24)

The *āyah* indicates that the report of a single person can be accepted for the information a man requires, what he needs to know regarding religious and worldly circumstances on which judgments are based and matters concerning the *ḥalāl* and *ḥarām*. The same thing exists in Islam as well. The Prophet ﷺ said to Hawāzin, 'Go back to your *'arīf*s (chiefs) and let them present your case.' Al-Bukhārī transmitted it. It is also evidence for the permissibility of using spies. Spying is to seek out information. The Prophet ﷺ sent Basbasah to act as a spy, as reported in Muslim. The ruling concerning spies will be dealt with in *al-Mumtahanah*.

The names of the leaders of the tribe of Israel [sent as spies] were mentioned by Muḥammad ibn Ḥabīb in *al-Muḥabbir*. He said: 'The leader of the tribe of Reuben was Shammua son of Zaccur, the leader of the tribe of Simeon was Shaphat son of Hori; of the tribe of Judah: Caleb son of Jephunneh; of the tribe of Issachar: Igal son of Joseph; of the tribe of Ephraim ben Joseph: Hoshea son of Nun; of the tribe of Benjamin: Palti son of Raphu; of the tribe of Zebulun: Gaddiel son of Sodi; of the tribe of Manasseh ben Joseph: Gaddi son of Susi; of the tribe of Dan: Ammiel son of Gemalli; of the tribe of Asher: Sethiur son of Michael; of the tribe of Naphtali: Nahbi [text has Yūhanna] son of Vopshi; and of the tribe of Gad: Geuel son of Machi. Two of them were believers: Hoshea and Caleb. Mūsā prayed against the rest and they were destroyed by Divine wrath.' Al-Māwardī said that. As for the leaders on the night of 'Aqabah, they are mentioned in the *Sīrah* of Ibn Isḥāq.

Allah said, 'I am with you. If you establish the prayer'

Ar-Rabī' ibn Anas said, 'He said that to the leaders.' Others said that He said it to the whole tribe of Israel. The participle '*inna*' takes a *kasrah* because it is inchoative. The preposition '*with you*' is in the accusative because it is an adverbial usage, i.e. 'with you with help and support.'

Then there is a new sentence. Allah tells them that if they do the things He mentions, He will admit them into Gardens. The *lām* on '*la-in*' is for stress and it has the meaning of an oath. It is also said that it means, 'If you establish the prayer, I will erase your evil deeds from you.' What He mentions is a precondition for expiation: 'If you do that, I will erase…' It is said that it means, 'If you establish the prayer' is the apodosis of 'I am with you' and the precondition is 'I will erase'.

and respect and support them

Ta'zīr means respect and esteem. Abū 'Ubaydah composed:

How many a person glorifies them, noble
    and Layth who is respected (*yu'azzaru*) in the assembly.

It means that he is esteemed and respected. *Ta'zīr* also is used for beating as a punishment less than the *ḥadd*. It is deterrence. You say, 'I disciplined (*'azzartu*) so-and-so' when you punished him and deterred him from what is ugly. So here it means 'I averted their enemies from them.'

make a generous loan to Allah,

The expression *'a generous loan'* here means *ṣadaqah*. Allah uses the form *qarḍ* and not *iqrāḍ*. This comes from the verbal noun as we see elsewhere. The adjective '*ḥasan*' (generous) can refer to what you are happy with, that by which you seek the face of Allah, or what is lawful. It is also possible that *qarḍ* is, in fact, a noun and not a verbal noun.

Any of you who disbelieve after that have gone astray from the right way.'

'*That*' means after making the Covenant. This means that they erred in the path.

فَبِمَا نَقْضِهِم مِّيثَٰقَهُمْ لَعَنَّٰهُمْ وَجَعَلْنَا قُلُوبَهُمْ قَٰسِيَةً يُحَرِّفُونَ
ٱلْكَلِمَ عَن مَّوَاضِعِهِۦ وَنَسُوا۟ حَظًّا مِّمَّا ذُكِّرُوا۟ بِهِۦ وَلَا تَزَالُ
تَطَّلِعُ عَلَىٰ خَآئِنَةٍ مِّنْهُمْ إِلَّا قَلِيلًا مِّنْهُمْ فَٱعْفُ
عَنْهُمْ وَٱصْفَحْ إِنَّ ٱللَّهَ يُحِبُّ ٱلْمُحْسِنِينَ ﴿١٣﴾

13 But because of their breaking of their covenant, We have cursed them and made their hearts hard. They distort the true meaning of words and have forgotten a good portion of what they were reminded of. You will never cease to come upon some act of treachery on their part, except for a few of them. Yet pardon them, and overlook. Allah loves good-doers.

But because of their breaking of their covenant,

The '*mā*' here is redundant and used for emphasis according to Qatādah and the great majority of scholars. That is because stressing the word is part of making it firm in the mind because of its excellent composition. Emphasis by using a marker is like emphasis through repetition. [POEM]

We have cursed them and made their hearts hard.

Ibn 'Abbās said that the words '*We have cursed them*' mean: 'We have punished them through the *jizyah*.' Al-Ḥasan and Muqātil said, 'It was by transmogrification.' 'Aṭā' said it means, 'We put them far away.' 'Cursing' (*la'n*) is to put afar away and expel from mercy. '*We made their hearts hard*' so they are not concerned with good nor do they do it. The word '*hard*' (*qāsiyah*) is read as *qasiyyah* by al-Kisā'ī and Ḥamzah, which was the reading of Ibn Mas'ūd, an-

Nakha'ī and Yaḥyā ibn Waththāb. A 'hard (*qasīy*) year' is one without rain. It is said that it comes from dirhams which are *qasīyah*, meaning unsound, and so it would mean that they do not have sincere faith in their hearts, but it is tainted with hypocrisy. An-Naḥḥās said, 'This is good because one calls a dirham "hard" (*qasiyy*) when it is adulterated with copper or other things. One says "a *qasiyy* dirham", like *shaqiyy* (wretched). It means that it is counterfeit. Abū 'Ubaydah mentioned that and said:

> They make a clinking in the stony ground of peace,
> as the counterfeit coins (*qasiyyāt*) shout in the hands of money-changers.

He is describing the sound of spades on stone. Al-Aṣma'ī and Abū 'Ubayd said that a counterfeit (*qasiyy*) dirham is as if it were an Arabicised version of *qāshī*.' Al-Qushayrī said, 'This is unlikely because there is nothing in the Qur'ān that is not from the language of the Arabs. Rather it comes from "hard" (*qasiyy*) and "rigid" because a small amount of molten ore becomes hard and rigid.' Al-A'mash recited '*qasiyah*' on the measure of *fa'ilah*. It comes from the verb *qasiya*, *yaqsā*, not from *qasā*, *yaqsū*. The rest recite it on the measure of *fā'ilah*. That is what is preferred by Abū 'Ubayd. They are two dialectal forms like *'aliyyah* and *'āliyah*, *zakiyyah* and *zākiyah*.

Abū Ja'far an-Naḥḥās said, 'What is more fitting concerning it is that *qasiyyah* means *qāsiyah* although the measure *fa'īlah* is more intensive than *fā'ilah*. It means, "We made their hearts coarse and far from faith and success in obedience." That is because the people were not described with any faith and so their hearts are described as having faith mixed with unbelief like a false dirham is mixed with something fraudulent.' [POEM]

They distort the true meaning of words and have forgotten a good portion of what they were reminded of.

This means that they interpret them incorrectly and then teach this to the common people. It is said that it means that they change their letters. It means: 'We made their hearts hard, distorting.' As-Sulamī and an-Nakha'ī recited '*al-kalām*'. That is because they changed the description of Muḥammad ﷺ and the verse about stoning. They have forgotten the contract which Allah has made with the Prophets to believe in Muḥammad ﷺ and to make his description clear.

You will never cease to come upon some act of treachery on their part, except for a few of them.

This is addressed to Muḥammad and means 'You continue to find.' *Khā'inah* [an active participle] means *khiyānah* (treachery) as Qatādah said. This is linguistically permitted. It is like saying *'qā'ilah'* meaning *'qaylūlah'* for a midday nap. It is also said that it is a description of something elided, which implies: 'a treacherous group'. The word can be used for a single person to emphasise his treacherous nature. It is like when one says that a man is *nassābah* (genealogist) and *'allāmah* (scholar). According to this, *khā'inah* is for emphasis. A man is called *khā'inah* when you stress his quality of being treacherous. A poet said:

> You called yourself faithful, and not
> treacherous (*khā'inah*), indulging in perfidy

Ibn 'Abbās said that treachery is disobedience to Allah. It is said that it is lying and impiety and that their treachery was breaking the contract between them and the Messenger of Allah ﷺ and their support of the idolaters in fighting the Messenger of Allah ﷺ, as on the Day of the Parties and their intention to kill him and abuse him. *'Except a few of them'* who were not treacherous. This is an exception connected to the pronoun *'hum'* in *'on their part'*.

Yet pardon them, and overlook.

Two things are said about the meaning of this. One is that you should pardon and overlook while there is a treaty between you and them, referring to the people of the *dhimmah*. The other view is that it was abrogated by the *Āyah* of the Sword or, it is said, by Allah's words: *'If you fear treachery on the part of a people.'* (8:58)

وَمِنَ ٱلَّذِينَ قَالُوٓاْ إِنَّا نَصَٰرَىٰٓ أَخَذۡنَا مِيثَٰقَهُمۡ فَنَسُواْ حَظّٗا
مِّمَّا ذُكِّرُواْ بِهِۦ فَأَغۡرَيۡنَا بَيۡنَهُمُ ٱلۡعَدَاوَةَ وَٱلۡبَغۡضَآءَ إِلَىٰ
يَوۡمِ ٱلۡقِيَٰمَةِۚ وَسَوۡفَ يُنَبِّئُهُمُ ٱللَّهُ بِمَا كَانُواْ يَصۡنَعُونَ ١٤
يَٰٓأَهۡلَ ٱلۡكِتَٰبِ قَدۡ جَآءَكُمۡ رَسُولُنَا يُبَيِّنُ لَكُمۡ كَثِيرٗا
مِّمَّا كُنتُمۡ تُخۡفُونَ مِنَ ٱلۡكِتَٰبِ وَيَعۡفُواْ عَن كَثِيرٖۚ قَدۡ جَآءَكُم
مِّنَ ٱللَّهِ نُورٞ وَكِتَٰبٞ مُّبِينٞ ١٥ يَهۡدِي بِهِ ٱللَّهُ مَنِ ٱتَّبَعَ
رِضۡوَٰنَهُۥ سُبُلَ ٱلسَّلَٰمِ وَيُخۡرِجُهُم مِّنَ ٱلظُّلُمَٰتِ إِلَى
ٱلنُّورِ بِإِذۡنِهِۦ وَيَهۡدِيهِمۡ إِلَىٰ صِرَٰطٖ مُّسۡتَقِيمٖ ١٦

14-16 We also made a covenant with those who say, 'We are Christians,' and they too forgot a good portion of what they were reminded of. So We stirred up enmity and hatred between them until the Day of Rising when Allah will inform them about what they did. People of the Book! Our Messenger has come to you, making clear to you much of the Book that you have kept concealed, and passing over a lot. A Light has come to you from Allah and a Clear Book. By it, Allah guides those who follow what pleases Him to the ways of Peace. He will bring them from the darkness to the light by His permission, and guide them to a straight path.

We also made a covenant with those who say, 'We are Christians,'

This means We made a covenant with them regarding *tawḥīd* and belief in Muḥammad ﷺ since he is mentioned in the Gospel.

and they too forgot a good portion of what they were reminded of.

This refers to belief in Muḥammad ﷺ, meaning that they did not do what they were commanded and that passion and deviation became a reason for rejecting Muḥammad ﷺ. The words: '*We made a covenant*' (literally 'took their covenant') is as you say, 'I took Zayd's garment and dirham from him.' Al-Akhfash said that. The word order implies 'We made a covenant with those who say, "We are Christians"' because it is in the position of the second object of the verb '*We took*'. According to the Kufans, it implies: 'Among those who said, "We are Christians" are those with whom We made a covenant,' and the pronoun '*hum*' refers to an elided '*man*' (who). According to the first position, it refers to '*alladhīna*'.

Grammarians do not permit the order '*akhadhnā mīthāqahum min alladhīna qālū*' because a concealed pronoun cannot come before an explicit pronoun. The fact that it does not say, 'from the Christians' indicates that they innovated Christianity and then called themselves that. Something similar is reported from al-Ḥasan.

So We stirred up enmity and hatred between them until the Day of Rising

We incited them, or We made it cling to them. The verb is derived from *ghirā'* which is that which makes something stick to something else, like glue. The verb *gharā, yaghrā, gharā* and *ghirā'* is to glue. Ar-Rummānī said that *ighrā'* means to set one against another. It is said that it means sow discord, and its root is attach to something. One says, '*gharītu bi'r-rajul gharan*' when you are very attached to him. Kuthayyir said:

> When it is said, 'Take it easy,' the eye speaks with weeping
> copiously (*ghirā'*), replenished by flows of tears.

You say, '*aghraytu Zaydan ḥattā ghariya bihi*', 'I incited Zayd until he stuck to it.' Part of that is the *ghirā'*, the glue which is used for sticking. *Ighrā'* is to adhere to a thing in order to control it. The verb is used for inciting a dog to go after game.

The word '*between them*' is a preposition describing enmity. The noun *baghḍā'* means hatred. It indicates that the Jews and Christians – as was mentioned by as-Suddī and Qatādah – are enemies of one another. It is said that it specifically indicates the divisions of the Christians. Ar-Rabī' ibn Anas said that because they are the most recently mentioned group. They divided into Monophysites, Nestorians, Melchites, and others, and call one another unbelievers. An-Naḥḥās said that the best of what is said about this is that Allah commanded enmity and hatred of the unbelievers, each group being commanded to hate the other because they are unbelievers. The words: '*Allah will inform them about what they did*' are a threat and refer to the repayment the will incur for breaking their covenant.

People of the Book! Our Messenger has come to you, making clear to you much of the Book that you have kept concealed, and passing over a lot.

The word '*Book*' is generic here, meaning 'Books' in general and so all of them are addressed. '*Our Messenger*' is Muḥammad ﷺ. He makes clear to you what your Books say concerning belief in him, the verse of stoning, and the story of those who broke the Sabbath being transformed into apes, which they had concealed.

The expression *'passing over a lot'* means leaving it without making it clear. He made clear the things that proved his Prophethood and indicated his truthfulness and attested to his Message and left what did not need to be made clear. It is said that it means He passed over much and did not speak of it.

It is mentioned that one of the Jews came to the Prophet ﷺ and asked, 'You! Have you pardoned us? [using the same verb]' The Messenger of Allah ﷺ turned away from him without explaining it. The Jew wanted to be able to contradict his words, and when he did not explain it, he left and told his friends, 'I think that he speaks the truth about what he says because he has found in His Book that he should not explain everything he is asked about.'

A Light has come to you from Allah and a Clear Book.

The word *'Light'* can refer to illumination or Islam. Az-Zajjāj said that it means Muḥammad ﷺ. The *'Clear Book'* is the Qur'ān which makes rulings clear.

By it, Allah guides those who follow what pleases Him to the ways of Peace.

'The ways of Peace' are the paths of peace which lead to the Abode of Peace free from every disaster and safe from every fear: the Garden. Al-Ḥasan and as-Suddī say that it means Allah, as Peace is one of His Names. It can mean the *Dīn* of Allah which is Islam as He says: *'The dīn in the sight of Allah is Islam.'* (3:19) He will bring them out of the darkness of disbelief and ignorance into the light of Islam and guidance. *'By His permission'* means by His giving success and by His will.

لَّقَدْ كَفَرَ ٱلَّذِينَ قَالُوٓا۟ إِنَّ ٱللَّهَ هُوَ ٱلْمَسِيحُ ٱبْنُ مَرْيَمَ
قُلْ فَمَن يَمْلِكُ مِنَ ٱللَّهِ شَيْـًٔا إِنْ أَرَادَ أَن يُهْلِكَ ٱلْمَسِيحَ ٱبْنَ
مَرْيَمَ وَأُمَّهُۥ وَمَن فِى ٱلْأَرْضِ جَمِيعًا وَلِلَّهِ مُلْكُ ٱلسَّمَٰوَٰتِ
وَٱلْأَرْضِ وَمَا بَيْنَهُمَا يَخْلُقُ مَا يَشَآءُ وَٱللَّهُ عَلَىٰ كُلِّ شَىْءٍ
قَدِيرٌ ﴿١٧﴾

17 Those who say, 'Allah is the Messiah, son of Maryam,' have rejected. Say: 'Who possesses any power at all over Allah if He desires to destroy the Messiah, son of Maryam, and his mother, and everyone else on earth?' He creates whatever He wills. Allah has power over all things.

Those who say, 'Allah is the Messiah, son of Maryam,' have rejected.

This was discussed at the end of *an-Nisa'* (4:171). The disbelief of the Christians is indicated by their words, 'Allah is the Messiah, son of Maryam,' by way of religious dogma. If they had merely recounted that expression while denying it, they would not have disbelieved.

Say: 'Who possesses any power at all over Allah if He desires to destroy the Messiah, son of Maryam, and his mother, and everyone else on earth?'

'*Over Allah*' means 'over Allah's command.' The verb '*yamliku*' means 'has the power'. You say, 'I had power (*malaktu*) over the business of so-and-so.' Who has the power to prevent any of that? Allah informs us that if the Messiah had been a god he would have been able to avert what happened to him and others. His mother died and he was unable to avert her death. If Allah were to make him die, who could defend him from that or avert it from him?

The kingdom of the heavens and the earth and everything between them belongs to Allah.

The Messiah and his mother were creatures who were limited and confined. That which can be encompassed by limits and confined cannot be considered to have divine status. Allah says: '*between them*' using the dual pronoun and does not use the feminine plural because He means two types and categories. [POEM]

He creates whatever He wills.

He created 'Īsā without a father as a sign for His slaves.

وَقَالَتِ ٱلْيَهُودُ وَٱلنَّصَٰرَىٰ نَحْنُ أَبْنَٰٓؤُا۟ ٱللَّهِ وَأَحِبَّٰٓؤُهُۥ ۚ قُلْ فَلِمَ يُعَذِّبُكُم
بِذُنُوبِكُم ۖ بَلْ أَنتُم بَشَرٌ مِّمَّنْ خَلَقَ ۚ يَغْفِرُ لِمَن يَشَآءُ وَيُعَذِّبُ مَن يَشَآءُ ۚ
وَلِلَّهِ مُلْكُ ٱلسَّمَٰوَٰتِ وَٱلْأَرْضِ وَمَا بَيْنَهُمَا ۖ وَإِلَيْهِ ٱلْمَصِيرُ ﴿١٨﴾

18 The Jews and Christians say, 'We are Allah's children and His loved ones.' Say: 'Why, then, does He punish you for your wrong actions? No, you are merely human beings among those He has created. He forgives whoever He wills and He punishes whoever He wills. The kingdom of the heavens and the earth and everything between them belongs to Allah. He is our final destination.'

The Jews and Christians say, 'We are Allah's children and His loved ones.'

Ibn 'Abbās said, 'The Messenger of Allah ﷺ threatened some of the Jews with Divine punishment and they said, "We are not afraid. We are the sons of Allah and those He loves," and the *āyah* was revealed.' Ibn Isḥāq said, 'The Messenger of Allah ﷺ went to Nu'mān ibn Aḍā, Baḥrī ibn 'Amr and Sha's ibn 'Adī and they spoke together. He called them to Allah and warned them about His retribution and they said, "Why are you trying to frighten us in this way, Muḥammad? We are the sons of Allah and those He loves," as the Christians also said, and so Allah revealed this.'

Mu'ādh ibn Jabal, Sa'd ibn 'Ubādah and 'Uqbah ibn Wahb said, 'Company of Jews, fear Allah! By Allah, you know that he is the Messenger of Allah and you mentioned him to us before he was sent and described him to us.' Rafī' ibn Ḥuraymalah and Wahb ibn Yahūdhā said, 'We did not say this to you. Allah has not revealed any Book after Mūsā nor sent any bringer of good news or warner after him.' Allah revealed: *'People of the Book! Our Messenger has come to you, making things clear to you after a period with no Messengers…'* (5:19)

As-Suddī said, 'The Jews claimed that Allah revealed to Israel, "You are My firstborn."' Another said, 'The Christians said, "We are the sons of Allah because the Gospel reports that 'Īsā said, 'I go to my father and your father.'"' It is said that it means, 'We are the sons of the Messengers of Allah,' and there is elision. In general, they thought that they had superiority over others. They are refuted by the question: *'Why, then, does He punish you for your wrong actions?'*

Why, then, does He punish you for your wrong actions?

This demands one of two responses. Either they will say that He will punish them and then they are told, 'So you are not His children and those He loves. A lover does not punish the one he loves. You affirm the punishment and that indicates that you are lying.' Debaters call this the proof of disparity. Or they will say that He will not punish them and thereby deny what their Scriptures contain and what their Messengers brought. They consider acts by which one disobeys Allah to be permissible even while admitting that their rebels will be punished. This is what the rulings of their Scriptures demand.

It is said that 'punish you' means 'punished you' in the past, meaning 'Why did He turn you into monkeys and pigs and why did He previously punish Jews and Christians like you with various sorts of punishment?' That is because Allah does not use an unlikely argument against them because they might say, 'He will not punish us in the future.' Rather He used what they knew as an argument.

You are merely human beings among those He has created.

This means: 'You are like the rest of His creation. He will call you to account for obedience and disobedience. He will repay each for what He did.' *'He forgives whomever He wills'* among the Jews and *'punishes whoever He wills'* of those who have died in the Next World.

يَٰٓأَهۡلَ ٱلۡكِتَٰبِ قَدۡ جَآءَكُمۡ رَسُولُنَا يُبَيِّنُ لَكُمۡ عَلَىٰ فَتۡرَةٖ مِّنَ ٱلرُّسُلِ
أَن تَقُولُواْ مَا جَآءَنَا مِنۢ بَشِيرٖ وَلَا نَذِيرٖۖ فَقَدۡ جَآءَكُم بَشِيرٞ وَنَذِيرٞۗ وَٱللَّهُ
عَلَىٰ كُلِّ شَيۡءٖ قَدِيرٞ ١٩

19 People of the Book! Our Messenger has come to you, making things clear to you, after a period with no Messengers, lest you should say, 'No one came to us bringing good news or warning.' Someone has come to you bringing good news and a warning. Allah has power over all things.

People of the Book! Our Messenger has come to you,

This means Muḥammad ﷺ. He puts an end to their argument and they cannot say, 'No Messenger has come to us.' The noun '*fatrah*' indicates a stillness in something and the verb *fatara* means to be still. Here it means a break between the Prophets as Abū 'Alī and a group of the people of knowledge stated. Ar-Rummānī reported that. He said, 'The basic meaning is that of stopping an action or flagging in it.' It used for water when it becomes lukewarm. A woman who is described as having '*fātiratu't-ṭarf*' does not have a sharp look. *Futūr* in relation to the body is limpness, similar to water being lukewarm. *Fitr* describes the area between the forefinger and thumb when they are open. It here refers to the gap between him ﷺ and the Messengers before him.

There is disagreement about the length of this gap. In the *Ṭabaqāt*, Muḥammad ibn Sa'd quoted Ibn 'Abbās as stating that there were 1700 years between Mūsā and 'Īsā and no gap without a Prophet during that time. Between them He sent a thousand Prophets from the tribe of Israel in addition to those he sent to others. There were five hundred and sixty-nine years between the birth of 'Īsā and that of the Prophet Muḥammad ﷺ. At the beginning of that time three Prophets were sent, which is the meaning of the words of the Almighty: *'When We sent them two and they denied them both and We reinforced them with a third.'* (36:14) The one with whom He strengthened them was Simon, who was one of the Apostles. The gap during which Allah sent no Messenger was four hundred and thirty-four years.

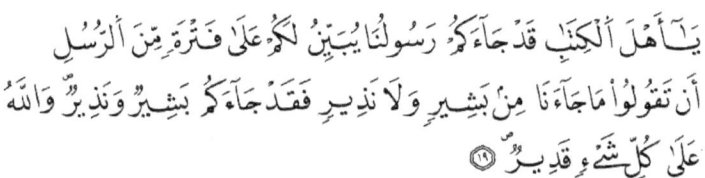

Al-Kalbī said that there were five hundred and sixty-nine years between 'Īsā and Muḥammad ﷺ, and there were four Prophets between them, one from the Arabs among the Banū 'Abs, who was Khālid ibn Sinān. Al-Qushayrī said, 'Things like this can only be known by a sound report.' Qatādah said that there were six hundred years between 'Īsā and Muḥammad ﷺ. Muqātil, aḍ-Ḍaḥḥāk and Wahb ibn Munabbih said that, although Wahb added twenty years. Aḍ-Ḍaḥḥāk also said that it was about four hundred and thirty years.

Ibn Sa'd mentioned that 'Ikrimah said, 'There were ten generations between Ādam and Nūḥ, all of whom had Islam (as their deen).' Ibn Sa'd said that Muḥammad ibn 'Amr ibn Wāqid al-Aslamī reported that more than one person had said that there were ten generations between Ādam and Nūḥ. A generation was a hundred years. There were ten generations between Nūḥ and Ibrāhīm. A generation was a hundred years. There were ten generations between Ibrāhīm and Mūsā ibn 'Imrān. A generation was a hundred years. These are the generations and years between Ādam and Muḥammad ﷺ.' Allah knows best.

lest you should say, 'No one came to us bringing good news or warning.'

This is in order that they should not be able to say that. A *bashīr* is someone who brings good news and a *nadhīr* is someone who brings a warning. Ibn 'Abbās said, 'Mu'ādh ibn Jabal, Sa'd ibn 'Ubādah and 'Uqbah ibn Wahb said to the Jews, "Company of Jews! Fear Allah! By Allah, you know that Muḥammad is the Messenger of Allah! You mentioned him to us before he was sent and described him to us." They said, "Allah has not revealed any Book after Mūsā and has not sent any bringer of good news or warner after him!" So Allah revealed the *āyah*.'

Allah has power over all things.

He has the power to send any of His creatures that He wishes. It is said that He has the power to bring about that about which there was good or news or warning.

وَإِذْ قَالَ مُوسَىٰ لِقَوْمِهِۦ يَٰقَوْمِ ٱذْكُرُوا۟ نِعْمَةَ ٱللَّهِ عَلَيْكُمْ إِذْ جَعَلَ فِيكُمْ
أَنۢبِيَآءَ وَجَعَلَكُم مُّلُوكًا وَءَاتَىٰكُم مَّا لَمْ يُؤْتِ أَحَدًا مِّنَ ٱلْعَٰلَمِينَ ﴿٢٠﴾ يَٰقَوْمِ
ٱدْخُلُوا۟ ٱلْأَرْضَ ٱلْمُقَدَّسَةَ ٱلَّتِى كَتَبَ ٱللَّهُ لَكُمْ وَلَا تَرْتَدُّوا۟ عَلَىٰٓ أَدْبَارِكُمْ
فَتَنقَلِبُوا۟ خَٰسِرِينَ ﴿٢١﴾ قَالُوا۟ يَٰمُوسَىٰٓ إِنَّ فِيهَا قَوْمًا جَبَّارِينَ وَإِنَّا لَن
نَّدْخُلَهَا حَتَّىٰ يَخْرُجُوا۟ مِنْهَا فَإِن يَخْرُجُوا۟ مِنْهَا فَإِنَّا دَٰخِلُونَ ﴿٢٢﴾ قَالَ
رَجُلَانِ مِنَ ٱلَّذِينَ يَخَافُونَ أَنْعَمَ ٱللَّهُ عَلَيْهِمَا ٱدْخُلُوا۟ عَلَيْهِمُ ٱلْبَابَ فَإِذَا
دَخَلْتُمُوهُ فَإِنَّكُمْ غَٰلِبُونَ وَعَلَى ٱللَّهِ فَتَوَكَّلُوٓا۟ إِن كُنتُم
مُّؤْمِنِينَ ﴿٢٣﴾ قَالُوا۟ يَٰمُوسَىٰٓ إِنَّا لَن نَّدْخُلَهَآ أَبَدًا مَّا دَامُوا۟ فِيهَا فَٱذْهَبْ
أَنتَ وَرَبُّكَ فَقَٰتِلَآ إِنَّا هَٰهُنَا قَٰعِدُونَ ﴿٢٤﴾ قَالَ رَبِّ إِنِّى لَآ أَمْلِكُ
إِلَّا نَفْسِى وَأَخِى فَٱفْرُقْ بَيْنَنَا وَبَيْنَ ٱلْقَوْمِ ٱلْفَٰسِقِينَ ﴿٢٥﴾ قَالَ فَإِنَّهَا
مُحَرَّمَةٌ عَلَيْهِمْ أَرْبَعِينَ سَنَةً يَتِيهُونَ فِى ٱلْأَرْضِ فَلَا تَأْسَ عَلَى
ٱلْقَوْمِ ٱلْفَٰسِقِينَ ﴿٢٦﴾

20-26 Remember when Mūsā said to his people, 'My people! remember Allah's blessing to you when He appointed Prophets among you and made you kings, and gave you what He had not given to anyone else in all the worlds! 'My people! enter the Holy Land which Allah has ordained for you. Do not turn back in your tracks and so become transformed into losers.' They said, 'There are giants in it, Mūsā. We will not enter it until they leave. If they leave it, then we will go in.' Two men among those who were afraid, but whom Allah had blessed, said, 'Enter the gate against them! Once you have entered it, you will be victorious. Put your trust in Allah if you are believers.' They said, 'We will never enter it, Mūsā, as long as they are there. So you and your Lord go and fight. We will stay sitting here.' He said, 'My Lord, I have no control over anyone but myself and my brother, so make a clear distinction between us and this deviant people.' He said, 'The land will be forbidden to them for forty years during which they will wander aimlessly about the earth. Do not waste grief on this deviant people.'

Remember when Mūsā said to his people, 'My people! remember Allah's blessing to you

Allah made it clear that their ancestors were recalcitrant towards Mūsā and disobeyed him. That is also how they behaved towards Muḥammad ﷺ. This is to console him, meaning, 'O you who believe, remember Allah's blessings to you and remember the story of Mūsā.' It is related that 'Abdullāh ibn Kathīr recited '*yā qawmu*' with rather than '*yā qawmi*'.

when He appointed Prophets among you

It is not inflected because it has the feminine *alif.*

and made you kings,

The meaning of the words '*made you kings*' is that you have control over your own affairs and no one has overpowered you since the time that you were slaves and subject to Pharaoh. Allah saved you from him by drowning him. That is how they were kings and that is what as-Suddī, al-Ḥasan and others said. As-Suddī said, 'Every one of them had power over himself, his family and his property.'

Qatādah said, 'Allah says: "*made you kings*" because we are told that they were the first of the descendants of Ādam to be be served by servants. 'Aṭā' said, 'This is weak because the ancient Egyptians engaged the services of the tribe of Israel, and it is clear that it is part of the human condition that some people subjugate others, and this has been the case since they propagated and multiplied. Nations only differ in the meaning of ownership.' It is said that it means, 'He gave you houses which none will enter except with your permission,' and a group of scholars say something similar. Ibn 'Abbās said, 'When no one enters a man's house without his permission, he is a king (*malik*).' Al-Ḥasan and Zayd ibn Aslam said that if someone has a house, wife and servant, he is a king. That is the position of 'Abdullāh ibn 'Amr as we find in *Saḥīḥ Muslim* which reports that he was asked, 'Are we not the poor *Muhājirūn*?' 'Abdullāh asked the questioner, 'Do you have a wife to whom you go?' 'Yes,' the asker replied. 'Abdullāh asked, 'Do you have a house where you live?' 'Yes,' the man answered. He said, 'Then you are one of the wealthy.' The man said, 'I have a servant.' He said, 'Then you are a king among kings.'

Ibn al-'Arabī said, 'The point of this is that when a man has to do *kaffārah,* and owns a house and servant he can sell for the *kaffārah*, then he is not permitted to fast because he is capable of owning slaves, and kings do not carry out *kaffārah* by fasting and they are not described as being unable to emancipate.' Ibn 'Abbās and Mujāhid said that He made them kings by giving them manna and quail, the

Stone and the Cloud, meaning that they were served like kings. Ibn 'Abbās said that it means having a servant and a house. Mujāhid, 'Ikrimah and al-Ḥakam ibn 'Uyaynah said that and added a wife. That is like what Zayd ibn Aslam said, although it is known that he said that the Prophet ﷺ said, 'Anyone who has a house (or a dwelling) in which he can shelter, a wife and a servant who serves him is a king.' An-Naḥḥās mentioned it. It is said that anyone who is free of the need of others is a king. This is like what the Prophet ﷺ said: 'Whoever is safe in the morning in his burrow, healthy in his body and possesses food for the day is like someone who owns the entire world.'

and gave you what He had not given to anyone else in all the worlds!

According to most commentators Mūsā is speaking to his people. Mujāhid said that it means the manna and quail, the stone and the cloud. It is said that it refers to the great number of Prophets among them and the Signs that they brought. It is also said that it means hearts free of rancour and deceit. It is said that it is making it lawful to take and use booty. This last statement is rejected: booty was only made lawful for this community as confirmed in the *Ṣaḥīḥ*. This will be explained, Allah willing. What Mūsā said was to prepare them to be strong and enter the land of the giants with force, and those whom Allah exalted and raised carried that out. The expression *'in all worlds'* here means all the people of their time, as al-Hasan said. Ibn Jubayr and Abū Mālik said that it is addressed to the Community of Muhammad ﷺ but this is deviating from the apparent meaning of the words in an improper matter.

History supports the fact that Damascus was the capital of the giants (*jabbārūn*). It is called 'Holy' (*muqaddasah*), meaning purified. Mujāhid said that it means blessed. *Barakah* is purification from drought, hunger and the like. Qatādah said that it is Syria as a whole. Mujāhid said it is Sinai and the area around it. Ibn 'Abbās, as-Suddī, and Ibn Zayd said that it is Jericho. Az-Zajjāj said that is Damascus, Palestine and part of Jordan. Qatādah's statement is the most comprehensive.

which Allah has ordained for you

Which He has obliged you to enter and promised you that you would enter and dwell in. When the tribe of Israel left Egypt, He commanded them to fight the people of Jericho in Palestine. They said, 'We know nothing about that place.' So by Allah's command twelve leaders were sent, one from each tribe, to spy out the land. They saw the dwellings of the tyrants who were the Amalekites, who were giants. It is said one of them saw their leaders and put them in his sleeve with the fruit he carried from his garden and took them to the king and scattered them before him, saying, 'This lot wants to fight us.' The king said to them, 'Go back to your man and tell him about us.' It is said that when they returned, they took a bunch of the grapes of that land. It is said that one man carried them, and it is said that the twelve leaders carried them. This is more likely. It is said that when they reached the Amalekites, they found that two of their men could enter into the sleeve of one of them. It took five of them to carry one of their bunches on a piece of wood. Four or five could get into half of a pomegranate.

This and the first account are not contradictory. That Amalekite who put them in his sleeve was 'Ūj ibn 'Anāq (Og). He was the tallest of them in stature and greatest in size as will be mentioned Allah willing. The height of the rest of them was nine and a half cubits according to Muqātil. Al-Kalbī said that each of them was eight cubits tall. Allah knows best. When, with the exception of Hosea (Joshua) and Caleb, they spread the news and the tribe of Israel refused to fight, they were punished by wandering in the wilderness for forty years until those rebels died and their children grew up. They then fought the Amalekites and were victorious.

Do not turn back in your tracks

'Do not stop obeying Me and what I command you to do with regard to fighting the giants.' It is said, 'Do not return to disobedience from obedience,' and the meaning is the same.

They said, 'There are giants in it, Mūsā,'

There are people there who are immensely tall in stature. *Jabbārah* is used of a tree which is very tall. Someone who is *jabbār* is exalted and protected from abasement and poverty. Az-Zajjāj said that it means that they are tyrants who compel people to do what they want. According to this, its root is *ijbār*, which is compulsion, compelling someone to do act as one wants. It is said that it is taken from mending (*jabr*) a bone, and so the root comes from the one who straightens things out. Then it is used for someone who brings benefit to himself, rightly or falsely. Al-Farrā' said, 'I have not heard of the form *fa''āl* coming from *af'ala* except in two cases: *jabbār* from *ajbara* and *darrāk* from *adraka*.'

Then it is said that those people were remnants of the people of 'Ād. It is also said that they were the descendants of Esau, the son of Isḥāq, and that they were Greeks. 'Uj (Og) ibn 'Anaq was with them. His height was three thousand three hundred and thirty-three cubits, as Ibn 'Umar said. He used to take hold of the clouds and drink from them, and take fish from the bottom of the sea and roast them by the eye of the sun itself and then eat them. He was present at the Flood of Nūḥ and it did not pass his knees. He lived to the age of three thousand six hundred. He wrenched up a stone the size of Mūsā's army with which to crush them and Allah sent a bird that pecked it so that it fell on his neck and knocked him down. Mūsā advanced to him and his staff was ten cubits long. He jumped ten cubits into the sky and only hit his ankle. It felled him and he killed him. It is said that it struck him in a vein under his ankle and he fell and died. He fell on the river Nile in Egypt and was a bridge for them for a year. This story is mentioned in various versions by Muḥammad ibn Isḥāq, aṭ-Ṭabarī, Makkī and others. Al-Kalbī said that Og was one of the children of Mārūt and Hārūt. Allah knows best.

We will not enter it until they leave.

'It' refers to Jerusalem or Jericho. They said, 'We will not enter it until they leave and surrender it to us without fighting.' It is said that they said that out of fear of the giants, without intending disobedience.

Two men among those who were afraid, but whom Allah had blessed

Ibn 'Abbās and others said that the two men were Yūsha' (Hosea/Joshua) and Kālib ibn Yūfanā or ibn Qaniya [Caleb, son of Jephunneh]. They were among the twelve leaders. They *'were afraid'* of the giants. Qatādah says, 'They had fear of Allah.' Aḍ-Ḍaḥḥāk said, 'They were two men in the city of the giants who followed the *dīn* of Mūsā. So it means they were afraid of the Amalekites and that their faith would be discovered and they would be tested, but they trusted in Allah.' It is said that they were afraid of the weakness and cowardice of the tribe of Israel. Mujāhid and Ibn Jubayr recited *'yukhāfūna'* which strengthens the idea that they were not from Mūsā's people. The words: *'but whom Allah had blessed'* mean that they were blessed with Islam or with certainty and righteousness.

Enter the gate against them!

They said to the tribe of Israel, 'Do not let the size of their bodies make you falter, for their hearts are full of terror of you. Their bodies are huge but their hearts are weak.' They knew that when they entered that gate, they would be victorious and they said that out of their trust in Allah's promise. Then they added: *'Put your trust in Allah if you are believers* and affirm him. He will help you.' According to the first view, when they said this, the tribe of Israel wanted to stone them, saying, 'Should we believe you two and abandon what the other ten say!'

They said, 'We will never enter it, Mūsā, as long as they are there. So you and your Lord go and fight.'

The Israelis said this to Mūsā. This was obstinacy, turning away from fighting and despair of gaining victory. Furthermore, they were ignorant of the nature of their Lord and said, *'you and your Lord go and fight.'* They described Him as 'going' when Allah is exalted above that. This indicates that they were anthropomorphists, and it is the sense of what al-Ḥasan said. It constitutes disbelief in Allah on their part. That is clear from the meaning of their words. It is also said that it means: 'The help of your Lord is better for you than our help, and His fighting with you, if you are His Messenger, is better than our fighting.' This would also be disbelief on their part because it constitutes doubt about his Messengership. It is said that it means, 'Go and fight and let your Lord help you!' It is also said that 'Lord' here means Hārūn, who was older than Mūsā and he would obey him. In general, they deviated by what they said since Allah says: *'Do not waste grief on this deviant people.'*

He said, 'My Lord, I have no control over anyone but myself and my brother'

That was because his brother obeyed him. It is said that it means, 'I have no control over anyone but myself,' and then a new sentence, 'and my brother,' meaning that his brother only has control over himself. According to the first view, '*my brother*' is in the accusative, added to '*myself*'. According to the second, it is in the nominative. If you wish, it is added to the noun of *inna*, which is *yā'*, i.e. 'I (*innī*) and my brother only have control over ourselves.' Or, if you wish, it could be added to what is implied in '*amliku*' and it is as if he were saying 'I and my brother only have control over ourselves.'

So make a clear distinction between us and this deviant people.

There are various responses to the question of how Allah was to make a distinction between him and them. The first is that it is indicated by their distance from the truth and abandonment of correct behaviour in the way they disobeyed. That is why they were cast out into the wilderness. The second is by being set aside from them and not included with them in the punishment. It is said that it means: 'Judge between us and them by protecting us from the disobedience they committed'. That possibility can be seen in the words of the Almighty: *'During it every wise decree is specified.'* (44:4) That was done when Allah caused them to die in the wilderness. It is said that it refers to the Next World, in other words: 'Put us in the Garden and do not put us with them in the Fire.' A poem bears witness to the great distance that this kind of separation can involve:

O Lord, separate him from me
with the greatest separation there can be between two!

Ibn 'Uyaynah related from 'Amr ibn Dīnār that 'Ubayd ibn 'Umayr recited '*ifriq*' with *kasrah* on the *rā'*.

He said, 'The land will be forbidden to them for forty years during which they will wander aimlessly about the earth.'

Allah answered his supplication and punished them in the wilderness for forty years. The linguistic root of wilderness (*tīh*) is confusion and the verb *tāha* taken from the root means to be confused and lost. A land which is *tayhā'* is one in which there is no guidance. So the land is *tīh* or *tayhā'*. [POEMS ILLUSTRATING]

They used to travel a few parasangs (c. four miles), and it is said that it was about six, in twenty-four hours and then they would be back where they had started out. They were constantly travelling without respite. There is disagreement about whether Mūsā and Hārūn were with them. It is said that they were not because the wilderness was a punishment and the years in the wilderness were equal to the number of days they worshipped the Calf, a year for every day. Musa had said: *'Make a clear distinction between us and this deviant people.'* It is said that they were with them and that Allah made it easy for them, as He made the fire coolness and peace for Ibrāhīm.

The adjective '*forbidden*' in this context means that they were forbidden to enter it in the same way as it is said, 'Allah has forbidden your face to the Fire' and 'I have forbidden you to enter the house.' So this *taḥrīm* implies prevention, not the prohibition of the *Sharī'ah*. This is what most commentators say. A poet said:

She went around to make me fall and I told her, 'Stop it.
I am a man whom you are forbidden to make fall.'

It means: that you cannot make me fall.

Abū 'Alī said, 'It is possible that it was a form of worship.' It is asked how could a large group of intelligent people travel a few parasangs and not be guided to get out of it? Abū 'Alī said, 'Allah turned around the land they were on when they slept and so they were returned back to the place from which they started. There was nothing physical to prevent them leaving, but it was like a miracle which is outside of normal things.' The number '*forty*' describes the amount time they spent in the wildness.

Al-Ḥasan and Qatādah said that none of them entered it, and so the stop is at 'forbidden to them'. Ar-Rabī' ibn Anas and others said that the stop is at '*forty years.*' According to the first, their children entered it, as Ibn 'Abbās said, and only Joshua and Caleb remained of them. Joshua led them with their descendants to that city and conquered it. According to the second, those who were still alive after forty years entered it. Ibn 'Abbās reported that Mūsā and Hārūn died in the wilderness.

Someone else said that Allah informed Joshua and told him to fight the giants and held back the sun until he entered the city. In it he burned those who had things that had been pilfered from the booty in their possession. When they took booty, a white fire would descend from heaven and consume it. That was a sign of acceptance. But if booty had been pilfered, it would not be consumed by the fire and beasts of prey and wild animals would come and eat it. The fire descended but did not consume their booty. He said, 'There is booty that has been pilfered from it. Let every tribe come and offer me a pledge. They did so and the hand of one man among them stuck to his hand. He said, 'You have stolen some booty.' He brought out something like the head of a gold ox. Then the fire descended and burned up the booty. It was a white fire like silver with a noise like that of wind in trees and the wings of birds. They mentioned that it burned the one who had stolen it and his goods in a depression now called Ghawr 'Ājiz known as al-Ghāll (the misappropriator). His name was 'Ājiz (Achan).

This tells us the punishment of those before us who misappropriated from the booty. We have already mentioned its rulings in our religion (2:254) and the clarification of the name of the Prophet and the misappropriator concerned in the sound *ḥadīth* from Abū Hurayrah in which the Messenger of Allah ﷺ said, 'One of the Prophets went on an expedition…' Muslim transmitted it. We find in it: 'He went on the expedition and approached the city when it was the time of the *'Aṣr* prayer or close to it. He said to the sun, "You are commanded and I am commanded. O Allah, hold it back for us for a while!" It was held for him until Allah granted him victory.' He said, 'They collected the booty and the fire advanced to consume it but refused to consume it. He said, "There has been some misappropriation among you. Let a man from each tribe pledge himself to me." The hands of two or three stuck to him. He said to them, "You have misappropriated."'

Our scholars said that the wisdom in holding back the sun for Joshua when he was fighting the people of Jericho, his looking to conquer it in the evening of Friday, and his fear of the sun setting before conquest, is that if the sun had set before he had conquered, he would have been forbidden to fight because it would have been the Sabbath. His enemies knew that and would attack and slaughter them with the sword. That was a personal Sign for him after his Prophethood was confirmed by what Mūsā ﷺ reported. Allah knows best. The Prophet ﷺ said in this *ḥadīth*: 'Booty was not made lawful for anyone before us.' That was because Allah Almighty saw our weakness and lack of power and was good to us. This refutes the position of those who interpret His words: *'He gave you what He had not given to anyone else in all the worlds'*, as meaning making booty lawful as well as its use.

'Amr ibn Maynūn al-Awdī was one of those who said that Mūsā died in the wilderness. He added that Hārūn did as well. They left the wilderness and went to a cave. Hārūn died and Mūsā buried him and went to the tribe of Israel. They asked, 'What happened to Hārūn?' 'He died,' he answered. They said, 'You have lied! You killed him because of our love for him!' He was loved among the tribe of Israel. Allah revealed to him that he should take them to his grave. He said, 'I will resurrect him so that he can inform them that he died a natural death and that you did not kill him.' He took them to his grave and called out, 'Hārūn!' He came out of his grave, shaking his head. He said, 'Did I kill you?' 'No,' he answered, 'I died.' He said, 'Return to your resting place,' and left.

Al-Ḥasan said that Mūsā did not die in the wilderness. Someone else said that Mūsā conquered Jericho with Joshua in the vanguard. He fought the giants who were there and then Mūsā led the tribe of Israel into it and they remained there for as long as Allah made them remain. Then Allah took him to back Himself and no creature knows where his grave is. Ath-Tha'labī said that is the soundest of views.

Muslim related that Abū Hurayrah said, 'The Angel of Death was sent to Mūsā. When he came to him, Mūsā struck him and gouged out his eye. He returned to his Lord and said, "You sent me to a servant who does not want to die." Allah restored his eye and told him, "Return to him and tell him, 'Put your hand on the back of an ox. You will have a year for every hair your hand covers.'" He asked, "What will happen then?" "Then death," he answered. He said, "Now then." He asked Allah to bury him a stone's throw from the Holy Land."' The Messenger of Allah ﷺ said, 'If I had been there, I would show you his grave beside the path under the red dune.' This Prophet of ours ﷺ knew his grave and described its location. He saw him standing and praying in it as we find in the *ḥadīth* of the Night Journey. It is possible that Allah concealed it from other people and did not let it be known among them. Perhaps that was in order to prevent it from being worshipped. Allah knows best. 'The path' means the path to Jerusalem. One of the transmissions says the path beside Mount Sinai.

Scholars disagree about the interpretation of Mūsā striking the Angel of Death and gouging out his eye. One of them is that it was an imaginary and not actual eye. This is false because it would lead to saying that what the Prophets saw of the forms of angels was not real. Another view is that it is a semantic eye and he gouged it out by the proof. This is a metaphorical understanding and not an actual occurrence. Another view is that he did not recognise the Angel of death and saw a man entering his dwelling without permission to attack him and so he defended himself and hit his eye and gouged it out. Self-defence is completely permissible in this instance. This is a good approach because it is actual with respect to the eye and blow. Imam Abū Bakr ibn Khuzaymah said that although it is at variance with what is in the *ḥadīth*, which is that when the Angel of Death returned to Allah Almighty, he said, 'Lord, You sent me to a servant who does not want to die.' If Mūsā had not recognised him, the words of the Angel of Death would not be true. Furthermore, it says in another variant, 'Answer your Lord,' indicating that he identified himself. Allah knows best.

Another view is that Mūsā was quick to anger. When he became angry, smoke rose from his cap and the hair of his body raised his jubbah. His quickness to anger was the reason he struck the Angel of Death. Ibn al-'Arabī said, 'This is as you see. The Prophets are protected from initiating the like of this in pleasure or anger.' Another view, and the soundest of them, is that Mūsā recognised the Angel of Death and that he had come to take his soul, but he came with the resolve of someone commanded to take his soul without giving him any choice. Mūsā knew, as the text that has come from our Prophet Muḥammad ﷺ states, that Allah does not take the soul of a Prophet until he is given a choice. When the angel came in other than the manner about which he had been informed, because of his energy and strength, he hastened to discipline him and struck him, gouging out his eye, to test the Angel of Death since he did not give him the choice. One thing that indicates the soundness of this is that when the Angel of Death returned to him, he gave him the choice between life and death and he chose death and submitted. Allah has more wisdom and better knows His Unseen. This is the soundest of what is said about the death of Mūsā. Commentators have mentioned other stories and reports about whose soundness Allah knows best. There is enough about it in the *Ṣaḥīḥ*.

Mūsā lived for 120 years. It is related that Joshua saw him in a dream after he had died and asked him, 'How did you find death?' He answered, 'Like a sheep skinned while it is still alive.' This meaning is sound. The Prophet ﷺ said in a sound *ḥadīth*, 'Death has throes' as we explained in *at-Tadhkirah*.

Do not waste grief on this deviant people.'

Do not be sad. *Asā* is sorrow and the verb is *asiya, ya'usā, asā*. A poet said:

They say, 'Do not die of sorrow (*asā*).

وَاتْلُ عَلَيْهِمْ نَبَأَ ابْنَيْ آدَمَ بِالْحَقِّ إِذْ قَرَّبَا قُرْبَانًا فَتُقُبِّلَ مِنْ أَحَدِهِمَا وَلَمْ
يُتَقَبَّلْ مِنَ الْآخَرِ قَالَ لَأَقْتُلَنَّكَ قَالَ إِنَّمَا يَتَقَبَّلُ اللَّهُ مِنَ الْمُتَّقِينَ ﴿٢٧﴾

27 Recite to them the true report of Ādam's two sons when they offered a sacrifice and it was accepted from one of them but not accepted from the other. The one said, 'I shall kill you.' The other said, 'Allah only accepts from people who are godfearing.

Recite to them the true report of Ādam's two sons when they offered a sacrifice

This *āyah* is connected to what came before it regarding Allah's clarification of the wrongdoing of the Jews and their breaking of their contracts and covenants, which is here compared to the son of Ādam wronging his brother. It means: 'Those Jews wanted to assassinate you, Muḥammad, just as they killed the Prophets before you and as Qābīl killed Hābīl.' Evil has ancient origins. Their mention of this story is true, not like other fabricated reports. That is to censure those who opposed Islam and to console the Prophet ﷺ.

There is disagreement about the sons of Ādam. Al-Ḥasan al-Baṣrī said, 'They were not his actual sons. They were two men of the tribe of Israel of whom Allah made an example to illustrate the envy of the Jews. They had a quarrel and brought offerings, and such offerings only took place among the tribe of Israel.' Ibn 'Aṭiyyah noted, 'This is weak. How could the form of burial be unknown among the tribe of Israel so that they would imitate a crow? The truth is that they were Adam's actual sons.' This is the position of most commentators and that of Ibn 'Abbās, Ibn 'Umar and others. They were Qābīl (Cain) and Hābīl (Abel). Qābīl offered a bundle of wheat because he was a farmer and he chose the worst of his crop. Then he found some good grain in it and removed it and ate it. The offering of Hābīl was a ram because he was a shepherd and he chose one of his best sheep.

and it was accepted from one of them but not accepted from the other.

'Accepted' means the ram was raised to the Garden. The ram continued to graze in the Garden until it was used to ransom the son of Ibrāhīm. Sa'īd ibn Jubayr and others said that. When Hābīl's sacrifice was accepted because he

was a believer, Qābīl, who was an unbeliever, told him out of envy, 'Are you to walk on the earth with people thinking you are better than me! *"I shall kill you'*!"'

It is said that the reason for offering this sacrifice was that Ḥawwā' used to bear twins - a boy and a girl - except for Shīth (Seth) who was born alone to replace Hābīl and was called Hibatu'llāh (the Gift of Allah), because when he was born, Jibrīl told Ḥawwā', 'This is the gift of Allah to replace Hābīl.' On the day Shīth was born Ādam was 130 years old. The male used to marry a female from another pregnancy and was not allowed to marry his twin. Qābīl's twin was beautiful and her name was Iqlīmiyā' (Aclima) and the twin of Hābīl was not beautiful, and was called Layūdhā (Jumella). When Ādam wanted them to marry, Qābīl said, 'I am more entitled to my sister!' Ādam commanded him and he did not obey. He chided him and he would not be restrained and so they agreed to offer sacrifices. This is according to a group of commentators, including Ibn Mas'ūd, and he related that Ādam was present at that. Allah knows best.

Regarding this topic it is related from Ja'far aṣ-Ṣādiq: 'Ādam did not give his daughter in marriage to his son. If Ādam had done that, then the Prophet ﷺ would not have been averse to it. The *dīn* of Ādam was the same as that of the Prophet ﷺ. When Allah sent down Ādam and Ḥawwā' to the earth and they joined together, Ḥawwā' bore a girl whom they called 'Anāq. She fornicated and was the first to fornicate on the surface of the earth. So Allah allowed her to be killed. Then Qābīl was born to Ādam and then Hābīl. When Qābīl came of age, Allah made a jinn girl called Jumālah appear to him in human form. Allah revealed to Ādam that he should marry her to Qābīl and he did so. When Hābīl came of age, Allah sent down to Ādam a houri in human form and created a womb in her. Her name was Bazlah. When Hābīl looked at her, he loved her, and Allah revealed to Ādam that he should marry her to Hābīl and he did so. Qābīl said, "Father, am I not older than my brother?" "Yes," he answered. He said, "I am more entitled to what you have done than he is!" Ādam said to him, "My son, Allah commanded me to do that. All favour is in Allah's hand and He gives it to whomever He wishes." He exclaimed, "No, by Allah! You have preferred him to me!" Ādam said, "Let both of you offer a sacrifice and whoever has his sacrifice accepted is more entitled to the favour."'

I do not think that this story from Ja'far is sound. The proper view is what we mentioned of a boy from one pregnancy marrying a girl from another pregnancy. The evidence for this is the words of Allah: *'O mankind! have taqwā of your Lord Who created you from a single self and created its mate from it and then disseminated many men and women from the two of them.'* (4:1) This is like a text which was then abrogated as was explained in *al-Baqarah.*

The total number of the children of Ḥawwā' was forty in twenty pregnancies. The first was Q̱ābīl and his twin Iqlīmiyā' and the last was 'Abd al-Mughīth. Then Allah blessed the progeny of Ādam. Ibn 'Abbās said, 'Ādam did not die until his descendants numbered 40,000.' As for what is related about her bearing a daughter who fornicated, it might be asked, 'With whom did she fornicate? With a jinn who seduced her?' Something like this requires sound and unimpaired transmission and that does not exist. Allah knows best.

Allah only accepts from people who are godfearing

Words before that are elided and imply: 'Why would you kill me when I have not done anything wrong and I have incurred no wrong action in Allah's accepting my sacrifice? I fear Him and I am on the path of the truth. Allah only accepts from people who are godfearing.' Ibn 'Aṭiyyah said that, by the consensus of the people of the *Sunnah,* what is meant by *taqwā* here is guarding against *shirk.* If someone is on guard against it and unifies Allah, all his actions in which his intention is sincere are accepted. As for the one who guards against *shirk* and acts of disobedience, he has a higher degree of acceptance and his seal is mercy. That is known by reports from Allah. It is not that it is obliged logically for Allah. 'Adī ibn Thābit and others said that the offering of the godfearing of this community is the prayer.

This is particular to a form of worship. Al-Bukhārī reported from Abū Hurayrah that the Messenger of Allah ﷺ said, 'Allah Almighty says, "I have declared war against anyone who shows enmity towards a friend of Mine. My slave does not draw near to Me with anything I love more than what I have made obligatory for him. Then My slave continues to draw near to Me with supererogatory actions until I love him. When I love him, I become his hearing with which he hears, his sight by which he sees, his hand with which he strikes and his foot with which he walks. If he asks of Me, I give to him. If he seeks refuge with Me, I give him refuge. I do not hesitate to do anything I do as I hesitate to take the soul of the believer who hates death and I dislike to vex him."'

لَئِنۢ بَسَطتَ إِلَيَّ يَدَكَ لِتَقۡتُلَنِي مَآ أَنَا۠ بِبَاسِطٖ يَدِيَ إِلَيۡكَ لِأَقۡتُلَكَۖ إِنِّيٓ
أَخَافُ ٱللَّهَ رَبَّ ٱلۡعَٰلَمِينَ ٢٨ إِنِّيٓ أُرِيدُ أَن تَبُوٓأَ بِإِثۡمِي وَإِثۡمِكَ فَتَكُونَ
مِنۡ أَصۡحَٰبِ ٱلنَّارِۚ وَذَٰلِكَ جَزَٰٓؤُاْ ٱلظَّٰلِمِينَ ٢٩

28-29 'Even if you do raise your hand against me to kill me, I am not going to raise my hand against you to kill you. Truly I fear Allah, the Lord of all the worlds. I want you to take on both my wrongdoing and your wrongdoing and so become one of the Companions of the Fire. That is the repayment of the wrongdoers.'

Even if you do raise your hand against me to kill me,

This means: 'If you intend to kill me, I do not intend to kill you.' This is submission on his part. We read the tradition: 'In a trial be like the better of the sons of Ādam.' Abū Dāwūd reported that Sa'd ibn Abi Waqqāṣ said, 'I said, "Messenger of Allah, what if someone enters my house and stretches out his hand to kill me?" The Messenger of Allah ﷺ replied, "Be like the better of the sons of Ādam," and he recited: *"Even if you do raise your hand against me to kill me."*' Mujāhid said, 'The obligation on them at that time was not to unsheathe a sword against anyone, even in self-defence.' Our scholars say that such behaviour was permitted as an act of devotion, but our *Sharī'ah* permits self-defence by consensus, and there is disagreement about whether it is obligatory. The soundest position is that it is mandatory since it is forbidding the bad. Some of the Ḥāshwiyyah do not permit the one attacked to defend himself, citing as evidence the *ḥadīth* of Abū Dharr. Scholars take it to mean not fighting in civil war and to refrain in case of doubt as we explained in our book, *at-Tadhikrah*.

'Abdullāh ibn 'Amr and the majority of people say that Hābīl was stronger than Qābīl, but he refused to fight back. Ibn 'Aṭiyyah said, 'This is more likely. It is strengthened by the fact that Qābīl was a rebel, not an unbeliever, because if he had been an unbeliever, he would not have been constrained at all. Hābīl was constrained because he would have had to kill a believer and was content to be wronged since he would be repaid in the Next World. This is like what 'Uthmān did.' It is said that it means, 'I do not intend to kill you, but to defend myself.' It is said that he was sleeping when Qābīl came and crushed his head with a stone. A person is permitted to defend himself against an aggressor, even to the extent of killing him. It is said that he meant, 'If you start to kill me, I will not start to kill.'

It is said that it means, 'If you raise your hand against me wrongfully, I am not a wrongdoer. I fear Allah, the Lord of the Worlds.'

I want you to take on both my wrongdoing and your wrongdoing

The meaning of these words is what is found in the words of the Prophet ﷺ, 'When two Muslims meet with their swords, the killer and the slain are both in the Fire.' They asked, 'Messenger of Allah, that is clear in the case of the killer, but why the victim?' He replied, 'He was also eager to kill his companion.' It is as if Hābīl meant: 'I am not eager to kill you. I want you to bear the sin which I would have had if I had wished to kill you on top of your wrongdoing in killing me.'

It is said that *'my wrongdoing'* means 'that in which I was remiss,' meaning: 'my evil deeds will be cast onto my brother because of his injustice in murdering me.' This is supported by what the Prophet ﷺ said, 'On the Day of Rising the wronger and the one he wronged will be brought and good deeds will be taken from the wrongdoer and added to the good deeds of the one he wronged until he has justice. If he does not have enough good deeds, then some of the evil deeds of the wronged one will be taken and cast on him.' Muslim has it. It is also supported by the words of Allah: *'They will bear their own burdens and other burdens together with their own.'* (29:12) This is clear without any uncertainty.

It is said that it means: 'so that you do not take on my wrongdoing and your wrongdoing' as the usage is seen in 16:15 and 4:176. I say that this is weak since the Prophet ﷺ said, 'No self is killed unjustly but that the burden of his blood rests on the first son of Ādam because he was the first to institute the *sunnah* of killing.' It is confirmed by this that the wrongdoing of killing is clear. That is why most scholars say, 'You will return with the wrong of my murder and your wrong which you did before killing me.' Ath-Tha'labī said that this is the position of most commentators.

It is said that it is a question: 'What do I want?' implying denial. That is because the desire to kill is disobedience to Allah. Al-Qushayrī related that Abū al-Ḥasan ibn Kaysān was asked, 'How can a believer want to wrong his brother and enter the Fire?' He said, 'The desire to do so happened before he stretched out his hand to kill him. So it means: "If you stretch forth your hand to kill me, I refuse to do that out of desire for the reward."' He was asked, 'Why does He say, *"My wrongdoing and your wrongdoing"*? What wrongdoing did he have when he was killed?' There are three answers to this question.

One is that it means: 'You take on the wrongdoing of killing me and the wrongdoing of your sin which prevented your sacrifice from being accepted.' This view was related from Mujāhid. The second is: 'You take on the wrongdoing of killing me and the wrongdoing of your aggression against me' because he sinned by his aggression, even when he had not yet killed him. The third is that he sins by stretching out his hand against him. He related that if someone refrains from doing that, the wrongdoing reverts back to the one who does it. So it is like the words: 'Wealth is between him and Zayd,' meaning it is shared between them. It means: 'You take on the burden of the wrongdoing of both of us.'

The root of *bā'* is returning to one's abode (*mabā'ah*). The meaning of 'return' is used elsewhere in the Qur'ān and was dealt with in *al-Baqarah*. A poet said:

Do kings not leave us alone and in fear
so that blood for our sacred things is not answered (*yabw'i*) with blood?

That is the repayment of the wrongdoers.

This indicates that at that time they were legally responsible because the threat and the promise applied to them. Some people take the words of Hābīl about Qābīl being in the Fire to indicate that he was an unbeliever because the term 'Companions of the Fire' normally applies to unbelievers in the Qur'ān. This view is rejected by the people of knowledge as we have already mentioned, and Allah knows best. 'One of the Companions of the Fire' indicates the period of your being in it. Allah knows best.

فَطَوَّعَتْ لَهُۥ نَفْسُهُۥ قَتْلَ أَخِيهِ فَقَتَلَهُۥ فَأَصْبَحَ مِنَ ٱلْخَٰسِرِينَ ﴿٣٠﴾

30 So his lower self persuaded him to kill his brother, and he killed him and became one of the lost.

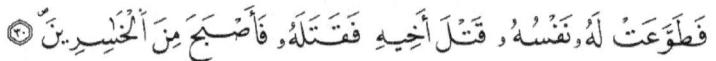

His lower self made it easy for him to do it and encouraged him with the idea of killing his brother. *Ṭā'a* means to make something easy and submissive. It is related that he did not know how to kill him and so Iblīs brought a bird or another animal and crushed its head between two stones so that Qābīl could imitate that. He did so. That is stated by Ibn Jurayj, Mujāhid and others. Ibn 'Abbās and Ibn Mas'ūd said that he found him asleep and crushed his head with a stone. That took place at Thawr, a mountain at Makkah, according to Ibn 'Abbās. Other places are mentioned: 'Aqabah Hirā', according to Muḥammad ibn Jarīr aṭ-Ṭabarī, and Basra at the site of the Great Mosque, according to Ja'far aṣ-Ṣādiq. Hābīl was twenty when he was killed. It is also said that Qābīl knew how to kill him, knowing that by his nature, because even though he did not know about killing, he naturally knew that the self could disappear and be destroyed. Therefore, he took a stone and killed him in India. Allah knows best. When he killed him, he regretted it and sat down at his head weeping. Two crows came and fought and one killed the other and then dug a hole with its beak and buried it, and so Qābīl did the same with brother.

'*Sawa'ah*' (in the next *āyah*) means 'private parts', but it is said that here it means the corpse of the victim. Then he fled to Aden in the Yemen and Iblīs came to him and said, 'The fire consumed the offering of your brother because he worshipped fire. So you should set up a fire for you and your descendants.' So he built a temple to fire and he was the first to worship fire as it is said, and Allah knows best.

It is related from Ibn 'Abbās that when he killed him while Ādam was in Makkah, the trees became thorned, food went bad, fruits became sour, water became salty and the earth dusty. Ādam said, 'Something has happened in the land.' He went to India and found that Qābīl had killed Hābil. It is also said that Qābīl is the one who went to Ādam. When he reached him, Ādam asked, 'Where is Hābīl?' He replied, 'I do not know. Did you charge me with looking after him?' Ādam said to him, 'Did you do it? By Allah, his blood calls out, "O Allah! Curse a land which drinks the blood of Hābīl."' Then Ādam remained for a hundred years without smiling until an angel came to him and said, 'May Allah prolong your life and delight you.' Ādam asked, 'What is "delight"?' He said, 'Making you laugh.' After Ādam was 130, five years after the death of Hābīl, Shīth was born. His name means 'Allah's gift' and he was to replace Hābīl.

Muqātil said, 'Before Qābīl killed Hābīl, the wild animals and birds were friendly with Ādam. When he killed him, they fled and Ādam knew that something had changed. It is related that Ādam recited:

The land is changed as well as those on it.
    The face of the earth is dusty and ugly.
Every taste and colour has changed.
    Rarely does a smile grace a comely face.

There are many verses which were mentioned by ath-Tha'labī. Al-Qushayrī and others said that Ibn 'Abbās said, 'Ādam did not compose poetry. Muḥammad and all the Prophets were the same in being forbidden to compose poetry, but when Hābīl was killed, Ādam elegised him in Syriac. His elegy in Syriac was bequeathed to his son Shīth. He said, "It is my testament to you, so preserve these words from me so that they will bequeathed." It was preserved from him until the time of Ya'rub ibn Qaḥṭān who translated it into Arabic and made it into a poem.'

It is related that Anas said, 'The Prophet ﷺ was asked about Tuesday and said, "It is the day of blood. On it Ḥawwā' menstruated and the son of Ādam killed his brother.' In *Ṣaḥīḥ Muslim* and elsewhere it is confirmed that 'Abdullāh said that the Messenger of Allah ﷺ said that Qābīl is responsible for the blood of everyone who is murdered, as we mentioned, just as Iblīs bears the responsibility of everyone who refuses to prostrate, because he was the first to disobey. The same principle applies to anyone who innovates something in the *dīn* which is an impermissible innovation or sect. The Messenger of Allah ﷺ said, 'Anyone who creates a good *sunnah* in Islam has its reward and the reward of whoever does it after him until the Day of Rising. Anyone who creates a bad *sunnah* in Islam bears its burden and the burden of whoever acts by it after him until the Day of Rising.' This is a text about good and evil. The Prophet ﷺ also said, 'My greatest fear for My community is a misguiding imām.'

All this is explicit and is sound text regarding the meaning of the *āyah*. This applies when the one who does that does not repent of his disobedience, because Ādam was the first to disobey by eating what he was commanded not to eat but he does not bear any of the burdens of those who disobey Allah by eating or drinking what is forbidden. There is a consensus regarding this because Ādam repented of that and Allah turned to him. So he became like someone who had not done it. Another reason is that, according to the sound position, he ate out of forgetfulness as we explained in *al-Baqarah* (2:35). Someone who does something out of forgetfulness does not sin and is not punished. This *āyah* demonstrates the state of the person who suffers from envy and shows that his envy can move him to destroy himself by killing his closest relatives and those to whom he should be merciful and kind.

and became one of the lost.

This means one of those whose good actions are lost. Mujāhid said, 'One of the legs of a murderer is chained by his calf to his thigh from today to the Day of Rising. His face is towards the sun wherever it moves. In the summer he has a fence of fire and in the winter a fence of ice.' Ibn 'Aṭiyyah said, 'If this is sound, it is part of the loss expressed in this *āyah*. Loss includes both this world and the Next.' This may refer to part of his punishment if he is a rebel and not an unbeliever and so the loss is in this world. Allah knows best.

فَبَعَثَ ٱللَّهُ غُرَابًا يَبْحَثُ فِي ٱلْأَرْضِ لِيُرِيَهُۥ كَيْفَ يُوَٰرِي سَوْءَةَ أَخِيهِ ۚ قَالَ يَٰوَيْلَتَىٰٓ أَعَجَزْتُ أَنْ أَكُونَ مِثْلَ هَٰذَا ٱلْغُرَابِ فَأُوَٰرِيَ سَوْءَةَ أَخِي ۖ فَأَصْبَحَ مِنَ ٱلنَّٰدِمِينَ ﴿٣١﴾

31 Then Allah sent a crow which scratched at the earth to show him how to conceal his brother's corpse. He said, 'Woe is me! Can I not even be like this crow and conceal my brother's corpse?' And he became one of those who suffer bitter remorse

Then Allah sent a crow which scratched at the earth

Mujāhid said, 'Allah sent two crows who fought and then the one who killed the other one dug a hole and buried it. The son of Ādam was the first man to be killed.' It is said that the crow scratched at the earth for its food to conceal it for the time it needed it as is the habit of crows. By that Qābīl learned how to conceal his brother. It is related that when Qābīl killed him, he put him in a bag and walked carrying him on his shoulder for a hundred years. Mujāhid said that. Ibn al-Qāsim reported from Mālik that he carried him for a year, and Ibn 'Abbās said that. It is said that it was until evening and he did not know what to do until he imitated the crow.

Anas reported that he heard the Messenger of Allah ﷺ say, 'Allah favoured the sons of Ādam with three after three: the smell after the departure of the *rūḥ*. If it had not been for the smell, no friend would have buried a friend. If it had not been for the worms in corpses, kings would have stored them up and they would have been more valuable than dirhams and dinars. A man becomes old until he is bored with himself and his family and children and relatives are bored with him, and then death conceals him.'

People said that Qābīl knew about burial but left Hābīl exposed, thinking little of it. Then Allah sent a crow to scratch the earth over him to bury him. Then Qābīl said: *'Woe is me! Can I not even be like this crow and conceal my brother's corpse?'* when he saw how Allah honoured Hābīl by sending the crow to bury him. It was not the regret of repentance. It is also said that his regret was for his loss, not for killing him or that his regret was not lasting. Ibn 'Abbās said that if he had truly regretted killing him, then the regret would have been true repentance. It is said that Ādam and Ḥawwā' came to his grave and wept for days. Then while Qābīl was on the top of a mountain, an ox gored him and he fell and was smashed at the foot of it. It is said that Ādam prayed against him and the earth swallowed him up. It is said that Qābīl was distressed after killing Hābīl and stayed in the wilderness. He could only eat from wild animals. When he caught an animal, he hit it until it died and then ate it. Ibn 'Abbās said that gored animals are forbidden because of what happened with Qābīl. He will be the first of human beings who will be driven to the Fire.' That is the words of Allah: *'Our Lord, show us those jinn and men who misguided us.'* (41:29) Iblīs is the leader of the unbelieving jinn and Qābīl is the leader of human beings who erred. This will be explained in *Fuṣṣilāt*, Allah willing. It is said that regret at that time was not repentance. Allah has more knowledge of all of that and greater wisdom.

The literal meaning of the *āyah* is that Hābīl was the first human being to die. That is why the custom of burial was unknown. That is what aṭ-Ṭabarī related from Ibn Isḥāq from one of the people with knowledge of what was contained in the first books. The verb 'scratched' (*yabḥathu*) means to peck at the earth with its beak and move it. That is why *Sūrat at-Tawbah* is called *al-Buḥūth* because it investigates the hypocrites. An example of that is the words of the poet:

If people cover me, I cover them.
    If they investigate me, they too have things that can be investigated.

The sending of the crow was an act of wisdom to show the son of Ādam how to bury. It is the meaning of the words of Allah: *'Then He causes him to die and buries him.'* (80:21) The action of the crow became an abiding custom among creatures, a general duty for people in general. If one person does it, the obligation is cancelled for others. Those most entitled to undertake it are someone's closest relatives, then their neighbours and then Muslims in general. As for the unbelievers, Abū Dāwūd related that 'Alī said, 'I said to the Prophet ﷺ, "Your old misguided uncle has died." He said, "Go and bury your father in the earth. Then do not do anything until you come to me." So I went and buried him and came to him and he told me to wash and made supplication for me.'

It is recommended to make a grave wide and good since Ibn Mājah reports from Hishām ibn 'Āmir that the Messenger of Allah ﷺ said, 'Dig and make it wide and make it good.' Al-Adra' as-Sulamī said, 'I came at night to guard the Prophet ﷺ and there was a man reciting in a loud voice. The Prophet ﷺ came out and I said, "Messenger of Allah, this one is showing off." The man died in Madīnah and they finished preparing him and carried his bier. The Messenger of Allah ﷺ said, "Be kind to him. Allah was kind to him. He loved Allah and His Messenger." When he was present at the burial, he said, "Make it wide. May Allah make it wide for him." One of his Companions asked, "Messenger of Allah, are you sad about him?" He answered, "Yes, he used to love Allah and His Messenger."'

Abū Bakr ibn Abī Shaybah transmitted it from Zayd ibn al-Ḥubāb from Mūsā ibn 'Ubaydah from Sa'īd ibn Abī Sa'īd. Abū 'Umar ibn 'Abd al-Barr said, 'Adra' as-Sulamī related one *ḥadīth* from the Prophet ﷺ.' Sa'īd ibn Abī Sa'īd al-Maqburī related from him. Hishām ibn 'Āmir ibn Umayyah ibn al-Ḥasḥās ibn 'Āmir ibn Ghanm ibn 'Adī ibn an-Najjār al-Anṣārī was named Shihāb in the Jāhiliyyah and the Prophet ﷺ changed his name to Hishām. His father 'Āmir was martyred in the Battle of Uḥud. Hishām settled in Basra and died there. This is mentioned in the Book of Companions.

It is said that the niche-grave (*laḥd*) is better than the *shaqq* grave. It is what Allah preferred for his Messenger ﷺ. When the Prophet ﷺ died in Madīnah, there were two grave-diggers, one of whom did *laḥd* and the other who did not. They said, 'Whichever of them comes first will do it his way.' The one who did *laḥd* came first and so that sort of grave was dug for the Messenger of Allah ﷺ. Mālik mentioned it in the *Muwaṭṭā'* from Hishām ibn 'Urwah from his father. Ibn Mājah transmitted it from Anas ibn Mālik and 'Ā'ishah. The two men were Abū Ṭalḥah and Abū 'Ubaydah. Abū Ṭalḥah did *laḥd* and Abū 'Ubaydah did *shaqq*.

A *laḥd* grave is one in which a niche is made in the side of the bottom of the grave when the earth is firm. The deceased is placed in the niche and then bricks are placed in it and then earth is put in the grave. Sa'd ibn Abī Waqqāṣ said in his final illness: 'Dig me a *laḥd* grave and put bricks for me as was done for the Messenger of Allah ﷺ. Muslim transmitted it. Ibn Mājah and others related that Ibn 'Abbās said, 'The Messenger of Allah ﷺ said, "The *laḥd* grave is for us and the *shaqq* for others."'

Ibn Mājah related from Sa'īd ibn Musayyab: 'I was at a funeral with Ibn 'Umar. When the body was placed in the niche, he said, "In the Name of Allah, and in the Way of Allah and on the religion of the Messenger of Allah ﷺ." When the bricks were level over the niche, he said, "O Allah, protect him from Shayṭān and the punishment of the grave. O Allah, keep the earth from his body and let his soul ascend. Give him pleasure from You." I said, "Ibn 'Umar, is this something you heard from the Messenger of Allah ﷺ or did you say it of your own accord?" He said, "As if I were able to speak! Indeed, I heard it from the Messenger of Allah ﷺ!"' It is related from Abū Hurayrah that the Messenger of Allah ﷺ stood at a funeral and then went to the grave of the decreased and put three handfuls of dirt on it towards the top. This is connected to the meaning of the *āyah* in rulings.

The root of 'Woe is me!' is *'yā waylatāy'* and the *yā'* has been replaced by an *alif*. Al-Ḥasan recited it with the *yā'* but the first is sounder because of the usual elision of the *yā'* in the vocative. It is an exclamation used by the Arabs in moments of destruction. Sībawayh said that. Al-Aṣma'ī said that the meaning of *'wayl'* is distance. Al-Ḥasan recited *'a a'jiztu'*. An-Naḥḥās said that it is an obscure dialect. One says *"ajazat al-imra'tu'* when a woman has a large posterior (*'ajīzah*), and the verb is used for being unable to do something with the nouns *'ajz*, *ma'jizah* and *ma'jazah*. Allah knows best.

مِنْ أَجْلِ ذَٰلِكَ كَتَبْنَا عَلَىٰ بَنِيٓ إِسْرَٰٓءِيلَ أَنَّهُۥ مَن قَتَلَ نَفْسًۢا
بِغَيْرِ نَفْسٍ أَوْ فَسَادٍ فِى ٱلْأَرْضِ فَكَأَنَّمَا قَتَلَ ٱلنَّاسَ جَمِيعًا وَمَنْ
أَحْيَاهَا فَكَأَنَّمَآ أَحْيَا ٱلنَّاسَ جَمِيعًا ۚ وَلَقَدْ جَآءَتْهُمْ
رُسُلُنَا بِٱلْبَيِّنَٰتِ ثُمَّ إِنَّ كَثِيرًا مِّنْهُم بَعْدَ ذَٰلِكَ فِى ٱلْأَرْضِ
لَمُسْرِفُونَ ﴿٣٢﴾

32 on account of that. So We decreed for the tribe of Israel that if someone kills another person – unless it is in retaliation for someone else or for causing corruption in the earth – it is as if he had murdered all mankind. And if anyone gives life to another person, it is as if he had given life to all mankind. Our Messengers came to them with Clear Signs but even after that many of them committed outrages in the earth.

on account of that.

On account of the guilt and crime of the killer. Az-Zajjāj says that it is on account of his crime. One says, 'He committed (*ajala*) evil against his family.' The verb is *ajala, ya'julu ajl* for committing a crime. It is like the verb *akhadha*. Al-Khinnawt says:

I was among the people of a righteous tent.
They fought hastily. I committed it.

'Adī ibn Zayd said:

Yes, Allah has preferred us
above those who tightened the contract by lineage.

The root of *ajila* means to commit and *ajal* is the time of its occurrence. Ājil (future) is the opposite of *'ājil*. It refers to what comes of a future matter. *'Ajal'* also means 'yes' because it is acquiescence with what occurs. *Ijl* is a kind of wild ox. Ar-

Rummānī said that. Abū Ja'far Yazīd ibn al-Qa'qā' recited *mini-jli'* with a *kasrah* on the *nūn* and the *hamzah* elided. It is a dialect. The root is '*min ijli*' and the *kasrah* of the *hamzah* has been put on the *nūn* and the *hamzah* elided.

It is said that it is possible that it is connected to the *āyah* before and so the stop is at '*on account of that*'. It is also possible that it is connected to what is after it, 'We decreed' and so '*on account of that*' is an inceptive of words which end at 'bitter remorse'. Most people say this, namely: 'because of this event We wrote.' The tribe of Israel is mentioned, even though nations before them were forbidden to commit murder, because they were the first community on whom the threat about murder descended in writing. Before that it was a general statement. The command was made more severe for the tribe of Israel by being written, according to their wrongdoing and shedding of blood. Allah mentions the exception because He forbade killing in all *Sharī'ahs* except in three cases: disbelief after belief, fornication after lawful marriage, or killing someone wrongly and unjustly '*or for causing corruption in the earth*,' meaning *shirk*. It is also said that it means highway robbery.

Al-Ḥasan recited '*fasādan*' in the accusative based on an implied elision of a verb which indicates it at the beginning of the words. It implies: 'causing corruption'. It is evidenced by the words because murder is one of the greatest forms of corruption. Most recite '*fasādin*' in the genitive, implying 'with other than corruption'.

it is as if he had murdered all mankind.

Commentators disagree about the exact nature of this resemblance because the punishment of one who kills all people is more than the one who kills one person. It is related from Ibn 'Abbās that the meaning is that if someone kills a Prophet or just ruler, it is as if he had killed all the people, and if someone gives life by strong support and help, it is as if he had given life to all mankind. It is also reported that he said that the meaning is: whoever kills one soul and violates the sanctity of life is like someone who kills all people. Whoever does not kill a single soul and protects the sanctity of life, and lets them live out of fear of Allah, is like someone who gives life to all mankind. Yet another interpretation is related from him: It is as if he killed all mankind for the victim. If someone saves him from destruction, it is as if he has given life to all mankind for the one saved.

Mujāhid said that the meaning is that if someone kills a believer deliberately, Allah will repay him with Hell and will be angry with him and curse him and inflict a terrible punishment on him. He says, 'If he had killed all of mankind, it would not be worse than that. The one who does not kill gives life to people.'

Ibn Zayd said that the meaning is that if someone kills someone, retaliation is inflicted on him as if he had killed all mankind. The one who gives life is the one who pardons. Al-Ḥasan also said that. It refers to pardon when having the power to kill. It is said that the meaning is: 'If someone kills someone, all the believers are his opponents because he has wronged all, and whoever lets someone live, has given life to all, meaning that all must thank him.' It is said that the sin of someone who kills one person is the sin of someone who kills all people and Allah can judge however he wishes. It is also said that this specifically applies to the tribe of Israel to be severe on them.

Ibn 'Aṭiyyah said, 'In general, the correspondence, according to what is said, applies to all. Someone who violates one is like someone who violates all. An example of that is that two men swear on two trees that they will not eat any of their fruit. Then one of them eats one fruit from his tree and the other eats all the fruits of his tree. They both break their oath.' It is said that the meaning is that someone who considers it lawful to kill one person considers it lawful to kill all of them because he denies the *Sharī'ah.*

If anyone saves another person's life.

It is metaphorical and designates not killing and saving someone from destruction. Bringing to life, in reality, belongs to Allah. This bringing to life is like the words of the accursed Nimrod: *'I too give life and cause to die.'* (2:258) So he referred to not killing as 'giving life'. Allah reports that the Messengers brought the tribe of Israel Clear Signs but most of them exceeded the limits and abandoned Allah's command.

إِنَّمَا جَزَٰٓؤُاْ ٱلَّذِينَ يُحَارِبُونَ ٱللَّهَ وَرَسُولَهُۥ وَيَسْعَوْنَ فِي ٱلْأَرْضِ
فَسَادًا أَن يُقَتَّلُوٓاْ أَوْ يُصَلَّبُوٓاْ أَوْ تُقَطَّعَ أَيْدِيهِمْ وَأَرْجُلُهُم مِّنْ
خِلَٰفٍ أَوْ يُنفَوْاْ مِنَ ٱلْأَرْضِ ذَٰلِكَ لَهُمْ خِزْيٌ فِي ٱلدُّنْيَا وَلَهُمْ
فِي ٱلْأَخِرَةِ عَذَابٌ عَظِيمٌ ٣٣ إِلَّا ٱلَّذِينَ تَابُواْ مِن قَبْلِ أَن تَقْدِرُواْ
عَلَيْهِمْ فَٱعْلَمُوٓاْ أَنَّ ٱللَّهَ غَفُورٌ رَّحِيمٌ ٣٤

33-34 The reprisal against those who wage war on Allah and His Messenger, and go about the earth corrupting it, is that they should be killed or crucified, or have their alternate hands and feet cut off, or be banished from the land. That will be their

degradation in this world and in the Next World they will have a terrible punishment, except for those who repent before you gain power over them. Know that Allah is Ever-Forgiving, Most Merciful.

People disagree about the reason for this *āyah* being revealed. What the majority say is that it was revealed about the 'Uraynīs. The Imāms relate this, as Abū Dāwūd reported from Anas ibn Mālik: 'Some people from 'Ukl – or 'Urayna – came to the Messenger of Allah ﷺ and fell ill on account of the climate of Madīnah. The Messenger of Allah ﷺ instructed them to go to the milk-camels and to drink their urine and milk [for their treatment] and so they went. When they recovered, they killed the herdsman of the Prophet ﷺ and stole the camels. The news arrived early in the day and the Prophet ﷺ sent people on their trail. They were brought to him in the middle of the day. He ordered that their hands and feet be cut off and nails were driven into their eyes and they were cast out into al-Ḥarrah. They asked for water but none was given to them.'

Abū Qilābah said, 'They were people who stole, murdered, disbelieved after belief, and fought Allah and His Messenger.' One variant has: 'He commanded that nails be heated up and applied to their eyes and their hands and feet cut off.' One variant has: 'The Messenger of Allah ﷺ sent a party to look for them and they were brought.' He said that Allah revealed about that: *'The reprisal against those who wage war on Allah and His Messenger, and go about the earth corrupting it.'* In one variant Anas said: 'I saw one of them biting the earth with his mouth out of thirst until they died.'

We find in al-Bukhārī that Jarīr ibn 'Abdullāh said, 'The Messenger of Allah ﷺ sent me out with a group of Muslims and we caught them when they were close to their land. We brought them to the Messenger of Allah ﷺ.' Jarīr said, 'They were saying, "Water!" and the Messenger of Allah ﷺ said, "Fire." Historians and biographers related that they cut off the hands and feet of the herdsman and stuck thorns in his eyes until he died. He was brought dead into Madīnah. His name was Yasār and he was a Nubian. The apostates did this in 6 AH. One of the variants from Anas states: 'The Messenger of Allah ﷺ burned them after they were killed.'

It is related from Ibn 'Abbās and aḍ-Ḍaḥḥāk that it was revealed because of some of the People of the Book who had a treaty with the Messenger of Allah ﷺ and then broke the treaty, acted as highwaymen and wrought corruption in the land.' We find in the *Muṣannaf* of Abū Dāwūd that Ibn 'Abbās said that this *āyah* was revealed about the idolaters and those of them who are taken before one has power over them: that does not prevent the *ḥadd* punishment they are due from being carried out on them. Among those who said that it was revealed about the idolaters were 'Ikrimah and al-Ḥasan. This is weak and is refuted by 8:38 and the words of the Prophet ﷺ: 'Islam wipes out what was before it.' Muslim transmitted it. The sound position is the first, based on the texts of well established *ḥadīth*s on the matter.

Mālik, ash-Shāfi'ī, Abu Thawr and the People of Opinion say that it was revealed about Muslims who go out to commit highway robbery and work corruption in the land. Ibn al-Mundhir said, 'The position of Mālik is sound, and Abū Thawr used as evidence for this position the fact that the *āyah* was revealed about other than the people of *shirk* as shown by the words: *"except for those who repent before you gain power over them."* They agree that when the people of *shirk* are captured by us and become Muslim, their blood is inviolable. That indicates that the *āyah* was revealed about people of Islam.'

Aṭ-Ṭabarī reported from people of knowledge that this *āyah* abrogated what the Prophet ﷺ did to the 'Uraynīs and the punishment was restricted to these *ḥudūd*. Muḥammad ibn Sīrīn reported that this occurred before the *ḥudūd* were revealed. Al-Layth ibn Sa'd also said that what was done to the 'Uraynīs was abrogated since it is not permitted to mutilate an apostate.

Abū az-Zinād said, 'When the Messenger of Allah ﷺ amputated and gouged out the eyes of those who stole the milk-camels, Allah Almighty rebuked him for that and revealed: *"The reprisal against those who wage war against Allah and His Messenger…"*' Abū Dāwūd transmitted it. Abū az-Zinād stated, 'When he was warned about mutilation and forbidden it, he did not repeat it.' One group do, however, say that this does not abrogate that action because that was against apostates. It is further confirmed in *Ṣaḥīḥ Muslim*, book of Abū Dāwūd and elsewhere that the Prophet ﷺ gouged the eyes of those people because they had done that to the herdsman and so it falls under the category of retaliation whereas this *āyah* concerns the believer who commits brigandage.

This is excellent, and it is what Mālik and ash-Shāfi'ī believed. That is why Allah says: *'except for those who repent before you gain power over them'*. It is known that the rulings regarding unbelievers do not change by cancelling the punishment when they repent either before or after they are taken. An apostate should be killed on the basis of apostasy rather than brigandage. He is not exiled nor are his hands or feet amputated nor is he let go. He is killed if he does not reaffirm Islam. He is not crucified. This indicates that the *āyah* is not about apostates. Allah says about the unbelievers: *'Say to those who disbelieve that if they stop, they will be forgiven what is past'* (8:38). and He says about brigands: '*...except for those who repent.'* This is clear. There can be no criticism of the punishment inflicted on the 'Uraynīs because Allah says: *'So if anyone oversteps the limits against you, overstep against him the same as he did to you.'* (2:194) They mutilated and so they were mutilated in return. It is possible that if the censure is sound, it is about what is more than killing, namely branding them with hot nails and leaving them to die of thirst. Allah knows best.

Aṭ-Ṭabarī related from as-Suddī that the Prophet ﷺ did not gouge out the eyes of the 'Uranīs. He wanted to do that and then the *āyah* was revealed which forbade doing that. This is very weak indeed. Firm reports have come about the gouging, as we saw in al-Bukhārī: 'He commanded that nails be heated up and applied to their eyes.' There is no disagreement among the people of knowledge that this *āyah* deals with the brigands of the people of Islam, even if it was revealed about apostates or Jews.

The usage of 'waging war against Allah and His Messenger' is metaphorical since one cannot wage war against Allah and He is above that as He possesses the qualities of perfection and He must be above equals and opposites. It means: they wage war against the friends of Allah. He uses Himself to designate them to demonstrate the enormity of harming them. This is as He uses Himself to designate the poor and weak when He says: *'Is there anyone who can make Allah a generous loan?'* (2:245) which encourages giving to them. It is like what is in the sound *Sunnah*: 'I asked you to feed Me and you did not feed Me.' Muslim transmitted that *ḥadīth* and it was mentioned in *al-Baqarah* (2:245).

Scholars disagree about who should be called a *muḥārib* (bandit). Mālik said, 'We consider it to refer to anyone who attacks people in a city or the countryside to take their lives and property without there being war, blood vengeance or invasion.' Ibn al-Mundhir said, 'Different things are reported from Mālik concerning this question. Sometimes he states that it can occur in a city and sometimes he denies that.'

One group say that the ruling applies to the city, houses, roads or dwellings of the people of the countryside and villages, and it carries the same *ḥudūd*. This is the position of ash-Shāfi'ī and Abū Thawr.' Ibn al-Mundhir added, 'That is the case. It is called banditry, and the topic is general. No one can remove a group of people from the sum of the *āyah* without proof.' Another group state that it cannot occur in a city, but must occur outside of it. This is the position of Sufyān ath-Thawrī, Isḥāq and an-Nu'mān. An assassin is like a *muḥārib*. He is someone who employs stratagems to kill someone in order to take his property. Even if the weapon is not known but he enters his house or accompanies him on a journey and feeds him poison so that he dies and so he murders him: he is killed by a *ḥadd*, not in retaliation.

There is disagreement about the ruling governing a *muḥārib*. One group say that he is dealt with according to his action. If someone alarms people on the road and robs them, his alternate hands and feet are amputated. If he robs and kills, his alternate hands and feet are amputated and then he is crucified. If he killed and did not rob, he is simply killed. If he did not rob or kill, he is exiled. Ibn 'Abbās said that. It is related from Abū Miljaz, an-Nakha'ī, 'Aṭā' al-Khurasānī and others. Abū Yūsuf said, 'If he robbed and killed, he is crucified and killed on a post.' Al-Layth said, 'Crucifixion is the punishment for banditry.' Abū Ḥanīfah said, 'If he killed, then he is killed. If he did not kill, his alternate hand and foot are amputated. If he robbed and killed, then the ruler can choose. If he wishes, he cuts off his hand and foot, or if he wishes, his hand and foot are not amputated and he is killed.' Abū Yūsuf says that execution satisfies all. Al-Awzā'ī says the same. Ash-Shāfi'ī said, 'If he steals property, his right hand is cut off. Then his left foot is cut off and he is left because this crime goes beyond theft by banditry. If he kills, he is killed. When he steals and kills, he is killed and crucified.' It is related from him that he is crucified for three days. He said, 'When he engages in it frequently and causes fear, mere imprisonment would abet the enemy.' Aḥmad says the same as ash-Shāfi'ī: 'If he kills, he is killed. If he steals property, his hand and foot are cut off.' Some people say that he should not be crucified before he is killed so that he is stopped from the prayer and eating and drinking. It is related that ash-Shāfi'ī said, 'I dislike someone being killed by crucifixion since the Messenger of Allah ﷺ forbade mutilation.'

Abu Thawr said, 'According to the literal meaning of the *āyah*, the ruler can choose.' That is what Mālik said and it is related from Ibn 'Abbās. It is also the position of Sa'īd ibn al-Musayyab, 'Umar ibn 'Abd al-'Azīz, Mujāhid, aḍ-Ḍaḥḥāk and an-Nakha'ī. They all said that the ruler can choose which ruling to impose on *muḥāribūn*. He can give whichever judgment of those which Allah has imposed he wishes: killing, crucifixion, amputation or exile according to the literal meaning of the *āyah*. Ibn 'Abbās said that when *'aw'* (or) is used in the Qur'ān, it is accompanied by choice. This position is taking cognizance of the literal meaning of the *āyah*. The people who take the first view say that *'aw'* is just used for order. Even if they disagree, you will find that their positions agree on the *ḥadd* punishment and say that bandits are killed and crucified. Some say that they are crucified and killed and some that their hand and foot are amputated and they are exiled. That is not how the *āyah* is and there would then be no sense to the words 'or' linguistically An-Naḥḥās said that.

The first group argue by aṭ-Ṭabarī's mention that Anas ibn Mālik said, 'The Messenger of Allah ﷺ asked Jibrīl about the ruling governing banditry and he said, "If someone causes fear on the roads and steals property, cut off his hand for taking and his foot to cause alarm. If he kills, then kill him. If he does all of this, crucify him."' Ibn 'Aṭiyyah said, 'Exile is only for someone who causes alarm. The one who causes alarm has the status of a killer. Furthermore, Mālik thinks that it is recommended to take the least of the punishments.'

or be banished from the land.

There is disagreement about the meaning of this. As-Suddī said that he is pursued by horses and men until he is captured and the *ḥadd* of Allah carried out on him or he leaves the Abode of Islam in flight. Ibn 'Abbās, Anas ibn Mālik, Mālik ibn Anas, al-Ḥasan, as-Suddī, aḍ-Daḥḥāk, Qatādah, Sa'īd ibn Jubayr, ar-Rabī' ibn Anas and az-Zuhrī related that. Ar-Rummānī related it in his book. It is related from ash-Shāfi'ī that they are driven from one town to another and are sought out in order for the *ḥadd* punishment to be imposed on them. Al-Layth ibn Sa'd and az-Zuhrī also said that.

Mālik said, 'A bandit is banished from the land in which he committed his crime to a different town and imprisoned like a person guilty of illicit sex.' The Kufans said that it means imprisonment and he is exiled from enjoying the expanse of the world to suffering its constriction and so it resembles imprisonment. He is exiled in the land from the place of his abode. They used as an argument the words of one of the people in prison:

We have left this world although we are its people.
We are neither dead or alive in it.
When the jailer comes to us one day for a need,
we are amazed and say, 'This one has come from the world!'

Makḥūl related that 'Umar ibn al-Khaṭṭāb was the first to imprison people. He said, 'I will imprison him until I know that he repents and I will not exile him to another land so that he can harm people there.' It is clear that the 'land' mentioned in the *āyah* is the land where it occurred. In the past people avoided a land in which people committed wrong actions. If the ruler thinks that this brigand who alarms the region will revert to banditry or corruption, he should imprison him in the land to which he is banished. If he did not cause alarm and he thinks that he will not revert to crime, he is let go. Ibn 'Aṭiyyah stated, 'This is the clear position of Mālik: that the person is banished and imprisoned until he is banished. This is because he usually causes alarm.' Aṭ-Ṭabarī preferred that. It is clear because expelling him from the land in which the crime occurred concurs with the text of the *āyah*. He is imprisoned after that according to the amount of alarm he causes. If he repents and his circumstances are known, he is let go.

The root of *nafy* (banishment) is destruction or to make non-existent, and it also is the opposite of affirmation. So *nafy* is destruction and eradication. *Nufāyah* is something which is of no use. *Nafiyy* is froth which rises from water. [POEM]

Ibn Khuwayzmindād says that there is no minimum amount in respect of the property taken by a bandit as there is in the case of the theft, where the minimum is a quarter of a dinar. Ibn al-'Arabī said that ash-Shāfi'ī and the people of opinion say that amputation is only inflicted on a highway robber when he takes the amount for which a thief has his hand cut off. Mālik said, 'The judgment on him is the same as the judgment on a bandit, and that is sound. The Prophet ﷺ specified the minimum in the case of theft, but did not in the case of banditry. He only mentioned the punishment of a bandit, and so it is applied however much he steals, even if it is only a single grain.' This analogy is one principle based on another, and it is disputed. The analogy of the superior applies to the less forceful and the less forceful to the lesser. That is the opposite of analogy. How can it be sound to make a bandit analogous to a thief who is seeking to steal property and if he is discovered, flees. So if a thief enters with weapons to search for property and is stopped or a shout is made about him and he fights, he becomes a bandit and the judgment of a bandit is carried out on him.

Qāḍī Ibn al-'Arabī said, 'During the time I was rendering judgment on people, someone brought a thief who had entered a house with a knife which he held against the heart of the owner, who was asleep, while his fellows were taking the man's goods. I judged that he was a bandit. You should understand this from the fundamental principle of the *dīn*. Rise to the pinnacle of knowledge from the nadir of ignorance.' 'Pinnacle' (*yafa'*) is the word for the summit of the mountain. A boy is described as *yafa'ah* when he reaches maturity. 'Nadir' (*ḥaḍīḍ*) is a hole in the lowest part of a valley. Linguists said that.

There is no disagreement that if a robber kills, he must be killed. If he is not the equal of the victim, ash-Shāfi'ī has two positions. One is that one considers equivalence as in retaliation, and this is weak because his execution is not for the act of killing itself, but for the general corruption of causing fear and stealing property. Allah says: *'The reprisal against those who wage war on Allah and His Messenger and go about the earth corrupting it, is that they should be killed.'* So Allah commanded that the *ḥadd* be imposed on a bandit if he commits robbery and strives to bring about corruption in the land. Class or status is not considered. The second position is that when brigands go out and fight with a caravan, some of the bandits kill and some do not. Ash-Shāfi'ī said, 'Only those who killed should be killed.' This is weak. Those present in the battle share in the booty, even if all of them did not kill. We agree that an [enemy] scout is killed, so it is even more likely to apply to a bandit.

When bandits cause fear on the road and cut it off, the ruler can fight them without having to invite them to desist, and the Muslims are obliged to assist in fighting them and stopping them from harming the Muslims. If they are defeated, those of them who flee are not pursued unless they have killed and robbed. If that has happened, then they are pursued and the punishment for their crimes carried out on them. If they are found in possession of stolen goods, the goods are returned to their owners or their heirs. If the owner cannot be found, then it is put in the treasury. They are liable for any property they have destroyed. There is no blood money for those of them who are killed when they are captured before they repent.

If brigands repent and come to the ruler, he has no way against them in respect of the *ḥadd*, but they are still liable for the rights due to other human beings and so are subject to retaliation for any killing and wounding they have done and they owe any property they have taken. Their victims are permitted to pardon them, as is the case with other crimes committed by people other than brigands. This is the position of Mālik, ash-Shāfi'ī, Abū Thawr and the People of Opinion. Property in their possession is taken from them and they are liable for the cost of anything they destroyed because that was impermissible usurpation. They are not permitted to be its owners and it is handed back to its owners or kept by the leader until its owner can be ascertained. Some of the Companions and Followers only took the property that was in their possession and did not issue a demand for what was destroyed. Aṭ-Ṭabarī mentioned that from Mālik via al-Walīd ibn Muslim. It appears to be what 'Alī ibn Abī Ṭālib did to Ḥārithah ibn Badr al-Ghudānī. He was a brigand who repented before he was caught.

Ibn Khuzayzimandād said that transmissions from Mālik vary about a brigand when the *ḥadd* punishment has been carried out and no property is found with him. Is it a debt to be pursued or is it cancelled as it is cancelled for a thief? Muslims and *dhimmīs* are the same in this respect. Scholars agree that the ruler is the *walī* of brigands, and if a brigand kills the brother or father of a person while a brigand, they cannot seek retaliation or blood money, and cannot pardon. It is the ruler who is in charge of that as that is like one of the *ḥudūd*. This is a summary of the rulings regarding brigands which we have mentioned, avoiding excessive detail.

Something strange is said about this *āyah* as when Mujāhid says that what is meant in it by the word *muḥārib* is fornication and theft, but that is not sound. Allah makes it clear in His Book and on the tongue of His Messenger that a thief has his hand cut off and a fornicator is flogged and exiled if he has not been married and is stoned if he has been married and is a *muḥṣan*. The rulings that apply to a brigand in this *āyah* are different, unless the reason for his causing alarm on the roads by a display of weapons is to gain power over women. That is the most atrocious and foul form of brigandage, worse than stealing property. It is included under Allah's words: '*...go about the earth corrupting it*'.

Our scholars say that robbers (*liṣṣ*) are threatened by Allah. If they refrain, they are left. If they refuse to refrain, they are killed. If you kill a robber, his blood is of no account. An-Nasā'ī related from Abū Hurayrah that a man came to the Messenger of Allah ﷺ and asked, 'Messenger of Allah, what do you think if I am attacked by someone for my property?' He said, 'Adjure him by Allah.' He asked, 'And if he comes back at me?' He said, 'Adjure him by Allah.' He asked, 'And if he comes back at me?' He said, 'Adjure him by Allah.' He asked again, 'And if he comes back at me?' He said, 'Adjure him by Allah.' He said, 'And if he comes back at me?' He answered. 'Then fight him. If you are killed, you will be in the Garden. If you kill him, he will be in the Fire.' Al-Bukhārī and Muslim transmitted it from Abū Hurayrah without mentioning the adjuring: 'A man came to the Messenger of Allah ﷺ and asked, "Messenger of Allah, what do you think if someone comes wanting to take my property?" He answered, "Do not give him your property." He asked, "What if he fights me?" "Fight him," he answered. He said, "What about if he kills me?" He replied, "You will be a martyr." He asked, "And if I kill him?" "He will be in the Fire," was his answer.'

Ibn al-Mundhir said, 'We related from a group of scholars who thought that one should fight thieves and defend one's life and property.' This is the position of Ibn 'Umar, al-Ḥasan al-Baṣrī, Ibrāhīm an-Nakha'ī, Qatādah, Mālik, ash-Shāfi'ī, Aḥmad, Isḥāq and an-Nu'mān. Indeed it is the view of most scholars: a man may defend himself, his family and his property when someone wants to do wrong to them, based on the reports which have come from the Prophet ﷺ, without specifying one time rather than another, one situation rather than another, except when it is the ruler. The group of the people of *ḥadīth* are like those who agree that someone who can only defend himself by going out against the ruler to fight him should not go out against him or fight him based on the *ḥadīths* from the Messenger of Allah ﷺ which contain the command to be steadfast in the face of their injustice and wrongdoing and not fight them and rebel against them as long as they establish the prayer.

There is disagreement when someone is asked for something insignificant like a garment and food and whether that should be given to them or they should be fought against. This disagreement is based on a principle, which is whether the command to fight them is because it is changing something wrong or because it is averting harm. This is also the basis of the disagreement about warning them before fighting. Allah knows best.

That will be their degradation in this world

That is because of the heinousness of banditry and the gravity of the harm it causes. It contains great harm because it bars people from earning, it being known that the greatest and most common form of earning is trade, whose support and pillar is travelling in the land as evinced by Allah's words: *'Others are travelling in the land seeking Allah's bounty.'* (73:20). If there is fear on the road, people are prevented from travelling and have to stay in their houses and so the door of trade is closed against them and their income stream is cut off. Therefore, Allah has prescribed severe *ḥudūd* punishments for highway robbery. That is degradation in this world to deter their evil deeds and to open the door to trade, which He has allowed for those of His slaves who wish to do it. He has promised such brigands a terrible punishment in the Next World. It is an act of disobedience of a different magnitude to others and an exception to the *ḥadīth* of 'Ubādah about the words of the Prophet ﷺ, 'If someone does any of those things and is punished in this world, that is its expiation for him.' Allah knows best.

It is possible that the degradation is for the one who is punished, and the punishment of the Next World is for the one who is preserved from punishment in this world, in which case this wrong action is like others. A believer will not be eternally in the Fire, as we mentioned, but the severity of his punishment will be according to the seriousness of his wrong action. Then he will be brought out of it either by intercession or being taken out in a handful [as stated in the *ḥadīth*]. This threat is contingent on being implemented by Divine Will as Allah says: *'He forgives whomever He wills for anything other than that'* (4:116). Fear predominates concerning them according to the threat and enormity of the disobedience.

except for those who repent before you gain power over them.

Allah makes an exception in the case of those who repent before there is power to seize them, and the punishment which is His right is cancelled in respect of them as He says: *'Know that Allah is Ever-Forgiving, Most Merciful.'* But where retaliation and the rights of people are concerned, there is no cancelation. If someone repents after being captured, that is of no use and the *ḥadd* punishment is still carried out on him. Ash-Shāfi'ī has a position in which every *ḥadd* punishment is cancelled by repentance, but the sound position in his school is that what is connected to a human being, retaliation or any other right, is not revoked by repentance before capture. It is also said that it means that when an idolater repents and believes before capture the *ḥudūd* are cancelled for him. This is weak because it is agreed that someone who embraces the faith even after he is taken is not killed by consensus.

It is also said that the *ḥadd* punishment is not revoked in the case of brigands after one has power over them, and Allah knows best, because they are suspected of lying in their claim to repent and of it being merely an affectation on their part after the ruler has them in his custody, or it is because, when there is power over them, they are subject to punishment and so their repentance is not accepted. It is like someone subject to punishment in the nations before us, or someone who is on the point of death who repents. When they repent before someone has power over them, then there is no suspicion. That benefits them as will be explained in *Sūrat Yūnus*.

As for drinkers, fornicators and thieves who repent and put things right and that is known about them and are then brought before the ruler, he should not impose the *ḥadd* on them. When they are arraigned and then say, 'We repent!' they are not excused. In this case they are like brigands who are overpowered. Allah knows best.

يَٰٓأَيُّهَا ٱلَّذِينَ ءَامَنُوا۟ ٱتَّقُوا۟ ٱللَّهَ وَٱبْتَغُوٓا۟ إِلَيْهِ ٱلْوَسِيلَةَ وَجَٰهِدُوا۟
فِى سَبِيلِهِۦ لَعَلَّكُمْ تُفْلِحُونَ ﴿٣٥﴾ إِنَّ ٱلَّذِينَ كَفَرُوا۟ لَوْ أَنَّ لَهُم مَّا
فِى ٱلْأَرْضِ جَمِيعًا وَمِثْلَهُۥ مَعَهُۥ لِيَفْتَدُوا۟ بِهِۦ مِنْ عَذَابِ يَوْمِ
ٱلْقِيَٰمَةِ مَا تُقُبِّلَ مِنْهُمْ وَلَهُمْ عَذَابٌ أَلِيمٌ ﴿٣٦﴾

35-36 You who believe! have *taqwā* of Allah and seek the means of drawing near to Him, and do *jihād* in His Way, so that hopefully you will be successful. As for those who disbelieve, if they had

everything on the earth and the same again with it to ransom themselves from the punishment of the Day of Rising, it would not be accepted from them. They will have a painful punishment.

The *wasīlah* is an act of devotion (*qurbah*), according to Abū Wā'il, al-Ḥasan, Mujāhid, Qatādah, 'Aṭā', as-Suddī, Ibn Zayd and 'Abdullāh ibn Kathīr. *Wasīlah* is the form *fa'īlah* from the verb *tawassala*, meaning to draw near. 'Antarah said:

Men have a means (*wasīlah*) to you
to take you as my kohl and dye.

The plural is *wasā'il*. He said:

When the critics are heedless, we revert to our connection,
and mutual friendship and means (*wasā'il*) between us resume.

It also means to ask for something. The *wasīlah* is an act of devotion which is very beneficial. The *wasīlah* is also a rank in the Garden as is found in the *ḥadīth*, 'If someone asks for the *wasīlah* for me, intercession is lawful for him.'

يُرِيدُونَ أَن يَخْرُجُوا۟ مِنَ ٱلنَّارِ وَمَا هُم بِخَٰرِجِينَ مِنْهَا ۖ وَلَهُمْ عَذَابٌ مُّقِيمٌ ۝٣٧

37 They will want to get out of the Fire but they will not be able to. They will have an everlasting punishment.

Yazīd al-Faqīr said, 'Someone said to Jābir ibn 'Abdullāh, "You Companions of Muḥammad say that some people will leave the Fire whereas Allah says: '… *but they will not be able to.*'" Jābir said, "You make the general particular and the particular general. That is about the unbelievers." I recited the entire verse and it is clear that it is about the unbelievers.' '*Muqīm*' means everlasting, constant and without change. A poet said:

If you have a day of distance from me,
you have a constant, everlasting (*maqīm*) punishment.

وَٱلسَّارِقُ وَٱلسَّارِقَةُ فَٱقۡطَعُوٓاْ أَيۡدِيَهُمَا جَزَآءَۢ بِمَا كَسَبَا نَكَٰلٗا
مِّنَ ٱللَّهِۗ وَٱللَّهُ عَزِيزٌ حَكِيمٞ ﴿٣٨﴾ فَمَن تَابَ مِنۢ بَعۡدِ ظُلۡمِهِۦ وَأَصۡلَحَ فَإِنَّ ٱللَّهَ
يَتُوبُ عَلَيۡهِۚ إِنَّ ٱللَّهَ غَفُورٞ رَّحِيمٌ ﴿٣٩﴾

38-39 As for thieves, both male and female, cut off their hands in reprisal for what they have done: an object lesson from Allah. Allah is Almighty, All-Wise. But if anyone repents after his wrongdoing and puts things right, Allah will turn towards him. Allah is Ever-Forgiving, Most Merciful.

As for thieves, both male and female, cut off their hands

After mentioning highway robbery and causing corruption in the land, Allah mentions the ruling of someone who steals without banditry as will be explained. He mentions the male thief first which is the reverse of what He says in respect of fornication. There was theft in the *Jāhiliyyah* and the first to judge amputation as a penalty for it in the Jāhiliyyah was al-Walīd ibn al-Mughīrah. Then Allah commanded amputation in Islam. The first man to have his hand amputated by the Messenger of Allah ﷺ in Islam for theft was al-Khiyār ibn 'Adī, and the first woman was Murrah bint Sufyān of Makhzūm. Abū Bakr cut off the hand of a Yemeni who stole a necklace and 'Umar cut off the hand of Samurah, the brother of 'Abd ar-Raḥmān ibn Samurah. There is no disagreement about that.

The apparent meaning of the *āyah* is that it is general to every theft, but that is not the case since the Prophet ﷺ, said, 'A thief does not have his hand cut off except for a quarter of a dinar or more.' So it is clear that the *āyah* means some thieves rather than others. Only a thief who steals a quarter of a dinar or something worth a quarter of a dinar has his hand cut off. This is the position of 'Umar ibn al-Khaṭṭāb, 'Uthmān ibn 'Affān, and 'Alī. It was taken by 'Umar ibn 'Abd al-'Azīz, al-Layth, ash-Shāfi'ī and Abū Thawr.

Mālik said, 'When a person's theft reaches a quarter of a dinar or more, his hand is cut off. If someone steals two dirhams which are equal to a quarter of a dinar because of the drop in the exchange rate, his hand is not cut off for them.' The hand is not cut off for goods unless their value reaches three dirhams, whatever the exchange rate. In his school, Mālik made gold and silver each their own principle. The equivalence in the case of goods is based on their value in dirhams in the well-known position.

Aḥmad and Isḥāq said that if someone steals gold, it is a quarter of a dinar. If he steals other than gold and silver, its value of is a quarter of a dinar or three dirhams of silver. This is close to the final position of Mālik. The evidence for the first position is the *ḥadīth* of Ibn 'Umar which mentions that a man stole a leather shield. He was brought to the Prophet ﷺ and it was estimated to be worth three dirhams. Ash-Shāfi'ī takes the *ḥadīth* of 'Ā'isha about a quarter of a dinar as the basis in estimating goods, not three dirhams, whether gold is cheap or dear. He ignored the *ḥadīth* of ibn 'Umar since he saw, and Allah knows best, that the Companions disagreed about the shield for which the Messenger of Allah ﷺ amputated the thief's hand. Ibn 'Umar said it was worth three dirhams and Ibn 'Abbās said ten dirhams and Anas said five dirhams.

The *ḥadīth* from 'Ā'ishah is sound and confirmed and there is no disagreement about it although some of them consider it to be *mawqūf*. Those who oblige acting by memory and integrity make it *marfū'*. Abū 'Umar and others said that. On this basis, when the stolen goods reach a quarter of a dinar in value through estimation, a thief's hand is cut off. That is the position of Isḥāq. Base yourself on these two bases. They are what is relied on in the topic. They are the soundest of what is said about it.

Abū Ḥanīfah and his two companions and ath-Thawrī said that a thief's hand is only cut off for ten dirhams in measure or a dinar in gold or weight, and it is not cut off until he has removed the goods from the possession of the owner. Their argument is the *ḥadīth* of Ibn 'Abbās who said, 'The value of the shield for which the Prophet ﷺ cut off the hand was estimated to be ten dirhams.' 'Amr ibn Shu'ayb related from his father from his grandfather: 'The price of the shield was ten dirhams.' Ad-Dāraquṭnī and others transmitted it.

There is a fourth view regarding the matter which was related by ad-Dāraquṭnī in which 'Umar said, 'Five are only cut off for five.' Sulaymān ibn Yasār, Ibn Abī Laylā and Ibn Shubrumah said that. Anas ibn Mālik said that Abū Bakr cut off a hand for a shield worth five dirhams. A fifth view is that the hand is cut off for four dirhams and more. It is related from Abū Hurayrah and Abū Sa'īd al-Khudrī. A sixth view is that the hand is cut off for a dirham or more, and 'Uthmān al-Battī said that. Aṭ-Ṭabarī mentioned that 'Abdullāh ibn az-Zubayr cut off the hand for a dirham. A seventh view is that the hand is cut off for anything that has any value based on the literal reading of the *āyah*. This is the position of the Khārijites. It is related from al-Ḥasan al-Baṣrī and is one of three transmissions from him. The second is what 'Umar related and the third was related by Qatādah who said, 'We debated about how much a hand was cut off for in the time of Ziyād. It happened that we thought that it was for two dirhams.' These are similar views and what is sound of them is what we already mentioned to you.

If it is said that al-Bukhārī, Muslim and others related from Abū Hurayrah that the Messenger of Allah ﷺ said, 'Allah curses the one who steals an egg (or helmet) and has his hand cut off, or steals a rope for which his hand is cut off.' This agrees with the literal meaning of the *āyah* about amputation being for both a little or a lot. The answer is that this is warning against a lot or a little, as encouraging a little is like a lot in the words of the Prophet ﷺ, 'If someone builds a mosque, even the size of the nest of a sand-grouse, Allah will build a house for him in the Garden.' It is said that this is metaphorical in another way. That is if someone desires to steal a little, he will also steal a lot and so his hand is cut off. Better than that is what al-A'mash said and al-Bukhārī mentioned at the end of the *ḥadīth* like a commentary: 'They used to think that the "egg" was an iron helmet and the rope was one that was worth a few dirhams.' I think that this is like a ship's rope and the like. Allah knows best.

Most people agree that amputation is only carried out when someone removes something from a secure place. Al-Ḥasan ibn Abī al-Ḥasan said, 'When garments are collected in a house, then there is amputation.' Al-Ḥasan ibn Abī al-Ḥasan also said in another view a similar position to that of the rest of scholars. So it becomes sound agreement. Allah knows best. A secure place is what is normally used to protect people's property and it varies according to the item as will be explained. Ibn al-Mundhir said, 'There is no sound report or position from scholars about this. That is like consensus from the people of knowledge.' It is related that al-Ḥasan and the literalists did not stipulate what a secure place was.

It is reported in the *Muwaṭṭā'* by Mālik from 'Abdullāh ibn 'Abd ar-Raḥmān that the Messenger of Allah ﷺ said, 'The hand is not cut off for fruit hanging on a tree or for sheep kept in the mountains. But when they are taken from the fold or the place where the fruit is dried, the hand should be cut off for whatever reaches the price of a shield.' Abū 'Umar said, 'The meaning of this *ḥadīth* is connected to the *ḥadīth* of 'Abdullāh ibn 'Amr ibn al-'Āṣ and others. This 'Abdullāh is considered reliable by all. Ahmād used to praise him.'

'Abdullāh ibn 'Amr reported that the Prophet ﷺ was asked about fruit hanging on the tree and said, 'Whoever takes some of it out of of need without putting any in his garment owes nothing. Anyone who takes away any of it has his hand cut off. Anyone who steals less than that is liable for its like and is punished.' One version has, '…is flogged as an example' instead of 'punished'. Scholars say that flogging was then abrogated and amputation replaced it. Abū 'Umar says that 'liable for its like' was abrogated. I do not know of any of the *fuqahā'* who state that, except that it is reported from 'Umar about the flour of Ḥāṭib ibn Abī Balta'ah, which Mālik transmitted as did Aḥmad ibn Ḥanbal. People say that there is a fine for it based on Allah's words: *'So if anyone oversteps the limits against you, overstep against him the same as he did to you.'* (2:194)

Abū Dāwūd reported that Ṣafwān ibn Umayyah said, 'I was sleeping in the mosque on a cloak of mine worth thirty dirhams. A man came and stole it from me. The man was taken and brought to the Messenger of Allah ﷺ and he commanded that his hand be cut off. I went to him and asked, "Will you cut it off for thirty dirhams? I would sell it to him and give him the price on credit." He said, "Why didn't you do it before you brought him to me?"'

Property was created ready for all creatures to use. Then the first ruling made about it is private ownership which is legal ownership, but others still covet it and hopes are fixed on it, but a few people refrain from it through noble character and religion while most people are restrained by its protection and secure location. When the owner puts them in a protected place, there is protection and security around it as much as is humanly possible. When that is violated, there is a crime and punishment is obliged.

If a group participate in removing the minimum amount from its place of safekeeping, then some of them may enable it to be brought out while others may simply support them. If it is the former, our scholars take two different positions. One is that their hands are cut off and the other that they are not, and that is the position of Abū Ḥanīfah and ash-Shāfi'ī who say that the hand is not cut for theft when it is a group unless the share of each of them reaches the minimum according to the words of the Prophet ﷺ, 'A thief's hand is only cut off for a quarter of a dinar or more.' None of them stole the minimum and so their hands are not cut off. The reason for cutting off the hands in the second view is that they share in the action and the penalty is not cancelled for them, as is the case in murder.

Ibn al-'Arabī said, 'How close the two are! We killed a group for one victim to protect blood so that they will not assist one another in shedding the blood of their enemies, the same is true of property, especially when ash-Shāfi'ī supported us by saying that when a group participate in what legitimates cutting off a man's hand, their hands are cut off and there is no difference between them. Secondly, if the item is something which can only be brought out by mutual help, there is agreement among scholars that all of them are subject to amputation.'

If they both participate, so that one breaks through the wall and the other removes the goods, they are helping one another and their hands are cut off. If one of them does it on his own without the agreement of the other, as when the latter comes and lets the first one out, the hand of one of them is not amputated.

If they both help to make the hole and only one brings it out, only that one has his hand amputated. Ash-Shāfi'ī said that there is no amputation at all because this one broke but did not steal and the other took it from a place where it was no longer secure. Abū Ḥanīfah said, 'If he takes part in the breaking and enters and takes it, his hand is cut off.' He did not stipulate participation in the piercing using a single implement. Succession of actions entails participation.

If one of them enters and brings the goods out of their secure place and the other puts his hand in and takes them, his hand is cut off and the first one is punished. Ashhab says that both their hands are cut off. If someone places it outside the place of protection, he has his hand cut off rather than the one who takes. If he places it in the middle of the hole and the other man takes and both their hands were involved in the piercing, they are both cut off.

Graves and mosques are places of security and a grave-robber has his hand amputated, except in the position of Abū Ḥanīfah who says that a grave has no owner because the dead have no ownership. Some of them deny that it is theft because there is no inhabitant in it: theft is from somewhere protected from eyes and guarded from people. The people of Transoxania say that it is not theft. The majority say that he is a thief because he uses the cover of night and avoids people's eyes and does it at a time in which no one is looking or passing by. It is the same position if he steals at the time when people go out for the 'Īd and the town is empty of all of them.

If you say that cattle are not in a place of protection, that is false because the protection of every thing is according to the circumstances possible for it. If you say that a dead person does not own anything, that is also false because it is not permitted to leave a corpse naked. This need is settled by the grave being a place of protection. Allah Almighty calls attention to this when He says: *'Did We not make the earth a receptacle for the living and the dead?'* (77:25-26) So the living live on it and the dead are buried in it. If they say that it is subject to destruction, all that a living person wears is subject to destruction and becoming tattered by being worn although the first is quicker than the second. Abū Dāwūd related that Abū Dharr said, 'The Messenger of Allah ﷺ summoned me and said, "How will you be when death befalls people and a grave costs the same as a slave?" I said, "Allah and His Messenger know best." He said, "You must be patient."' Ḥammād said, 'This is stated by those who say that a thief's hand is cut off because he has entered the house of the dead.'

As for mosques, whoever steals from one is confined and has his hand cut off. 'Īsā related that from Ibn al-Qāsim. Even if the mosque does not have a door, it is considered to be a place of security. If someone steals the doors, his hand is also cut off. It is also related from Ibn al-Qāsim that if someone steals its mats during the day, his hand is not cut off. If he climbs over the wall at night, his hand is cut off. It is mentioned from Saḥnūn that if the mats are stitched together, his hand is cut off. Otherwise, it is not. Aṣbagh said, 'If someone steals the mats, candles and paving stones of a mosque, his hand is cut off. The same holds if he steals its door or wood from its roof or one of its beams. Ashhab said in *Kitāb Muḥammad*: 'The hand is not cut off for any of the mats, candles or paving stones of the mosque.'

Scholars disagree about whether a thief who has had his hand amputated is liable for repayment or not. Abū Ḥanīfah says that liability and amputation are not combined because of what the *āyah* says. Allah does not mention liability. Ash-Shāfi'ī says that a thief is liable for the value of the stolen item, whether he is wealthy or insolvent, and it is a debt that he owes and must pay when his finances increase. That is the position of Aḥmad and Isḥāq. Our scholars, Mālik and his adherents, say that if he still has the item, he must return it. If it has been destroyed and he is wealthy, he is liable. If he is poor, it is not pursued as a debt and he owes nothing. Mālik related the like of that from az-Zuhrī.

Shaykh Abū Isḥāq said, 'It is said that it is pursued as a debt whether the thief is wealthy or poor.' He said, 'That is the view of more than one of our scholars from the people of Madīnah. The evidence for its validity is that both cases are rights owed to those who are entitled to it and it is not cancelled for any of them, as is the case with blood money and *kaffārah*.' Then he added, 'That is what I say.' Qāḍī Abū al-Ḥasan used as evidence the well-known statement of the Prophet ﷺ: 'When the *ḥadd* punishment has been carried out on someone, he has no liability.' He gives its *isnād* in his book. Some of them said that pursuing him for a debt is a punishment and amputation is a punishment and two punishments are not combined. Qāḍī 'Abd al-Wahhāb relied on that.

What is sound is the position of ash-Shāfi'ī and those who agree with him. Ash-Shāfi'ī said, 'A thief is liable for what he stole if he is wealthy or poor and whether or not his hand has been cut off. The same is true if he is a highwayman.' He said, 'The *ḥadd* punishment from Allah does not cancel out his liability for any property he has destroyed.' As for what our scholars use as an argument, taking the words of the *ḥadīth*, 'if he is poor,' that is also used by the Kufans as an argument. It is the position of aṭ-Ṭabarī. There is no proof in it. An-Nasā'ī and ad-Dāraquṭnī related it from 'Abd ar-Raḥmān ibn 'Awf. Abū 'Umar said, 'This *ḥadīth* is not strong nor is it used as an argument.' Ibn al-'Arabī said, 'This *ḥadīth* is false.' Aṭ-Ṭabarī said, 'The analogy taken from it is that a person is liable for what he destroys, but we abandon that based on the report on it.' Abū 'Umar said, 'Abandoning analogy in favour of a weak report is not permitted because that which is weak does not demand a ruling.'

They disagree about whether someone who steals stolen property from a thief has his hand cut off. Our scholars say that it is cut off. Ash-Shāfi'ī says that it is not because the person did not steal it from its owner or from a secure place. Our scholars say that the inviolability of the owner still applies and is not cancelled. A thief's hand is like no hand. It is like the case is with a misappropriator: if misappropriated property is stolen from him, the thief's hand is cut off. If it is said that you make its safe place like one that is not safe, we say that denomination 'safe place' still applies and ownership applies and is not invalidated in its case while they tell us that safe-keeping is invalidated.

There is disagreement about what happens when someone steals again after having his hand cut off for stealing. Most say that there is amputation. Abū Ḥanīfah said that there is no amputation. The general nature of the Qur'ān demands amputation and refutes his position. Abū Ḥanīfah also said that a thief can become the owner of the stolen item by purchase or a gift before amputation and then there is no amputation. But Allah says: *'As for thieves, male and female, cut off their hands,'* and so amputation is obliged as a right of Allah and not cancelled for anything.

Most recite *'as-sāriqu'* in the nominative. Sībawayh says that it means, 'What is obliged of you in the case of thieves, male and female. It is said that the nominative in the two nouns are the governor in the nominal sentence whose predicate is 'cut off their hands'. It does not indicate anyone in particular. If it had meant someone in particular, it would have had to be in the accusative. Az-Zajjāj says that this is preferred. It is recited as *'as-sāriqah'* in the accusative in which case it implies: 'cut off the hands of the thief.' Sībawayh preferred that because it is better to have a verb with a command and that the accusative is more common in Arabic. Ibn Mas'ūd recited it in the plural as *'as-sāriqūna wa's-sāriqātu faqṭa'ū aymānuhum'*. This reinforces the reading of the majority. *Sariq* and *sariqah* is the word used for the thing stolen. The verbal noun of *saraqa* is *saraq*. Al-Jawharī said that. The root meaning of this word is taking a thing secretly, hidden from eyes. Ancillary to that is eavesdropping (*istaraqqa-s-sama'*) and a stolen glance (*sāriqatu-n-naẓar*). Ibn 'Arafah said, 'According to the Arabs, a "*sāriq*" is someone who comes clandestinely to a protected place and takes from it what is not his. If he takes it openly, then he is a filcher (*mukhtalis*), a plunderer (*mustalib*), a looter (*muntahib*) and rustler (*muḥtaris*). If he does not have a right to what is in his possession, he is a usurper (*ghāṣib*).'

We find in a report from the Messenger of Allah ﷺ, 'The worst thief is the one who steals his prayer.' They asked, 'How can a person steal his prayer?' He answered, 'He does not complete its bowing or its prostration.' It is transmitted in the *Muwaṭṭā'* and elsewhere. He is called a thief, even though he is not an actual thief, by derivation. Usually stealing glances is not in it.

cut off their hands

This clearly means the physical removal of the hand. Certain conditions are necessary for this amputation to take place in respect of the thief, the object stolen and the place from which it is stolen. The thief must be adult, sane, not the owner of the stolen property and not entrusted with it, because a slave's hand is not cut off for taking his master's property nor is the hand of a master cut for taking his slave's property. A slave's hand is not cut off by the consensus of the Companions and the statement of the caliph, 'Your slave stole your goods.'

Ad-Dāraquṭnī mentioned from Ibn 'Abbās that the Messenger of Allah ﷺ said, 'If a runaway slave or a *dhimmī* steals, his hand is not cut off.' He said that only Fahd ibn Sulaymān has it *marfū'*. What is correct is that it is *mawqūf.* Ibn Mājah mentioned from Abū Hurayrah that the Messenger of Allah ﷺ said, 'If a slave steals, sell him, even for a *nashsh* (half an *ūqiyyah*).' It is transmitted from Abū Bakr ibn Abī Shaybah from Abū Usāmah from Abū 'Awānah from 'Umar ibn Abī Salamah from Abū Hurayah. Ibn Mājah related from Jubārāh ibn al-Mughallis from Ḥajjāj ibn Tamīm from Maymūn ibn Mihrān from Ibn 'Abbās that one of the slaves of the *khums* stole from the *khums* and was brought before the Prophet ﷺ and he did not cut off his hand. He said ﷺ, 'One part of Allah's property stole another part of it.' Jubārāh ibn al-Mughallis is abandoned. Abū Zur'ah ar-Rāzī said that. Nor is the hand of a child or a mad person subject to amputation. It is obliged for a *dhimmī*, a person with a treaty and a *ḥarbī* when he enters with a safe conduct.

As for the stolen item, it must have four qualities. One is that its value corresponds to the minimum amount. The second is that it is something which can be owned and lawfully sold. If it is something that cannot be owned and which it is not lawful to sell, such as wine or pigs, then there is agreement that the hand is not cut off for it except, according to Mālik and Ibn al-Qāsim, in the case of the abduction of a young free person. It is also said that the hand is not cut off, and ash-Shāfi'ī and Abū Ḥanīfah said that is because such a person is not property. Our scholars say that it is the most esteemed kind of property, and the hand of the thief is not cut off for the property itself, but because of people's attachment to it, and the attachment to a free minor is greater than the attachment to a slave.

If it is something that can be owned but not sold, like dogs that one is permitted to have and the meat of sacrifices, Ibn al-Qāsim and Ashhab disagree about it. Ibn al-Qāsim said that the hand of someone who steals a dog is not cut off while Ashhab says that that only applies to dogs which one is forbidden to have. As for permitted dogs, the thief's hand is cut off for them. He also said, 'If someone steals the meat or skin of a sacrificial animal, his hand is cut off if it is worth more than three dirhams.' Ibn Ḥabīb said that Aṣbagh said, 'If someone steals a sacrificial animal before it is slaughtered, his hand is cut off. If he steals it after the slaughter, his hand is not cut off.'

If it is something that can be owned and sold and then from it he makes something which it is not permitted to use, like a mandolin, flute, lute or similar instruments of entertainment, one investigates. If, after its form has been corrupted and intended use lost, there remains the value of a quarter of a dinar or more, his hand is cut off. That is also the ruling about gold and silver vessels which it is not permitted to use. It is commanded that they be broken up and the amount of gold or silver in them estimated rather than the work involved in their manufacture. The same is true of gold or silver crucifixes and impure oil, whose value reaches the minimum in spite of its impurity, his hand is cut off.

The third quality is that it is not in the possession of the thief at the time, as is the case if someone steals what is pledged with him or what he has hired. There must be no doubt about its ownership. There is a disagreement among our scholars and others about taking doubtfulness of ownership into consideration, as in the case of someone who steals from the booty or the treasury because he has a share in it. It is related that a man who had stolen a helmet from the *khums* was brought to 'Alī and he did not think that his hand should be cut off. He said, 'He has a share in it.' This is the basis of the position of the majority about the treasury as well. It is also said that the hand of such a person should be cut off based on the generality of the *āyah* and because it is part of what can be actually stolen, like a young slave and adult non-Arab, because the hand is not cut off for what cannot be actually stolen, like a slave who is fluent in the Arabic language.

As for what is considered about the place from which something is stolen, it has one quality: that it is a secure place for the type of thing that has been stolen. In short, the position about it is that everything has a known place and that place is considered to be secure, and everything has a protector and its protector is its secure place. So houses, dwellings and shops are a secure place for what is in them whether their people are present or absent. Similarly, the treasury is a secure place for all people and a thief is not entitled to any of it, even if, before the theft, he was someone to whom the ruler was permitted to give. The right of every Muslim becomes specific by the giving. Do you not see that the ruler is permitted to devote all of the money to one particular focus of best interest and not divide it out among people, or to spend it all in one town rather than another, and to deny certain people rather than others? The implication is that this thief is someone who has no right to it. The same is true of booty: specific ownership comes about through division. It is like what we mentioned about what is in the treasury. It can also become specific by being obtained on the field of battle. So one must consider the amount stolen and if it is more than the minimum, his hand is cut off. Otherwise it is not.

The backs of animals are a secure place for what they carry and courtyards of shops are secure places for what is placed in them for sale, even if there is no store there, and whether its people are there are or not, and whether it is in the day or the night. That applies to the site for sheep in a market, whether they are tied up or not tied up. Animals in their pens are in a place of security, whether the owner is with them or not. An animal at the door of the mosque or in the market, however, is not secure unless someone is looking after it.

A ship is a place of security for what is in it, whether it is moored or not. In respect of the ship itself, it is treated like an animal. If it is drifting, it is not protected. If its owner has tied it up and it is at anchor, tying it up renders it secure. Similarly if there is a watchman with it wherever it is, it is secure, unless they stop their boat in their journey and tie it up. Then it is secure whether or not the watchman is with it.

There is no disagreement that in the case of those who live in one house, like a hotel where each person has his own separate room, if one of them steals from another occupant, his hand is cut off when he takes and goes into the hall, even if he does not take it into his room or take it outside of the house. If someone steals something from the hallway, his hand is not cut off, even if he takes it into his room or out of the building because the hallway is a place where all are permitted to buy and sell, unless it is an animal in its stall or something similar.

Neither parent's hand is cut off for stealing from their child because the Prophet ﷺ said, 'You and your property belong to your father.' A child's hand is cut off for stealing their property because there is no ambiguity about ownership. It is also said that their hand is not cut off, and that is the position of Ibn Wahb and Ashhab because children often have the use of their father's property. Similarly, a slave does not have his hand cut off for stealing his master's property.

They disagree about grandfathers. Mālik and Ibn al-Qāsim said that his hand is not cut off while Ashhab says that it is. Mālik's view is sounder because he is a father. Mālik said, 'I prefer the hands of grandparents not to be cut off, even if their maintenance is not obliged.' Ibn al-Qāsim and Ashhab said that the hands of other relatives are cut off. Abū Ḥanīfah said that the hands of relatives who are *maḥram* are not cut off: such as paternal and maternal aunts, sisters and others. That is the position of ath-Thawrī. Mālik, ash-Shāfi'ī, Aḥmad and Isḥāq said, 'The hands of any of those who steal are cut off.' Abū Thawr said, 'The hand of anyone who steals is cut off unless there is a consensus about it, and then that consensus is accepted.' Allah knows best.

They disagree about stealing a copy of the Qur'ān. Ash-Shāfi'ī, Abū Yūsuf and Abū Thawr said that the hand is cut off if its value reaches the amount for which the hand is amputated. Ibn al-Qāsim also said that. An-Nu'mān said that the hand of someone who steals a copy of the Qur'ān is not cut off. Ibn al-Mundhir said that his hand is cut off.

They disagree about pickpockets who snatch something from a person's sleeve. One group said that if someone snatches something from inside or outside a sleeve, his hand is cut off. That is the position of Mālik, al-Awzā'ī, Abū Thawr and Ya'qūb. Abū Ḥanīfah, Muḥammad ibn al-Ḥasan and Isḥāq said that if some dirhams are placed in the outside of a sleeve and someone snatches them, thereby stealing them, his hand is not cut off. If they are placed inside the sleeve and someone puts his hand in and steals them, then his hand is cut off. Al-Ḥasan also said that his hand is cut off. Ibn al-Mundhir said that his hand is cut off for any manner in which he snatches them.

They disagree about cutting off the hand while travelling and imposing the *ḥadd* punishment while in the Abode of War. Mālik and al-Layth ibn Sa'd said that the *ḥudūd* punishments are carried out in the land of war and there is no difference between the land of war and land of Islam. Al-Awzā'ī said, 'The *ḥudūd* are carried out on an expedition by the one in charge of the army, even if he is not a governor of a city, within the army with the exception of one which involves amputation.' Abū Ḥanīfah said, 'When an army is on an expedition in the land of war and the army has a commander, he only carries out the *ḥudūd* within the army if he is the ruler of Egypt, Syria, Iraq or the like. Such a person can implement the *ḥudūd* within the army.' Al-Awzā'ī and those who take his view use as evidence the *ḥadīth* of Junādah ibn Abī Umayyah who said, 'We were at sea with Busr ibn Arṭāh and a thief called Miṣdar was brought to him. He had stolen a Bactrian camel. He said, "I heard the Messenger of Allah ﷺ say, 'Hands are not cut off on expeditions.' If it had not been for that, I would have cut his hand off."'

This Busr was said to have been born in the time of the Prophet ﷺ and there are reports of him inflicting harm on 'Alī and his people. He killed two children of 'Abdullāh ibn al-'Abbās. Their mother lost her wits and wandered about in her madness. 'Alī prayed against him, asking Allah to prolong his life and remove his wits and that was what happened. Yaḥyā ibn Ma'īn said, 'Busr ibn Arṭāh was an evil man.' Those who said that there is amputation deduced that from the generality of the *āyah*. That is sound, Allah willing. The most appropriate argument of those who forbade amputation and the *ḥadd* punishments in the land of the enemy is the fear that that will be connected to *shirk*. Allah knows best.

Where is the hand or foot amputated? The general position is that it is cut at wrist or ankle. Some of them said that it is cut at the elbow. The limb is cauterised. It is said that it is cut at the shoulder because *'yad'* includes that. 'Alī said that the front part of the foot is cut and the heel is left. That is the position of Aḥmad and Abū Thawr. Ibn al-Mundhir said, 'We related that the Prophet ﷺ commanded that a man's hand be cut off and said, "Cauterise it."' The *isnād* is questionable. A group of the related that, including ash-Shāfi'ī, Abū Thawr and others. This is better and quicker to heal and less likely to cause death. There is no disagreement that the right hand is what is amputated first. Then there is disagreement about what happens if there is a second theft. Mālik, the people of Madīnah, ash-Shāfi'ī, Abū Thawr and others said that the left foot is then amputated, and the left hand for the third and the right foot for the fourth crime. If there is another case after that, then he is disciplined and imprisoned.

Among our scholars, Abū Muṣ'ab said that he is killed after the fourth theft. He cited as evidence the *ḥadīth* of an-Nasā'ī from Ḥāṭib that a thief was brought to the Messenger of Allah ﷺ and he said, 'Kill him.' They said, 'Messenger of Allah, he has stolen.' 'Kill him,' he repeated. They repeated, 'Messenger of Allah, he has stolen.' He said, 'Cut off his hand.' He said, 'Then he stole and his foot was cut off, and then he stole again in the reign of Abū Bakr until all of his appendages had been cut off. Then he stole a fifth time. Abū Bakr said, 'The Messenger of Allah ﷺ knew that this would come. Kill him.' He was given to some young men of Quraysh to be killed. They included 'Abdullāh ibn az-Zubayr who wanted to be in command. He said, 'Put me in command over you.' They did so and they beat him to death. There is also the *ḥadīth* of Jābir that the Prophet ﷺ commanded that a thief be killed on the fifth occasion. Jābir said, 'We took him and killed him. Then we dragged him and threw him into a well and threw stones over him.' Abū Dāwūd related it and an-Nasā'ī transmitted it and said that it is a *munkar ḥadīth* and one of its narrators is not strong.

I do not know of any sound *ḥadīth* about this matter. Ibn al-Mundhir said, 'It is confirmed that Abū Bakr and 'Umar cut off the hand after the hand and the foot after the foot.' It is said that the second time the left foot is cut off and after that nothing is amputated. If he then does it again, he is disciplined and imprisoned. That is related from 'Alī ibn Abī Ṭālib, and it was the position of az-Zuhrī, Ḥammād ibn Abī Sulaymān and Aḥmad ibn Ḥanbal. Az-Zuhrī said, 'We have not heard in the *Sunnah* that anything more than a hand and foot are cut off.' 'Aṭā' said, 'His right hand is cut off and then nothing more is amputated.' Ibn al-'Arabī mentioned it and said, 'As for the view of 'Aṭā', the Companions before him said something different.'

There is disagreement about what happens when a ruler cuts off the left hand instead of the right hand. Qatādah says that the *ḥadd* has been carried out on him and nothing more is done to him. Mālik said that is the case if the amputator errs and cuts off the left hand. The People of Opinion recommended that. Abū Thawr said that the cutter owes blood money because he erred and then he cuts off the right hand unless it is forbidden by consensus.

Ibn al-Mundhir said that the left hand of the thief is cut off in one of two ways. One is that the amputator did it deliberately and so he is subject to retaliation. The other is that it was an accident and the *'āqilah* of the amputator owe blood money and he must cut off the right hand. It is not permitted to change what Allah has obliged on account of the transgression of a transgressor or the error of someone who errs. Ath-Thawrī said about the one who owes retaliation for the right hand that he puts forward his left hand which is cut off. He also said that it is the right hand which is cut off. Ibn al-Mundhir said that this is sound. One group said that his right hand is cut off if it was innocent. That is because he destroyed his left hand, and the amputator owes nothing according to the People of Opinion. It is analogous to the position of ash-Shāfi'ī. His right hand is cut off if it was innocent. Qatādah and ash-Sha'bī said, 'There is nothing against the amputator and it is according to what he cut off.'

The hand of the thief is hung from his neck. 'Abdullāh ibn Muḥayrīz said, 'I asked Faḍālah about hanging a thief's hand from his neck and whether it came from the *Sunnah*. He said, "A thief was brought to the Messenger of Allah ﷺ and his hand was cut off. Then he commanded that it be hung from his neck."' At-Tirmidhī transmitted it and said that it is a *ḥasan gharīb ḥadīth* as do Abū Dāwūd and an-Nasā'ī.

If someone has the *ḥadd* for theft obliged on him and then kills a man, Mālik said that he is executed and the amputation is included in that. Ash-Shāfi'ī says that he has his hand cut off and is killed because there are two rights which must be satisfied and each of them must be carried out. This is sound, Allah willing and it is preferred by Ibn al-'Arabī.

The word 'hands' here is in the plural but uses the dual pronoun. Linguists have discussed this. Ibn al-'Arabī said, 'The *fuqahā'* corroborated what the linguists said on the basis of their good opinion of them.' Al-Khalīl ibn Aḥmad and al-Farrā' say, 'Everything in the constitution of a human being which is single and is ascribed to two has the dual pronoun used. One says 'their heads' and 'their bellies (pl)' using the dual of 'theirs'" as in 'your hearts (pl)' in 66:4. That is why Allah says 'their' in the dual and 'hands' in the plural and not 'hands' in the dual. What is meant is: 'Cut off the right hand of this one and the right hand of that one.' It is also possible to have 'hands' in the dual, which is the basis. [POEM WITH BOTH]

Sībawayh said, 'When it is singular, it can be in the plural when you mean the dual. It is related from the Arabs, "*waḍa'ā riḥālahumā*" "they (dual) deposited their baggage" with baggage in the plural) when it means "the bags of both of them."' Ibn al-'Arabi said, 'This is based on the right hand alone being what is amputated. That is not the case. Hands and feet are amputated. So "*their hands*" in fact refers to four. It is the plural in the dual, and so it is part of eloquence. If Allah had said, "Cut off their hands" all in the plural, it would have been to the point because "male and female thieves" does not mean two particular individuals. They are generic names which are general and undefined.'

in reprisal for what they have done.

'Reprisal' is either a direct object or a verbal noun. *Nakāl* is an exemplary punishment for that action. The verb is *nakala*. It is used when you do to someone that which must be a deterrent to that action. Allah is Almighty and never overcome, and All-Wise in whatever He does.

But if anyone repents after his wrongdoing and puts things right

The words '*after his wrongdoing*' mean after his stealing. It means that if someone then repents, Allah will overlook it, but amputation is not revoked by repentance. 'Aṭā' and a group say that it is revoked if the thief repents before he is arrested. Some of the Shāfi'īs say that and attribute it to ash-Shāfi'ī and connect it to the words of Allah: '*except for those who repent before you gain power over them.*' That is an exception to the obligation. It is obliged to apply all *ḥudūd* to it.

Our scholars say, 'This is our exact proof because when Allah mentions the *ḥadd* for banditry, He says: "*...except for those who repent before you gain power over them.*" Then He adds to it the *ḥadd* for theft and says, "*If anyone repents after his wrongdoing and puts things right, Allah will turn towards him.*" If the ruling had been the same, He would not have changed the ruling between them.'

Ibn al-'Arabī said, 'Company of Shāfi'īs! Glory be to Allah! Where are the fine points of *fiqh* and legal rulings which you deduce in difficult cases? Do you not see that the bandit has independence and transgresses with his weapons and how a ruler must stir horses and riders against him? How can he revoke his punishment simply by repentance, ignoring all the circumstances involved? It is like what is done to an unbeliever in forgiving all he did before, starting anew with his Islam. As for a thief and fornicator, they are among the fold of Muslims and subject to the judgment of the ruler. What can revoke for them the ruling that is obliged for them? How can it be said that they are analogous to brigands? Wisdom and circumstances distinguish between them. This is not befitting for those like you, company of skilled scholars! If the *ḥadd* is confirmed, it cannot be revoked by repentance. Repentance is accepted and amputation is his expiation.'

'Puts things right' means: 'just as he repents from theft, so he also repents from every wrong action.' It is said that it means: if he abandons disobedience entirely. As for abandoning theft by fornication or by becoming a Jew or Christian, this is not repentance. Allah's turning to His servant is by giving him success in repenting. It is said that it means He accepts his repentance.

If it is asked what the wisdom is in Allah mentioning the male thief first before the female in this *āyah,* while in the case of fornication the female is mentioned first, the answer is that the reason for that is that men have greater love for wealth and women greater desire for pleasure. That is why He begins with each of them in the proper situation. This is an aspect which will be explained in *Sūrat an-Nūr* when fornication is discussed, Allah willing.

Allah prescribed amputation of the hand for theft, since it is used to take wealth, but did not prescribe castration (for fornication), even though the deed is perpetrated by the private parts. There are three reasons for that. One is that the thief has another similar hand to the one which was amputated. He can always use the other hand instead. A fornicator does not have another penis to replace the first and so has no other he can use. The second is that the *ḥadd* punishment is a deterrent to the perpetrator and others. Cutting off the hand is clear but castration is concealed. The third is that castration prevents progeny which amputation of the hand does not. Allah knows best.

أَلَمْ تَعْلَمْ أَنَّ ٱللَّهَ لَهُۥ مُلْكُ ٱلسَّمَٰوَٰتِ وَٱلْأَرْضِ يُعَذِّبُ مَن يَشَآءُ وَيَغْفِرُ
لِمَن يَشَآءُ ۗ وَٱللَّهُ عَلَىٰ كُلِّ شَىْءٍ قَدِيرٌ ٤٠

40 Do you not know that the kingdom of the heavens and earth belongs to Allah? He punishes whoever He wills and forgives whoever He wills. Allah has power over all things.

This is addressed to the Prophet ﷺ and others, meaning that there is no kinship between Allah Almighty and anyone else which might oblige mutual love so that someone could validly say, 'We are the sons of Allah and those He loves.' The *ḥadd* punishment is carried out on everyone on whom it is obliged, no matter who they are. It is said that it means that Allah makes whatever judgment He wills. This is why He distinguishes between a brigand and a thief who is not a brigand. Similar things to this *āyah* have already been mentioned and there is no point in repeating them. It is Allah Who gives success. These are the rulings connected to the *āyah* of theft. Allah knows best.

يَٰٓأَيُّهَا ٱلرَّسُولُ لَا يَحْزُنكَ ٱلَّذِينَ يُسَٰرِعُونَ فِى ٱلْكُفْرِ مِنَ ٱلَّذِينَ قَالُوٓا۟
ءَامَنَّا بِأَفْوَٰهِهِمْ وَلَمْ تُؤْمِن قُلُوبُهُمْ ۛ وَمِنَ ٱلَّذِينَ هَادُوا۟ ۛ سَمَّٰعُونَ
لِلْكَذِبِ سَمَّٰعُونَ لِقَوْمٍ ءَاخَرِينَ لَمْ يَأْتُوكَ ۖ يُحَرِّفُونَ ٱلْكَلِمَ
مِنۢ بَعْدِ مَوَاضِعِهِۦ ۖ يَقُولُونَ إِنْ أُوتِيتُمْ هَٰذَا فَخُذُوهُ وَإِن لَّمْ
تُؤْتَوْهُ فَٱحْذَرُوا۟ ۚ وَمَن يُرِدِ ٱللَّهُ فِتْنَتَهُۥ فَلَن تَمْلِكَ لَهُۥ
مِنَ ٱللَّهِ شَيْـًٔا ۚ أُو۟لَٰٓئِكَ ٱلَّذِينَ لَمْ يُرِدِ ٱللَّهُ أَن يُطَهِّرَ
قُلُوبَهُمْ ۚ لَهُمْ فِى ٱلدُّنْيَا خِزْىٌ ۖ وَلَهُمْ فِى ٱلْءَاخِرَةِ عَذَابٌ
عَظِيمٌ ﴿٤١﴾

41 O Messenger! do not be grieved by those who rush headlong into unbelief among those who say 'We believe' with their tongues when their hearts contain no belief, nor by those among the Jews who listen to lies, listen to other people who have not come to you, distorting words from their proper meanings, saying, 'If you are given this, then take it. If you are not given it, then beware!' If Allah desires misguidance for someone, you cannot help him against Allah in any way. Those are the people whose hearts Allah does not want to purify. They will have disgrace in this world and in the Next World they will have a terrible punishment.

O Messenger! do not be grieved

Three things are said about the reason for the revelation of this *āyah*. It is said that it was revealed about the Banū Qurayẓah and the Banū an-Naḍīr. A Qurayẓī man killed a Naḍirī man, and the custom was that when one of the Banū an-Naḍīr killed one of the Banū Qurayẓah, they did not give them retaliation, but paid them blood money. So they took the case to the Prophet ﷺ and he judged that the Qurayẓī and Naḍirī were the same. That annoyed them and they did not accept the judgment. It is also said that it was revealed about Abū Lubābah when the Prophet ﷺ sent him to the Banū Qurayẓah and he betrayed him by indicating to them that they would be killed. It is further said that it was revealed about two Jews who committed fornication and the concealment of the verse of stoning. This is the soundest view because the Imāms Mālik, al-Bukhārī, Muslim, At-Tirmidhī, and Abū Dāwūd related it.

Abū Dāwūd reported from Jābir ibn 'Abdullāh that the Messenger of Allah ﷺ told them, 'Bring me two of your most knowledgeable men.' They brought the two sons of Ṣūriyā and he asked them by Allah, 'What do you find is the ruling of these two in the Torah?' They answered, 'We find in the Torah that if there are four witnesses who testify that they saw his penis in her vagina – like the stick in the kohl bottle – they are stoned.' He asked, 'What keeps you from stoning them?' They replied, 'We no longer have sufficient authority and we dislike killing.' So the Prophet ﷺ called for witnesses and they came and testified that they saw his penis in her vagina like the stick in the kohl bottle, and so the Prophet ﷺ commanded that they be stoned.

Outside of the two *Ṣaḥīḥ* collections, ash-Sha'bī reported that Jābir ibn 'Abdullāh said, 'A man of the people of Fadak committed fornication and the people of Fadak wrote to some of the Jews in Madina, saying: "Ask Muḥammad about that. If he commands you to flog them, accept it. If he commands you to stone them, do not accept it." They asked him and he summoned Ibn Ṣūriyā, who was their scholar and a one-eyed man. The Messenger of Allah ﷺ said to him, "I ask you by Allah, what do you find in your Book about fornicators?" Ibn Ṣūriyā said, "Since you asked me by Allah, we find in the Torah that the glance is fornication. The embrace is fornication. Kissing is fornication. If four bear witness that they saw his penis in her vagina like a stick in a kohl bottle, then stoning is obliged." The Messenger of Allah ﷺ said, "It is that."'

We find in *Ṣaḥīḥ Muslim* that al-Barā' ibn 'Āzib said, 'The Prophet ﷺ passed by a Jew who had been flogged and his face blackened and he summoned them and asked, "Is that what you find to be the *ḥadd* punishment for illicit sex in your Book?" "Yes," they replied. So he summoned one of their scholars and said, "I ask You by Allah who revealed the Torah to Mūsā, is that what you find to be the *ḥadd* punishment for illicit sex in your Book" "No," he replied, "if it had not been that you asked me by Allah about this, I would not have told you. We find that it is stoning. However, it happened frequently among our nobles and so when we took a noble, we left him, and when we someone weak, we carried out the *ḥadd* punishment on him. We said, 'Let us agree to something which we will carry out on both the noble and base and so we made it blackening the face and flogging instead of stoning.'" The Messenger of Allah ﷺ said, "O Allah! I am the first to revive Your command when they do away with it!" He commanded stoning and Allah Almighty revealed: *"O Messenger! do not be grieved by those who rush headlong unbelief ... If you are given this, then take it."* They said, "Bring Muḥammad. If he commands blackening the face and flogging, take it. If he gives the decision of stoning, then beware." So Allah revealed 5:44-45. Allah revealed: *"Those who do not judge by what Allah has sent down: such people are deviators."* (5:48)' It was about all the unbelievers.

We find in this transmission, '[A Jew] passed by the Prophet ﷺ' We find in the *ḥadīth* of Ibn 'Umar: 'A Jew and a Jewess who had fornicated were brought and the Messenger of Allah ﷺ went to a Jew. He said, "What do you find in the Torah about someone who fornicates?"' One version has: 'The Jews brought a man and woman who had fornicated to the Messenger of Allah ﷺ.' We find in the book of Abū Dāwūd that Ibn 'Umar said, 'A group of Jews came and invited the Messenger of Allah ﷺ to go to al-Quff [*wādī*]. They went to the Bayt al-Midrās (Jewish place of learning) and said, "Abū'l-Qāsim, one of our men fornicated with a woman. Judge between them."' There is no contradiction in any of this. It is all one story.

Abū Dāwūd gives it from Abū Hurayrah in an excellent fashion. He said, 'A man of the Jews fornicated with a woman and they said to each other, "Let us go to this Prophet. He is a Prophet sent to make things easier. If he gives us a ruling less than stoning, we will take it and use it as an argument before Allah and will say, 'One of Your Prophets gave us that decision.'" They went to the Prophet ﷺ while he was sitting in the mosque among his Companions. They said, "Abū'l-Qāsim, what do you think about a man and woman who fornicate?' The Prophet ﷺ did not speak to them until he went to the Bayt al-Midrās. He stood at the door and said, "I ask you by Allah Who sent down the Torah to Mūsā, what do you find in the Torah about someone who fornicates when he has been previously married (*muḥṣan*)?" They answered, "His face is blackened, he is carried backwards on a donkey and flogged." One young man among them remained silent. When the

Prophet ﷺ saw that he was silent, he directed the request to him and he said, "O Allah! Since you have implored me by Allah, we do find stoning in the Torah."' The *ḥadīth* continues until it has: 'The Prophet ﷺ said, "I will judge by what is in the Torah," and he commanded that they be stoned.'

The conclusion from all these transmissions is that the Jews asked the Prophet ﷺ to give judgment and he gave them a judgment which was in accordance with the Torah. In that he relied on the position of Ibn Ṣūriyā. Then he heard testimony and acted on it. Islam is not a precondition for being *muḥṣan*. So there are four points here. When the people of the *dhimmah* present a case to the ruler and the case they present concerns wrongdoing like killing, assault or misappropriation, without disagreement he judges between them and prevents them from the wrongdoing. If that is not the case, then the ruler can choose between giving judgment or leaving it according to Mālik and ash-Shāfi'ī. Mālik, however, thought it is more fitting to leave it and that if he does give judgment, he gives the judgment of Islam.

Ash-Shāfi'ī said that the ruler should not judge between them in a case involving the *ḥudūd*. Abū Ḥanīfah said that he should judge between them in every case, and that is the position of az-Zuhrī, 'Umar ibn 'Abd al-'Azīz and al-Ḥakam. It is related from Ibn 'Abbās and is one of the two positions of ash-Shāfi'ī who based it on the words of Allah: *'Judge between them by what Allah has sent down.'* (5:49) This will be further explained there. Mālik's evidence for having a choice is: *'If they come to you, you can either judge between them or turn away from them.'* (5:42) It is a text giving choice.

Ibn al-Qāsim said, 'When bishops and a fornicating couple present themselves, the judge has a choice because carrying out the ruling [about the couple] is the bishops' duty.' Someone who disagrees says, '[When the judgment of the couple is handed over to the ruler, it is permitted to carry out the ruling] and then no attention is paid to the bishops.' Ibn al-'Arabī said, 'That is sounder because if two Muslims both give a judgment about a man, that judgment is carried out, and one does not consider the consent of the ruler. That applies even more to the Kitābīs.'

'Īsā said that Ibn al-Qāsim said that the people of the Dhimmah are not like the people of war. Ibn al-'Arabī said, 'What 'Īsā reported from him is discarded based on what aṭ-Ṭabarī and others related about a fornicating couple from the people of Khaybar or Fadak who fought the Messenger of Allah ﷺ. The name of the female fornicatress was Busrah. They sent to the Jews of Madīnah who told them, 'Ask Muḥammad about this. If he gives you a decision other than stoning, take it and accept it. If he gives you a decision of stoning, beware of it.'

Ibn al-'Arabī said, 'If this is sound, their presentation of the fornicators and request was after a treaty and safe conduct. If there is no treaty, *dhimmah* or abode, he can judge to refrain from them or to deliver justice to them. There is no proof in what 'Īsā transmitted about that. Allah reports about them: "*...they listen to lies, listen to other people who have not come to you.*" When they asked the Prophet ﷺ to judge them, the judgment was carried out on them and they could not retract (their request).

The basis of entrusting a man with the task of rendering a judgment in the *dīn* is this *āyah*. Mālik said, 'When a man gives judgment on another man, his judgment is carried out. When it is presented to the ruler, it should be carried out unless it is clear injustice.' Saḥnūn says that it is carried out if it appears to be correct. Ibn al-'Arabī said, 'That refers to judgments about property and rights that are demanded. As for the *ḥudūd*, only the ruler may render judgment in their case. The principle is that arbitration is permitted in every case where there are two litigants and the judgment of the arbiter should be carried out.'

The fact is that arbitration between people is their right, not the right of the ruler, although leaving a matter to arbitration is a gap in the principle of authority (*walāyah*) which can lead to donkey-like factiousness between people. There must be a clear decision. That is why the *Sharī'ah* sets up a ruler (*wālī*) to stop people killing one another. Permission for arbitration is given to lighten things for him and them in view of the difficulty of presenting all matters to him in order to achieve people's best interests and obtain benefit. Ash-Shāfi'ī and others said that the arbitration is permitted and it is a *fatwā*.

Some scholars said that the Prophet ﷺ ruled that the Jews should be subject to stoning in order to confirm the judgment contained in their Scripture when they had deviated from it and concealed it and failed to act on it. Do you not see that he said, 'O Allah, I am the first to bring Your command to life when they let it die out.' [It was also a time before the ruling of stoning had been revealed to the Prophet ﷺ. That is why some reports of this *ḥadīth* say that this occurred when he ﷺ first came to Madīnah. That was when the sons of Ṣūriyā verified the ruling of the Torah and he ﷺ made them swear to that.] The statements of unbelievers about *ḥudūd* and their testimony about it are not accepted by consensus, but he did that to make obligatory for them what was already obligatory for them and for them to act by it.

It is possible that obtaining that knowledge was by way of revelation or by what Allah inspired in him, verifying what the sons of Ṣūriyā said about it and not based purely on their word. Allah made it clear to the Prophet ﷺ and declared the legitimacy of stoning which began at that time. So he learned through his legitimisation of the ruling of the Torah, making it clear that it was also the ruling of his *Sharīʿah* and that the Torah also contained Allah's judgment, as the Almighty says: *'We sent down the Torah containing guidance and light, and the Prophets who had submitted themselves gave judgment by it'* (5:44), he ﷺ being one of the Prophets. Abū Hurayrah reported that he said, 'I judge by what is in the Torah.' Allah knows best.

Most scholars say that the testimony of a *dhimmī* is rejected because he is not one of the people who is allowed to give testimony. His testimony is not accepted against a Muslim or an unbeliever. A group of the *Tābiʿūn* did accept their testimony when no Muslim was available, based on what is specified at the end of the *sūrah.* If it is said that he ﷺ judged by their testimony in the story and stoned the adulterers, the response is that he carried out the judgment of the Torah on them and made them act on it, based on what the tribe of Israel had previously done, which proved the argument against them and showed how they had twisted and changed things. So he was carrying out the judgment, not giving it. This is based on the first interpretation and our assertion that it was a specific incident since there is no evidence that testimony of this kind was accepted at the beginning of Islam. Allah knows best.

Nāfiʿ reads *'do not be grieved'* as *'yaḥzinuka'* whereas the others read it *'yaḥzunuka'*. Sorrow *(ḥuzn* and *ḥazan)* is the opposite of happiness. The verb is *hazana* and a sad person is *hazin* and *hazīn*. The verbs *ahzana* and *hazana* both mean to cause sorrow to someone. Az-Zubaydī said that *ḥazana* is the dialect of Quraysh and *ahzana* that of Tamīm. Both are recited. Form VIII and Form V mean the same. The purpose of the *āyah* is to console the Prophet ﷺ, meaning, 'Do not let their haste to unbelief grieve you. Allah has promised promised you success.'

among those who say 'We believe' with their tongues when their hearts contain no belief, nor by those among the Jews

This refers to the hypocrites. This means that their hearts do not contain the faith which their tongues articulate. *'The Jews'* here refers to the Jews of Madīnah. This is the completion of the sentence.

who listen to lies

Then Allah begins a new sentence: *'those who listen to lies'*. It is like the phrase: *'moving around (*ṭawwāfūna*) among yourselves'*. (24:58) It is also said that the new sentence begins with *'And among the Jews'*, meaning among them are those who listen to lies, in other words who accept the lies of their leaders who distort the Torah. It is also said that it means: 'They listen to your words, Muḥammad, so that they can deny you.' There used to be those among them who would be present with the Prophet ﷺ and deny him with the common people and try to make them dislike him. There were hypocrites who used to do this. Al-Farrā' said that it could also be *'sammā'īna'* and *'ṭawwāfīna'* as is the case with *'muttaqīna'* in 33:61, *'fākihīna'* in 52:17-18, and *'ākhidhīna'* in 51:16.

Sufyān ibn 'Uyaynah said that Allah mentioned spies in the Qur'ān when He says: *'...listen to other people who have not come to you.'* The Prophet ﷺ, in spite of his knowledge of them, did not concern himself with them, because at that time the rulings of the *Sharī'ah* had not been confirmed and Islam was not consolidated. The ruling concerning spies will come in *al-Mumtahanah*, Allah willing.

distorting words from their proper meanings

They are interpreting them improperly after they have understood them from you and known what Allah desired by them and the rulings He had made clear through them. They said, 'It has been prescribed that stoning should be abandoned,' and they replaced stoning a person who has been married with forty lashes to alter the judgment of Allah.

'Distorting' describes 'those who listen' and it is not an adverbial *ḥāl* modifying the pronoun in 'who come to you' because when they did not come, they did not listen. *'Distorting'* comes from someone who is present and hears and then twists things. Those who distort were some of the Jews, not all of them. That is why the meaning is more likely to be applied to a group of *'those among the Jews'* who listened. The word *'saying'* is in the position of a *ḥāl* modifying the implied 'they' in *'distorting'*. The sentence: *"If you are given this, then take it. If you are not given it, then beware!'* means 'If Muḥammad ﷺ rules that flogging is the correct judgment, accept it. Otherwise do not.'

If Allah desires misguidance for someone, you cannot help him against Allah in any way.

This means if He desires to misguide him in this world and punish him in the Next. The words: *'...you cannot help him'* means 'you will not be able to benefit him.'

Those are the people whose hearts Allah does not want to purify.

He makes it clear that they are ordained to be unbelievers. The *āyah* indicates that misguidance is by the will of Allah, refuting those who have said something different to that, as we have already mentioned. It means that Allah does not wish to purify their hearts from the seal placed on them in the way He does purify the hearts of the believers to reward them.

They will have disgrace in this world.

It is said that it is their disgrace was when they denied stoning and then the Torah was brought and stoning was found in it. It is said that their disgrace in this world is paying *jizyah* and abasement. Allah knows best.

سَمَّٰعُونَ لِلْكَذِبِ أَكَّٰلُونَ لِلسُّحْتِ فَإِن جَآءُوكَ فَاحْكُم
بَيْنَهُمْ أَوْ أَعْرِضْ عَنْهُمْ وَإِن تُعْرِضْ عَنْهُمْ فَلَن يَضُرُّوكَ شَيْـًٔا وَإِنْ
حَكَمْتَ فَاحْكُم بَيْنَهُم بِالْقِسْطِ إِنَّ اللَّهَ يُحِبُّ الْمُقْسِطِينَ ﴿٤٢﴾

42 They are people who listen to lies and consume ill-gotten gains. If they come to you, you can either judge between them or turn away from them. If you turn away from them, they cannot harm you in any way. But if you do judge, judge between them justly. Allah loves the just.

They are people who listen to lies and consume ill-gotten gains.

It is repeated to emphasise the enormity of their action. This was already mentioned in *al-Baqarah*. The form of the word for '*consume*' stresses the repeated nature of their action. The root of *'ill-gotten gains'* or '*suḥt*' means destruction and hardship. Allah says: '*…or He will annihilate you (fa-yusḥitakum) with His punishment.*' (20:61) Al-Farazdaq said:

Ibn Marwān, the severity of time only leaves of one's wealth
In livestock that which is destroyed (*musḥat*) or only a remnant.

One says a shaver removes it all (*asḥata*). *'Ill-gotten gains'* are called that because they destroy acts of obedience and eradicate them. Al-Farrā' said, 'Its root is burning hunger.' A man described as '*masḥūt'* eats inordinately. So someone who takes bribes and consumes what is unlawful out of greed is like someone with insatiable hunger. It is said that unlawful property is called *suḥt* because it destroys a man's good character.

The first definition is more likely because when someone's *dīn* is removed, good character is also removed. There is no possibility of manly character for someone with no *dīn*. Ibn Mas'ūd and others said that the word *suḥt* means a bribe. 'Umar ibn al-Khaṭṭāb said, 'A bribe to a judge is *suḥt*.' The Prophet ﷺ said, 'The Fire is more entitled to any flesh which grows from *suḥt*.' They asked, 'Messenger of Allah, what is *suḥt*?' He replied, 'A bribe in exchange for judgment.' Ibn Mas'ūd also said, '*Suḥt* is that a man judges in favour of his brother's need and he gives him a wage which he accepts.' Ibn Khuwayzimandād said, 'An aspect of *suḥt* is that a man gains by virtue of his rank. That happens when he has a position with the ruler and a person asks him for something he needs but he will only judge in his favour if he receives a bribe.'

There is no disagreement among the *Salaf* that accepting a bribe to void a right or to allow what is not permitted is unlawful *suḥt*. Abū Ḥanīfah said, 'When a judge takes a bribe, he is immediately dismissed, if he does not resign, and all his judgments after that are null and void.' It cannot be disputed that accepting bribes is deviance (*fisq*) and the judgment of a deviant (*fāsiq*) is not allowed. Allah knows best. The Prophet ﷺ said, 'Allah has cursed anyone who gives a bribe and anyone who takes one.'

'Alī said, '*Suḥt* refers to bribes, the payment one gives to a soothsayer and taking a wage for judgment.' Wahb ibn Munabbih was asked, 'Is a bribe unlawful in every instance?' He replied, 'No, it is disliked to give a bribe so that you are given what is not yours to or avert something you owe. But if you give a bribe to protect your *dīn*, life and property, it is not unlawful.' The *faqīh* Abū al-Layth as-Samarqandī said, 'We take this view. There is nothing wrong with a man defending his life and property through bribes.' It is related that 'Abdullāh ibn Mas'ūd was in Abyssinia and gave a bribe of two dinars. He said, 'The sin is for the one who takes it, not the one who gives it.'

Al-Mahdawī said, 'If someone calls the earning of a cupper and those like him "*suḥt*", it means that the one who takes it shaves away his manliness.' What is sound is that the earnings of a cupper are good. If someone takes what is good, his manly character is not diminished nor his rank degraded. Mālik related from Ḥumayd aṭ-Ṭawīl that Anas said, 'The Messenger of Allah ﷺ was cupped by Abū Ṭayyibah. The Messenger of Allah ﷺ commanded that he be given a *ṣā'* of dates and told his owners to reduce his levy.' Ibn 'Abd al-Barr said, 'This indicates that the earnings of a cupper are good because the Messenger of Allah ﷺ would not assign a price, wage or recompense for anything false. This *ḥadīth* of Anas abrogates what the Prophet ﷺ forbade regarding the price of blood and it abrogates that he disliked the wages of a cupper. Al-Bukhārī and Abū Dāwūd related that Ibn 'Abbās said, 'The Messenger of Allah ﷺ was cupped and paid the cupper his wage.' If that had been '*suḥt*', he would not have given it to him.

Suḥut and *suḥt* are two dialectical variants, and it is recited in both ways. Abū 'Amr, Ibn Kathīr and al-Kisā'ī recite it as *suḥut* while the rest have *suḥt*. Al-'Abbās ibn al-Faḍl related from Khārijah ibn Muṣ'ab from Nāfi' '*akkālūna li's-sāḥt*'. This is the verbal noun from *saḥata*. It is said that *saḥata* and *asḥata* mean the same. Az-Zajjāj said that *saḥata* is to remove bit by bit.

If they come to you, you can either judge between them or turn away from them.

This is the option given by Allah. Al-Qushayrī mentioned it. We already mentioned that is about people with whom there is a treaty, not the people of *dhimmah*. When the Prophet ﷺ came to Madīnah, he made a treaty with the Jews and did not oblige us to judge between the unbelievers when they are not *dhimmīs*. It is permitted to so judge if we want to. As for the people of the *dhimmah*, is it mandatory for us to judge between them when they present a case to us? Ash-Shāfiʿī has two positions. If the dispute is with a Muslim, then we must judge. Al-Mahdawī said, 'Scholars agree that the judge decides between a Muslim and a *dhimmī*, but they disagree about two *dhimmīs*.' Some say that the *āyah* is one of judgment and the judge can choose. That is related from an-Nakhaʿī, ash-Shaʿbī and others. It is the position of Mālik, ash-Shāfiʿī and others except for what is related from Mālik about not carrying out the *ḥadd* punishment on the People of the Book for illicit sex. If a Muslim has illicit sex with a Kitābī woman, he receives the *ḥadd* punishment but she does not. If the pair are both *dhimmīs*, neither receives the *ḥadd*. That is the position of Abū Ḥanīfah, Muḥammad ibn al-Ḥasan and others. It is also related from Abū Ḥanīfah that they are flogged and not stoned. Ash-Shāfiʿī, Abū Yūsuf, Abū Thawr and others said that the *ḥadd* is carried out on them if they come content to accept our judgement.

Ibn Khuwayzimandād said, 'The ruler does not send for them when they commit aggression against one another and does not summon a litigant to his assembly unless it is something connected to injustices by which corruption spreads, such as killing, robbing homes and the like. As for debts, divorce and other transactions, one only judges between them when there is mutual consent. A judge can choose not to judge and refer them to their own judges. If he does judge between them, he gives the judgment of Islam.'

As for compelling them to accept the judgment of the Muslims regarding things from which corruption spreads, we did not give them the treaty on the basis of corruption, and corruption must be removed from them and others because that is preserving their property and lives. There may be something in their *dīn* which, if allowed, would spread corruption among us. That is why we forbid them to sell wine publicly and to have illicit sex openly and other disgusting acts, so that they do not corrupt foolish Muslims. But we do not force them to adopt rulings in respect of divorce, illicit sex and their like. To force judgment on them would harm their judges and alter their religion. That is not the case with debts and business transactions because judgments in these areas can both entail a form of injustice and also be a means of stopping corruption. Allah knows best.

There is a second position about the *āyah* related from 'Umar ibn 'Abd al-'Azīz and also from an-Nakha'ī: it is that the choice put forward in the *āyah* was abrogated by the words of Allah: *'Judge between them by what Allah has sent down'* (5:49) and so a judge should judge between them. That was the position of 'Aṭā' al-Khurasani, Abū Ḥanīfah and his people, and others. 'Ikrimah, however, says that this *āyah* was abrogated by 5:49. Mujāhid stated that only two *āyahs* in *al-Mā'idah* were abrogated: this *āyah* by 5:49, and the words: *'Do not profane the sacred rites of Allah'* (5:2) which were abrogated by: *'...kill the idolaters wherever you find them.'* (9:5)

Az-Zuhrī said, 'The *sunnah* is that the People of the Book are referred to the people of their own *dīn* in respect of their rights and inheritance, unless they come desiring the judgment of Allah, and then judgment is given according to the Book of Allah.' As-Samarqandī said that this tallies with the position of Abū Ḥanīfah that there is no judgment given when they do not both agree to our judgement.

An-Naḥḥās said in his book '*The Abrogating and Abrogated*' that this is abrogated because it was revealed when the Prophet ﷺ first came to Madīnah and there were a lot of Jews at there at that time. The most proper course was to refer them to their own judges. When Islam became strong, then Allah revealed: *'Judge between them by what Allah has sent down.'* (5:49) Ibn 'Abbās, Mujāhid, 'Ikrimah, az-Zuhrī, 'Umar ibn 'Abd al-'Azīz and as-Suddī all said that. It is the sound position of ash-Shāfi'ī who said in *Kitāb al-jizyah*: 'He has no choice when they ask him to judge since the Almighty says: "*...until they pay the jizyah with their own hands in a state of complete abasement.*" (9:29)'

An-Naḥḥās said, 'This is the soundest of arguments because Allah's words "*in a state of complete abasement*" mean that it is mandatory that the rulings of the Muslims be carried on them unless they resort to their own judges. If this is so, the *āyah* is abrogated.' It is also the position of the Kufans, Abū Ḥanīfah, Zufar, Abū Yūsuf and Muḥammad. There is no disagreement between them that when the People of the Book take a case to the ruler for judgment, he may not turn away from them, although Abū Ḥanīfah said, 'When a woman and her husband come, he must judge fairly between them. When a woman comes alone and her husband does not consent, he should not judge.' The rest say that he should.

It is confirmed that the position of most scholars is that the *āyah* is abrogated, apart from what is confirmed about the hesitation of Ibn 'Abbās. If it had not been for the *ḥadīth* from Ibn 'Abbās, reflection would demand that it should be abrogated, because there is general agreement that when the People of the Book present the ruler with a case, he must examine it. [Then they disagree about what happens when he turns away from them as we mentioned. It is mandatory for him to examine the case because that is correct] according to the majority unless he turns them away. According to some scholars, however, it is an obligation for him to turn them away since, if he did not, he would be doing something that is not lawful and which is outside his competence.

An-Naḥḥās said, 'Those Kufans who say that it is abrogated have other views. Some of them say that when the ruler knows that one of the *ḥudūd* of Allah Almighty is owed by the People of the Book, he must carry it out, even if they do not come to him for judgment. The proof is that the words of the Almighty: *"judge between them,"* can be interpreted in two ways. One is to judge between them when they ask you to judge. The other is that you judge between them, even if they do not request it, if you know that of them. They said, "We find in the Book of Allah and the *Sunnah* of His Messenger ﷺ evidence that obliges establishing the right on them, even if they do not ask us to judge." The evidence in the Book of Allah is: *"You you who believe! be upholders of justice, bearing witness for Allah alone."* (4:125) Then in the *Sunnah* is the *ḥadīth* of al-Barā' ibn 'Āzib who said, "A Jew who had been flogged and his face blackened was brought past the Messenger of Allah ﷺ and he said, 'Is this the *ḥadd* punishment for fornication among you?' 'Yes,' they replied. So he summoned one of their scholars and said, 'I ask you by Allah, is this the *ḥadd* punishment for a fornicator among you?' 'No,' he answered."" An-Naḥḥās said, 'They argued that the Prophet ﷺ judged between them and, in this *ḥadīth*, they did not come to him for judgment.'

If someone were to bring up the *ḥadīth* of Mālik from Nāfi' from Ibn 'Umar in which the Jews came to the Prophet ﷺ, he would be told that the *ḥadīth* of Mālik does not say that the couple who fornicated consented to judgment and yet the Prophet ﷺ ordered their stoning. Abū 'Umar ibn 'Abd al-Barr said, 'If someone uses the *ḥadīth* of al-Barā' as evidence, it does not in fact constitute evidence because the *ḥadīth* is a commentary on 5:41. It says, "If he gives you the judgment of flogging and blackening the face, take it. If he decides on stoning, then beware." This is evidence that they asked him to judge.' That is made clear in the *ḥadīth* of Ibn 'Umar and others. If someone says that the *ḥadīth* of Ibn 'Umar does not say that the fornicating couple asked the Messenger of Allah ﷺ to judge, nor that they consented to his judgment, the answer to this is that the *ḥadd* on the fornicator is one of the rights of Allah which the judge must carry out. It is known that the Jews had a judge who judged between them and implemented their *ḥudūd* on them. He is the one who asked the Messenger of Allah to judge. Allah knows best.

But if you do judge, judge between them justly.

An-Nasā'ī related from Ibn 'Abbās that the clan of an-Naḍīr was more noble than the clan of Qurayẓah and when a man of Qurayẓah killed a man of an-Naḍīr, he was killed in retaliation for him, but when a man of an-Naḍīr killed a man of Qurayẓah, the penalty was blood money of a hundred *wasq*s of dates. After the Messenger of Allah ﷺ was sent, a man of Qurayẓah killed a man of an-Naḍīr, and they said, 'Hand him over to us so that we can kill him.' They said, 'The Prophet ﷺ is between us and you.' Then this *āyah* was revealed and the ruling of a life for a life, and it was also revealed: *'Do they then seek the judgment of the Jāhiliyyah?'* (5:50)

وَكَيْفَ يُحَكِّمُونَكَ وَعِندَهُمُ ٱلتَّوْرَىٰةُ فِيهَا حُكْمُ ٱللَّهِ ثُمَّ يَتَوَلَّوْنَ مِنۢ بَعْدِ ذَٰلِكَ وَمَآ أُو۟لَٰٓئِكَ بِٱلْمُؤْمِنِينَ ﴿٤٣﴾

43 How can they make you their judge when they have the Torah with them which contains the judgment of Allah? Then even after that they turn their backs! Such people are certainly not believers.

Al-Ḥasan said that the judgment referred to here is stoning. Qatādah said that it is retaliation. It is asked whether the words *'which contains the judgment of Allah'* mean that it is not abrogated. The answer is as Abū 'Alī said, 'Yes, because if it had been abrogated, after it was abrogated it would not then have been called "the judgment of Allah" in the same way that it is not said that it is Allah's judgment to make wine lawful or the Sabbath sacred [for the Muslims].

The words: *'Such people are certainly not believers,'* refer to not believing that the judgment is from Allah. Abū 'Alī said, 'Anyone who seeks other than the judgment of Allah is an unbeliever. This is the state of the Jews.'

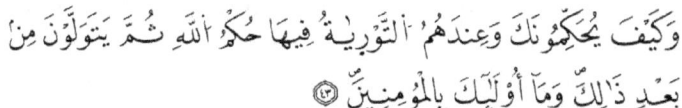

إِنَّآ أَنزَلۡنَا ٱلتَّوۡرَىٰةَ فِيهَا هُدٗى وَنُورٞۚ يَحۡكُمُ بِهَا ٱلنَّبِيُّونَ ٱلَّذِينَ
أَسۡلَمُواْ لِلَّذِينَ هَادُواْ وَٱلرَّبَّٰنِيُّونَ وَٱلۡأَحۡبَارُ بِمَا ٱسۡتُحۡفِظُواْ مِن كِتَٰبِ ٱللَّهِ
وَكَانُواْ عَلَيۡهِ شُهَدَآءَۚ فَلَا تَخۡشَوُاْ ٱلنَّاسَ وَٱخۡشَوۡنِ وَلَا
تَشۡتَرُواْ بِـَٔايَٰتِي ثَمَنٗا قَلِيلٗاۚ وَمَن لَّمۡ يَحۡكُم بِمَآ أَنزَلَ ٱللَّهُ
فَأُوْلَٰٓئِكَ هُمُ ٱلۡكَٰفِرُونَ ٤٤

44 We sent down the Torah containing guidance and light, and the Prophets who had submitted themselves gave judgment by it for the Jews – as did their scholars and their rabbis – by what they had been allowed to preserve of Allah's Book to which they were witnesses. Do not be afraid of people, be afraid of Me. And do not sell My Signs for a paltry price. Those who do not judge by what Allah has sent down, such people are unbelievers.

We sent down the Torah containing guidance and light, and the Prophets who had submitted themselves gave judgment by it for the Jews – as did their scholars and their rabbis –

This means clarification, illumination and declaration of the fact that Muḥammad ﷺ is true. '*Guidance*' is in the nominative by the inceptive and '*light*' is added to it. It is said that the word '*Prophets*' here refers to Muḥammad ﷺ, even though the plural is used. It is said that it means every Prophet sent after Mūsā to establish the Torah and that the Jews said, 'The Prophets were Jews,' and the Christians said, 'They were Christians,' and Allah exposed their lies. The word '*submitted*' here means that they affirmed the Torah from Mūsā until the time of 'Īsā, between whom were a thousand Prophets, or 4000 or more than that, all of whom gave judgment by the Torah. It is said that it means submitted to the command of Allah which they were sent to establish. It is said that it means, 'The Prophets who followed the *dīn* of Ibrāhīm judged by it.' The meaning is the same.

In '*for the Jews*' the particle '*li*' (for) actually means '*'alā*' (against). It is said that it means: 'the Prophets, who had submitted themselves, judged by it for and against those who were Jews' and 'against' is elided. Those who '*submitted themselves*' is an adjectival description which contains praise. The word '*h*ādū' means 'repent from disbelief'. It is said that there is a change of order in the sentence, i.e. 'We sent down the Torah, which contains guidance and light for those who are Jews, by which the Prophets, scholars and rabbis give judgement.' The scholars give judgment based on it. These scholars (*rabbāniyyūn*) are those who inculcate knowledge in people and teach them when they are young, as Ibn 'Abbās and others said. This was already discussed in *Āl 'Imrān* (3:79). Abū Razīn said, 'The scholars are those with knowledge and wisdom, and the rabbis, according to Ibn 'Abbās, are the *fuqahā'*.'

Ḥibr or *ḥabr* is a scholar. It is derived from *taḥbīr*, which means to embellish. They clarify knowledge and adorn it and it is embellished in their breasts. Mujāhid said that the *rabbāniyyūn* are above the scholars. The definite article is used for emphasis. Al-Jawharī said, '*Ḥibr* or *ḥabr*, the plural of which is *aḥbār*, are the rabbis of the Jews. *Ḥibr* is more eloquent because of the plural form.' Al-Farrā' said that *ḥibr* is used for a scholar. Ath-Thawrī said, 'I asked al-Farrā' why a scholar is called *ḥibr*. He answered, "A scholar is called that because of the ink of the *ḥibr* and 'ink' is elided."' He said, 'I asked al-Aṣma'ī and he said, "This is nothing. A person is called *ḥibr* because of his making a mark. One says that there is *ḥibr* on a person's teeth, meaning yellowness or black."'

Abū al-'Abbās said, 'The word *'ḥibr'* means the one who writes with ink (*ḥibr*), meaning he achieves it.' Abū 'Ubayd said, 'What I say is that the singular of *aḥbār* is *ḥabr* which means a scholar since he adorns words and knowledge.' He said that all *ḥadīth* scholars relate it as *ḥabr* and *ḥibr* is that with which one writes whose locus is a *miḥbarah* (ink-pot). *Ḥabr* is also a mark whose plural is *ḥubūr*, as Ya'qūb [ibn as-Sikkīt] said.

by what they had been allowed to preserve of Allah's Book

This means by what they retained of its knowledge. The *bā'* (by) is connected to *'their scholars and their rabbis'*. It is as if Allah were saying 'those with knowledge that they had preserved', or it is connected to *'give judgement'*, meaning 'giving judgment by what they had preserved'.

to which they were witnesses.

They witnessed that the Book was from Allah. Ibn 'Abbās said, 'Witnesses that the judgment of Muḥammad ﷺ is in the Torah.'

Do not be afraid of people, be afraid of Me.

Do not fear people where disclosing the description of Muhammad ﷺ and stoning are concerned. *'Be afraid of Me'* if you conceal that. This is addressed to the Jewish scholars. It also includes anyone who conceals a right he owes and does not disclose it. The meaning of selling Signs for a paltry price has already been discussed (2:41).

Those who do not judge by what Allah has sent down, such people are unbelievers.

The terms *kāfirūn*, *ẓālimūn* (wrongdoers) and *fāsiqūn* (deviators) used in this context were all revealed about the unbelievers. That is confirmed in *Ṣaḥīḥ Muslim* in the *ḥadīth* of al-Barā' which was already mentioned (5:41). It is the position of the vast majority. A Muslim does not become an unbeliever, even if he commits a major wrong action. It is said that there is some implied meaning in it: in other words, anyone who does not judge by what Allah has revealed, rejecting the Qur'ān and denying the words of the Messenger ﷺ, is an unbeliever. Ibn 'Abbas and Mujāhid said, 'According to this the *āyah* is general.' Ibn Mas'ūd and al-Hasan said, 'It is general to everyone among the Muslims, Jews and unbelievers, who do not judge by what Allah has revealed, who believe it to be acceptable to do that. As for someone who does that, knowing that he is doing something unlawful, he is one of the impious Muslims and his business is left up to Allah. If Allah wishes, he will punish him, and if He wishes, He will pardon him.' Ibn 'Abbās said in one version, 'Whoever does not judge by what Allah has revealed has done an action which resembles the actions of unbelief.' It is said that it means: anyone who does not judge by all that Allah has revealed is an unbeliever. As for one who judges by *tawḥīd* and does not judge by some of the laws, he is not included in this *āyah*.

The sound position is the first, except for what ash-Sha'bī said about it, meaning that it is just about the Jews, which an-Naḥḥās selected. He mentioned three points. One is that the Jews were mentioned earlier in the *āyah* and so the pronoun refers to them. Another point is the context of the words indicates that. It is also followed by: *'We prescribed for them'* which clearly refers to the Jews who denied stoning and retaliation. If it is said that the pronoun '*Those*' usually includes more than that and is general unless there is proof of its being specific, the response is that here '*those*' is a demonstrative pronoun, implying, 'Those Jews who do not judge by what Allah has revealed, they are the unbelievers.' This is the best of what is said about this. It is related that Ḥudhayfah was asked about these *āyah*s and whether they were about the tribe of Israel. He replied, 'Yes, they are about them and you will travel their path step by step.'

It is said that here 'unbelievers' refers to the Muslims, 'wrongdoers' to the Jews and 'deviators' to the Christians. This is preferred by Abū Bakr ibn al-'Arabī because it is the apparent meaning of the *āyah*. It is also preferred by Ibn 'Abbās, Jābir ibn Zayd, Ibn Abī Zā'idah, Ibn Shubrumah and ash-Sha'bī. Ṭāwūs and others said that one cannot use the term 'unbelief' except for actual unbelief, but it what is meant by the term here is an unbelief which is less than true unbelief. This differs: if he judges while knowing the judgment from Allah and then changes it, his changing it brings about a definitive judgment of unbelief against him, but if he judges by personal passion and disobedience, it is a wrong action which can be forgiven according to the principle of the people of the *Sunnah* regarding those who commit wrong actions.

Al-Qushayrī said that the position of the Khārijites is that anyone who takes a bribe or gives other than the judgment of Allah is an unbeliever. This is attributed to al-Ḥasan al-Baṣrī. Al-Ḥasan also said, 'Allah imposed three things on the judges: not to follow whims, not to fear people, but to fear Him, and not to sell His signs for a cheap price.'

وَكَتَبْنَا عَلَيْهِمْ فِيهَآ أَنَّ ٱلنَّفْسَ بِٱلنَّفْسِ وَٱلْعَيْنَ بِٱلْعَيْنِ وَٱلْأَنفَ
بِٱلْأَنفِ وَٱلْأُذُنَ بِٱلْأُذُنِ وَٱلسِّنَّ بِٱلسِّنِّ وَٱلْجُرُوحَ قِصَاصٌ
فَمَن تَصَدَّقَ بِهِۦ فَهُوَ كَفَّارَةٌ لَّهُۥ وَمَن لَّمْ يَحْكُم بِمَآ أَنزَلَ
ٱللَّهُ فَأُوْلَٰٓئِكَ هُمُ ٱلظَّٰلِمُونَ ﴿٤٥﴾

45 We prescribed for them in it: a life for a life, an eye for an eye, a nose for a nose, an ear for an ear, a tooth for a tooth, and retaliation for wounds. But if anyone forgoes that as a *ṣadaqah*, it will act as expiation for him. Those who do not judge by what Allah has sent down, such people are wrongdoers.

We prescribed for them in it: a life for a life,

It is clear that in the Torah Allah made a life equal to a life and they opposed that, and so were misguided. The blood money of a Naḍīrī was greater and a Naḍīrī was not killed for a Quraẓī, but a Quraẓī was killed for a Naḍīrī. When Islam came, the Banū Qurayẓah consulted the Messenger of Allah ﷺ about it and he judged that they were equal. The Banū an-Naḍīr said, 'You have abased us!' and the *āyah* was revealed. *'Prescribed'* means made obligatory. Their Law was retaliation or pardon and no blood money, as was dealt with in *Sūrat al-Baqarah* (2:178).

Abū Ḥanīfah and others commented on this *āyah* and said that a Muslim is killed for a *dhimmī* because it is a life for a life. This was also explained in *Sūrat al-Baqarah* (2:178). Abū Dāwūd, at-Tirmidhī and an-Nasā'ī reported that 'Alī was asked, 'Did the Messenger of Allah ﷺ give you anything specific?' He said, 'No, except for this,' and he produced a letter from the scabbard of his sword and which said: 'The blood of the believers is equal. They are one hand against others. A Muslim is not killed for an unbeliever nor for one with a treaty.' The *āyah* also refutes the Jews making disparity between tribes and taking a man for a man in the case of one tribe and two men for a man in the case of other tribes. The Shāfi'īs say that this is about the *Sharī'ah* before us, which is not prescribed for us. This was adequately refuted in *al-Baqarah* (2:178), Allah willing.

Another point is that Allah says: *'We prescribed in it for them: a life for a life.'* That was prescribed for the people of the Torah who are a single religion. They did not have *dhimmīs* in the same way that the Muslims do because *jizyah* is something which Allah has given the Muslims and no one before this community had it, and in the past there was no Prophet who was sent to other than his own people. Therefore, the *āyah* necessitates the judgment that the blood of individuals among the tribe of Israel is all the same. It is like the statement of one person from among us regarding the blood of the non-Muslim [i.e. in granting security.] *'A life for a life'* has two meanings in respect of a people: the ruling on these people is that one of their lives is taken for a life taken, and this *āyah* gives the judgment that there is a life for a life among the people of the Qur'ān. There is nothing in the Book of Allah that indicates this equivalence when people are from different religions.

The adherents of ash-Shāfi'ī and Abū Ḥanīfah say that when someone wounds another person or cuts off their ear or hand and then kills them, the same is done to him because of this *āyah*. Our scholars say that if he deliberately maims someone, the same is done to him, but if it is in the course of striking and defending, he is executed by the sword. That was said about mutilation because the Prophet ﷺ gouged out the eyes of the 'Uranīs as we already mentioned.

an eye for an eye

This is all recited by Nāfi', 'Āṣim, al-A'mash and Ḥamzah in the accusative. Ibn Kathīr, Ibn 'Āmir, Abū 'Amr and Abū Ja'far recite it all in the nominative except for *'wounds'*. Al-Kisā'ī and Abū 'Ubayd have them all in the nominative. Abū 'Ubayd said that Ḥajjāj related from Hārūn from 'Abbād ibn Kathīr from az-Zuhrī from Anas that the Prophet ﷺ recited it in the nominative. The nominative case is used based on the nominal subject and predicate and the meaning of the position of 'a life' because the meaning is: *'a life for a life'*. Another aspect was stated by az-Zajjāj, which is that it is added to what is implied in *'life'* because the pronoun in *'life'* is in the position of the nominative because it implies: 'the life which is taken for a life'. The nouns are added to it. Ibn al-Mundhir said, 'Someone who recites it in the nominative makes that the beginning of the phrases as a ruling for the Muslims.' This is the sounder of the two views. That is because it was the recitation of the Prophet ﷺ. It is addressed to the Muslims to whom the command is directed. If someone only makes *'wounds'* nominative, that is based on separating it from what is before and starting anew as if that alone was a command to the Muslims in particular and what was before it was not directed to them.

This *āyah* indicates that there is retaliation for wounds as is mentioned. Ibn Shubrumah explained the lack of specification as indicating that the right eye can be taken for the left and vice-versa and the same applies to limbs and teeth in that a front tooth can be taken for a molar or a molar for a front tooth. Those scholars of the community who disagree with him say that the right eye should be taken for the right if it exists. It is not permitted to go beyond that to the left, even with consent. That makes it clear to us that what is meant by the *āyah* is to fully observe similarity in the perpetrator and it is not permitted to go beyond it just as it is not permitted to go from a foot to a hand in all cases. This is clear.

Scholars agree that when both eyes are wounded accidentally, there is blood money owed for them. One eye incurs half of the blood money. When the eye of someone with only one eye is gouged out, full blood money is owed. That is related from 'Umar and 'Uthmān and it is the view of 'Abd al-Malik ibn Marwān, az-Zuhrī, Qatādah, Mālik, al-Layth ibn Sa'd, Aḥmad and Isḥāq. It is also said that only half of the blood money is owed. That is related from 'Abdullāh ibn al-Mughaffal, Masrūq and an-Nakha'ī, and it is the view of ath-Thawrī, ash-Shāfi'ī and an-Nu'mān. Ibn al-Mundhir said, 'That is what we say about the *ḥadīth* which says that there is full blood money for both eyes, and it is understood from that there is half blood money for one.' Ibn al-'Arabī said, 'That is a clear analogy, but our scholars say that someone with one eye has the benefit of sight similar or close to that of someone with full sight, and so the same blood money is obliged.'

There is disagreement about when the sound eye of someone with one eye is gouged out. It is related from 'Umar, 'Uthmān and 'Alī that there is no retaliation in that case, but there is full blood money. That position is taken by 'Aṭā', Sa'īd ibn al-Musayyab and Aḥmad ibn Ḥanbal. Mālik said that he can either take retaliation so that the perpetrator is left blind, or can take the full blood money. An-Nakha'ī said, 'If he wishes, he takes retaliation, and if he wishes, he takes half the blood money.' Ash-Shāfi'ī, Abū Ḥanīfah and ath-Thawrī said that there is retaliation against him. That is related from 'Alī, and it is the view of Masrūq, Ibn Sīrīn and Ibn Ma'qil. Ibn al-Munshir and Ibn al-'Arabī preferred that because Allah says, *'an eye for an eye'* and the Prophet ﷺ stipulated full blood money for both eyes, and there is half the blood money for one eye, and retaliation involving a sound eye and a blind eye is the same. Aḥmad ibn Ḥanbal explained retaliation as taking all sight for part sight and this is not equality. It is what is related from

'Umar, 'Uthmān and 'Alī about that. Mālik holds to the fact that when the evidence is contradictory, the victim is given a choice. Ibn al-'Arabī said, 'It is more appropriate to take the general terms of the Qur'ān. It is safer in the sight of Allah Almighty.'

They disagree about the loss of the sightless eye of a one-eyed man. It is related that Zayd ibn Thābit said that there is a hundred dinars for it. 'Umar ibn al-Khaṭṭāb said that there is a third of the blood money for it. That is what Isḥāq said. Mujāhid said that there is half the blood money in that instance. Masrūq, az-Zuhrī, Mālik, ash-Shāfi'ī, Abū Thawr and an-Nu'mān said that it is subject to arbitration. Ibn al-Mundhir said, 'That is what we say because it is the minimum of what is said.'

There is full blood money for causing the loss of sight while the eyes themselves remain in place. The blear-eyed and weak-sighted are the same in that respect. There is a half blood money for making one eye sightless while the other remains all right. Ibn al-Mundhir said, 'The best of what is said on that is what 'Alī ibn Abī Ṭālib did: he commanded that the person's sound eye should be covered and gave someone an egg who walked with it while he was looking until he could no longer see it. Then he commanded that a line be drawn in that place. Then he commanded that the other eye be covered and the sound eye uncovered and gave someone an egg who walked with it while the person was looking until he could no longer see it. Then a line was drawn there. Then he commanded that the person be taken to another place and the same done again. He found it to be the same and gave him the due compensation for his loss of sight from the property of the other. This is the position of the school of ash-Shāfi'ī.'

The position of our school is that there is no disagreement among the people of knowledge that there is no retaliation for partial loss of sight since it is not possible to replicate it. [For example], how can there be any retaliation for an injury to an eye which entails heating a mirror, placing cotton on the other eye and then bringing the mirror close up to the eye until its pupil dissolves? This was a case related from 'Alī and was mentioned by al-Mahdawī and Ibn al-'Arabī.

There is disagreement about eyelids. Zayd ibn Thābit said that there is a quarter of blood money for them. That is the position of ash-Sha'bī, al-Ḥasan, Qatādah, Abū Hāshim, ath-Thawrī, ash-Shāfi'ī and the People of Opinion. It is related that ash-Sha'bī said that there is a third of blood money for the top eyelid and two-thirds for the bottom. Mālik said that.

a nose for a nose

There is a *ḥadīth* from the Messenger of Allah ﷺ that says: 'There is blood money for a nose when it is removed.' Ibn al-Mundhir said, 'There is consensus of all the people of *ḥadīth* who are reported from that that is the position. There is retaliation for a nose when the crime is deliberate, just like the retaliation for other limbs according to the Book of Allah.' There is disagreement about a broken nose. Mālik thought that there was retaliation if it was deliberate and arbitration if it was accidental. Ibn Nāfi' related that there is no blood money for a nose unless it is completely removed. Abū Isḥāq at-Tūnisī said, 'This is aberrant and what is known is the first position.'

If we branch out from what is known, then there is blood money for part of the cartilage of the nose according to the cartilage removed. Ibn al-Mundhir said, 'It is according to how much of the nose is severed. That is related from 'Umar ibn 'Abd al-'Azīz and ash-Sha'bī.' That is also the position of ash-Shāfi'ī. There is disagreement about when the cartilage is cut but the nose is not completely removed. Mālik, ash-Shāfi'ī, Abū Ḥanīfah and his people believe that there is full blood money for that. Then there is arbitration when just part of it is cut. Mālik said, 'In the case of the nose, that for which there is full blood money is when the cartilage is cut. It is less than the bone.' Ibn al-Qāsim said, 'It is the same whether the cartilage is cut from the bone or the nose completely removed from the bone under the eyes: there is full blood money for it, as there is full blood money for removing the tip of the penis or for removing the whole penis.'

Ibn al-Qāsim said, 'When the nose is punctured or broken and then heals imperfectly, there is deliberation about it as there is no known amount of blood money for it. If it heals perfectly as when a head wound heals perfectly, there is nothing owed for it. That is because that is what has come in the *Sunnah*. There is nothing for piercing the nose. Mālik and ash-Shāfi'ī and their people agree that it is not a *jā'ifah* (penetrative wound) and believe that a *jā'ifah* only applies to the abdomen. *Mārin* (cartilage) is the soft tissue of the nose according to al-Khalīl and others. Abū 'Umar said, 'I think that *rawthah* is the cartilage and *arnab* is the tip of nose.' It is said that *arnabah*, *rawthah* and *'artamah* is the tip of the nose.' The position of Mālik, ash-Shāfi'ī, the Kufans and those who follow them is that when the sense of smell is diminished or eradicated, there is arbitration regarding it.

an ear for an ear

Our scholars say that there is arbitration when someone cuts off one of a man's ears. There is blood money for hearing loss analogous to loss of sight. For the loss of one of them only half the blood money is owed, even if one cannot hear from it, which is not the case with a one-eyed person for which there is full blood money, as already mentioned.

Ashhab said, 'If hearing is asked about, it is said that one source of hearing hears what two hear. So, in my view, it is like sight. When there is doubt about hearing, it is tested by shouting to him from a number of different places and that is compared. If they are equal or close to it, he is paid according to the hearing loss incurred and made to swear an oath to that effect.' Ashhab said, 'That is calculated for him according to the median level of men like him. If he is tested and what he says differs, then he has nothing.' 'Īsā ibn Dīnār said, 'If what he says differs, he is given the minimum when he swears an oath.'

a tooth for a tooth,

Ibn al-Mundhir said that it is confirmed from the Messenger of Allah ﷺ that there is retaliation for a tooth. He ﷺ said, 'Retaliation is in the Book of Allah.' We find in a *ḥadīth* that the Messenger of Allah ﷺ said, 'There are five camels for a tooth.' Ibn al-Mundhir said, 'The literal meaning of this ḥadith is that there is no preference for incisors over canines, molars and the teeth next to the incisors since all of them are included in the *ḥadīth.* That is the position of most of the people of knowledge.' Among those who took the literal meaning of the *ḥadīth* without preferring any tooth over another were 'Urwah ibn az-Zubayr, Ṭāwūs, az-Zuhrī, Qatādah, Mālik, ath-Thawrī, ash-Shāfi'ī, Aḥmad, Isḥāq, an-Nu'mān and Ibn al-Ḥasan. That is related from 'Alī ibn Abī Ṭālib and Mu'āwiyah.

There is a second view which is related from 'Umar ibn al-Khaṭṭāb. He judged that five camels should be given for all teeth in the front of the mouth. That is fifty dinars, each camel being worth ten dinars. There was one camel for each of the back teeth. 'Aṭā' used to say that there were five camels each for the two teeth near the incisors and the incisors and two camels for each of the other teeth, upper and lower being the same and back teeth being the same.

Abū 'Umar said, 'As for what Mālik related in the *Muwaṭṭā'* from Yaḥyā ibn Sa'īd from Sa'īd ibn al-Musayyab about 'Umar judging a camel each for molars, that means that there are twenty molars and twelve [front] teeth: four are the front incisors, four are the teeth next to them and there are two canines. Based on the view of 'Umar, the full blood money is eighty camels, five each for the front teeth and one each for the back teeth. According to the view of Mu'āwiyah about there being five camels each for both the front and back teeth, the full blood money is 160 camels. According to the view of Sa'īd ibn al-Musayyab about two camels being owed for each molar – there being twenty in total – making forty, and five for each of the front teeth, making sixty, then the total is a hundred. That is full blood money in camels. The difference between them is about back teeth, not front teeth.'

Abū 'Umar said, 'The disagreement between scholars among the Companions and *Tābi'ūn* about blood money for teeth is very great indeed. The argument for what the *fuqahā'*, Mālik, Abū Ḥanīfah and ath-Thawrī, believe is the literal words of the Messenger of Allah ﷺ, "There are five camels for a tooth." A molar is a tooth.' Ibn 'Abbās related that the Messenger of Allah ﷺ said, 'Fingers are the same. Teeth are the same. An incisor and molar are the same. This one and that one are the same.' This is a text transmitted by Abū Dāwūd. Abū Dāwūd also related that Ibn 'Abbās said, 'The Messenger of Allah ﷺ made fingers and toes the same.'

Abū 'Umar said, 'Most of the *fuqahā'* of the regions and other scholars take from these reports that all fingers are the same in respect of blood money and all teeth are the same in respect of blood money, whether incisors, molars or canines. There is no difference between any of them according to what is in the letter of 'Amr ibn Ḥazm.' Ath-Thawrī mentioned that Azhar ibn Muḥārib said, 'Two men took an argument to Shurayḥ. One of them had hit the incisor of the other while the other had hit the molar of the other. Shurayḥ said, "The incisor and its beauty and the molar and its use are single teeth in my estimation."' Abū 'Umar said, 'This is what the practice is today in all regions.' Allah knows best.

According to Mālik and al-Layth, if a tooth is hit and goes black, full blood money is owed for it. That is what Abū Ḥanīfah said and that is also related from Zayd ibn Thābit. It is the position of Sa'īd ibn al-Musayyab, az-Zuhrī, al-Ḥasan, Ibn Sīrīn and Shurayḥ. It is related from 'Umar ibn al-Khaṭṭāb that a third of blood money should be paid for it. That is the view of Aḥmad and Isḥāq, Ash-Shāfi'ī and Abū Thawr said that there is arbitration for it. Ibn al-'Arabī said, 'I consider this a disagreement that ends in agreement. If it is black, its benefit has gone but its shape remains, like a palsied hand and blind eye. There is no disagreement that blood money is obliged. Then if any or all of its use remains, arbitration is only obliged according to the loss of its use. What is related from 'Umar about there being a third of blood money for it does not have a sound *isnād* or text.'

There is disagreement about a child's tooth that is pulled out before they have lost their milk-teeth. Mālik, ash-Shāfi'ī and the People of Opinion say that if a child's tooth is pulled out and a new one grows, the one who pulled it out owes nothing, although Mālik and ash-Shāfi'ī said, 'If it grows to be shorter than those near it, there is a fine according to the decrease in size. One group said that there is arbitration for it. That is related from ash-Sha'bī and an-Nu'mān also stated that. Ibn al-Mundhir said, 'One waits until the time when experts say that it will no longer grow. If that is the case, then there is full blood money for it according to the literal meaning of the *ḥadīth*. If it then grows, the fine is returned. Most scholars who are reported from say that there is a delay of a year. That is related from 'Alī, Zayd, 'Umar ibn 'Abd al-'Azīz, Shurayḥ, an-Nakha'ī, Qatādah, Mālik and the People of Opinion. Ash-Shāfi'ī did not assign a known term for that.'

If the tooth of an adult is pulled out and he takes the blood money and then it grows back, Mālik says that he does not have to return what he took. The Kufans say that he must return it if it re-grows. Ash-Shāfi'ī has two positions: returned and not returned because this growth is not normal and a ruling is not confirmed by something unusual. This is the position of our scholars. The Kufans hold to the view that it is replaced if it grows and so the money should be returned. The basis is the same as a child's tooth. Ash-Shāfi'ī said, 'If someone injures it and it grows soundly, then there is a full fine for it.' Ibn al-Mundhir said, 'This is the sounder of the two positions because each of them removed a tooth. The Prophet ﷺ designated five camels for a tooth.'

If a man removes the tooth of another man and its owner puts it back and it sticks, we think that there is nothing owed for it. Ash-Shāfi'ī said, 'He cannot return it since it is an impurity. Ibn al-Musayyab and 'Aṭā' said that. If he returns it, then he must redo every prayer he prayed because it is carrion. The same is true if his ear is cut off and then returned with hot blood and it sticks.' 'Aṭā' said, 'The ruler makes him remove it because he has attached something dead to himself.'

Ibn al-'Arabī said, 'This is an error. He was ignorant and it was hidden from him that restoring it in its form does not oblige the ruling [of it being carrion] because the impurity only existed in it by virtue of its separation [from the body], but now it is reconnected to it. The rulings of the *Sharī'ah* do not describe specific instances. The rulings simply derive from what Allah says.' What Ibn al-'Arabī related from 'Aṭā' differs from what Ibn al-Mundhir said. He said, 'There is disagreement about a tooth removed in retaliation which is then put back and grows. 'Aṭā' al-Khurāsānī and 'Aṭā' ibn Abī Rabāḥ said that there is nothing wrong with that.' Ath-Thawrī, Aḥmad and Isḥāq said that it must be removed because retaliation is shame. Ash-Shāfi'ī said, 'He cannot return it because it is an impurity and the ruler must compel him to remove it.'

If he has an extra tooth which is removed, there is arbitration about it. That is the position of the *fuqahā'* of the regions. Zayd ibn Thābit said that there is a third of the blood money for it. Ibn al-'Arabī said, 'There is no evidence for the determination. Arbitration is fairer.' Ibn al-Mundhir said, 'What is related from Zayd is not sound.' It is related that 'Alī said, 'If part of a tooth is broken, the victim is paid according to the amount of it that has been lost.' This is the view of Mālik, ash-Shāfi'ī and others.

This ends what Allah says regarding the limbs. He makes no mention of the lips and tongue. The majority say that full blood money is owed for the lips and there is half the blood money for one of them. There is no difference between the upper and lower lips. It is related from Zayd ibn Thābit, Sa'īd ibn al-Musayyab and az-Zuhrī that there is a third of blood money for an upper lip and two-thirds for a lower lip. Ibn al-Mundhir said, 'I take the first view based on the *marfū' ḥadīth* in which the Messenger of Allah ﷺ said, "Blood money is owed for the lips" and because there is blood money for the hands whose benefit varies. Any severing of the lips is analogous to that.'

As for the tongue, a *ḥadīth* from the Messenger of Allah ﷺ states: 'Blood money is owed for the tongue.' Scholars among the people of Madīnah, the people of Kufa, the People of Hadith and the People of Opinion agree on that view. Ibn al-Mundhir said that. They disagree about when a man cuts off part of another man's tongue and impairs his speech. Most of the people of knowledge say that they calculate the loss of speech according to the letters of the alphabet and calculate his portion of blood money accordingly. If he has completely lost his speech, full blood money is owed. This is the position of Mālik, ash-Shāfi'ī, Aḥmad, Isḥāq and the People of Opinion. Mālik says that there is no retaliation since it is impossible to be proportionate. If proportionality is possible, it is the basis of what is done.

There is disagreement about injury to the tongue of someone who is mute. Ash-Sha'bī, Mālik, the people of Madīnah, ath-Thawrī, the people of Iraq, ash-Shāfi'ī, Abū Thawr, an-Nu'mān and his two companions say that there is arbitration regarding it. Ibn al-Mundhir said, 'There are two aberrant views regarding it. One is that of an-Nakha'ī who says that full blood money is owed for it. The second, which is that of Qatādah, is that a third of blood money should be paid for it.' Ibn al-Mundhir said, 'The first view is sounder because it is the minimum of what is said.'

Ibn al-'Arabī said, 'Allah speaks of the major limbs and leaves the rest because of the possibility of making analogy with them. So there is retaliation for each limb when it is possible and it is not feared that death will result from the injury. That is the case with every limb which loses its use while its physical form remains: there is no retaliation, but blood money is owed, because proportionate retaliation is not possible.'

and retaliation for wounds.

This was discussed in al-Baqarah (2:178). There is no retaliation even for a potentially fatal wound nor for a wound that reaches a level which would normally entail retaliation if the blow is accidental, whatever the extent of it. Retaliation only applies in the case of deliberate wounds when it is possible to take retaliation. All of this is about deliberate wounding. Blood money is, however, owed for accidental injury just as it is for accidental homicide.

In *Ṣaḥīḥ Muslim*, Anas reported that the sister of ar-Rubayyi', Umm Ḥārithah, injured someone and there was a dispute and the people went to Prophet ﷺ. The Messenger of Allah ﷺ said, 'Retaliation. Retaliation.' Umm ar-Rubayyi' said, 'Messenger of Allah, will retaliation be taken from so-and-so? By Allah, retaliation will not be taken from her!' The Messenger of Allah ﷺ said, 'Glory be to Allah, Umm ar-Rubayyi'! Retaliation is what is in the Book of Allah.' She said, 'No! By Allah, retaliation will never be taken from her!' She kept at it until they accepted the blood money. Then the Messenger of Allah ﷺ said, 'There are certain slaves of Allah who, if they make an oath by Allah, He will fulfil it.'

The injured party was a girl and the injury consisted of a broken incisor. An-Nasā'ī also transmitted from Anas that his aunt broke the incisor of a girl and the Prophet ﷺ judged that there should be retaliation for it. Her brother, Anas ibn an-Naḍr, said, 'Is the incisor of so-and-so to be broken? No, by the One Who sent you with the truth, her incisor will not be broken!' He said, 'Before that they had asked her family for pardon and offered to pay a fine. When her brother, the uncle of Anas who was martyred in the Battle of Uḥud, swore, the people agreed to pardon. The Prophet ﷺ said, 'There are certain slaves of Allah who, if they make an oath by Allah, He will fulfil it.' Abū Dāwūd transmitted it and said, 'I heard Aḥmad ibn Ḥanbal being asked how retaliation is taken for a tooth and he replied, "It is filed."' There is no contradiction between the two *ḥadīth*s. It is possible that each of them swore and Allah fulfilled their oaths. This indicates the miracles (*karāmāt*) of the *awliyā'* as will be explained in the story of al-Khiḍr, Allah willing. We ask Allah that we may remain firm in our belief in their miracles and to make us follow faithfully in their footsteps without trial or temptation.

Scholars agree that '*a tooth for a tooth*' is about deliberate injury. If the blow is deliberate, there is retaliation based on the *ḥadīth* of Anas. They disagree about the deliberate breaking of bones. Mālik said that there is retaliation for everything in the body except for that which might be life-threatening, like the thigh, spine, *ma'mūnah* (head wound exposing cerebral membrane), *munaqqilah* (displaced bone) and *hāshimah* (skull fracture), for which there is blood money. The Kufans say that there is no retaliation for a broken bone, except a tooth, based on Allah's words, '*a tooth for a tooth*'. That is the position of al-Layth and ash-Shāfi'ī. Ash-Shāfi'ī said, 'No two breaks are ever the same and so retaliation is forbidden.'

Aṭ-Ṭaḥāwī said, 'They agree that there is no retaliation for skull injuries, and the same holds true for other bones.' Mālik's argument is based on the *ḥadīth* of Anas about the tooth which is a bone. So the same is true of other bones except for those about which it is agreed that there is no retaliation because of fear of loss of life. Ibn al-Mundhir said, 'Those who say that there is no retaliation in the case of bones differ from the *ḥadīth*. It is not permitted to resort to something similar when a report exists.' This is also indicated by Allah's words: *'If anyone oversteps the limits against you, overstep against him in the same way as he did to you'* (2:194) and: *'If you want to retaliate, retaliate to the same degree as the injury done to you.'* (16:126) What they agree on is not included in the *āyah*s. Allah knows best and He is the One Who grants success.

Abū 'Ubayd said, regarding the *ḥadīth* of the Prophet ﷺ about the *mūḍiḥah* (a wound that bares the bone) and other head wounds and Al-Aṣma'ī and others said that the first form of head wound is a *ḥāriṣah,* which is when the skin is slightly scratched. The verb *ḥaraṣa* is used when fullers make a hole in a garment which is called a *ḥarṣah.* Then there is the *bāḍi'ah,* which is when the cut penetrates the skin into the adjacent flesh. Then there is the *mutalāḥimah* which is when the the skin is penetrated but not so deeply as in the case of a *samḥāq.* A *samḥāq* is when the cut reaches the fine membrane between the flesh and the bone. Al-Wāqidī says that this is called *'milṭayy'* and others call it *'milṭāh'* which is mentioned in *ḥadīth.* Then there is the *mūḍiḥah* which is when the skin is removed or the penetration is such that the bone begins to appear. Abū 'Ubayd said that there is no retaliation for any cutting wound except for the *mūḍiḥah* because other head wounds have no defined limit. Blood money is owed for all other cutting wounds. Then there is the *hāshimah* which is when the bone is crushed. Then comes the *munaqqilah* which causes the bones to move when they are broken so that the thin bones fly off. Then comes the *ammah* or *ma'mūnah* which is a cut that reaches the brain (*umm ar-ra's*).

Abū 'Ubayd said that when the cut is made, the judgment against him for what he cut is made immediately according to where the cut reaches, without any delay. He said that in the case of other than cuts, we wait to see what the outcome will be and then give judgment. Abū 'Ubayd said, 'Where all cuts and all wounds are concerned our method is to await the outcome.' Hushaym related that Ḥuṣayn said that 'Umar ibn 'Abd al-'Azīz said, 'Wounds less than a *mūḍiḥah* are considerd scratches and they should be dealt with by reconciliation.' Al-Ḥasan al-Baṣrī said, 'There is no retaliation for less than a *mūḍiḥah.'* Mālik said, 'There is retaliation for anything less than a *mūḍiḥah*: a *milṭayy, dāmiyyah, bādi'ah* and the like.' That is similar to what the Kufans said and they added the *samḥāq*. Ibn al-Mundhir related it.

Abū 'Ubayd said that a *dāmiyyah* is a wound which bleeds but without the blood flowing from it. A *dāmi'ah* is one from which the blood flows. There is no retaliation for anything less than a *mūḍiḥah*. Al-Jawharī also said that a *dāmiyyah* is a wound which bleeds without blood flowing from it. Our scholars have said that a *dāmiyyah* is a wound which bleeds. There is no retaliation for wounds beyond a *mūḍiḥah*: the *hāshimah* which is to the bone, the *munaqqilah* – with the disagreement about it – the *ammah* which reaches the brain, and the *dāmighah* which penetrates to the brain. There is retaliation for a *hāshimah* wound to the body unless it is to a part which is might be life-threatening, such as the thigh and its like. In the case of a head *hāshimah*, Ibn al-Qāsim says that there is no retaliation for it because it might become a *munaqqilah*. Ashhab said that there is retaliation for it unless the bone moves and it becomes a *munaqqilah* in which case there is no retaliation.

In the case of extremities, retaliation must be taken at the joint unless that endangers life. Included within the idea of 'joints' are the parts of the nasal cartilage, ears, penis, eyelids and lips because they allow for determination. Two things are related about the tongue. There is retaliation for breaking bones unless it might prove fatal, like the bones of the chest, neck, spine, thigh and the like. There is retaliation for breaking the bones of the arms. Abū Bakr ibn Muḥammad ibn 'Amr ibn Ḥazm ruled about a man who had broken the thigh of another man that his thigh should be broken. 'Abd al-'Azīz ibn 'Abdullāh ibn Khālid ibn Usayd did that in Makkah. It is related that 'Umar ibn 'Abd al-'Azīz also did that. This is the position of the school of Mālik as we mentioned. He said, 'That is what is agreed upon with them. What is done in our land is that if a man strikes another man who defends himself with his hand which is broken, then retaliation is taken from him.'

Scholars have said that *shijāj* are wounds to the head and *jirāḥ* are wounds to the body. Scholars agree that there should be a fine for less than a *mūḍiḥah* according to what Ibn al-Mundhir mentioned. There is disagreement about what that fine should be. There are five head wounds less than a *mūḍiḥah*: *dāmiyyah, dāmi'ah, bādi'ah, mutalāḥimah* and *samḥāq*. Mālik, ash-Shāfi'ī, Aḥmad, Isḥāq and the People of Opinion say that there should be arbitration in the case of a *dāmiyyah, bādi'ah,* and *mutalāḥimah.* 'Abd ar-Razzāq mentioned that Zayd ibn Thābit said, 'There is one camel for a *dāmiyyah,* two camels for a *bādi'ah,* three camels for a *mutalāḥimah,* four camels for a *samḥāq*, and five camels for a *mūḍiḥah.* There are ten camels for a *hāshimah,* fifteen for a *munaqqilah,* and a third of blood money for a *ma'mūnah.* If a man is struck so that his mind is lost, there full blood money for that. There is a quarter blood money for an eyelid and a quarter for a nipple.'

Ibn al-Mundhir said, 'A similar position about a *samḥāq* as that of Zayd is related from 'Alī.' It is related that 'Umar and 'Uthmān said that there is half of the retaliation owed for a *mūḍiḥah* for it.' Al-Ḥasan al-Baṣrī, 'Umar ibn 'Abd al-'Azīz and an-Nakha'ī said that there is arbitration for it. That is what Mālik, ash-Shāfi'ī and Aḥmad also said. There is no disagreement among scholars that five camels should be paid for a *mūḍiḥah* based on the *ḥadīth* of 'Amr ibn Ḥazm which says that five camels are owed for a *mūḍiḥah.*

Scholars agree that a *mūḍiḥah* is a wound on the head and face. They disagree about whether a *mūḍiḥah* on the face is worse than on the head. It is related from Abū Bakr and 'Umar that they are considered the same. A group of the *Tābi'ūn* took their view and it is stated by ash-Shāfi'ī and Isḥāq. It is related from Sa'īd ibn al-Musayyab that a *mūḍiḥah* on the face is worth twice as much as one on the head. Aḥmad said, 'It is more fitting to have an increase for a *mūḍiḥah* on the face.' Mālik said, 'A *ma'mūnah, munaqqilah* and *mūḍiḥah* are confined to the head and face, and a *ma'mūnah* is only on the head when it reaches the brain.' He said, 'A *mūḍiḥah* is on the skull, and anything below it on the neck is not a *mūḍiḥah.*' Mālik said that the nose is not part of the head and there is no *mūḍiḥah* where it is concerned. The same is true of the lower jaw: there is no *mūḍiḥah* in its case either.

They disagree about a *mūḍiḥah* on other than the face or the head. Ashhab and Ibn al-Qāsim said, 'A *mūḍiḥah, munaqqilah* and *ma'mūnah* on the body is a subject to discretion. There is no known fine for it.' Ibn al-Mundhir said, 'This is the view of Mālik, ath-Thawrī, ash-Shāfi'ī, Aḥmad and Isḥāq.' We also say that. It is related from 'Aṭā' al-Khurāsānī that when a *mūḍiḥah* is on a person's body, there is a fine of twenty-five dinars for it. Abū 'Umar said, 'Mālik, ash-Shāfi'ī and their people agree that if someone inflicts two, three or more *mūḍiḥah*s or *ma'mūnah*s on a man with a single blow, full money is owed for all of them, even if they overlap and become one. We believe that no blood money is owed for a *hāshimah*, but there is arbitration.'

Ibn al-Mundhir said, 'I do not find any mention of a *hāshimah* in the books of the Madinans. Mālik said that there is discretion if a man accidentally breaks someone else's nose.' Al-Ḥasan al-Baṣrī said, 'Nothing is stipulated about a *hāshimah.'* Abū Thawr said, 'If there is disagreement about something, arbitration should take place concerning it. Ibn al-Mundhir said, 'Investigation indicates this since there is no *Sunnah* or consensus on it.' Qāḍī Abū al-Walīd al-Bājī said, 'The same is owed for it as for a *mūḍiḥah.* If it becomes a *munaqillah,* then fifteen are owed for it. If it becomes a *ma'mūnah,* a third of blood money is due for it.' Ibn al-Mundhir said, 'We found that most of the scholars whom we met, and from whom we conveyed, assign ten camels for a *hāshimah.'* We related this position from Zayd ibn Thābit, and it is the position of Qatādah, 'Ubaydullāh ibn al-Ḥasan and ash-Shāfi'ī. Ath-Thawrī and the People of Opinion said that a thousand dirhams are owed for it, meaning a tenth of the blood money.

As for the *munaqqilah,* Ibn al-Mundhir said, 'A *ḥadīth* has come from the Prophet ﷺ in which he said, "Fifteen camels are owed for a *munaqqilah."* There is a consensus among scholars on this.' Ibn al-Mundhir also said, 'All the scholars who are reported from say that a *munaqqilah* is a wound in which bones are moved.' Mālik, ash-Shāfi'ī, Aḥmad and the People of Opinion said that there is no retaliation in the case of a *munaqqilah,* and that is the position of Qatādah and Ibn Shubrumah. We related that Ibn az-Zubayr – although it is not firm from him – took retaliation for a *munaqqilah.* Ibn al-Mundhir said, 'The first is more appropriate because I do not know of anyone who disagrees about that.'

As for a *ma'mūnah,* Ibn al-Mundhir said, 'A *ḥadīth* has come from the Prophet ﷺ in which he said, "A third of blood money is owed for a *ma'mūnah."'* Most people agree on that position and we do not know of anyone who disagrees with it except for Makḥūl who said, 'If a *ma'mūnah* is deliberate, two-thirds of the blood money is owed for it, and if it is accidental, then there is a third for it.' This is an aberrant view. I take the first position. There is disagreement about whether there should be retaliation for a *ma'mūnah.* Most scholars say that there is no retaliation for it. It is related that Ibn az-Zubayr did take retaliation for it. People deny that. 'Aṭā' said, 'We do not know of anyone who took retaliation for it before Ibn az-Zubayr.'

As for a *jā'ifah* (an internal wound), a third of the blood money is owed for it, based on the *ḥadīth* of 'Amr ibn Ḥazm. There is no disagreement about that except for what was related from Makḥūl who said, 'If it is deliberate, two-thirds of the blood money is owed for it, and if it is accidental, then a third is owed for it.' A *jā'ifah* is anything that penetrates, even if it is only a needle. If it goes right through from one side to the other, they consider that to be two *jā'ifah*s and two-thirds of the blood money is owed. Ashhab said, 'Abū Bakr aṣ-Siddīq judged that if a *jā'ifah* penetrates right through to the other side, the blood money for two *jā'ifahs* is due.' 'Aṭā', Mālik. Ash-Shāfi'ī and all the People of Opinion say that there is no retaliation for a *jā'ifah*.' Ibn al-Mundhir said, 'That is what we say.'

There is disagreement about whether there should be retaliation for a slap and similar things. Al-Bukhārī mentioned that Abū Bakr, 'Alī, Ibn az-Zubayr, and Suwayd ibn Muqarrin judged that there should be. The same is related from 'Uthmān and Khālid ibn al-Walīd. It is the view of ash-Sha'bī and a group of the people of *ḥadīth*. Al-Layth said, 'If it is a slap to the eye, there is no retaliation out of fear for the eye of the slapper and the ruler punishes him. If the slap is on the cheek, there is retaliation. Another group say that there is no retaliation and that is related from al-Ḥasan and Qatādah, and it is the position of Mālik, the Kufans and ash-Shāfi'ī. Mālik argued by saying, 'A slap by someone sick and weak is not the same as the slap of a strong person. A black slave does not slap like a man of substance. There is discretion employed in every instance since we are ignorant of the strength of the slap.'

They disagree about retaliation for the blow of a whip. Al-Layth and al-Ḥasan said that there is retaliation for it and more for assault. Ibn al-Qāsim said that there is retaliation while the Kufans and ash-Shāfi'ī say that there is no retaliation unless a wound is caused. Ash-Shāfi'ī said that if there is a wound, there is arbitration. Ibn al-Mundhir said, 'In the case of a blow from a whip, staff or stone which is less than fatal and is deliberate, there is retaliation.' This is the view of a group of the People of Hadith. We find in al-Bukhārī that 'Umar took retaliation by striking the perpetrator with a scourge. 'Alī ibn Abī Ṭālib took retaliation for three blows of a whip. Shurayḥ took retaliation for a whip blow that caused a scratch. Ibn Baṭṭāl said, 'The *ḥadīth* of the Prophet ﷺ forcing the people of a house to take the medicine [they had forced someone else to take] is evidence for those who assign retaliation for every pain, even if it is not an actual wound.'

There is disagreement about the blood money for wounds to women. We find in the *Muwaṭṭā'* that Mālik reported from Sa'īd ibn al-Musayyab: 'The blood-money for a woman is the same as that for a man up to one third of the blood-money. Her finger is like his finger, her tooth is like his tooth, her injury which lays bare the bone is like his, and her head wound which splinters the bone is like his.' Mālik said, 'If what she is owed exceeds a third of the blood-money of a man, she is given up to half of the blood-money of a man.'

Ibn al-Mundhir said, 'We related this position from Zayd ibn Thābit. It is also that of Sa'īd ibn al-Musayyab, 'Umar ibn 'Abd al-'Azīz, 'Urwah ibn az-Zubayr, az-Zuhrī, Qatādah, Ibn Hurmuz, Mālik, Aḥmad ibn Ḥanbal, and Ibn al-Mājishūn.' One group said that it is half that of a man in any case, whatever injury it is. We related that position from 'Alī ibn Abī Ṭālib. That is the position of ath-Thawrī, ash-Shāfi'ī, Abū Thawr, an-Nu'mān and their companions. They argue that when they agree on a lot, which is full blood money, then the same agreement applies to a lesser amount. We say that.

Qāḍī 'Abd al-Wahhāb said that there is arbitration for anything that is a matter of beauty but not of use, such eyebrows, the beard, hair on the head, and the chests and buttocks of men. One assesses the value of the injured party according to what it would be if he were a healthy slave and then one assesses how much the injury would reduce his price and that is made a part of the blood money, however much it is. Ibn al-Mundhir related that from all the people of scholarship who are recorded. He added, 'In it one accepts the view of two trustworthy men among experts in that field.' It is also said that the statement of one man is accepted. Allah knows best.

This is a summary of the rulings on limbs contained in the meaning of this *āyah*. It is brief but adequate. Allah is the One Who grants success by His grace and favour.

But if anyone forgoes that as a *ṣadaqah*, it will act as expiation for him.

If someone forgoes retaliation, and pardons, that is expiation for him, meaning for the one who forgoes it. It is also said that it is expiation for the one who caused the injury who is not harmed for it in the Next World because it takes the place of the right and the forgoer is rewarded. Ibn 'Abbās mentioned both views. Most of the Companions and later people take the first view. The second is reported from Ibn 'Abbās and Mujāhid. Something different was related from Ibrāhīm an-Nakha'ī and ash-Sha'bī. The first view is more evident because it refers to what was mentioned, which is '*anyone*'.

Abū ad-Dardā' said that the Prophet ﷺ said, 'There is no Muslim who is afflicted by anything in his body and then he forgoes his right to retaliation from him [the one who inflicted that] without Allah elevating him one degree and removing one error from him.' Ibn al-'Arabī said, 'The statement of someone who says that if the injured party pardons, Allah pardons him, is not based on any evidence and so it has no meaning.'

وَقَفَّيْنَا عَلَىٰٓ ءَاثَٰرِهِم بِعِيسَى ٱبْنِ مَرْيَمَ مُصَدِّقًا لِّمَا بَيْنَ يَدَيْهِ مِنَ
ٱلتَّوْرَىٰةِ ۖ وَءَاتَيْنَٰهُ ٱلْإِنجِيلَ فِيهِ هُدًى وَنُورٌ وَمُصَدِّقًا لِّمَا بَيْنَ يَدَيْهِ
مِنَ ٱلتَّوْرَىٰةِ وَهُدًى وَمَوْعِظَةً لِّلْمُتَّقِينَ ﴿٤٦﴾ وَلْيَحْكُمْ أَهْلُ
ٱلْإِنجِيلِ بِمَآ أَنزَلَ ٱللَّهُ فِيهِ ۚ وَمَن لَّمْ يَحْكُم بِمَآ أَنزَلَ ٱللَّهُ فَأُو۟لَٰٓئِكَ هُمُ
ٱلْفَٰسِقُونَ ﴿٤٧﴾

46-47 And We sent 'Īsā son of Maryam following in their footsteps, confirming the Torah that came before him. We gave him the Gospel containing guidance and light, confirming the Torah that came before it, and as guidance and admonition for the godfearing. The people of the Gospel should judge by what Allah sent down in it. Those who do not judge by what Allah has sent down, such people are deviators.

It means: We caused 'Īsā to follow in the footsteps of the Prophets who submitted, confirming that which was true in the Torah before him and the obligation to act by it until it is abrogated. '*Confirming*' is in the accusative as a *ḥāl* modifying 'Īsā. There are two possible aspects to the second '*confirming*'. It may refer to 'Īsā and is then added to the first '*confirming*', and it may also modify the word '*Gospel*', and so would imply, 'We gave him the Gospel containing guidance, light and confirmation.' '*The godfearing*' are mentioned because they are the ones who will benefit from it. It may also be in the nominative as added to 'containing guidance and light'.

The people of the Gospel should judge by what Allah sent down in it.

Al-A'mash and Ḥamzah read '*judge*' as '*yaḥkumu*' with a *lām* attached to the beginning, meaning 'in order to', and the others read it in the apocopate form: *yaḥkum*, as a command. In the first reading, the words are connected to '*We gave him*' and it is not permitted to stop, implying 'We gave him the Gospel so that his people would judge by what Allah revealed in it.' If it is read as a command, then it is like the words: '*Judge between them.*' (5:49), starting a new sentence meaning: 'Let the people of the Gospel judge at that time.' Now it is abrogated. It is said that it is a command to the Christians to now believe in Muḥammad ﷺ. The obligation to believe in him is found in the Gospel. Abrogation is conceivable in secondary rulings, not in basic principles. Makkī said, 'The command is preferred because the majority have it and because what comes after it is a threat which indicates that it is an obligation from Allah Almighty for the people of the Gospel.' An-Naḥḥās said, 'What I believe to be correct is that they are both good readings because Allah only revealed a Scripture in order for it to be acted on and He commanded that people should act by what is in it. So both are sound.'

وَأَنزَلْنَآ إِلَيْكَ ٱلْكِتَٰبَ بِٱلْحَقِّ مُصَدِّقًا لِّمَا بَيْنَ يَدَيْهِ مِنَ ٱلْكِتَٰبِ
وَمُهَيْمِنًا عَلَيْهِ فَٱحْكُم بَيْنَهُم بِمَآ أَنزَلَ ٱللَّهُ وَلَا تَتَّبِعْ أَهْوَآءَهُمْ عَمَّا
جَآءَكَ مِنَ ٱلْحَقِّ لِكُلٍّ جَعَلْنَا مِنكُمْ شِرْعَةً وَمِنْهَاجًا وَلَوْ شَآءَ ٱللَّهُ
لَجَعَلَكُمْ أُمَّةً وَٰحِدَةً وَلَٰكِن لِّيَبْلُوَكُمْ فِى مَآ ءَاتَىٰكُمْ فَٱسْتَبِقُوا۟ ٱلْخَيْرَٰتِ
إِلَى ٱللَّهِ مَرْجِعُكُمْ جَمِيعًا فَيُنَبِّئُكُم بِمَا كُنتُمْ فِيهِ تَخْتَلِفُونَ ﴿٤٨﴾

48 And We have sent down the Book to you with truth, confirming and conserving the previous Books. So judge between them by what Allah has sent down and do not follow their whims and desires, deviating from the Truth that has come to you. We have appointed a law and a practice for every one of you. Had Allah willed, He would have made you a single community, but He wanted to test you regarding what has come to you. So compete with each other in doing good. Every one of you will return to Allah and He will inform you regarding the things about which you differed.

And We have sent down the Book to you with truth, confirming and conserving the previous Books.

This is addressed to Muḥammad ﷺ. The *'Book'* is the Qur'ān. The word *'truth'* here means commanding the truth. The adjective *'conserving'* implies being above them and elevated over them. This validates the interpretation of those who say there is preference in terms of the size of the reward, as is indicated in *al-Fātiḥah*. Ibn al-Ḥaṣṣār prefers this in *Kitab Sharḥ as-Sunnah*. We mentioned what he said in *Sharḥ al-Asmā' al-Ḥusnā*. Qatādah said that the word *muhaymin* means 'testifying to', or 'conserving.' It is said that it means 'preserving'. Al-Ḥasan said it also means 'confirming' as in the poem:

The Book confirms (*muhaymin*) our Prophet
and those with intelligence recognise the truth.

Ibn 'Abbās said it means ensuring it. Sa'īd ibn Jubayr said, 'The Qur'ān secures the Books before it.' Ibn 'Abbās and al-Ḥasan that *muhaymin* means trustworthy. Al-Mubarrad said that its root is *mu'aymin* and the *hamzah* has changed into a *hā'*. Az-Zajjāj and Abū 'Alī said that it is declined and the verb is *haymana yuhīmanu, haymanah*. A person who is *muhaymin* is trustworthy. Al-Jawharī said that it is someone who makes another person safe from fear and that its root has two *hamzahs*. The verb is used for someone protecting someone else, as Abū 'Ubayd said. Mujāhid and Ibn Muḥayṣin recited '*muhayman*'. Mujāhid said that it means that Muḥammad ﷺ is the conserver of the Qur'ān.

So judge between them by what Allah has sent down

Judgment is mandatory. It is said that this abrogated the choice given in the earlier *āyah*. It is also said that this does not make it mandatory but means: 'Judge between them if you wish' since it is not obliged for us to judge between them if they are not *dhimmīs*. The issue of judging the *dhimmīs* was discussed earlier. It is said that it means: 'Judge between creatures. This is mandatory.'

do not follow their whims and desires

This means: do not act by their whims and desires contrary to the truth that has come to you, in other words: 'Do not abandon judging by the truth and rulings that Allah has made clear in the Qur'ān.' The noun *'ahwā'* is the plural of *hawā* and its meaning was discussed in *al-Baqarah* (2:87). Allah forbade him to follow what they desired. It indicates the falsity of someone who says that the value of wine is estimated against someone who destroys it, on the basis that it is not their property so that someone who destroys it is liable. This is because obliging liability for its destruction would be ruling by the whims of the Jews. We are commanded differently to that.

We have appointed a law and a practice for every one of you.

This indicates our disconnection from any earlier *Sharī'ahs*. *Shir'ah* and *sharī'ah* means a clear road which leads to salvation. Linguistically the word *sharī'ah* means a road leading to water. The *Sharī'ah* is what Allah has legislated for His slaves with respect to the *dīn*. He prescribed (*shara'a*) the path for them. *Shāri'* is the main road and *shir'ah* is also a string of a musical instrument. The plural is *shira'* and *shir'*, and *shirā'* is the plural of plurals as Abū 'Ubayd said. It is a shared noun. *Minhāj* is an unobstructed path, in other words it is clear. It can be *nahj* and *manhaj*. A poet said:

If someone has doubt, this is an entry
to quenching water and an unobstructed (*nahj*) path.

Abū al-'Abbās Muḥammad ibn Yazīd said that the word *sharī'ah* means the beginning of the road and *minhāj* is the illuminated path. Ibn 'Abbās, al-Ḥasan and others said that it is a *sunnah* and a way.

The meaning of the *āyah* is that He designated the Torah for its people, the Gospel for its people and the Qur'ān for its people. This is in respect of laws and acts of worship. The unifying basis is *tawḥīd* without dispute. Mujāhid said, '*Shir'ah* and *minhaj* both designate the *dīn* of Muḥammad ﷺ which abrogates others.'

Had Allah willed, He would have made you a single community

He would have made your *Sharī'ah* one so that you would all be following the truth. So it is clear that He intended difference as some people believe and others reject. This is a test. He made your Laws differ in order to test you. The verb *ibtilā'* means testing.

So compete with each other in doing good.

Race each other to acts of obedience. This indicates that it is better to perform obligations sooner rather than later. There is no disagreement about that regarding all acts of obedience except for the prayer at the beginning of its time. Abū Ḥanīfah thinks that it is better to delay it. The general meaning of the *āyah* indicates that and aṭ-Ṭabarī stated it. It indicates that it is better to fast on a journey than to not fast. All of this was discussed in *al-Baqarah* (2:148). '*He will inform you regarding the things about which you differed*' and remove all doubts.

وَأَنِ ٱحْكُم بَيْنَهُم بِمَآ أَنزَلَ ٱللَّهُ وَلَا تَتَّبِعْ أَهْوَآءَهُمْ وَٱحْذَرْهُمْ أَن يَفْتِنُوكَ عَنۢ
بَعْضِ مَآ أَنزَلَ ٱللَّهُ إِلَيْكَ فَإِن تَوَلَّوْا۟ فَٱعْلَمْ أَنَّمَا يُرِيدُ ٱللَّهُ أَن يُصِيبَهُم بِبَعْضِ ذُنُوبِهِمْ
وَإِنَّ كَثِيرًا مِّنَ ٱلنَّاسِ لَفَٰسِقُونَ ﴿٤٩﴾

49 Judge between them by what Allah has sent down and do not follow their whims and desires. And beware of them lest they lure you away from some of what Allah has sent down to you. If they turn their backs, then know that Allah wants to afflict them with some of their wrong actions. Many of mankind are deviators.

Judge between them by what Allah has sent down and do not follow their whims and desires.

This was discussed above as well as the fact that it abrogates having a choice about it. Ibn al-'Arabī said, 'This is a wide claim. There are four preconditions for abrogation. One of them is knowing the relative dates of revelation, which was first and which later. That is not known in the case of these two *āyahs* and so it is impossible to say which one abrogates the other. So the matter remains unchanged.'

Responding to this, we already mentioned from Abū Ja'far an-Naḥḥās that this *āyah* was revealed later and so it abrogates unless it is implied that the words: '*judge between them by what Allah has sent down*', implies 'if you so wish', because the matter of choice regarding it has already been discussed. So the idea of choice is implied in the later words because the earlier words indicate it by the fact that it is added to them. Therefore, the ruling regarding choice is also applicable to the previous ruling so that they both share in the matter of choosing. The later words cannot be considered separate from what preceded them since that would be meaningless and unsound. On this basis Allah's words: '*judge between them by what Allah has sent down*', are connected to His prior words: '*But if you do judge, judge between them justly*' (5:42) and His words: '*If they come to you, you can either judge between them or turn away from them.*' (5:42) It therefore means: 'Judge according to that criterion if you so wish and choose to.' So none of that is abrogated because what abrogates is not connected to what it abrogates by being added to it. The Prophet ﷺ had a choice regarding that and having that choice has not been not abrogated. Makkī said that.

The '*an*' before '*judge*' is in the position of the accusative case [by having the sense of an object] as added to '*the Book*' and means: 'We revealed to you that you should judge between them according to what Allah has revealed,' meaning according to the judgment of Allah He has sent down to you in His Book.

And beware of them lest they lure you away from some of what Allah has sent down to you.

Ibn Isḥāq reported that Ibn 'Abbās said, 'Some of the rabbis gathered, and they included Ibn Ṣūriyā, Ka'b ibn Asad, Ibn Ṣālūbā and Sha's ibn 'Adī. They said, "Let us go to Muḥammad. Perhaps we will manage to lure him away from his *dīn*. He is a human being." They went to him and said, "Muḥammad, you know that we are the rabbis of the Jews. If we follow you, none of the Jews will oppose you. There is a dispute between us and some people. We will present it to you for judgment. Give judgment in our favour against them and we will believe in you." The Messenger of Allah ﷺ refused and the *āyah* was revealed.'

The root of the word *fitnah* is testing and then the meaning varies. Here it means to 'block you and turn you aside'. *Fitnah* can mean idolatry as in Allah's words: *'Fitnah is worse than killing'* (2:217) and *'Fight them until there is no fitnah'* (8:39). *Fitnah* can also mean trial or test, as in Allah's words: *'Do not make us a fitnah for those who reject.'* (10:85) *Fitnah* can also signify barring people from the path, as in this *āyah.*

The repetition of the verb '*judge*' is then for emphasis or it may refer to circumstances and rulings. The command is to judge in every case by what Allah has revealed. The *āyah* contains evidence that it is permitted for the Prophet ﷺ to forget because Allah says: '*...lest they lure you*' and that would result from forgetfulness, not deliberation. It is said that it is addressed to the Prophet ﷺ while others are meant. Allah willing, this will be explained in *al-An'ām*. The phrase: '*...some of what Allah has sent down*' here means all that Allah has sent down to you. The word '*some*' (*ba'ḍ*) can also mean 'all'. [POEM] Ibn al-'Arabī said, 'What is sound is that '*ba'ḍ*' has its normal meaning in this *āyah.* It refers to the *āyah* of stoning or the judgment which they wanted. They did not intend to tempt him away from everything.' Allah knows best.

'If they turn their backs' – and refuse to let you judge – *'know that Allah wants to afflict them with some of their wrong actions.'* He will punish them with exile, *jizyah* and killing as happened. He says '*some*' because that is sufficient to destroy them. '*Many of mankind*' here refers to the Jews.

أَفَحُكْمَ ٱلْجَٰهِلِيَّةِ يَبْغُونَ ۚ وَمَنْ أَحْسَنُ مِنَ ٱللَّهِ حُكْمًا لِّقَوْمٍ يُوقِنُونَ ۝٥٠

50 Do they then seek the judgment of the Time of Ignorance? Who could be better at giving judgment than Allah for people with certainty?

Do they then seek the judgment of the Time of Ignorance?

The meaning is that in the days of the Jāhiliyyah the rulings for the nobility were different from the rulings for ordinary people, as is stated in more than one place. The Jews limited the *ḥudūd* to the weak and poor and did not carry them out on the strong and rich and in that respect they resembled the Jāhiliyyah.

Sufyān ibn 'Uyaynah reported that when they asked Ṭāwūs about a man preferring one of his children over another, he recited this *āyah.* He said, 'No one should prefer one child over another (in gifts). If he does so, his desire is not carried out and the action is void.' This is the position of the literalists. The same is reported from Aḥmad ibn Ḥanbal. Ath-Thawrī, Ibn al-Mubārak and

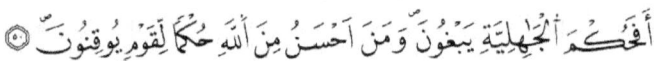

Isḥāq disliked it but said that if someone does it, what he wants is carried out and not rejected. Mālik, ath-Thawrī, al-Layth, ash-Shāfi'ī and the people of opinion permitted it, using as evidence what Abū Bakr did in giving a gift to 'Ā'ishah and not his other children and the words of the Prophet ﷺ, 'Take back your gift' and 'Ask someone other than me to bear witness to this.'

The first group cite as evidence for not doing this the words of the Prophet ﷺ to Bashīr, 'Do you have any other children?' When he said, 'Yes,' he asked, 'Did you give all of them the same as this?' When he answered, 'No,' he said ﷺ, 'Do not make me a witness for I will not be a witness to an injustice.' One variant has 'I only bear witness to a right.' They say, 'Something that is an injustice and not right is wrong and not permitted. When he said ﷺ, "Ask someone other than me to bear witness to this," that was not permission for someone to give testimony, but rather to prevent it because the Prophet ﷺ called it an injustice and refused to attest to it. Therefore, it is not possible for any Muslim to testify to that in any way. What Abū Bakr did is not contrary to the words of the Prophet ﷺ. It is possible that he had given his other children equivalent gifts.'

If it is said that the basic principle is that a person has absolute disposal of his property, it is confirmed that the general principle is indeed universal, but the actuality is specific and may differ from that basis [in the ruling] in such a way that there is no contradiction between them, as is the case with the general and specific in other instances. In the *uṣūl*, the sound position is that the undefined general ruling is based on the defined particular ruling. A consequence of that action may be filial disobedience, which is the greatest of wrong actions and is forbidden, and what leads to the forbidden is prohibited. That is why the Prophet ﷺ said, 'Fear Allah and be fair between your children.' An-Nu'mān said, 'My father went and took back that *ṣadaqah*.' It is, nevertheless, agreed that a father should not take back *ṣadaqah*, so the words of the Prophet, 'Take back your gift' mean to cancel it. Cancelling it would invalidate the original gift as in the words of the Prophet ﷺ, 'If someone does any action against what we have commanded, it is rescinded,' meaning cancelled. All of this is clear and strong. Open preference [between children] is prohibited.

Ibn Wahhāb and an-Nakha'ī recited '*fa-ḥukmu*' in the nominative, meaning 'they seek it' and the *hā'* (it) is elided. It implies: 'Is the judgment of the Time of Ignorance the judgment they seek?' Al-Ḥasan, Qatādah and al-A'mash recite '*ḥakama*' referring to the common reading since what is meant is not '*ḥakam*' (judge), but '*ḥukm*' (judgment). It is as if Allah were saying, 'Do they seek the judgment of a judge of the Time of Ignorance?' *Ḥakam* and *ḥākim* both mean 'judge'. It is as if Allah means a soothsayer and those like them who were the judges of the time of the Jāhiliyyah and so what is meant by that is general and generic since it does not mean a specific judge. Ibn 'Āmir recited '*tabghūna*' in the second person rather than the third person, '*yabghūna*', that the rest have.

Who could be better at giving judgment than Allah for people with certainty?

This is a question which demands denial, meaning, 'No one could be better.' It is inceptive and predicate and the noun '*judgment*' is in the accusative for clarification. The expression '*people with certainty*' means 'some of the people of certainty.'

يَٰٓأَيُّهَا ٱلَّذِينَ ءَامَنُواْ لَا تَتَّخِذُواْ ٱلۡيَهُودَ وَٱلنَّصَٰرَىٰٓ أَوۡلِيَآءَۘ بَعۡضُهُمۡ أَوۡلِيَآءُ بَعۡضٖۚ
وَمَن يَتَوَلَّهُم مِّنكُمۡ فَإِنَّهُۥ مِنۡهُمۡۗ إِنَّ ٱللَّهَ لَا يَهۡدِي ٱلۡقَوۡمَ ٱلظَّٰلِمِينَ ٥١

51 You who believe! do not take the Jews and Christians as your friends; they are the friends of one another. Any of you who takes them as friends is one of them. Allah does not guide wrongdoing people.

You who have believe! do not take the Jews and Christians as your friends; they are the friends of one another.

This indicates that this bar on befriending is part of the *Sharī'ah.* It was already clarified in *Āl 'Imrān* (3:118). Then it is said that the people addressed are the hypocrites and so it means: 'O you who believe outwardly!' They used to befriend the idolaters and tell them the secrets of the Muslims.

It is said that it was revealed about Abū Lubābah, as 'Ikrimah said. As-Suddī said, 'It was revealed about the expedition of Uḥud when the Muslims were so afraid that the some of them befriended the Jews and Christians. It is also said that it was revealed about 'Ubādah ibn aṣ-Ṣāmit and 'Abdullāh ibn Ubayy ibn Salūl. 'Ubādah freed himself from the friendship of the Jews and Ibn Ubayy maintained it, saying that he feared that there would be a reverse of fortune. The phrase: '*they are friends of one another*' indicates that that the *Sharī'ah* affirmed friendship between them so that Jews inherited from the Christians and vice versa.

Any of you who takes them as friends is one of them.

This means anyone who supports them against the Muslims. If he does that, Allah makes it clear that the judgment of him is the same as them. It forbids a

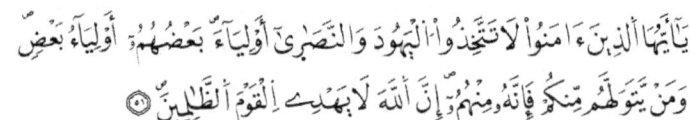

Muslim from inheriting from an apostate. The one who befriended them was Ibn Ubayy. This ruling, however, will remain until the Day of Rising. Allah Almighty says: *'Do not rely on those who do wrong thus causing the Fire to afflict you'* (11:113) and: *'The believers should not take the unbelievers as friends rather than the believers.'* (3:28), and: *'Do not take any outside yourselves as intimates.'* (3:118) This was already discussed. *'Friends of one another'* means with regards to help and support. Such a person is one of them because He is opposing Allah and His Messenger just as they do, and the Fire is obliged for him as it is for them. He is one of them.

فَتَرَى الَّذِينَ فِي قُلُوبِهِم مَّرَضٌ يُسَارِعُونَ فِيهِمْ يَقُولُونَ نَخْشَىٰ أَن تُصِيبَنَا دَآئِرَةٌ
فَعَسَى اللَّهُ أَن يَأْتِيَ بِالْفَتْحِ أَوْ أَمْرٍ مِّنْ عِندِهِۦ فَيُصْبِحُوا عَلَىٰ مَا أَسَرُّوا فِي أَنفُسِهِمْ
نَادِمِينَ ﴿٥٢﴾ يَقُولُ الَّذِينَ ءَامَنُوا أَهَٰؤُلَاءِ الَّذِينَ أَقْسَمُوا بِاللَّهِ جَهْدَ أَيْمَانِهِمْ إِنَّهُمْ
لَمَعَكُمْ حَبِطَتْ أَعْمَالُهُمْ فَأَصْبَحُوا خَاسِرِينَ ﴿٥٣﴾

52-53 Yet you see those with sickness in their hearts rushing to them, saying, 'We fear the wheel of fate may turn against us.' But it may well be that Allah will bring about victory or some other contingency from Him. Then they will deeply regret their secret thoughts. Those who believe say, 'Are these the people who swore by Allah, with their most earnest oaths, that they were with you?' Their actions have come to nothing and they now are losers.

Yet you see those with sickness in their hearts rushing to them, saying, 'We fear the wheel of fate may turn against us.'

The sickness they have is doubt and hypocrisy which was mentioned in *al-Baqarah* (2:10). What is meant is Ibn Ubayy and his companions who befriended and helped them. They say: *'We fear the wheel of fate may turn against us,'* meaning that we may, for instance, suffer drought and that if that happens they will not prefer us and give us their surplus, or that if the Jews are victorious over the Muslims, Muḥammad ﷺ will not remain in charge. This view is similar in meaning, because it is as things change and means fear of a change in authority. That is indicated by His words: *'...it may be that Allah will bring about victory.'* A poet says:

Turn from yourself the fate decreed.
    Changes in fortune will occur.

It means that the vicissitudes of time will go from one people to another.

But it may well be that Allah will bring about victory or some other contingency from Him.

There is disagreement about the meaning of '*fatḥ*' (victory). It is said that it means decision and judgment according to Qatādah and others. Ibn 'Abbās said, 'Allah brought victory and the fighters of the Banū Qurayẓah were killed and their dependants captured and the Banū an-Nadir exiled.' Abū 'Alī said that it refers to the conquest of the land of the idolaters by the Muslims. As-Suddī says that it means the conquest of Makkah. *'Some other contingency from Him'* is a reference to *jizyah* according to as-Suddī. Al-Ḥasan said that it refers to the exposure of the hypocrites and their names and the command to kill them. It is said that it is fertility and wealth for the Muslims.

Then they will deeply regret their secret thoughts.

They will regret befriending the unbelievers when they see that Allah has granted victory to the believers and when they see the consequences of it at death, when they will be given the news of the punishment.

Those who believe say,

The people of Madīnah and Syria read this without the *wāw* (and) as *'yaqūla'* whereas Abū 'Amr and Ibn Abī Isḥāq read it *'wa yaqūla'* added to *'an ya'tā'* according to most grammarians. It implies: 'Perhaps Allah will bring victory and perhaps they will say.' It is said that it is joined in meaning since it means 'Perhaps Allah will bring victory' since it is not permitted to *say "asā' Zaydun an ya'tā wa yaqūma 'Amr'* because the meaning is not sound when you say, '*'asā' Zaydun an yaqūma 'Amr'*. But if you say, '*'asā' an yaqūma Zaydun wa ya'tā 'Amr'*, it is good. If you advance *'an ya'tā'* beside *"asā'*, it is good because it implies: 'perhaps he will come and perhaps he will say.' {WORD ORDER+POEMS} It is also permitted to make *'an ya'tā'* an appositive for the Name of Allah and so it implies: 'Perhaps Allah will bring about' and perhaps those who believe ill say.' The Kufans read it *'wa yaqūlu'*, starting a new sentence.

'Are these the people who swore by Allah,

'The people' here are the hypocrites. They swear their strongest oaths. The believers will say this to the Jews by way of rebuke: 'Are those the ones who swore the most earnest oaths by Allah that they would help you against Muḥammad?' It is also possible that the believers are speaking to one another after the hypocrites have been exposed by Allah.

Their actions have come to nothing

This is because their actions were invalidated by their hypocrisy and they have lost any reward. It is said that they become losers by befriending the Jews which brought them no benefit after the Jews were killed and exiled.

يَٰٓأَيُّهَا ٱلَّذِينَ ءَامَنُواْ مَن يَرْتَدِدْ مِنكُمْ عَن دِينِهِۦ فَسَوْفَ يَأْتِي ٱللَّهُ بِقَوْمٍ يُحِبُّهُمْ وَيُحِبُّونَهُۥٓ
أَذِلَّةٍ عَلَى ٱلْمُؤْمِنِينَ أَعِزَّةٍ عَلَى ٱلْكَٰفِرِينَ يُجَٰهِدُونَ فِي سَبِيلِ ٱللَّهِ وَلَا يَخَافُونَ لَوْمَةَ
لَآئِمٍ ذَٰلِكَ فَضْلُ ٱللَّهِ يُؤْتِيهِ مَن يَشَآءُ وَٱللَّهُ وَٰسِعٌ عَلِيمٌ ﴿٥٦﴾

54 You who believe! if any of you renounce your *dīn*, Allah will bring forward a people whom He loves and who love Him, humble to the believers, fierce to the unbelievers, who strive in the Way of Allah and do not fear the blame of any censurer. That is the unbounded favour of Allah which He gives to whoever He wills. Allah is Boundless, All-Knowing.

You who believe! if any of you renounce your *dīn*,

The people of Madīnah and Syria read it as '*yartadid*' whereas the others read it as '*yartadda*'. This *āyah* is an example of the inimitability of the Qur'ān. The Prophet ﷺ informed us about their apostasy which did not occur while he was alive, and so it was an aspect of the unseen and only occurred later after his death. Ibn Isḥāq said, 'When the Messenger of Allah ﷺ died, the Arabs apostatised except for three mosques: Madīnah, Makkah and Jawathā. They fell into two groups in their apostasy: one group cast aside the entire *Sharī'ah* and left it completely and one group abandoned the obligation of *zakāt* while acknowledging the obligation of the rest of it, saying, "We will fast and pray but not pay *zakāt*." Abū Bakr fought all of them. He sent Khālid ibn al-Walīd against them with his armies and he fought and captured them as is well known from the histories.'

Allah will bring forward a people whom He loves and who love Him,

Al-Ḥasan, Qatādah and others said that it was revealed about Abū Bakr aṣ-Ṣiddīq and his household. As-Suddī said that it was revealed about the Anṣār. It is said that it indicates some people who did not exist at the time of the revelation of the *āyah* and Abū Bakr fought the people of *Riddah* with them. They were some of the tribes of Yemen from Kindah and Bajīlah and some of Ashja'.

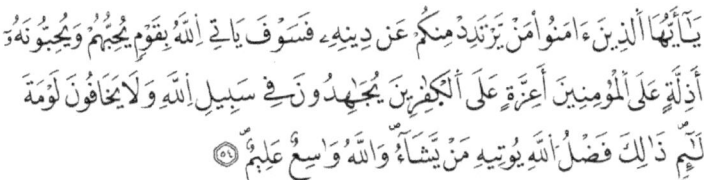

It is also said that it was revealed about the Ash'arites. It is reported that shortly after it was revealed, the Ash'ari brothers and the tribes of Yemen came by sea. They endured affliction in Islam during the lifetime of the Messenger of Allah ﷺ. The conquest of Iraq in the time of 'Umar was mostly carried out by the tribes of the Yemen. This is the soundest of what is said about this, and Allah knows best. Al-Ḥakim Abū 'Abdallāh reported in *al-Mustadrak* that when this was revealed, the Messenger of Allah ﷺ pointed at Abū Mūsā al-Ash'arī and said, 'They are these people.' Al-Qushayrī said, 'So it is the followers of Abū al-Ḥasan from his people who are meant, because when someone is named after the place he comes from that also includes his followers.'

humble to the believers, fierce to the unbelievers,

'*Humble*' and '*fierce*' are adjectives describing the '*people*' referred to. They show kindness and mercy to the believers and are kind and gentle with them. *Adhillah* is taken from the plural of *dhalūl*, which refers to an animal that is tractable and easy to lead. They are harsh to the unbelievers and hostile towards them. Ibn 'Abbās said, 'The believers are like a father with his child and a master with his slave. They are harsh to the unbelievers like wild beasts to their prey.' Allah also says: '*Fierce to the unbelievers, merciful to one another.*' (48:29) The word '*humble*' can also be in the accusative as an adverbial *ḥāl*, meaning 'He loves them and they love Him in this state.' The meaning of Allah's love for His slaves and theirs for Him was already discussed (3:31).

who strive in the Way of Allah and do not fear the blame of any censurer.

This differs from the hypocrites who fear reverses. It indicates the confirmation of the leadership of Abū Bakr, 'Umar, 'Uthmān and 'Alī because they strove in the Way of Allah while the Messenger of Allah ﷺ was alive and fought the apostates after him. It is known that whoever has these attributes is a friend of Allah. It is said that the *āyah* is general to all who strive against the unbelievers until the Day of Rising, and Allah knows best. '*Allah is Boundless*' in bestowing His favour, '*All-Knowing*' of the best interests of His creatures.

إِنَّمَا وَلِيُّكُمُ ٱللَّهُ وَرَسُولُهُۥ وَٱلَّذِينَ ءَامَنُوا۟ ٱلَّذِينَ يُقِيمُونَ ٱلصَّلَوٰةَ وَيُؤْتُونَ
ٱلزَّكَوٰةَ وَهُمْ رَٰكِعُونَ ٥٥

55 Your friend is only Allah and His Messenger and those who believe: those who establish the prayer and pay *zakāt*, and bow,

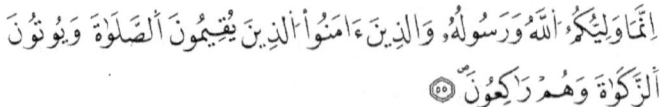

Your friend is only Allah and His Messenger and those who believe:

Jābir ibn 'Abdullāh mentioned that 'Abdullāh ibn Salām said to the Prophet ﷺ, 'Our people of Qurayẓah and an-Naḍīr have shunned us and have sworn that they will not sit with us nor are we able to sit with our companions because of the distance of their houses from us.' Then this *āyah* was revealed and he said, 'We are satisfied with Allah, His Messenger and the believers as friends.'

The word '*those*' is generally applicable to all believers. Abū Ja'far Muḥammad ibn 'Alī ibn al-Ḥusayn ibn 'Alī ibn Abī Ṭālib was asked about the meaning of this and whether it was 'Ali who was meant. He replied, "Alī is one of the believers,' indicating that it refers to all believers. An-Naḥḥās said, 'This is evident since "those" is a plural.' Ibn 'Abbās said, 'It was revealed about Abū Bakr.' Another report from him says that it was about 'Alī, and Mujāhid and as-Suddī also said that. The rest of the *āyah* moved them to say that.

those who establish the prayer and pay *zakāt*, and bow.

It is said that a beggar begged in the mosque of the Messenger of Allah ﷺ but no one gave him anything. 'Alī was in *rukū'* in the prayer and had a ring on his right hand. He gestured to the beggar with his hand to take it. Aṭ-Ṭabarī said, 'This indicates that a minor extraneous action does not invalidate the prayer since he gave the ring as *ṣadaqah* while praying without that invalidating his prayer.' The use of the expression '*pay zakāt*' here indicates that voluntary *ṣadaqah* can be called *zakāt*. 'Alī gave his ring as *ṣadaqah* while in *rukū'*. It is similar to Allah's words: '*Anything you give as zakāt, seeking the Face of Allah – all who do that will get back twice as much.*' (30:39) It includes the obligatory and the voluntary and so the word *zakāt* includes both as does *ṣadaqah*, and the word *ṣalāt* also contains two matters.

What is meant by *zakāt* according to this giving of the ring is *ṣadaqah* rather than the specific obligation to give it as *zakāt* because *zakāt* in its specific meaning is obligatory *zakāt* as explained at the beginning of the *sūrah*. Allah also says before that: '*...establish the prayer*' and it means to establish it at its time with all its duties and what is meant is the obligatory prayer. Then the word '*bow*' signifies the supererogatory prayers. It is said that bowing is mentioned to honour it. It is said that when it was revealed, the believers were between the completion of the prayer and bowing.

Ibn Khuwayzimandād said that the *āyah* gives permission for insignificant extra actions in the prayer. It takes the form of praise and the minimum of what praise can be directed towards is something permissible. As we said, it is related that 'Alī ibn Abī Ṭālib gave a beggar something while he was praying. It is possible that he was performing a supererogatory prayer at the time and that it is disliked in the obligatory prayer. It is said that praise is directed towards combining the two things as if Allah was describing here the person who believes in the obligatory nature of both the prayer and *zakāt*. The prayer is designated by 'bowing' as well as the belief in the obligation to act as you might say, 'The Muslims are those who pray.' You do not mean that they only pray in that situation. Praise is not directed at the simple doing of the prayer. It means the one who both performs this action and believes in it.

وَمَن يَتَوَلَّ ٱللَّهَ وَرَسُولَهُۥ وَٱلَّذِينَ ءَامَنُواْ فَإِنَّ حِزۡبَ ٱللَّهِ هُمُ ٱلۡغَٰلِبُونَ ٥٦

56 As for those who make Allah their friend, and His Messenger and those who believe: it is the party of Allah who are victorious!

This means those who entrust their affair to Allah and obey the command of His Messenger and befriend the Muslims: they are the party of Allah. It is said that it means those who undertake to obey Allah and help His Messenger and the believers.

it is the party of Allah who are victorious!

Al-Ḥasan said, 'The party of Allah is the army of Allah.' Someone else said that it is the helpers of Allah. A poet said:

How can I be harmed when Bilāl is my party?

He means, 'my helper'. The believers are the party of Allah and they defeated the Jews by capture, killing, exile and imposition of *jizyah*.

The noun *ḥizb* means a portion of people. Its root means 'to befall someone or press him'. It is as if those in a party collect together like people in the face of a disaster. A man's party are his friends. *Ḥizb* also means a portion of one's recitation. *Ḥizb* is the group and the verb *taḥazzaba* is to join together and *aḥzāb* are the parties who combined to fight the Prophets. The verb *ḥazaba* is used for something afflicting someone.

يَٰٓأَيُّهَا ٱلَّذِينَ ءَامَنُواْ لَا تَتَّخِذُواْ ٱلَّذِينَ ٱتَّخَذُواْ دِينَكُمۡ هُزُوٗا وَلَعِبٗا مِّنَ ٱلَّذِينَ
أُوتُواْ ٱلۡكِتَٰبَ مِن قَبۡلِكُمۡ وَٱلۡكُفَّارَ أَوۡلِيَآءَۚ وَٱتَّقُواْ ٱللَّهَ إِن كُنتُم مُّؤۡمِنِينَ ٥٧

57 You who believe! do not take as friends any of those given the Book before you or the unbelievers who make a mockery and a game out of your *dīn*. Have *taqwā* of Allah if you are believers.

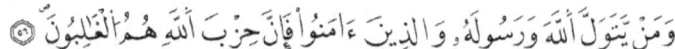

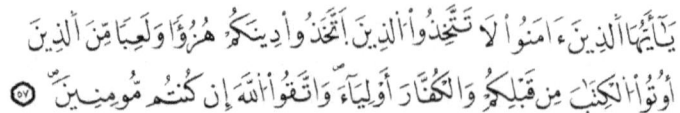

It is related from Ibn 'Abbās that some of the Jews and idolaters laughed at the Muslims while they were prostrating and Allah revealed this. The meaning of 'mocking' was mentioned in *al-Baqarah* (2:67). Abū 'Amr and al-Kisā'ī recited *'al-kuffāri'* in the genitive, meaning 'among the unbelievers'. The variant of Ubayy has *'mina-l-kuffāri'* as a generic clarifier. To have it in the accusative (*al-kuffāra*) is clearer as an-Naḥḥās said. It is said that it is added to the closest regent which is '*those given the Book*'. Allah forbids the Muslims to take the Jews and idolaters as friends and informs them that the two groups mock the *dīn* of the believers. If it is in the accusative, it is added to the first '*those*', meaning 'Do not take those and those as friends.' According to this, it is only the Jews who are described with mockery and games. It is forbidden to take Jews and idolaters as friends. In the reading in the genitive, both groups are described as making a mockery and playing games.

Makkī said, 'Were it not that the community agree on the accusative, I would have preferred the genitive because of its strength in syntax, meaning, commentary and proximity to what it is added to.' It is said that it means: 'Do not take the idolaters and hypocrites as friends since they say: *"We were only mocking."* (2:14)' All the idolaters are unbelievers, but the expression *kuffār* is usually used for the idolaters which is why the People of the Book are mentioned separately from the *kāfirūn*.

Ibn Khuwayzimandād said, 'This *āyah* is similar to Allah's words: *"Do not take the Jews and Christians as your friends"* (5:51) and: *"Do not take any outside yourselves as intimates."* (3:118) It is a prohibition against seeking the help and support of the idolaters.' Jābir said, 'When the Prophet ﷺ wanted to go to Uḥud, some of the Jews came to him and said, "We will go with you." He replied, "We do not seek help from idolaters in our affairs." This is considered to be the sound position in the school of ash-Shāfi'ī. Abū Ḥanīfah allows the Muslims to seek their help against idolaters. The text of the Book and what has come of the *Sunnah* regarding that differs from what they say, and Allah knows best.'

وَإِذَا نَادَيْتُمْ إِلَى الصَّلَوٰةِ اتَّخَذُوهَا هُزُوًا وَلَعِبًا ذَٰلِكَ بِأَنَّهُمْ قَوْمٌ لَّا يَعْقِلُونَ ۝٥٨

58 When you call to the prayer they make a mockery and a game of it. That is because they are people who do not use their intellect.

Al-Kalbī said, 'When the *mu'adhdhin* gave the call and the Muslims stood for the prayer, the Jews said, while laughing, "They stood. They did not stand." When the Muslims bowed and prostrated, they said in respect of the *adhān*, "You have innovated something which has not been heard of in the past nations. Why do you shout like an ass brays? What an ugly sound and what a loathsome business!'"

It is said that when the *mu'adhdhin* gave the *adhān*, they would laugh with one another and make mocking gestures to inculcate ignorance in their people and make people averse to it and averse to being called to it. It is said that they used to think that the one who called the prayer was like a joker by doing it, due to their ignorance of it and this was revealed. Allah also revealed: *'Who could say anything better than someone who summons to Allah?'* (41:33) The term used for 'call' here (*nadā'*) means 'to summon by raising the voice.' It includes supplication, braying and shouting. The only mention of the *adhān* in the Qur'ān is in this *āyah*. It is mentioned about Friday and so it is particular.

Scholars have said, 'In Makkah before the Hijrah the *adhān* was not called. They used to announce the prayer by saying, *"Aṣ-ṣalātu jāmi'ah."* (The prayer is gathered.) When the Prophet ﷺ made *hijrah* and the *qiblah* was changed to the Ka'bah, the *adhān* was commanded and the idea implicit in the words *"The prayer is gathered (aṣ-ṣalātu jāmi'ah)"* is taken for granted.' The Prophet ﷺ was concerned with the matter of the *adhān*. He heard the *adhān* during the Night Journey.

As for the dreams which 'Abdullāh ibn Zayd al-Khazrajī al-Anṣārī and 'Umar ibn al-Khaṭṭāb had about it, they are well-known. 'Abdullāh ibn Zayd told it to the Prophet ﷺ on the night he had the dream, and 'Umar said, 'In the morning, I told the Prophet ﷺ and he commanded Bilāl to give the *adhān* for the prayer. In the morning Bilāl added, "Prayer is better than sleep," and the Messenger of Allah ﷺ affirmed it. It was not from the dream of the Anṣārī.' Ibn Sa'd mentioned it from Ibn 'Umar. Ad-Dāraquṭnī mentioned that Abū Bakr dreamed the *adhān* and told the Prophet ﷺ who commanded Bilāl to give the *adhan* before the Anṣārī mentioned it. He mentioned this in a *ḥadīth* from Abū Bakr.

Scholars disagree about whether the *adhān* and the *iqāmah* are obligatory or not. Mālik and his people say that the *adhān* is mandatory in mosques where people gather for group prayers. Mālik stated that in the *Muwaṭṭā'*. The later Mālikīs have two positions: one is that it is a stressed *sunnah* which is mandatory (*wājibah*) for all in cities and in towns which are like cities. Others said that it is an obligation (*farḍ*) for all. The Shāfi'īs have the same disagreement. Aṭ-Ṭabarī reported from Mālik, 'If the people of a city deliberately abandon the *adhān*, they must repeat the prayer.' Abū 'Umar said, 'I do not know of any disagreement about the obligation of the *adhān* in general for the people of a city because the *adhān* is the sign which indicates the difference between the Abode of Islam and the Abode of Disbelief.' We read in *Ṣaḥīḥ Muslim*: 'When the Messenger of Allah

ﷺ sent out an expedition, he told them, "If you hear the *adhān*, refrain and hold back. If you do not hear the *adhān*, attack."'

'Aṭā', Mujāhid, al-Awzā'ī and Dāwūd said that the *adhān* is *farḍ*, and they did not say a communal obligation. Aṭ-Ṭabarī said, 'The *adhān* is *sunnah* and not mandatory.' Ashhab mentioned that Mālik said, 'If a traveller deliberately omits the *adhān*, he must repeat the prayer.' The Kufans disliked travellers praying without an *adhān* and *iqāmah*. They said, 'It is recommended for a city dweller to give the *adhān* and *iqāmah*. If he is content with the *adhān* and *iqāmah* of the people, that is allowed.' Ath-Thawrī said, 'The *iqāmah* is permitted without the *adhān* on a journey but if you wish, you can give both the *adhān* and the *iqāmah*.' Aḥmad ibn Ḥanbal said, 'According to the *ḥadīth* of Mālik ibn al-Ḥuwayrith travellers should make the *adhān*.' Dāwūd said, 'The *adhān* is obligatory for every traveller specifically, and so is the *iqāmah* based on the *ḥadīth* of Mālik ibn al-Ḥuwayrith: "When you travel, give the *adhān* and the *iqāmah*. The elder of you should lead two of you in the prayer."' Al-Bukhārī transmitted it and it is the position of the literalists.

Ibn al-Mundhir said, 'It is confirmed that the Messenger of Allah ﷺ said to Mālik ibn al-Ḥuwayrith and his cousin, "When you travel, give the *adhān* and the *iqāmah*. The elder of you should lead the two of you in the prayer."' Ibn al-Mundhir said, 'The *adhān* and the *iqāmah* are obligatory for every group, whether resident or travelling, because the Prophet ﷺ commanded the calling of the *adhān* and his command is an obligation.' Abū 'Umar said, 'Ash-Shāfi'ī, Abū Ḥanīfah and his people, ath-Thawrī, Aḥmad, Isḥāq, Abū Thawr and aṭ-Ṭabarī all agree that if a traveller omits the *adhān* either deliberately or forgetfully, his prayer is allowed. They believe that that is also the case if he omits the *iqāmah*, but they strongly dislike abandoning the *iqāmah*.' Ash-Shāfi'ī argues that the *adhān* is not mandatory and that it is not one of the obligations of the prayer since the *adhān* is dropped when joining at 'Arafah and Muzdalifah. The final position of Mālik regarding the *adhān* while travelling is the same as that of ash-Shāfi'ī.

Mālik and ash-Shāfi'ī and their people agree that the words of the *adhān* are repeated twice whereas those of the *iqāmah* are done once, although ash-Shāfi'ī makes the first *takbīr* four as reported in the *ḥadīth* of Abū Mahdhūrah. In the *ḥadīth* of 'Abdullāh ibn Zayd, he said, 'It is an addition which must be accepted.' Ash-Shāfi'ī said that that was the way it was done in Makkah. It continued like that in the family of Abū Mahdhūrah until his time. His people said, 'That is how it is now with them.' What Mālik believed also exists in the sound *ḥadīth*s about the *adhān* of Abū Mahdhūrah and that of 'Abdullāh ibn Zayd. The practice with the people in Madīnah is like that among the family of Sa'd al-Quraẓī until their time.

Mālik and ash-Shāfi'ī agree that there is *tarjī'* in the *adhān*. So after the *mu'adhdhin* has repeated the *shahādah* twice, he then raises his voice loudly. There is no disagreement between Mālik and ash-Shāfi'ī about the *iqāmah* except for the words *'qad qāmāti-ṣ-ṣalātu.'* Mālik says it once and ash-Shāfi'ī twice. Most scholars take the position of ash-Shāfi'ī and traditions have come about it. Abū Ḥanīfah and his people, ath-Thawrī, and al-Ḥasan ibn Ḥayy said that the expressions of the *adhān* and the *iqāmah* are all done in twos and they say that there are four *takbīr*s at the beginning of the *adhān* and *iqāmah*. They say that there is no *tarjī'* in the *adhān*. Their evidence for that is the *ḥadīth* of 'Abd ar-Raḥmān ibn Abī Laylā. He said, 'The Companions of the Messenger of Allah ﷺ related to us that 'Abdullāh ibn Zayd went to the Prophet ﷺ and said, "Messenger of Allah, I dreamt that a man wearing two green mantles stood at the foot of a wall and gave the *adhān* in twos and *iqāmah* in twos, sitting down between them." Bilāl heard that and stood and gave the *adhān* in twos, sat down, and then gave the *iqāmah* in twos.' Al-A'mash and others related it from 'Amr ibn Murrah from Ibn Abī Laylā. That is the position of most of the *Tābi'ūn* and *fuqahā'* in Iraq.

Abū Isḥāq as-Sabī'ī said, 'The people of 'Alī and 'Abdullāh [ibn Mas'ūd] doubled the expressions of the *adhān* and *iqāmah*. This is the *adhān* of Kufans which they have inherited and accordingly acted on generation after generation just as the people of the Hijaz inherited theirs. Their *adhān* has four *takbīr*s like that of the Makkans. Then the *shahādah* is done once and the 'Come to's' once. Then the *mu'adhdhin* repeats it with a loud voice and does the entire *adhān* with two phrases.'

Abū 'Umar said that Aḥmad ibn Ḥanbal, Isḥāq ibn Rāhawayh, Dāwūd ibn 'Alī, and aṭ-Ṭabarī believed that it is permitted to do the *adhān* in any manner which is related from the Messenger of Allah ﷺ. They say that that is permitted and up to one's choice. They say that all of that is permitted because all of that is confirmed from the Messenger of Allah ﷺ and was done by his Companions. If one wishes, you can say *'Allāhu akbar'* twice at the beginning of the *adhān* or you can say it four times. If you wish, you can use *tarjī'* in the *adhān* or not use it if you wish. You can double the expressions in the *iqāmah* or say them singly except for *'qad qāmāti-ṣ-ṣalātu'* which is twice in every case.

They disagree about the *tathwīb* in the *Ṣubḥ* prayer which is the words of the *mu'adhdhin*: 'Prayer is better than sleep.' Mālik, ath-Thawrī and al-Layth say that the *mu'adhdhin* says it twice after 'Come to success'. That was the position of ash-Shāfi'ī in Iraq. When he was in Egypt, he said that it is not said. Abū Ḥanīfah and his people say that he can say it after he finishes the *adhān* if he wishes. It is related from them that it is in the *adhān*. That is the position of people in the *adhān* for *Fajr*.

Abū 'Umar said that it is related that the Prophet ﷺ told Abū Maḥdhūrah to say in the *adhān* for *Ṣubḥ*: 'Prayer is better than sleep.' That is also related from 'Abdullāh ibn Zayd. Anas said that it is part of the *sunnah* to say that. It is related that Ibn 'Umar used to say it. As for the statement of Mālik in the *Muwaṭṭā'* that he heard that the *mu'adhdhin* came to 'Umar ibn al-Khaṭṭāb to call him to the *Ṣubḥ* prayer and found him sleeping, so he said, 'Prayer is better than sleep,' and 'Umar commanded him to put that in the *adhān* for *Ṣubḥ*, I do not know that this is related from 'Umar by an authoritative path of transmission whose soundness is known. There is the *ḥadīth* of Hishām ibn 'Urwah from a man called Ismā'īl whom he identified. Ibn Abī Shaybah mentioned from 'Abdah ibn Sulaymān from Hishām ibn 'Urwah from a man called Ismā'īl who said, 'The *mu'adhdhin* came to 'Umar to announce the *Ṣubḥ* prayer and said, "Prayer is better than sleep." 'Umar liked it and told the *mu'adhdhin*, "Keep it in your *adhān*."'

Abū 'Umar said, 'I believe that it means that he told him, "The call for *Ṣubḥ* is the place to say this, not here." It was as if he disliked there being another call at the door of the commander as rulers initiated later.' Abū 'Umar said, 'I was moved to this interpretation, even if the literal wording of the report differs, because the *tathwīb* is too well known by scholars and the common people in the *Ṣubḥ* prayer for anyone to suppose that 'Umar was ignorant of something of the *Sunnah* of the Messenger of Allah ﷺ and which he had commanded to be done by his *mu'adhdhins*, Bilāl in Madīnah and Abū Maḥdhūrah in Makkah. It is preserved and known by scholars in the *adhān* of Bilāl and the *adhān* of Abū Maḥdhūrah in the *Ṣubḥ* prayer for the Prophet ﷺ.'

Wakī' related from Sufyān from 'Imrān ibn Suwayd from Suwayd ibn Ghafalah that he sent for his *mu'adhdhin* when he reached, 'Come to success,' and said, 'Say, "Prayer is better than sleep." It is the *adhān* of Bilāl.' It is known that Bilāl never called the *adhān* for 'Umar nor was he ever to call the *adhān* after the Messenger of Allah ﷺ except for once when he entered Syria.

The people of knowledge agree that it is *sunnah* to only give the *adhān* after the time has come except in the case of *Fajr*. According to Mālik, ash-Shāfi'ī, Aḥmad, Isḥāq and Abū Thawr, it may be given before dawn. Their proof is the words of the Messenger of Allah ﷺ, 'Bilāl calls the *adhān* at night, so eat and drink until Ibn Umm Maktūm calls it.' Abū Ḥanīfah, ath-Thawrī and Muḥammad ibn al-Ḥasan said that the *adhān* for *Ṣubḥ* should only be called after the time based on what the Messenger of Allah ﷺ said to Mālik ibn al-Ḥuwayrith and his companion: 'When it is time for the prayer, you two should give the *adhān* and then the *iqāmah* and the elder of the two of you should lead the prayer,' and by analogy with other prayers.

One group of the People of Ḥadīth said, 'When a mosque has two *mu'adhdhins*, one of them gives an *adhān* before the breaking of dawn and the other after the breaking of dawn.'

They disagree about one person giving the *adhān* and another the *iqāmah.* Mālik, Abū Ḥanīfah and their people say that there is no harm in it based on the *ḥadīth* of Muḥammad ibn 'Abdullāh ibn Zayd from his father when the Messenger of Allah ﷺ commanded him to teach it to Bilāl after he had a dream about it. Bilāl gave the *adhān* and 'Abdullāh ibn Zayd gave the *iqāmah.* Ath-Thawrī, al-Layth and ash-Shāfi'ī said that the one who gives the *adhān* also gives the *iqāmah* based on the *ḥadīth* of 'Abd ar-Raḥmān ibn Ziyād that Ziyād ibn al-Ḥarith aṣ-Ṣudā'ī said, 'I went to the Messenger of Allah ﷺ and at the beginning of *Ṣubḥ,* he told me to give the *adhān.* Then he stood up to pray and Bilāl came to give the *iqāmah* and the Messenger of Allah ﷺ said, "The brother of Ṣudā' gave the *adhan.* The one who gives the *adhān* should also give the *iqāmah.*"'

Abū 'Umar said, "Abd ar-Raḥmān ibn Ziyād is al-Ifrīqī. Most of them consider him to be weak. He is the only one to relate this *ḥadīth.* The first one has a better *isnād,* Allah willing. Even if the *ḥadīth* of al-Ifrīqī is strong – he was one of the people of knowledge who is trusted and praised – I say that the first *ḥadīth* is better because it is a text in an area of dispute and, furthermore, it is later than the story of 'Abdullāh ibn Zayd with Bilāl. It is more appropriate to follow the final command of the Messenger of Allah ﷺ. Moreover, when there is a single regular *mu'adhdhin,* I recommend that he also do the *iqāmah.* If someone else does the *iqāmah,* the prayer is acceptable by consensus.' Praise be to Allah.

The *mu'adhdhin* should call the *adhān* in straightforward way and not use musical melodies as some ignorant people do today. Many of the common people go even further and do many repetitions and breaks so that what is being said cannot be understood nor what one is being directed to. Ad-Dāraquṭnī related from Ibn Jurayj from 'Aṭā' that Ibn 'Abbās said, 'The Messenger of Allah ﷺ had a *mu'adhdhin* who used to warble. The Messenger of Allah ﷺ said, "The *adhān* is plain and easy. If your *adhān* is not plain and easy, do not give it."'

Most scholars say that the *mu'adhdhin* should face the qiblah and turn his head right and left when he says the 'Come to's'. Aḥmad said that he should not turn around unless he is on a *minbar* and wants to make the people hear. Isḥāq said that. It is better to be in a state of purity when calling the *adhān.*

It is recommended that someone who hears the *adhān* should repeat it to the end of the *shahādah* and it is permitted for him to complete it based on the *ḥadīth* of Abū Sa'īd. In *Ṣaḥīḥ Muslim,* 'Umar ibn al-Khaṭṭāb said that the Messenger of

Allah ﷺ said, 'If, when the *mu'adhdhin* says, "Allah is greater, Allah is greater," someone says, "Allah is greater, Allah is greater," and when he says, "I testify that there no god but Allah," he repeats, "I testify that there no god but Allah," and when he says, "I testify that Muḥammad is the Messenger of Allah," he repeats "I testify that Muḥammad is the Messenger of Allah," and when he says, "Come to prayer," he says, "There is no power nor strength except by Allah," and when he says, "Come to success," he says, "There is no power nor strength except by Allah," and when he says, "Allah is greater, Allah is greater," he says, "Allah is greater, Allah is greater," and when he says, "There is no god but Allah," he says, "There is no god but Allah" from his heart, he will enter the Garden.' Sa'd ibn Abī Waqqāṣ said that the Messenger of Allah ﷺ said, 'If, when someone hears the *adhān*, he says, "I testify that there is no god but Allah alone with no partner and Muḥammad is His slave and Messenger, and I am pleased with Allah as a Lord, Muḥammad as a Messenger, and Islam as a *dīn*," he will be forgiven his prior wrong actions.'

There are many sound reports about the excellence of the *adhān* and the one who gives it. One of them is what Muslim related from Abū Hurayrah that the Prophet ﷺ said, 'When the call to prayer is done Shayṭān retreats, farting, so that he will not hear it.' It is enough for you that it is the token of Islam and a sign of belief. As for the *mu'adhdhin*, Muslim related that Mu'āwiyah said, 'I heard the Messenger of Allah ﷺ, say, "The *mu'adhdhins* will be the people with the longest necks on the Day of Rising."' This indicates security from the terror of that day, and Allah knows best. 'Long necks' is used by the Arabs as a metaphor for the nobles of a people.

In the *Muwaṭṭā'*, it states that Abū Sa'īd al-Khudrī heard the Messenger of Allah ﷺ say, 'No jinn or man or anything within range hears the voice of the *mu'adhdhin* without bearing witness for him on the Day of Rising.' We find in the *Sunan* of Ibn Mājah that Ibn 'Abbās said, 'If someone gives the *adhān* for seven years with expectation of the reward, freedom from the Fire will be recorded for him.' Regarding it Ibn 'Umar related that the Messenger of Allah ﷺ said, 'If someone gives the *adhān* for ten years, the Garden is obliged for him and sixty good deeds are recorded for his *adhān* every day and thirty for his *iqāmah*.' Abū Ḥātim said, 'This *isnād* is *munkar* while the *ḥadīth* is sound.'

'Uthmān ibn Abi-l-'Āṣ said, 'The last instruction that the Prophet ﷺ gave me was: "Appoint a *mu'adhdhin* who does not take a wage for his *adhān*."' It is a firm *ḥadīth*. There is, however, disagreement about receiving a wage for giving the *adhān*. Al-Qāsim ibn 'Abd ar-Raḥmān and the People of Opinion disliked it.

Mālik made an allowance for it and said that there is no harm in it. Al-Awzā'ī said that it is disliked, but there is no harm in taking payment from the treasury for it. Ash-Shāfi'ī said that a *mu'adhdhin* is only paid from the fifth of the *khums*, the share of the Prophet ﷺ. Ibn al-Mundhir said that it is not permitted to take a wage for the *adhān*.

Our scholars deduce from the *ḥadīth* of Abū Maḥdhūrah that a wage can be taken. It is debatable. It is transmitted by an-Nasā'ī, Ibn Mājah and others. He said, 'I set out with a group of people and when we had gone part of the way, the *mu'adhdhin* of the Messenger of Allah ﷺ gave the *adhān* for the prayer in the presence of the Messenger of Allah ﷺ. We heard the voice of the *mu'adhdhin* while we were shunning it and we shouted out repeating it, in mockery of it. The Messenger of Allah ﷺ heard that and sent some people to us and had us sit in front of him. He asked, "Whose voice among you did I hear raised?" All the people pointed at me and they spoke the truth. He sent all of them away and kept me. He told me, "Stand and give the *adhān*." I stood, and I did not dislike anything more than the business of the Messenger of Allah ﷺ and what he was commanding me to do. I stood before the Messenger of Allah ﷺ and the Messenger of Allah ﷺ himself taught me the *adhān*. He said, "Say: 'Allah is greater. Allah is greater. Allah is greater. Allah is greater. I testify that there is no god but Allah. I testify that there is no god but Allah. I testify that Muḥammad is the Messenger of Allah. I testify that Muḥammad is the Messenger of Allah.'" Then he told me, "Raise and extend your voice: 'I testify that there is no god but Allah. I testify that there is no god but Allah. I testify that Muḥammad is the Messenger of Allah. I testify that Muḥammad is the Messenger of Allah. Come to the prayer. Come to the prayer. Come to success. Come to success. Allah is greater. Allah is greater. There is no god but Allah." Then he called me when I had finished the *adhān* and gave me a bag with some silver.' Then he put his hand on the forelock of Abū Maḥdhūrah and passed it over his face, then over his breasts, then over his liver until the hand of the Messenger of Allah ﷺ reached the navel of Abū Maḥdhūrah. Then the Messenger of Allah ﷺ said, 'May Allah give blessing for you and blessing on you.' 'I said, "Messenger of Allah, appoint me to give the *adhān* in Makkah." "I have done so," he replied. All of the dislike which I had felt for the Messenger of Allah ﷺ departed and turned into love for the Messenger of Allah ﷺ. I went to 'Attāb ibn Usayd, the governor of Makkah for the Messenger of Allah ﷺ and gave the *adhān* for the prayer with him at the command of the Messenger of Allah ﷺ.' This is the version of Ibn Mājah.

That is because they are people who do not use their intellect.

They are in the position of people with no intelligence to prevent them from engaging ugly matters. It is related that when a Christian man who was in Madīnah heard the *mu'adhdhin* say, 'Muḥammad is the Messenger of Allah,' he said, 'The liar will be burned.' While he was asleep in his house, some sparks jumped from the fire and the house was locked, and the house and that unbeliever were burned. It was a lesson for people. 'Affliction stems from issued words.' They were given a respite with the Prophet ﷺ until they were conquered after which there was no respite. Ibn al-'Arabī mentioned it.

قُلْ يَٰٓأَهْلَ ٱلْكِتَٰبِ هَلْ تَنقِمُونَ مِنَّآ إِلَّآ أَنْ ءَامَنَّا بِٱللَّهِ وَمَآ أُنزِلَ إِلَيْنَا وَمَآ أُنزِلَ مِن قَبْلُ
وَأَنَّ أَكْثَرَكُمْ فَٰسِقُونَ ﴿٥٩﴾ قُلْ هَلْ أُنَبِّئُكُم بِشَرٍّ مِّن ذَٰلِكَ مَثُوبَةً عِندَ ٱللَّهِ مَن لَّعَنَهُ
ٱللَّهُ وَغَضِبَ عَلَيْهِ وَجَعَلَ مِنْهُمُ ٱلْقِرَدَةَ وَٱلْخَنَازِيرَ وَعَبَدَ ٱلطَّٰغُوتَ أُو۟لَٰٓئِكَ شَرٌّ
مَّكَانًا وَأَضَلُّ عَن سَوَآءِ ٱلسَّبِيلِ ﴿٦٠﴾

59-60 Say: 'People of the Book! do you resent us for any other reason than that we believe in Allah and what was sent down to us, and what was sent down before, and because most of you are deviators?' Say: 'Shall I tell you of a reward with Allah far worse than that: that of those whom Allah has cursed and with whom He is angry – turning some of them into monkeys and into pigs – and who worshipped false gods? Such people are in a worse situation and further from the right way.'

Say: 'People of the Book! do you resent us for any other reason

Ibn 'Abbās said, 'Some Jews, who included Abū Yāsir ibn Akhṭab and Rāfi' ibn Abī Rāfi', came to the Prophet ﷺ and asked him about which of the Messengers he believed in. He replied: *"We believe in Allah and what has been sent down to us and what was sent down to Ibrāhīm and Ismā'īl and Isḥāq and Ya'qūb and the Tribes, and what Mūsā and 'Īsā were given, and what all the Prophets were given by their Lord. We do not differentiate between any of them. We are Muslims submitted to Him."* (2:133) When he mentioned 'Īsā, they denied his Prophethood and said, "By Allah, we do not know of the people of a religion with a smaller portion in this world and the Next than you nor a *dīn* worse than your *dīn*!" Then this and what follows it were revealed.' This *āyah* is connected to what was previously mentioned about the denial of the *adhān*. So it is joined to testifying to Allah's unity and to the Prophethood of Muḥammad and refutes the *dīn* of those who make distinctions between the Prophets of Allah, not the *dīn* of those who believe in all of them. It is permitted to assimilate the *lām* into the *tā'* because it is close to it.

As for the word, *'tanqimūma'* (resent), it is said that it means 'hate or resent,' and it is said that it means 'refuse to acknowledge.' The meanings are similar. The verb *naqama, yanqimu* or *naqima, yanqamu* means to dislike something. *Naqama* is more frequently used. 'Ubaydullāh ibn Qays ar-Ruqayyāt said:

> Do they resent anything in the Banū Umayyah
> other than the fact that they are forbearing when they are angered?

We see its usage elsewhere in the Revelation: '*The only reason they punished (*naqamū*) them….*' (85:8) One says *'naqimtu 'alā'* for 'I was hostile towards someone.' *Nāqim* is someone who punishes. Al-Kisā'ī said that *naqima* is a dialectical form. *Naqama* and *naqima* also mean to hate something. *Intiqama* is used for Allah imposing a penalty on someone. The noun is *naqmah* or *naqamah*. The plurals are *naqimāt* and *niqam*, like *kalimah* and *kalimāt* and *kalim*. If you wish, the *qāf* can be silent and its vowel moved to the *nūn* and it is *niqmah* whose plural is *niqam*, like *ni'mah* and *ni'am*. The phrase '*…for any other reason that we believe in Allah*' is in the position of the accusative and means 'Do you criticise us for anything except the fact that we believe in Allah when you know that I am based on the truth?'

because most of you are deviators?

You are deviators in abandoning faith and not obeying the command of Allah. It is said that this is like a speaker saying, 'Do you resent me for other than the fact that I am chaste while you are lewd?' Most of you have left faith and ceased to obey Allah's command.

Say: 'Shall I tell you of a reward with Allah far worse than that?'

This means 'worse than your resentment of us.' It is said: 'worse than the hateful things you desire for us.' This is a response to their words, 'We do not know of a worse religion than your religion.' The noun *'reward'* is in the accusative for clarification. Its root is the passive participle and the vowel of the *wāw* is moved to the *thā'* and the *wāw* is silent and after it there is a silent *wāw* and one of them is elided for that reason. It is like *maqūlah*, *majūrah* and *maḍūfah* with the meaning of a verbal noun. [POEM]

In the phrase *'whom Allah has cursed'* the pronoun *'man'* is in the nominative as we see in 22:72. It implies: 'It is the curse of the one whom Allah has cursed.' It is also possible that it is in the accusative with the meaning: 'Shall I tell you of worse than that? Those whom Allah has cursed.' It can also be in the genitive as an appositive for '*worse*' and implies: 'Shall I tell you of those whom Allah has cursed?' meaning the Jews.

We have already discussed *ṭāghūt* (false gods) (2:256). It means that He made some of them people who worshipped false gods. According to al-Farrā', the conjunct is elided. The Basrans said that it is not permitted to elide the conjunct and it means: 'those whom Allah has cursed and [who] worshipped false gods.' Ibn Waththāb and an-Nakha'ī recited '*unbi'ukum*'. Ḥamzah recited "*abuda-ṭ-ṭāghūti*", making it a noun expressing emphasis (worshippers) and their being numerous, like *yaquẓ*, *nadus*, and *ḥadhur.* Its root is an adjective. [POEM ILLUS] It is in the accusative as the object of '*ja'ala'* which can mean 'created' and so it means 'He created some of them to be worshippers of false gods.' 'Worshippers' is ascribed to 'false gods' which is therefore in the genitive case. It means: 'He made some of them go to excess in worshipping false gods.'

The rest recite "*abada-ṭ-ṭāghūta*", making it a verb in the past tense and adding it to the previous verbs, and they say that it means: 'Among them are those whom Allah has cursed and those who worship idols.' Or it can be in the accusative by '*ja'ala*' and means: 'Allah made some of them monkeys and pigs and worshippers of idols.' The pronoun (used for worshippers) is in the singular, referring to '*man*' (who) outside its normal meaning. Ubayy and Ibn Mas'ūd recited "*abadū-ṭ-ṭāghūta*" with the same meaning. Ibn 'Abbas has "*ubuda-ṭ-ṭāghūti*" which can be the plural of "*abd*" as in *rahn* and *ruhun*, *saqf* and *suquf*, or the plural of "*ibād*" like *mithāl* and *muthul*, or or the plural of "*abīd*" like *raghīf* and *rughuf*, or the plural of '*ābid*' like *bāzil* and *buzul*. It then means 'servants of idols'.

Ibn 'Abbas also recited "*ubbada-ṭ-ṭāghūta*" as the plural of "*ābid*" like *shāhid* and *shuhhad* and *ghā'ib* and *ghuyyab*. Abū Wāqid recited "*ubbāda-ṭ-ṭāghūti*", which is a form used for emphasis and is also the plural of '*ābid*, like '*āmil* and '*ummāl*, and *ḍārib* and *ḍurrāb*. Maḥbūb mentioned that the Basrans recited "*ibāda-ṭ-ṭāghūti*", which is also the plural of '*ābid*, like *qā'im* and *qiyām*. It can also be the plural of '*abd*. Abū Ja'far ar-Ru'āsī recited "*ubida-ṭ-ṭāghūtu*" in the passive. It implies: 'False gods were worshipped among them.' 'Awn al-'Uqaylī and Ibn Buraydah recited "ābida-*ṭ-ṭāghūti*" in the singular while it refers to a group. Ibn Mas'ūd also recited "*ubada-ṭ-ṭāghūti*", and he and Ubayy also recited "*ubidati-ṭ-ṭāghūtu*" in the feminine plural as we see in 49:14. 'Ubayd ibn 'Umayr recited '*a'badu-ṭ-ṭāghūti*', like *kalb* and *aklab*. There are twelve forms.

Such people are in a worse situation

That is because their situation is the Fire. The believers will have nothing evil in their situation. Az-Zajjāj said that it means: 'Such people are in a worse situation according to your words.' An-Naḥḥās said, 'One of the best things said about it is that those whom Allah has cursed will have a worse situation in the Next World than your situation in this world because of the evil which will overtake them.' It is said that those ones whom Allah has cursed are in a worse situation than those who resent you. It is said that those who resent you are in a worse position than those whom Allah has cursed. When this *āyah* was revealed, the Muslims said to them, 'O brothers of monkeys and pigs, bow your heads in shame!' A poet says about them:

Allah's curse is on the Jews. The Jews are the brothers of monkeys.

وَإِذَا جَآءُوكُمْ قَالُوٓاْ ءَامَنَّا وَقَد دَّخَلُواْ بِٱلْكُفْرِ وَهُمْ قَدْ خَرَجُواْ بِهِۦ وَٱللَّهُ أَعْلَمُ بِمَا كَانُواْ
يَكْتُمُونَ ﴿٦١﴾ وَتَرَىٰ كَثِيرًا مِّنْهُمْ يُسَٰرِعُونَ فِى ٱلْإِثْمِ وَٱلْعُدْوَٰنِ وَأَكْلِهِمُ
ٱلسُّحْتَ لَبِئْسَ مَا كَانُواْ يَعْمَلُونَ ﴿٦٢﴾ لَوْلَا يَنْهَىٰهُمُ ٱلرَّبَّٰنِيُّونَ وَٱلْأَحْبَارُ عَن قَوْلِهِمُ
ٱلْإِثْمَ وَأَكْلِهِمُ ٱلسُّحْتَ لَبِئْسَ مَا كَانُواْ يَصْنَعُونَ ﴿٦٣﴾

61-63 When they come to you, they say, 'We believe.' But they entered with unbelief and left with it. Allah knows best what they were hiding. You see many of them rushing to wrongdoing and enmity and acquiring ill-gotten gains. What an evil thing they do! Why do their scholars and rabbis not prohibit them from evil speech and acquiring ill-gotten gains? What an evil thing they invent!

When they come to you, they say, 'We believe.' But they entered with unbelief and left with it. Allah knows best what they were hiding.

This is a description of the hypocrites. They did not benefit from anything they heard. They entered as unbelievers and left as unbelievers. *'Allah knows best what they were hiding'* of their hypocrisy. It is said that what is meant are the Jews who said, 'Believe in that which was revealed to those who believe at the beginning of the day when you enter Madīnah and reject it at the end of the day when you return to your houses.' What is before and after it about them indicates that. *'You see many of them'* means the Jews who hasten to acts of disobedience and wrongdoing.

Why do their scholars and rabbis not prohibit them

The word '*lawlā*' means 'Did they not?' '*Prohibit them*' means 'restrain them'. The word for scholars, *rabbāniyyūn*, means Christian scholars whereas *aḥbār* refers to the Jewish scholars. Al-Ḥasan said that. It is said that both terms apply to the Jews because these *āyahs* are about them. Their scholars are then rebuked for not prohibiting them. The words: *'What an evil thing they invent!'* continues the rebuke of them as they were criticised for their actions in *'What an evil thing they do!'* The *āyah* indicates that someone who fails to forbid the wrong is like someone who actually commits it. The *āyah* rebukes scholars for not commanding the right and forbidding the wrong. This was already discussed in *al-Baqarah* (2:43) and *Āl 'Imrān* (3:21-228).

Sufyān ibn 'Uyaynah related from Sufyān ibn Sa'īd that Mis'ar said, 'I heard that an angel was commanded to make a town sink into the earth. He said, "O Lord, so-and-so the worshipper is in it." Allah revealed to him, "Begin with him. His face did not show any anger at all."' There is a *ḥadīth* in at-Tirmidhī which states, 'When people see a wrongdoer and do not restrain his hands, Allah is about to envelop them in a punishment from Him.' *Sun'* here means action, but it means done well. A sword which is *ṣanī'* is well made.

وَقَالَتِ ٱلْيَهُودُ يَدُ ٱللَّهِ مَغْلُولَةٌ ۚ غُلَّتْ أَيْدِيهِمْ وَلُعِنُوا۟ بِمَا قَالُوا۟ ۘ بَلْ يَدَاهُ مَبْسُوطَتَانِ
يُنفِقُ كَيْفَ يَشَآءُ ۚ وَلَيَزِيدَنَّ كَثِيرًا مِّنْهُم مَّآ أُنزِلَ إِلَيْكَ مِن رَّبِّكَ طُغْيَٰنًا
وَكُفْرًا ۚ وَأَلْقَيْنَا بَيْنَهُمُ ٱلْعَدَٰوَةَ وَٱلْبَغْضَآءَ إِلَىٰ يَوْمِ ٱلْقِيَٰمَةِ ۚ كُلَّمَآ
أَوْقَدُوا۟ نَارًا لِّلْحَرْبِ أَطْفَأَهَا ٱللَّهُ ۚ وَيَسْعَوْنَ فِى ٱلْأَرْضِ فَسَادًا ۚ
وَٱللَّهُ لَا يُحِبُّ ٱلْمُفْسِدِينَ ﴿٦٤﴾

64 The Jews say, 'Allah's hand is chained.' Their hands are chained and they are cursed for what they say! No! Both His hands are open wide and He gives however He wills. What has been sent down to you from your Lord increases many of them in insolence and disbelief. We have incited enmity and hatred between them until the Day of Rising. Each time they kindle the fire of war, Allah extinguishes it. They rush about the earth corrupting it. Allah does not love corrupters.

The Jews say, 'Allah's hand is chained.'

'Ikrimah said, 'Finḥāṣ ibn 'Āzūra' and his people said this – may Allah curse them. They had property, and when they rejected Muḥammad ﷺ, their wealth diminished. So they said, 'Allah is miserly and Allah's hand refrains from giving to us,' and so the *āyah* is particular to some of them. It is said that when the others did not object to what they said, they became like them. Al-Ḥasan said, 'The meaning is: "Allah's hand is kept from punishing us."'

It is also said that when they saw the Prophet ﷺ in poverty and need and heard the words: *'Is there anyone who will make Allah a generous loan?'* (2:245) and saw that the Messenger of Allah ﷺ had to ask for their assistance in paying blood money, they said, 'The God of Muḥammad is poor,' or 'miserly'. This is what is meant by *'Allah's hand is chained.'* It is a metaphor like, *'Do not keep your hand chained to your neck.'* (17:29). A miser is said to be 'stiff-fingered', to have 'a closed hand' and 'tight fingers' and 'chained hand'. A poet said:

Khorasan was a land which enjoyed increase
and every door of blessings was open.
After him it has become tight-fingered,
as if its face was splashed with vinegar.

In Arabic, the word 'hand' (*yad*) can designate the actual limb as in *'Take a bundle of rushes in your hand (*bi-yadika*)'* (38:44), but this is impossible in respect of Allah Almighty. It can describe a blessing as in the expression, 'How many blessings I have had at the hand of so-and-so!' (lit. 'How many hands!') It can designate strength as Allah says: *'Remember Our slave Dāwūd, who possessed true strength (dhā-l-aydī).'* (38:18). It can mean ownership and power as Allah says: *'Say, "All favour is in the Hand of Allah and He gives it to whoever He wills."'* (3:73) It can mean direct connection as Allah says: *'We created for them, by Our own handiwork, livestock'* (36: 71), meaning 'We did it.' He also says: *'Or the one in charge (bi-yadihi) of the marriage contract forgoes it'* (2:237) which means the one with authority over the marriage contract. It can mean support and help as the Prophet ﷺ said, 'The hand of Allah is with the qāḍī so long as he divides and the distributor so long as he distributes.' It can be used to denote honour and nobility, as when Allah says: *'Iblīs! What prevented you prostrating to what I created with My own Hands?'* (38:75)

So it is not permitted to take it to mean the actual limb because the Creator cannot be divided into parts. It cannot be used for strength, ownership, blessing and direct connection because then there would be sharing between His friend Ādam and His enemy Iblīs. It is invalid to mention it as bounty since that particular meaning is invalid. There only remain two possible usages: attaching it to the creation of Ādam to honour him and connecting power to the object of power, not directly nor by actual touch. The like of that is what is related that Allah 'wrote the Torah with His hand,' 'He planted the Abode of Nobility with His own Hand for the people of the Garden' and other such usages which are taken accordingly.

What has been sent down to you from your Lord increases many of them in insolence and disbelief. Their hands are chained and they are cursed for what they say!

The *ḍammah* is elided from the *yā'* because it is heavy. Their hands will be chained in the Next World. It is possible that it is a supplication against them. The same is true of 'They are cursed for what they say.' It is meant to teach us as when Allah says: *'You will enter the Masjid al-Ḥarām in safety, Allah willing.'* (48:27) That teaches us to make the exception, *'Allah willing'* and He taught us the invocation against Abū Lahab when He says, *'Ruin to the hands of Abū Lahab!'* (111:1) It is said that what is meant is that they are the most miserly of people and so they are all blameworthy. There is an implied 'and' in the sentence. The word *'cursed'* means put far away.

No! Both His hands are open wide.

His blessing is outspread. Here the 'hand' means 'blessing'. Some say that this is an error, for the blessings of Allah are too great to be numbered, so how can it be only two outspread blessings? The answer to this is that the dual is used here is generic and not the singular, and so it is like the words of the Prophet ﷺ: 'The metaphor of the hypocrite is that of a lost sheep between two flocks of sheep.' One hand is the blessing of this world and the other the blessing of the Next World. It is said that the two blessings of this world are outward and inward, as Allah says elsewhere: *'He has showered His blessings upon you, both outwardly and inwardly?'* (31:20)

It is related from Ibn 'Abbās that the Prophet ﷺ said about this, 'The outward blessing is the good aspects of your character and the inward the concealing of your bad actions.' It is also said that the two blessings are rain and plants. It is said that the blessing is for emphasis as the Arabs say, *'Labbayka wa sa'dayka'* and it does not mean to confine it to two times. Someone might say, 'I do not have a hand (i.e. strength) for this business.'

As-Suddī said that the two hands may mean reward and punishment, which differs from what the Jews said, 'His hand is kept from punishing us.' In *Ṣaḥīḥ Muslim*, Abū Hurayrah reported that the Prophet ﷺ said, 'Allah said to me, "Spend and I will spend on you."' The Messenger of Allah ﷺ said, 'The right hand of Allah is full. Its outflowing by night and day does not decrease it. Do you not see what He has spent since the time He created the heavens and the earth? He is not stingy with what is in His right hand.' He also said ﷺ, 'His Throne is over the water. His other (left) hand constricts. He raises and lowers.' Similar to this *ḥadīth* are Allah's words: *'Allah contracts and expands.'* (2:245)

In the reading of Ibn Mas'ūd, the word in this *āyah* is '*busuṭān*'. Al-Akhfash related it. He said that a hand which is '*busṭah*' is one that is giving and expansive. The phrase *'He gives however He wills'* means that He provides in any way He wishes. It is also possible that the '*hand*' in this verse signifies 'power,' meaning that His power is comprehensive. If He likes, He gives expansion, and if He wishes, He contracts.

We have incited enmity and hatred between them

The *lām* is the *lām* of the oath. '*What has been sent down to you*' means 'by means of what was sent down to you.' *'In insolence and unbelief'* means: when something of the Qur'ān was revealed, they disbelieved and their disbelief increased. Mujāhid said that this means between the Jews and Christians because Allah says before this: *'Do not take the Jews and Christians as friends.'* (5:51) It is also said that it means between the parties of the Jews as He says: *'You consider them united but their hearts are scattered.'* (59:14) They hate one another and are not in harmony and so they are hated by people.

Each time they kindle the fire of war.

This refers to the Jews. '*Kullamā*' is an adverb. It means: whenever they gather and attack, Allah will cause them to fall into schisms. It is said that when the Jews became corrupted and opposed the Book of Allah, the Torah, Allah sent Nebuchadnezzar against them. Then they became corrupted again and He sent the Romans against them. Then they became corrupted and He sent the Magians against them. Then they became corrupted and He sent the Muslims against them. Whenever their affair was in order, Allah dissolved their unity, so whenever they kindled a fire, in other words provoked evil and agreed to fight the Prophet ﷺ, 'Allah extinguished it,' and defeated them and caused them to weaken. Fire is a metaphor. Qatādah said, 'Allah humiliated them. He sent the Prophet ﷺ while they were subjected to the Magians.'

They rush about the earth corrupting it.

They rush to undermine Islam, and doing that is the greatest possible kind of corruption, and Allah knows best. It is said that '*fire*' here means anger, meaning that whenever the fire of anger is kindled in them and they gather their physical and psychological force, Allah extinguishes it so that they become weak. That is an aspect of the terror through which the Prophet ﷺ is helped.

وَلَوْ أَنَّ أَهْلَ الْكِتَٰبِ ءَامَنُوا وَاتَّقَوْا لَكَفَّرْنَا عَنْهُمْ سَيِّـَٔاتِهِمْ وَلَأَدْخَلْنَٰهُمْ
جَنَّٰتِ النَّعِيمِ ﴿٦٥﴾ وَلَوْ أَنَّهُمْ أَقَامُوا التَّوْرَىٰةَ وَالْإِنجِيلَ وَمَا أُنزِلَ إِلَيْهِم
مِّن رَّبِّهِمْ لَأَكَلُوا مِن فَوْقِهِمْ وَمِن تَحْتِ أَرْجُلِهِم مِّنْهُمْ أُمَّةٌ مُّقْتَصِدَةٌ
وَكَثِيرٌ مِّنْهُمْ سَآءَ مَا يَعْمَلُونَ ﴿٦٦﴾

65-66 If only the People of the Book had believed and been godfearing, We would have erased their evil deeds from them and admitted them into Gardens of Delight. If only they had implemented the Torah and the Gospel and what was sent down to them from their Lord, they would have been fed from above their heads and beneath their feet. Among them there is a moderate group but what most of them do is evil.

If only the People of the Book had believed and been godfearing,

If only they had affirmed the truth and been careful to avoid *shirk* and disobedience. The word '*erased*' means 'covered over' and the *lām* is the *lām* of the apodosis of '*law*'. That means they should have implemented the Torah and Gospel by acting according to them and not altering them. This was adequately discussed in *Sūrat al-Baqarah* (2:63-64). What is meant by the words *'what was sent down to them'* is the Qur'ān or the Books of their Prophets.

they would have been fed from above their heads and beneath their feet.

Ibn 'Abbās and others said that this is a reference to rain and plants. This indicates that they were suffering a drought. It is also said that it means: 'We would have expanded their provision to them and they would have eaten continuously.' Also the prepositions '*above*' and '*below*' are used to emphasise what is given to them of this world. Similar to this are the words of Allah: *'Whoever has taqwā of Allah – He will give him a way out and provide for him from where he does not expect'* (65:2) and: *'If only they were to go straight on the Path, We would give them abundant water to drink'* (72:16) and: *'If only the people of the cities had believed and been godfearing, We would have opened up to them blessings from heaven and earth.'* (7:96) In these *āyah*s Allah makes it clear that *taqwā* is one of the causes of provision and promises increase for those who are thankful in His words: *'If you are grateful, I will certainly give you increase.'* (14:7)

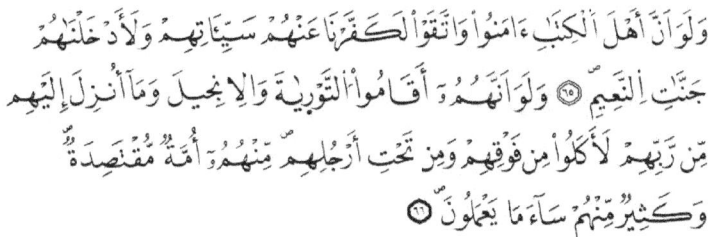

Among them there is a moderate group but what most of them do is evil.

Then Allah informs us that some of them are *'moderate'*. They are the believers among them, such as the Negus, Salmān and 'Abdullāh ibn Salām. They were moderate and did not say anything about 'Īsā and Muḥammad ﷺ except what was fitting for them. It is said that by the adjective *'moderate'* Allah means people who have not actually believed, but do not harm or mock. Allah knows best. Moderation (*iqtiṣād*) is balance in action. It is derived from the word *qaṣd* which signifies aiming for something. The verb *qaṣada* means the same when it takes a direct object or uses the particles *li* and *ilā*. *'What most of them do'* is deny the Messengers, alter the Books and take bribes.

يَٰٓأَيُّهَا ٱلرَّسُولُ بَلِّغۡ مَآ أُنزِلَ إِلَيۡكَ مِن رَّبِّكَۖ وَإِن لَّمۡ تَفۡعَلۡ فَمَا بَلَّغۡتَ رِسَالَتَهُۥۚ
وَٱللَّهُ يَعۡصِمُكَ مِنَ ٱلنَّاسِۗ إِنَّ ٱللَّهَ لَا يَهۡدِي ٱلۡقَوۡمَ ٱلۡكَٰفِرِينَ ٦٧

67 O Messenger! transmit what has been sent down to you from your Lord. If you do not do it you will not have transmitted His Message. Allah will protect you from people. Allah does not guide the people of the unbelievers.

O Messenger! transmit what has been sent down to you from your Lord.

It is said that this means to make the conveying of the Message public because in the beginning of Islam the Prophet ﷺ concealed it out of fear of the idolaters and then he was commanded in this *āyah* to make it public and Allah informed him that He would protect him from people. 'Umar was the first to openly display his Islam. He said, 'We do not worship Allah secretly.' About that Allah says: *'O Prophet! Allah is enough for you, and for the believers who follow you'* (8:64).

The *āyah* refutes those who claim that the Prophet ﷺ concealed something of the *dīn* out of *taqiyyah*. It is what the Rāfiḍites say and it is false. It indicates that he ﷺ did not make anything of the *dīn* confidential to anyone in particular because the meaning is, 'Convey all that was conveyed to you openly.' If it had not been for this, there would be no point in Allah's words: *'If you do not do it you will not have transmitted His Message.'* It is said that it means: 'Convey what has been conveyed to you from your Lord about Zaynab bint Jaḥsh.' Other things are said. The sound view is that it is general.

Ibn 'Abbās said, 'The meaning is: convey all that was revealed to you from your Lord. If you conceal any of it, you have not conveyed His Message.' This is teaching the Prophet ﷺ and teaching those who bear knowledge among his community not to conceal any of the *Sharī'ah*. Allah said that His Prophet ﷺ does not conceal any of His Revelation. We find in *Ṣaḥīḥ Muslim* that Masrūq reported that 'Ā'ishah said, 'Anyone who tells you that Muḥammad ﷺ concealed any of the Revelation has lied.' This refutes what the Rāfiḍites say about the Prophet ﷺ concealing some of the revelation from Allah to him.

Allah will protect you from people.

This is proof of his Prophethood because Allah informs us that he is protected. If Allah guarantees protection for someone, it is not possible for him to abandon anything which Allah has commanded him to do. The reason for the revelation of this *āyah* was that the Prophet ﷺ stopped under a tree and a bedouin surprised him. The bedouin drew his sword and said to the Prophet ﷺ, 'Who will protect you from me?' 'Allah,' he replied. The hand of the Bedouin shook and he dropped the sword and hit his head against the tree until his brains were splattered. Al-Mahdawī mentioned the story. In the *Shifā'*, Qāḍī 'Iyāḍ said, 'I was told that this story is true and that the person concerned was Ghuwayrith ibn al-Ḥārith. The Prophet ﷺ pardoned him and he returned to his people and said, "I have come to you from the best of people."' This was extensively discussed under *āyah* 11. It was also discussed in *Sūrat an-Nisā'* in the context of the Fear prayer (4:102).

In *Ṣaḥīḥ Muslim*, Jābir ibn 'Abdullāh said, 'We went on a raid with the Messenger of Allah ﷺ in the direction of Najd. Midday overtook us in a valley with a lot of large thorn-trees in it. The Messenger of Allah ﷺ alighted and the people split up to seek the shade of the trees. The Messenger of Allah ﷺ settled under a tree and hung his sword on one of its branches. The Messenger of Allah ﷺ said, "A man came to me while I was asleep and took the sword. I awoke and he was standing at my head. I was only aware of the sword gleaming in his hand. He said to me, 'Who will protect you from me?' I said, 'Allah.' He asked a second time. 'Who will protect you from me?' I said, 'Allah.' He sheathed the sword and he is sitting there now."' Then the Messenger of Allah ﷺ did not touch him.'

Ibn 'Abbās reported that the Prophet ﷺ said, 'When Allah sent me with His Message, I was constricted and saw those people who denied me, and so Allah revealed this *āyah*.' Abū Ṭalib used to send two men of the Banū Hāshim every day to guard him until Allah revealed this. Then the Prophet ﷺ said, 'Uncle, Allah has protected me from jinn and men, so I have no need of any guards.'

If it is said that this would mean that the *āyah* is Makkan, that is not the case. There is consensus that the *sūrah* is Madinan. One thing that indicates that the *āyah* is Madinan is what Muslim transmitted in the *Ṣaḥīḥ* from 'Ā'ishah: 'The

Messenger of Allah ﷺ was awake one night after arriving in Madīnah. He said, "Would that there was a righteous man among my Companions who would guard me tonight!" While we were like that we heard the rattle of weapons. He said, "Who is it?" "Sa'd ibn Abī Waqqāṣ," came the reply. The Messenger of Allah ﷺ asked him, "What has brought you?" He replied, "I felt frightened for the Messenger of Allah ﷺ, so I came to guard him." The Messenger of Allah ﷺ made supplication for him and then went to sleep.' In another variant not in the *Ṣaḥīḥ*, she said, 'While we were like that we heard the sound of weapons.' He asked, 'Who is it?' and the reply was, 'Sa'd and Ḥudhayfah. We have come to guard you.' 'Ā'ishah said, 'He slept until he snored and then this *āyah* was revealed. The Messenger of Allah put his head out of the tent and said, "Go, people. Allah has protected me."'

The people of Madīnah read *'risālātihi'* [in the plural] while Abū 'Amr and the people of Kufa have it *'risālatihi'* in the singular. An-Naḥḥās says that both are good, but the plural is clearer because the Messenger of Allah ﷺ received revelation time after time, and then made it clear. If it is singular, it indicates the plural as frequently happens with a verbal noun which is usually neither in the plural or dual when it indicates something generic. This usage is seen with 'blessing' in the singular in 14:24. It is said: 'Convey. Guidance is up to Us.' It is like Allah's words: *'The Messenger is only responsible for transmission.'* (5:99) Allah knows best.

قُلْ يَٰٓأَهْلَ ٱلْكِتَٰبِ لَسْتُمْ عَلَىٰ شَىْءٍ حَتَّىٰ تُقِيمُوا۟ ٱلتَّوْرَىٰةَ وَٱلْإِنجِيلَ
وَمَآ أُنزِلَ إِلَيْكُم مِّن رَّبِّكُمْ ۗ وَلَيَزِيدَنَّ كَثِيرًا مِّنْهُم مَّآ أُنزِلَ إِلَيْكَ مِن
رَّبِّكَ طُغْيَٰنًا وَكُفْرًا ۖ فَلَا تَأْسَ عَلَى ٱلْقَوْمِ ٱلْكَٰفِرِينَ ٦٨

68 Say: 'People of the Book! you have nothing to stand on until you implement the Torah and the Gospel and what has been sent down to you from your Lord.' What has been sent down to you from your Lord increases many of them in insolence and disbelief. So do not waste your grief on the people of the unbelievers.

Ibn 'Abbās said, 'A group of Jews came to the Prophet ﷺ and said, "Do you not affirm that the Torah is truly from Allah?" "Yes," he replied. They said, "We believe in it and do not believe in anything else." Then the *āyah* was revealed, and it means: "You have nothing of the *dīn* until you recognise what the two Books contain regarding belief in Muḥammad ﷺ and acting by what that necessitates."' Abū 'Alī said, 'It is possible that that was before they were abrogated.'

What has been sent down to you from your Lord increases many of them in insolence and disbelief.

They reject it and that increases them in disbelief on top of their earlier disbelief. The meaning of *tughyān* is to go beyond the limits in wrongdoing (*ẓulm*) and to be excessive in it. That is because some wrongdoing is minor and some is major. When someone goes beyond the limits of the minor, he has been insolent (*ṭaghā*). Exemplifying that is Allah's words: *'No indeed! Truly man is unbridled (yaṭghā)'* (96:6), meaning he has exceeded the limits in leaving the truth.

So do not waste your grief on the people of the unbelievers.

This means: do not be sad about them. The verb *asiya, ya'sā, asā* means to be sad. A poet said:

She made her eyes milk from excess of sorrow (*asā*).

This is solace for the Prophet ﷺ and not a prohibition of sorrow on his part because that is something of which one is incapable. It is solace and a prohibition against demonstrating excessive sorrow. This was discussed adequately at the end of *Āl 'Imrān* (3:176).

إِنَّ ٱلَّذِينَ ءَامَنُوا۟ وَٱلَّذِينَ هَادُوا۟ وَٱلصَّٰبِـُٔونَ وَٱلنَّصَٰرَىٰ
مَنْ ءَامَنَ بِٱللَّهِ وَٱلْيَوْمِ ٱلْءَاخِرِ وَعَمِلَ صَٰلِحًا فَلَا خَوْفٌ عَلَيْهِمْ
وَلَا هُمْ يَحْزَنُونَ ﴿٦٩﴾

69 Those who believe and those who are Jews and the Sabaeans and the Christians, all who believe in Allah and the Last Day and act rightly will feel no fear and will know no sorrow.

All of this has already been discussed (2:62). The word '*Sabaeans*' is added to the hidden pronoun in '*those who are Jews*' according to al-Kisā'ī and al-Akhfash. An-Naḥḥās said that he heard az-Zajjāj say that this statement is erroneous in two ways. One is that it is ugly to add to a nominative implied pronoun without it being stressed. The other is that what is added to it shares with what it is added to and therefore the meaning would be that the Sabaeans are included among the Jews, and this is not the case.

Al-Farrā' said that '*Sabaeans*' can be in the nominative because '*inna*' is weak and only affects the subject and not the predicate. The syntax of '*those*' here is not clear. Both things proceed in the same manner, and so it is possible for 'Sabaeans' to be in the nominative, referring to the basis of the words. Az-Zajjāj said, 'The method used to understand something whose syntax is unclear and something whose syntax is clear is the same.' Al-Khalīl and Sībawayh said that the nominative case is based on a change in normal order. It implies: 'those who believe and those who are Jews who believe in Allah and the Last Day and act rightly will feel no fear and know no sorrow, and the Sabaeans and Christians are like that.' Sībawayh quotes its like:

Know that I and you
are rebels [nom.] as long as we are in schism.

[ANOTHER POEM] It is said that '*inna*' here means 'yes' and so '*Sabaeans*' is in the nominative by the inceptive and the predicate is elided because the second predicate indicates it. So, according to this assumption, the conjunction is after the end of the words and end of the noun and predicate. [POEM]

لَقَدْ أَخَذْنَا مِيثَٰقَ بَنِىٓ إِسْرَٰٓءِيلَ وَأَرْسَلْنَآ إِلَيْهِمْ رُسُلًا ۖ كُلَّمَا جَآءَهُمْ
رَسُولٌۢ بِمَا لَا تَهْوَىٰٓ أَنفُسُهُمْ فَرِيقًا كَذَّبُوا۟ وَفَرِيقًا يَقْتُلُونَ ٧٠

70 We made a covenant with the tribe of Israel and We sent Messengers to them. Each time a Messenger came to them with something their lower selves did not desire, they denied some and they murdered others.

The covenant was discussed in *al-Baqarah* (2:27). It means to worship only Allah. In this *āyah*, the meaning is: 'Do not despair about the unbelievers. We have warned them and sent Messengers, but they broke their covenants.' This refers back to the words at the beginning of the *sūrah*: *'Fulfil contracts.'*

Whenever a Messenger came to the Jews with anything that went against what they desired, they did this. They denied 'Īsā and those Prophets like him and killed Zakariyyā, Yaḥyā and other Prophets. Allah says *'yaqtulūna'* to agree with the ends of the other *āyahs*. It is said: a group of them denied and a group of them killed. Such was their custom. It is said that one group denied but did not kill them, and another killed them and so denied. Allah knows best.

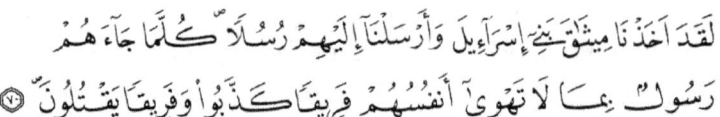

وَحَسِبُوٓاْ أَلَّا تَكُونَ فِتْنَةٌ فَعَمُواْ وَصَمُّواْ ثُمَّ تَابَ ٱللَّهُ
عَلَيْهِمْ ثُمَّ عَمُواْ وَصَمُّواْ كَثِيرٌ مِّنْهُمْ وَٱللَّهُ بَصِيرٌۢ بِمَا
يَعْمَلُونَ ﴿٧١﴾

71 They thought there would be no *fitnah*. They were blind and deaf. Then Allah turned towards them. Then many of them went blind and deaf again. Allah sees what they do.

They thought there would be no *fitnah*.

It means that those who made the covenant thought that Allah would not test them with hardships, just as they were deluded when they said, 'We are the sons of Allah and those He loves.' They were deluded by the long deferral they were granted.

Abū 'Amr, Ḥamzah and al-Kisā'ī read *takūnu* and the rest read *takūna*. If it is *takūnu*, it means: 'they were certain' and '*an*' is lightened and '*lā*' added to replace the lightening. The pronoun is elided because it is disliked for the verb to follow it. It is not part of its ruling to have it added to it and so they are separated by '*lā*'. The other reading makes '*an*' accusative by the verb and *ḥasiba* keeps its normal meaning with doubt and other things [they supposed, thought]. Sībawayh said that '*ḥasibtu allā yaqūlu dhāka*' means 'I supposed that he said.' He said that it can be in the accusative if you wish. An-Naḥḥās said, 'According to grammarians, it is better to have the nominative with *ḥasiba* and its sisters as he said:

Does Basbāsah claim today that I (*annanī*) am old
And that those like me do not (*allā*) attend amusement?

The nominative is better because the verb *ḥasiba* and its sisters denote something firm and known.'

Then many of them went blind and deaf again.

They were blind to guidance and deaf to hearing the Truth because they did not benefit from what they heard.

Then Allah turned towards them.

There is something implied here: They were tested and repented and so Allah turned to them by removing the drought or by sending Muḥammad ﷺ to inform them that Allah would turn to them if they believed. This means: Allah will turn to them as long as they believe and affirm, not that they in fact repented.

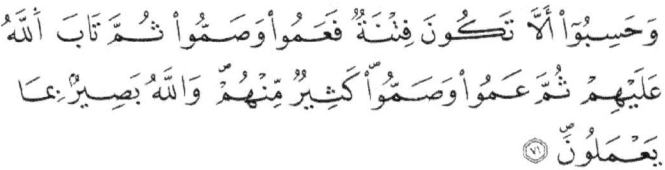

Then many of them went blind and deaf again.

Many were blind and deaf after the truth was made clear to them about Muḥammad ﷺ. 'Many' is in the nominative. Al-Akhfash said, 'It is as you say, "I saw two-thirds of your people" which is literally, "I saw your people, two-thirds of them."' If you wish, it can be based on an implied inchoative, i.e. 'Blind and deaf are many of them." If you wish, it can imply, "The blind and deaf among them are many."

لَقَدْ كَفَرَ ٱلَّذِينَ قَالُوٓا۟ إِنَّ ٱللَّهَ هُوَ ٱلْمَسِيحُ ٱبْنُ مَرْيَمَ ۖ وَقَالَ
ٱلْمَسِيحُ يَـٰبَنِىٓ إِسْرَٰٓءِيلَ ٱعْبُدُوا۟ ٱللَّهَ رَبِّى وَرَبَّكُمْ ۖ إِنَّهُۥ
مَن يُشْرِكْ بِٱللَّهِ فَقَدْ حَرَّمَ ٱللَّهُ عَلَيْهِ ٱلْجَنَّةَ وَمَأْوَىٰهُ ٱلنَّارُ ۖ
وَمَا لِلظَّـٰلِمِينَ مِنْ أَنصَارٍ ﴿٧٢﴾

72 Those who say that the Messiah, son of Maryam, is Allah have disbelieved. The Messiah said, 'Tribe of Israel! worship Allah, my Lord and your Lord. If anyone associates anything with Allah, Allah has forbidden him the Garden and his refuge will be the Fire.' The wrongdoers will have no helpers.

This is the position of the Jacobite sect. Allah refuted them with a definitive proof taken from what they affirm. The Messiah used to say, 'O Lord! O Allah!' So how would he call himself that and ask himself? This is impossible. *'If anyone associates anything with Allah...'* are either words of ʿĪsā or spoken by Allah. Associating with Him is to believe that something exists together with Him. 'Messiah' and its derivation was already discussed in *Āl ʿImrān* (3:45-46).

لَّقَدْ كَفَرَ ٱلَّذِينَ قَالُوٓا۟ إِنَّ ٱللَّهَ ثَالِثُ ثَلَـٰثَةٍ ۘ وَمَا مِنْ
إِلَـٰهٍ إِلَّآ إِلَـٰهٌ وَٰحِدٌ ۚ وَإِن لَّمْ يَنتَهُوا۟ عَمَّا يَقُولُونَ لَيَمَسَّنَّ
ٱلَّذِينَ كَفَرُوا۟ مِنْهُمْ عَذَابٌ أَلِيمٌ ﴿٧٣﴾ أَفَلَا يَتُوبُونَ إِلَى
ٱللَّهِ وَيَسْتَغْفِرُونَهُۥ ۚ وَٱللَّهُ غَفُورٌ رَّحِيمٌ ﴿٧٤﴾

73-74 Those who say that Allah is the third of three are unbelievers. There is no god but One God. If they do not stop saying what they say, a painful punishment will afflict those among them who disbelieve. Why do they not turn to Allah and ask for His forgiveness? Allah is Ever-Forgiving, Most Merciful.

Those who say that Allah is the third of three are unbelievers.

This means one of three. Az-Zajjāj and others said that *tanwīn* is not permitted in it. The Arabs had yet another position, which is saying, 'the fourth of three'. On this basis both the genitive and accusative are possible, meaning that what is three becomes four in their view. That is like when you say, 'Third of two' and *tanwīn* is permitted.

This is the position of groups of the Monophysite Christians: Melkites, Nestorians, and Jacobites, because they say that the Father, the son and the Holy Ghost are one God, not three gods, and that is their creed. They deny what the expression in fact obliges them to believe. One judges, however, by what the expression actually means, which is that they are saying that the son is a god, the Father is a god, and the Holy Ghost is a god. This was discussed in *an-Nisā'* (4:171). Because of their saying this, Allah states that they are unbelievers. The words *'There is no god but One God'* show that He is not multiple, which is what is obliged by their profession of trinitarianism, even if they do not explicitly say that. The meaning of *'One'* in this context was discussed in *al-Baqarah* (2:163).

'If they do not stop saying what they say' about the trinity, a painful punishment will afflict them in this world and the Next. *'Why do they not turn to Allah?'* This is affirmation and rebuke. They should turn to Him and ask Him to veil their sins. This refers to the unbelievers among them. The unbelievers are singled out because it is they who say this rather than the believers.

مَّا ٱلْمَسِيحُ ٱبْنُ مَرْيَمَ إِلَّا رَسُولٌ قَدْ خَلَتْ مِن قَبْلِهِ
ٱلرُّسُلُ وَأُمُّهُۥ صِدِّيقَةٌ كَانَا يَأْكُلَانِ ٱلطَّعَامَ
ٱنظُرْ كَيْفَ نُبَيِّنُ لَهُمُ ٱلْـَٔايَٰتِ ثُمَّ ٱنظُرْ أَنَّىٰ يُؤْفَكُونَ ٧٥

75 The Messiah, the son of Maryam, was only a Messenger, before whom other Messengers came and went. His mother was a woman of truth. Both of them ate food. See how We make the Signs clear to them! Then see how they are perverted!

The Messiah, the son of Maryam, was only a Messenger, before whom other Messengers came and went.

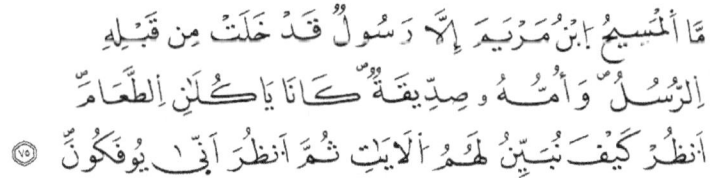

The Messiah had miraculous signs manifest at his hands as other Messengers had. If he had been a god, then they also would have been gods. This refutes what they say. The argument goes on to mention his mother. Someone who is born of a mother and eats food is a temporal creature like other creatures and none of them claims to be divine. When can a vassal be a Lord? As for their words that he ate by his human nature, not his divine nature, that leads to mixture and the divine cannot be mixed with another. If that were possible, the eternal would be mixed with the temporal, and it would be possible for the eternal to become temporal. If that was true for 'Īsā, it would be true for other creatures so that it could be said that divinity (*lāhūt*) is mixed with every temporal creature. Some commentators say that 'eating food' alludes to the need to urinate and defecate. This indicates mortality.

Those who say that Maryam was not a Prophet use this *āyah* as evidence. This is questionable since it is possible for someone who is truthful (*ṣiddīq*) to also be a Prophet, like Idrīs, and Allah knows best. She is called *ṣiddīqah* since she confirmed the signs of her Lord and those of her son in what she reported from him. Al-Ḥasan and others said that, and Allah knows best. '*The Signs*' are the proofs. '*Then see how they are perverted!*' in turning from the truth after this clarification. This refutes the Qadariyyah and Mu'tazilites. '*Perverted*' is *afaka* which means to divert something.

قُلْ أَتَعْبُدُونَ مِن دُونِ ٱللَّهِ مَا لَا يَمْلِكُ لَكُمْ ضَرًّا وَلَا نَفْعًا ۚ وَٱللَّهُ هُوَ ٱلسَّمِيعُ ٱلْعَلِيمُ ﴿٧٦﴾

76 Say: 'Do you worship, besides Allah, something which has no power to harm or help you when Allah is the All-Hearing, the All-Knowing?'

This is further clarification and establishing the evidence against them: 'Do you not affirm that 'Īsā was a foetus in his mother's womb, not possessing harm or benefit for anything, and affirm that 'Īsā was in a state in which he did not see or hear or know nor help nor harm. How, therefore, could he be a God? Allah is the One who continues to hear and know and who alone possesses the power harm and benefit. Such a One is the true God.' Allah knows best.

قُلْ يَٰٓأَهْلَ ٱلْكِتَٰبِ لَا تَغْلُوا۟ فِى دِينِكُمْ غَيْرَ ٱلْحَقِّ وَلَا تَتَّبِعُوٓا۟ أَهْوَآءَ قَوْمٍ قَدْ ضَلُّوا۟ مِن قَبْلُ وَأَضَلُّوا۟ كَثِيرًا وَضَلُّوا۟ عَن سَوَآءِ ٱلسَّبِيلِ ﴿٧٧﴾

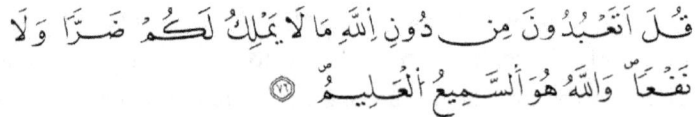

77 Say: 'People of the Book! do not go to extremes in your *dīn*, asserting other than the truth, and do not follow the whims and desires of people who were misguided previously and have misguided many others, and are far from the right way.'

Say: 'People of the Book! do not go to extremes in your *dīn*,

Do not go to excess as the Jews and Christians went to excess where 'Īsā was concerned. The Jews went to extremes in denigrating him and the Christians went to the other extreme in deifying him. 'Going to extremes' (*ghuluw*) is exceeding the proper limits. This was discussed in *Sūrat an-Nisā'* (4:171).

do not follow the whims and desires of people

This was discussed in *al-Baqarah* (2:249). *Ahwā'* is the plural of *hawā* (whim/desire). Desire is called that because it makes the person fall (*yahwī*) into the Fire. Mujāhid and al-Ḥasan said that those *'who were misguided previously'* are the Jews. *'They are far from the right way,'* which is the path of Muḥammad ﷺ. *'Misguiding'* is repeated because they misguided others before and then later. This means that their ancestors made a custom of misguidance and this was acted on by the leaders of the Jews and the Christians.

لُعِنَ ٱلَّذِينَ كَفَرُوا۟ مِنۢ بَنِىٓ إِسْرَٰٓءِيلَ عَلَىٰ لِسَانِ
دَاوُۥدَ وَعِيسَى ٱبْنِ مَرْيَمَ ۚ ذَٰلِكَ بِمَا عَصَوا۟ وَّكَانُوا۟
يَعْتَدُونَ ﴿٧٨﴾

78 Those among the tribe of Israel who disbelieved were cursed on the tongue of Dāwūd and that of 'Īsā son of Maryam. That is because they rebelled and overstepped the limits.

This contains the permission to curse unbelievers even if they are the sons of Prophets. Noble lineage does not prevent the curse on them. *'On the tongue of Dāwūd and that of 'Īsā, son of Maryam'* means in both the Psalms and also the Gospel, which were pronounced by the tongues of those two Prophets. That means that they were cursed in those two Books. Mujāhid and aḍ-Ḍaḥḥāk said that their cursing took the form of their transformation into monkeys and pigs. Abū Mālik said, 'Those who were cursed on the tongue of Dāwūd were transformed into monkeys and those who were cursed by 'Īsā were transformed into pigs.' Ibn 'Abbās said that those cursed by Dāwūd were those who violated the Sabbath and those cursed by 'Īsa were those who rejected the Table after it descended. Something similar is reported from the Prophet ﷺ. It is said that the early and later generations who disbelieved in Muḥammad ﷺ were the same as those cursed on the tongues of Dāwūd and 'Īsā because they both taught that Muḥammad ﷺ was a Prophet who would be sent and cursed those who rejected him. The word '*That*' in the second sentence means 'that curse' which was because of their disobedience. That was done to them because of their disobedience and transgression.

كَانُوا لَا يَتَنَاهَوْنَ عَن مُّنكَرٍ فَعَلُوهُ لَبِئْسَ مَا
كَانُوا يَفْعَلُونَ ٧٩

79 They would not restrain one another from any of the wrong things that they did. How evil were the things they used to do!

They would not restrain one another

They are censured for not forbidding one another from doing actions after those actions had been censured. Abū Dāwūd reported from 'Abdullāh ibn Mas'ūd that the Messenger of Allah ﷺ said, 'The first fault to enter the tribe of Israel was that a man would meet another man and say to him, "O so-and-so! Fear Allah and stop what you are doing. It is not lawful for you." But then he would meet him again the following day and find him still doing the same thing. That would not, however, prevent him from eating, drinking and sitting with him. When they did this, Allah caused the hearts of some of them to be tainted by others.' Then he recited this. Then the Prophet ﷺ added, 'No, by Allah, you should command the right and forbid the wrong, and you should restrain the unjust and turn them towards the truth and confine them to it or Allah will cause the hearts of some of you to be tainted by others. And then He will curse you as He cursed them.' At-Tirmidhī transmitted it.

Ibn 'Aṭiyyah said that there is consensus that the prohibition of evil is an obligation for the one who is able to do it and is safe from harm to himself and the Muslims. If he fears that, he must object in his heart and shun the one doing wrong and not mix with him.' Astute scholars have said, 'It is not a condition for the one who forbids to be safe from disobedience himself, rather those who are disobedient should forbid one another.' Some legal theorists have said, 'It is an obligation for those who pass cups of wine to one another to forbid one another based on this *āyah* which demands both their participation in the action and also censure for not forbidding one another to do it.'

The *āyah* also indicates that it is forbidden to sit with wrongdoers and they should be shunned. That is stressed by Allah's words in objecting to the Jews: *'You see many of them taking those who disbelieve as their friends.'*

The negative participle *mā* in *'mā kānū'* is in the accusative and what follows it describes it. It implies: 'Evil is the thing that they used to do.' Or it is in the nominative and then means 'which'.

تَرَىٰ كَثِيرًا مِّنْهُمْ يَتَوَلَّوْنَ ٱلَّذِينَ كَفَرُواْ لَبِيسَ مَا
قَدَّمَتْ لَهُمُۥٓ أَنفُسُهُمُۥٓ أَن سَخِطَ ٱللَّهُ عَلَيْهِمْ وَفِي
ٱلْعَذَابِ هُمْ خَٰلِدُونَ ﴿٨٠﴾

80 You see many of them taking those who disbelieve as their friends. What their lower selves have advanced for them is evil indeed, bringing Allah's anger down upon them. They will suffer punishment timelessly, for ever.

'Many of them' refers to the Jews. It is said that it is Ka'b ibn al-Ashraf and his people. Mujāhid said that it refers to the hypocrites. The words *'those who disbelieve'* refer to the idolaters who did not have their religion. The verb *'advanced'* here means 'made attractive.' It is also said that *'advanced for them'* is a reference to the Next World. In the phrase *'bringing Allah's anger down upon them'*, *'an'* is in the nominative based on an implied inchoative. It is similar to the words, 'What an evil man Zayd is!' [where Zayd is in the nominative.] It is said that it is an appositive for the *ma* in the phrase *'is evil indeed' (bi'sa mā)* on the basis that *mā* is indefinite, and so it is also in the nominative. It is also possible that it is in the accusative meaning 'because Allah is angry with them'.

وَلَوْ كَانُواْ يُومِنُونَ بِاللَّهِ وَالنَّبِيٓءِ وَمَآ أُنزِلَ إِلَيْهِ مَا
ٱتَّخَذُوهُمُۥٓ أَوْلِيَآءَ وَلَٰكِنَّ كَثِيرًا مِّنْهُمْ فَٰسِقُونَ ﴿٨١﴾

81 If they had believed in Allah and the Prophet and what has been sent down to him, they would not have taken them as friends. But most of them are deviators.

This indicates that those who take unbelievers as friends are not really believers since that indicates that they believe in what those friends believe in and are satisfied with their actions. *"Most of them"* are outside of faith by their adopting their deviation, or outside of belief in Muḥammad ﷺ because of their hypocrisy.

لَتَجِدَنَّ أَشَدَّ ٱلنَّاسِ عَدَٰوَةً لِّلَّذِينَ ءَامَنُوا۟ ٱلْيَهُودَ وَٱلَّذِينَ
أَشْرَكُوا۟ ۖ وَلَتَجِدَنَّ أَقْرَبَهُم مَّوَدَّةً لِّلَّذِينَ ءَامَنُوا۟ ٱلَّذِينَ
قَالُوٓا۟ إِنَّا نَصَٰرَىٰ ۚ ذَٰلِكَ بِأَنَّ مِنْهُمْ قِسِّيسِينَ وَرُهْبَانًا
وَأَنَّهُمْ لَا يَسْتَكْبِرُونَ ﴿٨٢﴾

82 You will find that the people most hostile to those who believe are the Jews and the idolaters. You will find the people most affectionate to those who believe are those who say, 'We are Christians.' That is because some of them are priests and monks and because they are not arrogant.

You will find that the people most hostile

The *lām* is the *lām* of the oath. According to al-Khalīl, the *nūn* [on the verb] is added to the verb to distinguish between the present and future. This *āyah* was revealed about the Negus and his people when the Muslims went to them in the first hijrah, fearing the idolaters and their persecution, according to the famous report in the *Sīrah* of Ibn Isḥāq and others. There were a number of them. Then the Prophet ﷺ emigrated to Madīnah and the idolaters were not able to get at him and there was war between them and the Messenger of Allah ﷺ. At Badr, Allah brought about the death of the leaders of the unbelievers and Quraysh said, 'Take your revenge in Abyssinia! Send two men holding your opinion to them. Perhaps they will give you those who are with them and you can kill them in exchange for those of you who were killed at Badr.'

So the unbelievers of Quraysh sent 'Amr ibn al-'Āṣ and 'Abdullāh ibn Abī Rabī'ah with gifts for the Negus. The Messenger of Allah ﷺ heard about that and sent 'Amr ibn Umayyah aḍ-Ḍamrī with a letter to the Negus. He came to the Negus and read the letter of the Messenger of Allah ﷺ to him. Then he summoned Ja'far ibn Abī Ṭālib and the Muhājirūn and sent for monks and priests to gather. Then he ordered Ja'far to recite the Qur'ān to them and he recited *Sūrat Maryam* and they began to weep. This was revealed about them.

Abū Dāwūd related from Muḥammad ibn Salamah al-Murādī from Ibn Wahb from Yūnus from Ibn Shihāb from Abū Bakr ibn 'Abd ar-Raḥmān ibn al-Ḥārith ibn Hishām, and from Sa'īd ibn al-Musayyab and from 'Urwah ibn az-Zubayr that the first hijrah was the hijrah of the Muslims to Abysinnia. He gave the whole account.

Al-Bayhaqī mentioned that Ibn Isḥāq said, 'When news of the Prophet ﷺ became known in Abyssinia, twenty men came to him. They found him in the mosque and spoke to him and questioned him while some of the men of Quraysh were sitting in their meeting places around the Ka'bah. When they had finished asking the questions they wanted to ask the Messenger of Allah ﷺ, the Messenger of Allah ﷺ invited them to Islam and recited the Qur'ān to them. When they heard it, their eyes overflowed with tears. They responded to him, believed in him, affirmed him and recognised him from the description of him found in their Scripture. When they stood up to leave him, Abū Jahl accosted them with a group of Quraysh. They said, "May Allah disappoint your troop! Those of the people of your religion you have come from sent you for a purpose and to bring them information about the man. You have no sooner sat with him than you have abandoned your religion and affirmed what he told you. We do not know of any retinue more stupid than you!" or words to that effect. They replied, "Peace be upon you. We do not ignore you. We have our actions and you have your actions. We do not neglect good for ourselves." It is also said that they were Christians from the people of Najrān. It is also said that the following verses were revealed about them: *"Those We gave the Book before this believe in it. … 'We do not desire the company of the ignorant.'"* (28:52-55)

It is said that it was Ja'far and his people who came to the Prophet ﷺ with seventy men wearing woollen garments, including sixty-two of them from Abyssinia and eight from Syria. They were Baḥīrā' the monk, Idrīs, Ashraf, Abrahah, Thumāmah, Qutham, Durīd and Ayman. The Messenger of Allah ﷺ recited *Sūrat Yasin* to them and they wept when they heard it and believed. They said, 'This is like what was revealed to 'Īsā.' This was then revealed about them, the delegation of the Negus, and they were monks.

Sa'īd ibn Jubayr said, 'Allah also revealed about them: "*Those We gave the Book before this believe in it. … They will be given their reward twice over*" (28:52-54). Muqātil and al-Kalbī said that it was forty men from the people of Najrān of the Banū al-Ḥārith, thirty-two Abyssinians and sixty-two Syrians. Qatādah said that it was revealed about some of the People of the Book who had a true *Sharī'ah* which 'Īsā had brought. When Allah sent Muḥammad ﷺ, they believed and Allah praised them for that.

That is because some of them are priests and monks

The singular of *qissīsīn* (priests) is *qass* and *qissīs*. Quṭrub said that. *Qissīs* means a scholar [in Greek]. Its root is *qassa*, to pursue and search for a thing. A poet said:

In the morning they were heedless about seeking (*qass*) annoyance.

Taqassasa is to listen to voices at night. *Qass* also means slander. The word also means a Christian who is a leader in religion and knowledge. The plural of that is *qusūs*. The same is true of *qissīs*. The *qissīsūn* are those who are followed as scholars and worshippers. It is also said that the plural of *qissīs* is *qasāwisah* where one of the *sīn*s has been replaced by a *wāw*. The word may be Arabic or it may have been derived from Greek and then became Arabicised. There is nothing in the Book which is not Arabic as we already stated.

Abū Bakr al-Anbārī related from his father from Naṣr ibn Dāwūd from Abū 'Ubayd who related from Mu'āwiyah ibn Hishām from Naṣīr aṭ-Ṭā'ī from aṣ-Ṣalt that Ḥāmiyyah ibn Ri'āb said, 'I said to Sulaymān, *"among them are priests and monks."* He said, "Leave the priests in the monasteries and cells. Did not the Messenger of Allah ﷺ recite to me: 'true (*ṣiddīqīn*) and monks'?"' 'Urwah ibn az-Zubayr said, 'The Christians lost the Gospel and added to it things which are not part of it. Four people changed it: Lūqās (Luke), Marqūs (Mark), Yuḥannas (John), and Maqbūs [Matthew? Marcion?]. A *qissīs* remained with the truth and what is straight and correct. Anyone who is followed in his religion and guidance is a *qissīs*.'

Rubhān (monks) is the plural of *rāhib*. It is the plural of *rāhib* like *rukbān* and *rākib*. An-Nābighah said:

Had she appeared for a grizzle-haired monk (*rāhib*)
    who worshipped God in celibate worship,
He would have been delighted at her sight and beautiful conversation
    and he would have thought it to be guidance even if it did not guide

The verb from which it comes, *rahaba, yarhabu* means to fear and the verbal nouns are *rahb*, *rahab* and *rahbah*. *Rahbāniyah* and *tarahhub* are worship in a hermitage. Abū 'Ubayd said that *ruhbān* is used for both the singular and the plural. Al-Farrā' said, '*Ruhbān* is the plural when the singular is *rahābinah* and *rahābīn*, like *qurbān* and *qarābīn*. Jarīr said, using the plural:

If the monks (*ruhbān*) of Madyan had seen you, they would descend,
    and the old antelopes from the refuge at the top of the mountain.

In the verse, *fādir* are old antelopes. It is also said that it is large as is *fadūr*. The plural is *fudr* and *fudur*, and the place is *mafdarah*. Al-Jawharī said that. Another uses it in the singular:

If she had seen the monk (*ruhbān*) of a hermitage in the mountain,
the monk would have come running while he was praying.

Rahābah is having a large sternum which hangs over the belly, like a tongue.

This *āyah* expresses praise for those of them who believed in Muḥammad ﷺ rather than remaining firm in disbelief. *'They are not too arrogant'* to obey the truth.

وَإِذَا سَمِعُوا۟ مَآ أُنزِلَ إِلَى ٱلرَّسُولِ تَرَىٰٓ أَعْيُنَهُمْ تَفِيضُ مِنَ
ٱلدَّمْعِ مِمَّا عَرَفُوا۟ مِنَ ٱلْحَقِّ يَقُولُونَ رَبَّنَآ ءَامَنَّا فَٱكْتُبْنَا مَعَ
ٱلشَّٰهِدِينَ ﴿٨٣﴾

83 When they listen to what has been sent down to the Messenger, you see their eyes overflowing with tears because of what they recognise of the truth. They say, 'Our Lord, we believe! So write us down among the witnesses.

'Eyes overflowing with tears' is in the position of a *ḥāl* as in *'They say'*. Imru' l-Qays said:

The tears from my eyes overflowed out of passion
Onto my chest until my tears made my shoulder holster wet.

A report is described as *mustafīḍ* (exhaustive) when it is numerous and widespread, like water is described with *fayḍ* when it is copious. This is the state of scholars who weep but do not faint, ask but do not shout, show sorrow but do not feign weakness. It is as Allah says: *'Allah has sent down the Supreme Discourse, a Book consistent in its frequent repetitions. The skins of those who fear their Lord tremble at it and then their skins and hearts yield softly to the remembrance of Allah,'* (39:23) and: *'The believers are those whose hearts tremble when Allah is mentioned.'* (8:2)

Allah makes it clear in these *āyahs* that the most hostile and obdurate of opponents of the Muslims are the Jews, helped by the idolaters. Allah knows best. It is clear that the closest in love are the Christians, and Allah knows best.

'So write us down among the witnesses' means among the community of Muḥammad ﷺ who bear witness to the Truth as Allah says: *'We have made you a middlemost community, so that you may act as witnesses against mankind.'* (2:143) Ibn

'Abbās and Ibn Jurayj said that. Al-Ḥasan said that it means those who testify to belief. Abū 'Alī said that it is those who affirm your Prophet and your Book. The meaning of the verb '*write*' here is place us among those who are recorded and registered.

وَمَا لَنَا لَا نُؤْمِنُ بِٱللَّهِ وَمَا جَآءَنَا مِنَ ٱلْحَقِّ وَنَطْمَعُ أَن يُدْخِلَنَا
رَبُّنَا مَعَ ٱلْقَوْمِ ٱلصَّٰلِحِينَ ﴿٨٤﴾

84 How could we not believe in Allah, and the truth that has come to us, when we long for our Lord to include us among the righteous?'

'How could we not believe' makes clear their insight into the *dīn* and that they can indeed do nothing but believe. *'The righteous'* here are the Community of Muḥammad ﷺ since Allah says elsewhere: *'It is My righteous slaves who will inherit the earth'* (21:105), meaning the Community of Muḥammad ﷺ. There is some elision in the words which implies: 'We want our Lord to admit us into the Garden.' It is said that the preposition '*ma'* ' (with) here means 'among'. You say, 'I was among those who met the amīr,' meaning 'with those who met the amir.'

The verb '*long*' can be the lightened form as well as the unlightened. One says *ṭami'a*, with the nouns *ṭama'*, *ṭamā'ah* and *ṭamā'īyah*.

فَأَثَٰبَهُمُ ٱللَّهُ بِمَا قَالُوا۟ جَنَّٰتٍ تَجْرِى مِن تَحْتِهَا ٱلْأَنْهَٰرُ خَٰلِدِينَ فِيهَا
وَذَٰلِكَ جَزَآءُ ٱلْمُحْسِنِينَ ﴿٨٥﴾ وَٱلَّذِينَ كَفَرُوا۟ وَكَذَّبُوا۟ بِـَٔايَٰتِنَآ
أُو۟لَٰٓئِكَ أَصْحَٰبُ ٱلْجَحِيمِ ﴿٨٦﴾

85-86 Allah will reward them for what they say with Gardens with rivers flowing under them, remaining in them timelessly, for ever. That is the recompense of the good-doers. As for those who disbelieve and deny Our Signs, they are the Companions of the Blazing Fire.

This is evidence of the sincerity of their belief and their sincerity in what they say. Allah answers their request and gives them what they desire. That is for those who have sincere faith and true certainty, their reward is the Garden. Then He talks of '*those who disbelieve*' among the Jews, Christians and idolaters. The noun

Jaḥīm designates a fire that blazes fiercely. The verb *jaḥama* is to stir up a fire. You can say that the eye of a lion is blazing (*jaḥmah*) because of its intensity. The same is true of war as the poet said:

Because of its fierce blaze, war does not leave pride or energy,
only a youth steadfast in hardship and steady horse.

يَٰٓأَيُّهَا ٱلَّذِينَ ءَامَنُواْ لَا تُحَرِّمُواْ طَيِّبَٰتِ مَآ أَحَلَّ ٱللَّهُ لَكُمۡ وَلَا
تَعۡتَدُوٓاْۚ إِنَّ ٱللَّهَ لَا يُحِبُّ ٱلۡمُعۡتَدِينَ ٨٧

87 You who believe! do not make unlawful the good things Allah has made lawful for you, and do not overstep the limits. Allah does not love people who overstep the limits.

Aṭ-Ṭabarī quotes Ibn 'Abbās as saying that this *āyah* was revealed because of a man who came to the Prophet ﷺ and said, 'Messenger of Allah, when I get some meat, I become expansive and my passion overtakes me and so I have made meat unlawful,' and Allah revealed this *āyah*. It is also said that it was revealed because a group of the Companions of the Prophet ﷺ, including Abū Bakr, 'Alī, Ibn Mas'ūd, 'Abdullāh ibn 'Umar, Abū Dharr al-Ghifārī, Sālim, the client of Abū Ḥudhayfah, al-Miqdād ibn al-Aswad, Salmān al-Fārisī, and Ma'qīl ibn Muqarrin met in the house of 'Uthmān ibn Maẓ'ūn and agreed to fast in the day and pray at night and not sleep in beds nor eat meat nor eat fat nor go near women and nor wear perfume. They would wear hair shirts and reject this world, wander in the land, be monk-like and do *dhikr* of Allah. Allah then revealed this *āyah*. And there are several other similar reports about reason for the revelation of this *āyah*.

Muslim transmitted from Anas that a group of the Companions asked the wives of the Prophet ﷺ about his private behaviour. One of them then said, 'I will not marry women.' Another said, 'I will not eat meat.' Yet another said, 'I will not sleep on beds.' The Prophet ﷺ praised Allah and said, 'What is wrong with these people who said such-and-such? I pray and I sleep. I fast and I break the fast. I marry women. Whoever disdains my *Sunnah* is not with me.'

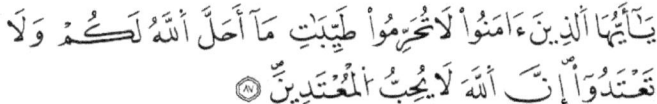

Al-Bukhārī also transmitted it from Anas. In his version we find: 'A group of three men went to the wives of the Prophet ﷺ and asked about his worship. When they were told about it, it was as if they thought it little. They remarked, "Where are we in respect of the Messenger of Allah ﷺ? Allah has forgiven him any past and future wrong actions." One of them said, "As for myself, I will always pray at night." The second said, "As for me, I will fast constantly and not break the fast." The last one said, "As for me, I will withdraw from women and never marry." When the Messenger of Allah ﷺ came out, he said, "Are you the ones who said such-and-such? By Allah, I am the one among you with the most fear and awareness of Allah, but I fast and break the fast, I pray and I sleep, and I marry women. Whoever disdains my *Sunnah* is not with me."' Both Muslim and al-Bukhārī transmitted that Sa'd ibn Abī Waqqāṣ said, "Uthmān ibn Maẓ'ūn wanted to be celibate and the Prophet ﷺ forbade him to do that. If he had permitted him to do it, we would have castrated ourselves.'

In the *Musnad* of Ibn Ḥanbal, it is reported from Abū al-Mughīrah from Mu'ān ibn Rifā'ah from 'Alī ibn Yazīd from al-Qāsim that Abū Umāma al-Bāhilī said, 'We went out with the Messenger of Allah ﷺ on an expedition. We passed by a man in a cave where there was some water. He had decided to live in that cave, subsisting on water and some of the plants around it. He had abandoned the world. I said, "I will go to the Prophet ﷺ, and mention that to him. If he gives me permission, I too will do it. Otherwise I will not." I went to him and said, "Prophet of Allah, I passed by a cave which has water and plants and I thought I should stay there and abandon the world." The Prophet ﷺ said, "I was not sent with Judaism or Christianity; I was sent with the pure Ḥanīfiyyah religion. By the One who has the soul of Muḥammad in His hand, a morning or evening in the Way of Allah is better than this world and all it contains! The standing of one of you in the prayer row is better than sixty years of prayer (alone)."'

Our scholars say that this *āyah* and those like it, and the *ḥadīth*s reported that have a similar meaning, refute the excessive ascetics and the false Sufis since such groups deviate from the Path and its reality. Aṭ-Ṭabarī said, 'It is not permitted for any Muslim to forbid for himself anything which Allah has made lawful for His believing slaves, in terms of good food, clothes and marriage, out of the fear that allowing himself those things will result in the hardening of his heart. That was the reason for the reply of the Prophet ﷺ to 'Uthmān ibn Maẓ'ūn. There is no virtue in abandoning anything which Allah has allowed His slaves. Virtue and piety lie in doing what He has recommended His slaves to do and following how the Messenger of Allah ﷺ acted and what he made a *sunnah* for his community and the method that was followed by the rightly-guided leaders, because the best guidance is that of our Prophet Muḥammad ﷺ. So it is a mistake to prefer wool and coarse garments to cotton and linen, when one is able to wear what is lawful, or to eat coarse food and leave meat in order to avoid having need of women.'

Aṭ-Ṭabarī continued, 'Anyone who thinks that good lies in other than what we have mentioned, preferring coarse garments and food and making things hard for themselves and giving away what is excess in value to the people of need, is in error. It is more fitting for a person to put himself right and to enable himself to obey his lord. There is nothing more injurious to the body than poor food since it corrupts the mind and flesh. A man went to al-Ḥasan al-Baṣrī and said, "I have a neighbour who does not eat *faludhaj* [a sweet similar to fudge]." "Why?" he asked. He said, "He said that he would not be able to be properly be thankful for it." He asked, "Does he drink cold water?" "Yes," the man replied. Al-Hasan said, "Your neighbour is ignorant. The blessing of Allah gives us in cold water is more than His blessing in *faludhaj*!"'

Ibn al-'Arabī said, 'Our scholars said, "This was when the *dīn* was straight and property not unlawful. When the *dīn* has been corrupted by people and the unlawful is widespread, then asceticism (*tabattul*) is better and leaving pleasures more fitting. When the lawful is widespread, then the state of the Prophet ﷺ is better and higher.' Al-Muhallab said, 'The Prophet ﷺ forbade asceticism (*tabattul*) and monkhood since he wanted his community to be numerous on the Day of Rising, and in this world to fight the parties of the unbelievers and at the end of time to fight the Dajjāl. Therefore, the Messenger of Allah ﷺ wanted people to have many children.'

Do not overstep the limits.

It is said that the meaning is: 'Do not overstep and make lawful what has been forbidden by Allah.' So, according to this, the two prohibitions include both aims: do not be severe and make the lawful unlawful and do not be lax and make the unlawful lawful. Al-Ḥasan al-Baṣrī said that. It is said that it is meant to reinforce the words: *'do not make unlawful'*. As-Suddī, 'Ikrimah and others said that, but the first is more likely and Allah knows best.

If someone forbids himself food or drink or his slave-girl or anything which Allah has made lawful, that is not binding and, according to Mālik, there is no expiation for going back on any of that, unless, by making the slave-girl unlawful for himself, he intended to free her. Then she becomes free and unlawful to him unless there is a new marriage after she is free. That is also the case when someone says to his wife, 'You are unlawful me.' She is trebly divorced from him. That is because Allah allowed him to make his wife forbidden to him by divorce, explicitly or by allusion. Being unlawful is an allusion to divorce, and that topic will be dealt with fully in *Sūrat at-Taḥrīm*, Allah willing.

Abū Ḥanīfah said, 'If someone forbids himself something, it becomes forbidden for him. If he then goes back on it, he owes *kaffārah*.' This is unlikely and the *āyah* refutes it. Sa'īd ibn Jubayr said, 'Inadvertent oaths forbid the unlawful,' and it is what ash-Shāfi'ī said, as will be dealt with later.

وَكُلُوا۟ مِمَّا رَزَقَكُمُ ٱللَّهُ حَلَٰلًا طَيِّبًا ۚ وَٱتَّقُوا۟ ٱللَّهَ ٱلَّذِىٓ
أَنتُم بِهِۦ مُؤْمِنُونَ ﴿٨٨﴾

88 Eat the lawful and good things Allah has provided for you, and have *taqwā* of Allah, Him in Whom you believe.

The verb '*eat*' in this *āyah* refers to experiencing enjoyment through eating, drinking, wearing clothes, riding and the like and it is used because it is the greatest aim and gives the most personal benefit. The rulings connected with food, drink and clothing will come in *al-A'rāf*, Allah willing.

As for our appetite for pleasant things and opposing the self in its desire to satisfy different types of appetites, people's position about allowing the self to indulge in them varies considerably. Some think that turning the self away from them and preventing it from pursuing its appetites is better than giving it free rein and being easy on it in that respect. If someone gives the self what it wants, he becomes the slave of his appetites and subjected to them. It is related that Abū Ḥāzim passed by some fruit and desired them. He said, 'The place where you are promised is the Garden.'

Others say that allowing the self to enjoy them is more fitting since they give it rest and allow it to generate energy. Yet others say that it is better to follow a middle way because in giving in to the self on some occasions and denying it at others they are combining both sides. That is fairness without blemish. Balance and provision were discussed in *al-Baqarah* (2:3 & 2:62), and praise belongs to Allah.

لَا يُؤَاخِذُكُمُ ٱللَّهُ بِٱللَّغْوِ فِىٓ أَيْمَٰنِكُمْ وَلَٰكِن يُؤَاخِذُكُم بِمَا عَقَّدتُّمُ ٱلْأَيْمَٰنَ ۖ
فَكَفَّٰرَتُهُۥٓ إِطْعَامُ عَشَرَةِ مَسَٰكِينَ مِنْ أَوْسَطِ مَا تُطْعِمُونَ أَهْلِيكُمْ
أَوْ كِسْوَتُهُمْ أَوْ تَحْرِيرُ رَقَبَةٍ ۖ فَمَن لَّمْ يَجِدْ فَصِيَامُ ثَلَٰثَةِ أَيَّامٍ ۚ ذَٰلِكَ كَفَّٰرَةُ
أَيْمَٰنِكُمْ إِذَا حَلَفْتُمْ ۚ وَٱحْفَظُوٓا۟ أَيْمَٰنَكُمْ ۚ كَذَٰلِكَ يُبَيِّنُ ٱللَّهُ لَكُمْ ءَايَٰتِهِۦ لَعَلَّكُمْ
تَشْكُرُونَ ﴿٨٩﴾

89 Allah does not take you to task for your inadvertent oaths, but He will take you to task for oaths you make intentionally. The expiation in that case is to feed ten poor people with the average amount you feed your family, or clothe them, or free a slave. Anyone without the means to do so should fast three days. That is the expiation for breaking oaths when you have sworn them. Keep your oaths. In this way Allah makes His Signs clear to you, so that hopefully you will be thankful.

Allah does not take you to task for your inadvertent oaths

The term '*laghw*' (inadvertent, null, foolish) was discussed in *al-Baqarah* (2:225). The word used for oaths is *aymān*, the plural of *yamīn*. *Yamīn* is derived from *yumn*, which means blessing and Allah has called it that because it protects people's rights. *Yamīn* can be masculine or feminine, and the plurals are *aymān* and *ayman*. [POEM] There is disagreement about the reason for the revelation of this *āyah*. Ibn 'Abbās said that it was because of some people who forbade themselves good food, clothes and marriage. They vowed that and the earlier *āyah*: '*...do not make unlawful the good things Allah has made lawful for you*' (5:87) was revealed. Then they asked, 'What should we do about our oaths?' and this *āyah* was revealed.

According to this, the meaning is, 'If you make oaths and then annul them – in other words rescind their ruling by expiation – and you have expiated them, Allah will not take you to task for that. He will only take you to task for what you stand by and do not expiate.' This makes it clear that an oath does not definitively forbid anything. It is the evidence of ash-Shāfi'ī that an oath cannot make the lawful unlawful and that making something lawful unlawful is inadvertent – just as making something unlawful lawful is inadvertent – in that it does not make it forbidden. It is as if someone saying, 'I have made wine lawful.' According to this, the *āyah* says that Allah called making something lawful unlawful inadvertent because it does not actually make it unlawful.

It is related that 'Abdullāh ibn Rawāḥah had orphans in his care and a guest. He returned from his work late in the night and said, 'Have you fed my guests?' They said, 'We were waiting for you.' He said, 'No, by Allah, I will not eat tonight!' His guest said, 'I will not be the one to eat.' His orphans said, 'We will not eat either.' When he saw that, he ate and they ate. Then he went to the Prophet ﷺ and told him and he said, 'You have obeyed the All-Merciful and disobeyed Shayṭān.' The *āyah* was then revealed.

There are four categories of oaths in the *Sharī'ah*; expiation is possible for two of them but there is no expiation for the other two. In his *Sunan*, ad-Dāraquṭnī transmitted that 'Abdullāh said, 'There are four types of oaths: two types require expiation and two cannot be expiated. The two types of oaths which can be expiated are when a man swears, "By Allah, I will not do such-and-such," and he does it, and when a man says, "By Allah, I will do such-and-such, and does not do it." The two which cannot be expiated are when a man swears, "By Allah I did not do such-and-such," when he did it and a man swears, "I did such and such," which he did not do.' Ibn 'Abd al-Barr said, 'This is also mentioned by Sufyān ath-Thawrī in his *Jāmi'* and by al-Marwazī.' Sufyān said, 'There are four oaths. Two can be expiated. This is when a man says, "By Allah, I will not do it," and he does it, or he says, "By Allah, I will do it," and does not do it. There are two oaths for which there is no expiation. They are when a man says, "By Allah, I did not do it" when he did it, or he says, "By Allah, I did it" when he did not do it.'

Al-Marwazī said, 'Regarding the first two oaths, there is no disagreement among scholars about what Sufyān said. Regarding the last two, there is disagreement. If someone swears an oath that he did not do a certain thing or that he did a certain thing and believes what he said to be true, he owes no expiation and commits no sin according to Mālik, Sufyān ath-Thawrī and the People of Opinion, as well as Aḥmad and Abū 'Ubayd. Ash-Shāfi'ī says that he commits no sin, but owes expiation.' A similar position to that of ash-Shāfi'ī is related from some of the *Tābi'ūn*. Al-Marwazī says that he inclines to the position of Mālik and Aḥmad. He said, 'According to most scholars, an inadvertent oath is a man saying, "No, by Allah" and "Yes, by Allah" when he talks not actually really intending any oath.' Ash-Shāfi'ī says that the inadvertent applies to what is said in insistence, anger and haste.

but He will take you to task for oaths you make intentionally.

'Aqd is of two sorts: physical, like the knot of rope, and in principle like a sale. A poet said:

When people make a contract (*'aqd*) with their neighbour,
 they bind it twice over.

An oath which is binding (*mun'aqidah*, from the measure *mufa'ilah*) comes from the root *'aqd*. It is when the heart resolves in the future not to do something or to do something and then does not carry that out. This is what can only be remedied by uttering the exception (if Allah wills) or through expiation as will come.

As well as the reading *'aqadtum*, the word is also read as *'āqadtum*, which is Form III. That usually only refers to two people, although it can be between two or more. The second party is the one to whom the oath is made. It can also mean 'for the oaths you made' because the verb *'āqada* is close in meaning to *'āhada* and becomes transitive with a genitive particle as we see in 48:10. The verb *nāda* is transitive in 5:58 and is used with *'ilā'* and on its own, as in 'I called Zayd.' It is also seen in 19:52. But when it means 'call', it is transitive with the particle *ilā* as we see in 41:33. Then it is expanded in Allah's words *'āqadtum* and the genitive particle is elided and the verb is connected to the object and it becomes *"āqadtumūhu'* and the *hā'* is elided as in 15:94. Or it is possible that '*fā'ala'* means *'fa'ala'* as we see in 9:30 where *qātalahum* means *qatalahum*. Sometimes in Arabic *mufā'ilah* can refer to one person without the normal meaning of Form III as when you say, *'sāfaratu'* (I travelled) and *'ẓāhartu'* (I helped).

It is also read as Form II (*'aqqadtum*), and Mujāhid said that it then means 'what you intended'. It is related from Ibn 'Umar that if it is read in Form II, it requires repetition, meaning that there is no expiation obliged except for what is repeated. This is countered by the report that the Prophet ﷺ said, 'By Allah, if Allah wills, I will never make an oath and then see something better than it without doing expiation for my oath and doing the thing that is better.' So he mentioned the necessity of expiation for an oath which is not repeated. Abū 'Ubayd said, 'The reading *'aqqadtum* demands repetition and the one who takes this reading does not oblige expiation for a single oath, only when it is repeated.' This position is contrary to the consensus. Nāfi' reported that when Ibn 'Umar broke an oath without stressing it, he fed ten poor people. When he had stressed an oath, he freed a slave. Nāfi' said that stressing the oath meant repeating it.

They disagree about deliberate false oaths and whether they are considered binding or not. The majority say that this refers to a deceitful oath, to treachery and to lies and is not binding nor is there expiation for it. Ash-Shāfi'ī, however, says that it is a binding oath because it is made with the heart and accompanied by an oath in the name of Allah and so there is expiation owed for it. The sound view is the first. Ibn al-Mundhir said, 'This is the position of Mālik ibn Anas and those of the people of Madīnah who follow him. It is the view of al-Awzā'ī and those Syrians who agree with him, and the position of ath-Thawrī and the people of Iraq.' It is the position of Aḥmad, Isḥāq, Abū Thawr, Abū 'Ubayd, the People of Hadith, and the People of Opinion from the people of Kufa.'

Abū Bakr said, 'The words of the Prophet ﷺ, "Anyone who swears an oath and then sees something better than it should expiate his oath and do the thing which is better" and, "Let him expiate his oath and do what is better", indicate that expiation is obliged for someone who swears to do an action in the future and then does not do it, or not to do something in the future which he then does.'

There is a second view regarding this matter – that of ash-Shafi'ī – which is that even if he sins and deliberately makes a false oath by Allah he should still make expiation. Abū Bakr adds, 'We do not know of any other report which indicates this position. The Book and *Sunnah* indicate the first view. Allah says: *"Do not, by your oaths, make Allah a pretext to avoid good actions and being godfearing and putting things right between people."* (2:224)' Ibn 'Abbās said, 'This is when a man swears that he will not give to his relatives and Allah gives him a way out of that by expiation. He should not use Allah as an excuse, but should expiate his oath.'

Reports indicate that an oath by which a man swears to take unlawful property is the greatest of the oaths which can be expiated. Ibn al-'Arabī said, 'The *āyah* brings two forms of oaths: inadvertent and intentional. It concentrates on the majority of oaths and leaves others, which amount to a hundred kinds of oaths with no form of expiation.' Al-Bukhari transmitted that 'Abdullāh ibn 'Amr said: 'A desert Arab came to the Prophet ﷺ and asked, "Messenger of Allah, what are the serious wrong actions?" He answered, "Associating others with Allah." He asked, "Then what?" He said, "Lack of respect towards parents." He asked, "Then what?" He replied, "False oaths." He asked, "What is a false oath?" He said ﷺ, "One by which a person takes the property of another Muslim and lies about it."'

Muslim transmitted from Abū Umāmah that the Messenger of Allah ﷺ said, 'If someone takes the right of another Muslim by his [false] oath, Allah has obliged the Fire for him and forbidden the Garden to him.' A man asked, 'Even if it is something insignificant, Messenger of Allah?' He answered, 'Even if it is a stick of arak.' We find in the *ḥadīth* of 'Abdullāh ibn Mas'ūd: 'The Messenger of Allah ﷺ said, 'Whoever swears a false oath in order to take the property of a Muslim will find Allah angry with him when he meets Him.' So it was revealed: *'Those who sell Allah's contract and their own oaths for a paltry price…'* (3:77) He did not mention expiation. If Allah had made expiation obligatory for us, the crime of that person would be annulled and he would find Allah pleased with him when he met Him and not merit the threat. How could that be when this person has sworn a false oath to appropriate someone else's property and made light of swearing an oath by Allah, disdained it and thought this world great? He has made little of what Allah made great and made great what Allah disdains. That is enough for you. This is why a false oath is called *'ghamūs'* (calamitous) because it plunges the one who swears it into the Fire.

If someone swears that he has not done a good action which he has done, his doing that breaks his oath and he is obliged to make expiation because of the difference between what he says and does. It is the same if he says, 'If I have done it.' When he then swears that he will do it, he immediately breaks his oath if he does the good action because of the existence of difference. It is the same if he says, 'If I did not do it.'

The words of someone who swears an oath, 'I will do it,' if he does not do it has the status of a command and his words, 'I will not do it' and 'If I do it' have the status of a prohibition. In the first case, it is not fulfilled until he does all that he swore to do, as when he swears, 'I will eat this loaf.' If he only eats part of it, the oath is not fulfilled until he has eaten all of it because eating all of it is what he swore to do. If he only says, 'I will eat' without definition, the oath is fulfilled by the minimum amount to which the word eating can be applied because the manner of eating exists.

In the case of a prohibition, he breaks the oath by doing the minimum of what he swore to because it demands that he does not broach the slightest amount of what he made forbidden to himself. If he swears, for instance, that he will not enter a house and puts just one of his feet inside, he breaks his oath. The evidence for that is that we find that the Lawgiver strengthened the prohibition at the very start of what is prohibited in His words: *'Do not marry any women your fathers married.'* (4:22) So if someone makes a marriage contract with a woman, she is unlawful to his father and son even if it is not consummated. The same is not true of a marriage designed to make remarriage with a previous husband lawful, as he ﷺ said, 'Not until you taste his sweetness' [i.e. the marriage has been consummated.]

What oaths should be sworn by is Allah and His Beautiful Names, such as the All Merciful, Most Merciful, All-Hearing, All-Seeing, Ever-Forbearing, and others of His Names and sublime attributes, like His Might, Power, Knowledge, Will, Greatness, Immensity, His covenant, His contract, and all the attributes of His Essence. This is because it is then an oath sworn by what is timeless and not temporal. So the one who swears by it like someone who swears by the Essence.

At-Tirmidhī, an-Nasā'ī and others related that when Jibrīl looked at the Garden and returned to Allah Almighty, he said, 'By Your might, no one will hear of it but that he will enter it!' Similarly he said of the Fire, 'By Your might, no one will hear of it and enter it!' They and others also transmitted that Ibn 'Umar said, 'The oath of the Prophet ﷺ was, 'No, by the Overturner of hearts!' One variant has, 'No, by the Director of hearts.' Scholars agree that if anyone swears an oath and says, *'wa'llāhi'*, *'billāhi'*, or *'tallāhi'* and then breaks his oath, he owes expiation. Ibn al-Mundhir said, 'Mālik, ash-Shāfi'ī, Abū 'Ubayd, Abū Thawr, Isḥāq and the People of Opinion say that if someone swears by one of the Names of Allah and breaks his oath, he owes expiation. That is what we say and I do not know of any disagreement about that.'

It is, however, transmitted in the Chapter of the one who swears by the Qur'ān that Ya'qūb said, 'If someone swears by the All-Merciful and breaks his oath, he owes no expiation.' There is consensus that the All-Merciful is one of the Names of Allah and there is no disagreement about it. There is disagreement about the expressions, 'by the Right of Allah' or 'the immensity of Allah', 'the Power of Allah', 'the Knowledge of Allah', 'the Life of Allah' and 'the Days of Allah'. Mālik said that all of them are oaths which demand expiation. Ash-Shāfi'ī said that the expressions 'by the Right of Allah', 'the Majesty of Allah', 'the Immensity of Allah', and 'the Power of Allah' only become oaths if an oath is intended by them. If an oath is not intended, then they are not oaths because it is possible that the right of Allah is obligatory and His power has been achieved. He said that using the expression 'trust (*amānah*) of Allah' is not an oath. This is also the case with 'by the life of Allah' and '*ayamullah*': if an oath is not intended by the use of the expression, it is not an oath.

The People of Opinion say that if someone says, 'by the immensity of Allah', 'might of Allah', 'majesty of Allah', 'greatness of Allah' and' 'trust of Allah' and breaks it, then he owes expiation. [Muḥammad ibn] al-Ḥasan said that 'by the right of Allah' is not an oath and there is no expiation for it. That is the position of Abū Ḥanīfah which ar-Rāzī related from him. That is also the case with swearing by the covenant, contract and trust of Allah: it is not an oath. Some of his people, however, say that it is an oath. Aṭ-Ṭaḥāwī said that it is not an oath, and the same is true of saying, 'by Allah's knowledge'. According to Abū Ḥanīfah, it is not an oath. His companion, Abū Yūsuf, disagreed with him and said that it is an oath.

Ibn al-'Arabī said, 'That which he concludes respecting that is that knowledge can be applied to anything that is known, which can be something temporal, and so the expression does not amount to a proper oath. He ignores the fact that the word "power" can be applied to what is decreed. The same judgment that can be made about what is decreed can be made about something that is known.'

Ibn al-Mundhir said, 'It is confirmed that the Messenger of Allah ﷺ said, "By Allah (*ayamu'llāh*), he is right for leadership" in the story of Zayd and his son Usāmah. Ibn 'Abbās used to say, "*ayamu'llāh*" as did Ibn 'Umar.' Isḥāq said, 'If he means an oath by the term "*ayamu'llāh*", it is an oath based on volition and the resolve of the heart.'

There is disagreement about swearing by the Qur'ān. Ibn Mas'ūd said, 'There is an oath by every *āyah*.' Al-Ḥasan al-Baṣrī and Ibn Mubārak said that. Aḥmad said, 'I do not know of anything to refute it.' Abū 'Ubayd said, 'It is one oath.' Abū Ḥanīfah said that there is no expiation for it. Qatādah said that he swears by a copy of the Qur'ān. Aḥmad and Isḥāq said, 'We do not dislike this.'

What is considered to be a binding oath is only one sworn by Allah and His Names and Attributes. Aḥmad ibn Ḥanbal, however, says that an oath is binding if someone swears by the Prophet ﷺ because he has sworn by something without which faith is not complete and so expiation is necessary for him in the same way as if he had sworn by Allah, although this is refuted by what is found in the two *Ṣaḥīḥ* collections and elsewhere in that the Messenger of Allah ﷺ caught up to 'Umar ibn al-Khaṭṭāb in a retinue while 'Umar was swearing by his father. The Messenger of Allah ﷺ called out to him: 'Allah Almighty forbids you to swear an oath by your fathers. If someone swears an oath, he should swear by Allah or be silent.' This involves not swearing by anything other than Allah Almighty and His Names and attributes, as we already mentioned. One thing that verifies that is what Abū Dāwūd, an-Nasā'ī and others related from Abū Hurayrah: the Messenger of Allah ﷺ said, 'Do not swear by your fathers or your mothers or equals. Only swear by Allah and you will be truthful.' He said that anyone who says, 'By Ādam and Ibrāhīm' and breaks that oath owes no expiation. He has sworn by something that does not constitute an oath.

The Imams related from Abū Hurayrah that the Messenger of Allah ﷺ said, 'If any of you swears and says, "By al-Lāt," he should say "There is no god but Allah." If someone says to his companion, "Come and let us bet," should give *ṣadaqah*.' An-Nasā'ī transmitted from Muṣ'ab ibn Sa'd that his father said, 'I had recently been in the state of Jāhiliyyah and I swore by al-Lāt and al-'Uzzā. Some of the Companions of the Messenger of Allah ﷺ said to me, "What you have said is very bad!" (In another variant, 'I used foul language.') So I went to the Messenger of Allah ﷺ and mentioned that to him and he said, "Say: 'There is no god but Allah alone with no partner. His is the kingdom and praise is His. He has power over all things.' Then spit three times to your left and seek refuge with Allah from Shayṭān. Then do not repeat it."'

Scholars say that the command of the Messenger of Allah ﷺ to him to say that is because saying 'There is no god but Allah' after it expiates those words, reminds against heedlessness and completes the blessing. He mentioned al-Lāt because that was what was most frequently said by them. Mentioning the names of other gods has the same rulings because there is no difference between them.

It is like that when someone says to friend, 'Come and let us bet.' It is like what he said about al-Lāt because they used to gamble and it is falsely consuming wealth.

Abū Ḥanīfah said about a man who says in his oath that he is a Jew, a Christian, free of Islam or the Prophet or the Qur'ān, or that he will disbelieve in Allah, that *kaffārah* is obliged for that oath and he is not obliged to fulfil it when he says Judaism, Christianity, the Prophet and the Ka'bah, even though it is a form of oath. One holds to what ad-Dāraquṭnī related from Abū Rāfi' that his female emancipator wanted to part him from his wife. She said that one day she would be Jewish and one day Christian, and that all her slaves would be freed and all of her wealth given in the Way of Allah, and that she must walk to the House of Allah, if they did not separate.' He said, 'I asked 'Ā'ishah, Ḥafṣah, Ibn 'Umar, Ibn 'Abbās and Umm Salamah, and they all said to her, 'Do you want to be like Hārūt and Mārūt?' They commanded her to expiate her oath and leave them alone.

It is also transmitted that he said, 'My female emancipator said, "I will part you and your wife," and that all of her property would be for the Ka'bah and she would be Jewish one day, Christian one day and Magian one day if she did not part him from his wife! I went to *Umm al-Mu'minīn* Umm Salamah and said, "My female client wants to part me from my wife." She said, "Go to your female client and tell her, 'It is not lawful for you to do that.'" So I returned to her Then I went to Ibn 'Umar and told him and he came to the door and said, "Here are Hārūt and Mārūt." She said, "I assigned all of my wealth to the Ka'bah?" He said, "And what will you eat from?" She said, "I said that I would be Jewish one day, Christian one day and Magian one day." He said, "If you become Jewish, you will be killed. If you become Christian, you will be killed. If you become Magian, you will be killed." She asked, "Then what do you command me?" He said, "Expiate your oath and join your slave and slavegirl."'

Scholars agree that when someone says, 'I swear by Allah,' it is an oath. They disagree about when someone swears or testifies that such-and-such will happen but does not mention Allah. According to Mālik, they are oaths if he means by Allah. If he does not mean by Allah, they are not oaths to be expiated. Abū Ḥanīfah, al-Awzā'ī, al-Ḥasan and an-Nakha'ī said that both cases are oaths. Ash-Shāfi'ī said that they are not oaths until he mentions Allah. This is what al-Muzanī transmitted from him. Ar-Rabī' related from him a similar position to that of Mālik. If someone says, 'I swear to you that you will do it,' and means a request, there is no *kaffārah* and it is not an oath. If he meant it as an oath, it is as we already said. If someone swears by something ascribed to Allah which is not an attribute, like 'the creation of Allah', 'Allah's provision', or the 'House of Allah', he owes nothing because it is not a permissible oath since it is not swearing by Allah.

When someone makes a binding oath, it is undone by expiation or making an exception (by saying 'Allah willing'). Ibn al-Mājishūn said that the exception is instead of the *kaffārah* and does not undo the oath. Ibn al-Qāsim said that it undoes the oath. Ibn al-'Arabī said that it is the school of the *fuqahā'* of the cities, and it is sound. It is a precondition which is verbally connected to it, based on what an-Nasā'ī and Abū Dāwūd related from Ibn 'Umar that the Prophet ﷺ said: 'If someone swears an oath and makes an exception, he can carry it out if he wishes, and he can leave it without any oath-breaking.' If he intends it without speaking or stops without an excuse, it does not help him.

Muḥammad ibn al-Mawwāz said, 'The exception ('Allah willing') is connected to the oath by belief, even if comes after an intervening expression.' He said, 'When someone finishes his oath and then makes an exception, that does not help him because the oath finished without the exception being made. The fact that it come after it makes it of no effect like being remiss. This is refuted by the *ḥadīth*, "If someone swears an oath and makes an exception." The *fā'* is for the consequence and that is the position of most of the people of knowledge. That would also lead to dissolving an oath when it is contracted and that is false.'

Ibn Khuwayzimandād said, 'Our colleagues disagree about when someone makes the exception internally to qualify the oath he made. Some of our people said that his exception is sound and he wronged the one to whom he swore. Some of them said that it is not valid unless it is heard by the one to whom he swore. Some said that it is sound when his tongue and lips move with it, even if the one to whom he swore did not hear it.'

Ibn Khuwayzimandād said, 'We say that the exception is sound in itself. That is because oaths are considered according to their intentions. We say that it is not sound unless his tongue and lips move with it. If his tongue and lips do not move with it, he is not speaking, and an exception involves speech rather than something else. We say that it is not sound in any case and that is because it is the right of the one to whom he swore it. It is according to what the judge gives him in full. Then it is not an oath based on the choice of the swearer. Rather it is taken in full from him and it has no effectiveness in it.'

Ibn 'Abbās said, 'The exception to an oath extends to a year.' He is followed in that view by Abū al-'Āliyah and al-Ḥasan, and it is connected to Allah's words: '*...those who do not call on any other god together with Allah.*' (25:68) After a year the revelation came: '*...except for those who repent.*' (19:60) Mujāhid said, 'It is allowed if someone says it after two years, Allah willing.' Sa'īd ibn Jubayr said, 'It is allowed if he says it after four months.' Ṭāwūs said, 'He can make an exception for as long as he is in the gathering.' Qatādah said, 'If he says it before he rises or speaks, the exception is valid.' Aḥmad ibn Ḥanbal and Isḥāq said, 'He can make an exception as long as he is in that business.' 'Aṭā' said, 'He can do it for as long as it takes to milk a camel with abundant milk.'

Ibn al-'Arabī said, 'As for Ibn 'Abbās's commentary on the *āyah*, it does not count because the two *āyahs* were connected in Allah's knowledge and His Tablet. The revelation was delayed because of a wisdom which Allah knew about. An excellent secondary ruling ensues from it, which is that if someone swears, "By Allah, I will not enter the house," or "You are divorced if I enter the house," and he makes the exception in his heart of "Allah willing" in the first oath, and also makes an exception to the second oath in his heart in the form of a proper exception which frees him from the oath after a period of time, or for some reason he stipulates, or because someone else wanted him to swear it, and he did not outwardly state the exception in any way out of fear of the one to whom he swore it, that will be effective for him and the two oaths are not binding on him. This is about divorce as long as clear evidence is not present. If there is clear evidence, his claim of the exception is not accepted. That benefits him when he comes asking for a *fatwā*.' The manner of the exception is that Allah manifested the first *āyah* and concealed the second. That is also the case when someone swears an oath out of fear and conceals the exception. Allah knows best.

Ibn al-'Arabī said, 'Abū al-Faḍl al-Marāghī used to study in Madīnah as-Salām. Letters would come to him from his land and he would put them in a box without reading them out of fear that he would see in them something which would upset him and divert him from his quest. After five years when he had achieved his goal in seeking knowledge and had resolved to travel, he put his saddle on and brought out those letters. In them he read that which, if he had read them after his arrival, would have prevented him from learning even an iota of knowledge. He praised Allah and put his cloth on the camel and went out to the Bāb al-Ḥalbah on the road to Khorasan. The one who had hired the camel to him went ahead of him and he stopped at a vendor to buy his travel requirements from him. While he was attempting to do that he heard him say to another vendor, "Did you hear the preacher say that Ibn 'Abbās permitted making an exception even after a year. My mind was occupied with that when I heard it and I continued to reflect on it. If that was correct, then why did Allah Almighty say to Ayyūb: *"Take a bundle of rushes in your hand and strike with that, but do no break your oath."* (38:44) What prevented Him from saying, "Say: 'If Allah wishes'"? When he heard him say that, he said, "How can I leave land in which vendors have knowledge like this and this rank for Marāghah? I will never do that." He went after the hired man and released him from his hire and remained there until his death.'

Saying, 'If Allah wills' annuls the oath by Allah since it is an allowance from Allah, and there is no disagreement about that. There is disagreement about an oath by other than Allah. Ash-Shāfi'ī and Abū Ḥanīfah say that it applies to all oaths, such as oaths to divorce, emancipate and the like. Abū 'Umar said, 'What they agree on is the truth. It has come that there is a stop on an oath by Allah through the exception, but not in anything else.'

The expiation in that case

Scholars disagree about doing expiation before breaking an oath and whether that is adequate, while there is consensus that expiation is preferred after breaking it, and it is more appropriate. There are three positions. One is that it is absolutely permitted, and it is the position of twenty-four Companions and a group of *fuqahā'*, and is the well-known view of Mālik. Abū Ḥanīfah and his people say that doing that is not allowed at all. One piece of evidence for its permissibility is related by Abū Mūsā al-Ash'arī. The Messenger of Allah ﷺ said, 'By Allah, if Allah wills, I will never make an oath and then see something better than it without doing expiation for my oath and doing the thing that is better.' Abū Dāwūd transmitted it.

In terms of meaning, the oath is the reason for the expiation since Allah says here: *'That is the expiation for breaking oaths when you have sworn them,'* and so expiation is connected to the oath, and meanings are related to their causes. If expiation replaces the fulfilment of the oath, it is permitted for it to be done before breaking the oath. The reason for its prohibition is what Muslim related from 'Adī ibn Ḥātim who said that he heard the Messenger of Allah ﷺ say, 'Whoever swears an oath and then sees something else is better than it, should do the thing which is better.' An-Nasā'ī added, 'and then expiate his oath.' In corroboration of this is the fact that expiation removes the sin. So if the oath has not been broken, there is nothing to be removed and so there is no point in the action. The words *'you make'* imply both swearing and then breaking the oath. Any action which is done before it is mandatory is not valid. That applies to the prayers and other acts of worship. Ash-Shāfi'ī said anticipatory expiation is satisfied by feeding, freeing and clothing, but not by fasting because the physical actions may not be advanced before their time. In other things expiation is advance is allowed, and this is the third view.

Allah mentions three means of expiation and gives us a choice between them. If these three are not possible, then there is fasting. He began with feeding because it was the best option in the Hijaz owing to the great need for it. There is no disagreement that there is a choice in how oaths may be expiated. Ibn al-'Arabī says: 'My view is that it should be according to the circumstances. If there are a lot of people in need, feeding is better because when you free someone, you do not satisfy their need for food but actually increase it. Clothing is next. Since Allah knew the need, He began with the most pressing one.'

is to feed ten poor people

According to us and to ash-Shāfi'ī poor people have complete ownership of what is given to them, and it is given to them so that they own it and can dispose of it since Allah says: *'He who feeds and is not fed'* (6:12) and in the *ḥadīth*: 'The Messenger of Allah ﷺ gave [lit. 'fed'] the grandfather a sixth.' It is a form of expiation and is only satisfied by transfer of ownership. Abū Ḥanīfah said, 'If someone gives them a midday and evening meal, that is sufficient.' This is the preference of Ibn al-Mājishūn among our scholars. He said that 'Transfer of ownership of food is feeding.' Allah says: *'They give food, despite their love of it, to the poor and orphans and captives.'* (76:8) Any manner of feeding is included in the *āyah.*

with the average amount you feed your family,

This was spoken of in *al-Baqarah* (2:143) where the adjective *'average'* (*wasṭ*) actually means 'the best'. Here it indicates a median position, as in the *ḥadīth*: 'The best of affairs is the middle one.' Ibn Mājah reports from Muḥammad ibn Yaḥyā from 'Abd ar-Raḥmān ibn Mahdī from Sufyān ibn 'Uyaynah from Sulaymān ibn Abī al-Mughīrah from Sa'īd ibn Jubayr from Ibn 'Abbās: 'A man may feed his family from a position of wealth and may also feed his family when he is in a state of hardship.' So this *āyah* was revealed. This indicates that it means the middle of two things.

Feeding, according to Mālik, consists of a *mudd* for each of the ten poor people if it is in the city of the Prophet ﷺ. Ash-Shāfi'ī and the people of Madīnah said that. Sulaymān ibn Yasār said, 'I met people who had been the recipients of the expiation of an oath. They were given a *mudd* of wheat measured by the lesser *mudd.* They saw that as being allowed.' It is position of Ibn 'Umar, Ibn 'Abbās, and Zayd ibn Thābit. 'Aṭā' ibn Abī Rabāḥ said that. There is disagreement when it is other than that. Ibn al-Qāsim said, 'A *mudd* satisfies it in every place.' Ibn al-Mawwāz said, 'Ibn Wahb gave a *fatwā* in Egypt for a *mudd* and a half. Ashhab said a *mudd* and a third and stated, "A *mudd* and a third is the median amount of what is common for midday and evening meals in cities."'

Abū Ḥanīfah said, 'It should be half a *ṣā'* of wheat, and a *ṣā'* of dates and barley according to the *ḥadīth* of 'Abdullāh ibn Tha'labah from his father who said, "The Messenger of Allah ﷺ stood up to speak and commanded a *ṣā'* of dates for the *zakāt al-fiṭr* or a *ṣā'* of barley of every sort or a *ṣā'* of the two varieties of wheat."' That was the view of Sufyān and Ibn al-Mubārak. It is related from 'Alī, 'Umar, Ibn 'Umar, and 'Ā'isha and it is the position of Sa'īd ibn al-Musayyab and that of most of the *fuqahā'* of Iraq since Ibn 'Abbās related it.' The Messenger of Allah ﷺ expiated with a *ṣā'* of dates and commanded people to do that. If someone did not have that, then a *ṣā'* of medium wheat with which you feed your family. Ibn Mājah transmitted it in the *Sunan*.

It is not permitted to feed a wealthy person or a relative whom someone is meant to support anyway. If he is a relative whom he is not required to support, Mālik says, 'I do not like someone feeding him, but if he does so and the relative is poor, that satisfies it.' If someone feeds a wealthy person, being ignorant of his wealth, according to the *Mudawwanah* and elsewhere, it does not satisfy it, whereas it does according to the *Asadiyyah*.

A man should give the sort of food that he himself eats. Ibn al-'Arabī said, 'Here a group of scholars have erred and said, "If someone eats barley and most people eat wheat, he should give what most people eat." This is clear heedlessness. If the one expiating is not able to buy other than barley for himself, he is not obliged to feed other people something else. The Prophet ﷺ said, "A *ṣā'* of food: a *ṣā'* of barley." He mentioned them separately and everyone pays his due from what he eats. This is not concealed.'

Mālik said, 'A midday meal for ten poor people satisfies it.' Ash-Shāfi'ī said, 'It is not permitted to feed them all at the same time, because people vary in when they eat, but he should give each poor person a *mudd*.' It is related that 'Alī ibn Abī Ṭālib said, 'Feeding ten is not satisfied by one meal,' in other words providing them with a midday meal without an evening one or vice versa. Abū 'Umar said, 'This is the position of the imāms of *fatwā* in the cities.'

Ibn Ḥabīb said, 'The requirement is not satisfied by giving bread alone. Rather someone should give it together with it its accompaniment in the form of oil, savoury sauce or what is feasible.' Ibn al-'Arabī said, 'I do not think that this addition is obligatory. It is either recommended to give bread along with sugar, or better still, with meat, or it might be said that there is no way to specify the accompaniment that goes with "food" because of the comprehensive nature of the term.'

The *āyah* was revealed about median fare which necessarily entails bread and oil or vinegar, and similar things such as cheese and other condiments as Ibn Ḥabīb said. The Messenger of Allah ﷺ said, 'The best condiment is vinegar.' Al-Ḥasan al-Baṣrī said that expiation is satisfied if someone feeds them bread and meat or bread and oil once a day until they are full. It is the position of Ibn Sīrīn, Jābir ibn Zayd and Makḥūl. That is related from Anas ibn Mālik.

It is not permitted to give *kaffārah* to one poor person. That is the position of ash-Shāfiʿī. The Ḥanafīs forbid giving all to one person at one time, but they disagree about when it is all given in the same day with different payments. Some permit that, and others say that it is permitted to give it to the same person over different days to make up the number of poor people. Abū Ḥanīfah said that that is permitted because the aim of the *āyah* is according to what he feeds. If he gives that amount to one person, that satisfies the requirement. Our evidence is that the text of Allah states '*ten*' and it is not permitted to turn from it. It also contains giving life and sufficiency to a group of Muslims for one day in which they can devote themselves to worshipping Allah and calling on Him and He will forgive the expiator because of that. Allah knows best.

According to grammatical usage, the pronoun in '*its expiation*' refers to '*mā*'. In this place it can mean 'which' or it can have the function of a verbal noun or refer to the wrong action for breaking the oath, even if it was not explicitly mentioned since the meaning demands it. '*Ahlīkum*' ('your family') is the sound plural of '*ahl*'. Jaʿfar ibn Muḥammad aṣ-Ṣādiq recited it as '*ahālīkum*' which is a broken plural. Abū al-Fatḥ said that *ahālī* is like *layālī*. The singular is *ahlāt* and *laylāt*. The Arabs say *ahl* and *ahlah*. [POEM]

or clothe them,

The word '*clothe*' is recited as *kiswah* and *kuswah* which are two dialectical forms. Saʿīd ibn Jubayr and Muḥammad ibn as-Samayfaʿ al-Yamānī recited '*ka'iswatihim*'. Clothing in respect of men is one garment that covers the entire body, and for women, the minimum is that which will allow the prayer, which is a dress and scarf. The same applies to children. In *al-ʿUtibyyah*, Ibn al-Qāsim said that a female child is clothed in one large garment and a boy in one large garment, analogous with feeding. Ash-Shāfiʿī, Abū Ḥanīfah, ath-Thawrī and al-Awzāʿī said that it is the minimum to which the word may be applied: one garment. In a transmission reported by Abū al-Faraj from Mālik, and stated by Ibrāhīm an-Nakhaʿī and Mughīrah: 'It is what covers the body based on the fact that the prayer is not permitted in less than that.'

It is related that Salmān said, 'The best garment is a *tubbān* (breeches).' Aṭ-Ṭabarī has its *isnād.* Al-Ḥakam ibn 'Utaybah said that it is satisfied by a turban which is wrapped around the head. That is the position of ath-Thawrī. Ibn al-'Arabī said, 'I would like it to be said that it is only satisfied by a garment that protects a person from heat and cold, as one must feed in a manner that satisfies hunger. That is what I say. I do not know of the position that a single waist-wrapper is sufficient. May Allah give us and you knowledge by His help!'

People take into consideration people's ordinary and customary dress. Some say that the requirement is not satisfied by one garment unless it is what is normally worn, like a robe or a wrapper. The Ḥanafīs say that clothing for the expiation of an oath should be a garment and waist-wrapper for every poor person, or a cloak, or a shirt, or gown. Abū Mūsā al-Ash'arī reported that he gave each person two garments. Ibn Sīrīn said, 'This is what is meant by what Ibn al-'Arabī said that he preferred.' Allah knows best.

Money to cover the cost of food or clothing does not satisfy the requirement, as ash-Shāfi'ī said. Abū Ḥanīfah, however, says that it does, and he also says that since paying the price satisfies *zakāt*, it does for *kaffārah* as well. Ibn al-'Arabī said, 'He relied on the aim of expiation being to satisfy need and remove it, which paying the price does.' Our answer is that if we look at settling need, where is the worship? Where is the text of the Qur'ān regarding the three categories and the clarification of moving from one category to another?

If the clothing is given to a *dhimmī* or a slave, it does not satisfy the requirement. Abū Ḥanīfah said that it does because they are included under the category of 'poor' and included in the generality of the *āyah*. We say that that this specifies that part of wealth must be given to the poor and it is not permitted to give it to an unbeliever. The basis for this is *zakāt* and we agree that it is not permitted to give *zakāt* to an apostate. Every evidence specific to an apostate is our proof about a *dhimmī*. A slave is not considered to be poor since his maintenance is undertaken by his master. Therefore, as is the case with someone wealthy, expiation may not be given to him.

or free a slave.

Freeing someone is to deliver them from servitude. The term (*taḥrīr*) is used for freeing captives and being freed of hardships and the toil of this world, and similar things as when the mother of Maryam said: *'I have pledged to you what is in my womb, devoting it to your service (muḥarrar).'* (3:35) This means that that person will be free of the toils of this world. Elaborating that are the words of al-Farazdaq ibn Ghālib when he said:

Banū Ghudānah, I have freed you,
and I have given you to 'Aṭiyyah ibn Ji'āl.

It means: 'I have freed you from mockery.' The neck is singled out in a person since it is the part of the body which is normally bound and shackled. So it is the site of ownership and freeing is ascribed to it.

Only fully freeing a believer satisfies the requirement. There can be no partial emancipation or freeing after a term or a *kitābah* or *tadbīr.* Being an *umm walad* does not satisfy it nor someone a person is under obligation to set free nor an old slave nor someone chronically ill which would impair his earning ability. Dāwūd disagrees and allows freeing someone with a defect. Abū Ḥanīfah says that it is permitted to free an unbelieving woman because the generality of the term entails that. Our argument is that it is an obligatory act of worship and so an unbeliever is not appropriate in this case as is the case with *zakāt.* Furthermore, everything undefined (*muṭlaq*) regarding this in the Qur'ān goes back to something which is elsewhere defined (*muqayyad*) regarding freeing a slave for accidental killing.

We said that there can be no sharing in it because Allah says: *'free a slave (neck)'* (4:92), and freeing part of a neck is not the same as a whole neck. We say that there is no contract of emancipation (*'atq*) in this instance because freeing (*taḥrīr*) demands initiating emancipation without the need for any prior emancipation agreement. We say that the slave must be 'sound' since Allah says: *'free a slave'*, and the implementation of that demands freeing a complete slave and a blind slave has a defect and is not, therefore, whole. We find in the *Ṣaḥīḥ* that the Prophet ﷺ said, 'If a Muslim frees a Muslim, it will free him from the Fire, each of his limbs for the emancipated limbs, even the genitals.' This is a text. Two positions are related about someone with only eye, someone who is deaf and eunuchs.

If someone produces money with which to free a slave for *kaffārah* and it is lost, he still owes the *kaffārah* which is not the case with money for *zakāt* given to someone to feed the poor or buy a slave. If that is lost, he owes nothing since he has obeyed the command.

There is disagreement about *kaffārah* if the person who made the oath dies. Ash-Shāfi'ī and Abū Thawr said that it must be taken from the capital of his estate. Abū Ḥanīfah said that it is taken from the third [for bequests]. Mālik said that that is the case when he leaves instructions to that effect. If someone makes an oath when he is wealthy and does not expiate it until he is poor, or breaks an oath when he is poor and does not expiate it until he becomes wealthy, or breaks an oath when he is a slave and then becomes free, it is the time that the oath is expiated that is considered, not the time when the oath was broken.

Muslim related from Abū Hurayrah that the Messenger of Allah ﷺ said, 'By Allah, it is more sinful in the sight of Allah for one of you to insist on fulfilling his oath about his family than for him to pay the expiation which Allah has imposed.' Insisting on the oath is to carry out what it demands. Obliging himself to do that entails constriction and hardship and abandoning that which contains immediate or later benefit. If anything like that is involved, it is more appropriate for him to break the oath and do the expiation and not the use the oath as an excuse. This is borne out by Allah's words: *'Do not, by your oaths, make Allah a pretext.'* (2:224) And the Prophet ﷺ said, 'If someone swears an oath and sees something better than it, he should expiate his oath and do what is better.'

Muslim related from Abū Hurayrah that the Messenger of Allah ﷺ said, 'The oath of someone who swears an oath is according to his intention.' Scholars say that that means that if someone obliges a right on himself by an oath, it is mandatory for him, and if he swears the oath intending something else, his intention does not help him and that does not remove him from the sin of that oath. That is the meaning of another *ḥadīth*: 'Your oath should be about something about which your companion will believe you.' Muslim transmitted it.

Mālik said, 'If someone swears an oath to a claimant about a right due to him and makes the exception ('if Allah wills') in his oath or moves his tongue and lips with it or utters it, his exception does not help him because the intention is that of the one to whom he made the oath because the oath is his right. It is according to what the judge presents to him, not the choice of the one who gives the oath which is accepted from him.' This is a summary of his school and position.

Anyone without the means to do so should fast

This means by consensus: if he is unable to do any of these three: feeding, clothing or freeing. If someone lacks the means to do any of these three, then he should fast. There are two forms of lacking the means: either the temporary absence of them or actual lack of them. The former is when they are in another place. If there is someone who can lend them to him, he is not permitted to fast. If he does not find anyone to lend them to him, there is disagreement. It is said that that he should wait until he reaches the place where they are. Ibn al-'Arabī said that he is not obliged to do that, but should fulfil the expiation by fasting because the obligation is his responsibility and the precondition of lack has been realised and there is no reason to delay it. He should expiate where he is due to his lack of ability to do one of the other three since Allah says: *'Anyone without the means...'*

It is said that this refers to someone who does not have anything left over from his capital on which he subsists. He is the one who does not possess the means. It is said that it only applies to someone who only has food for a day and a night and nothing more with which to feed himself. Ash-Shāfi'ī said that and aṭ-Ṭabarī preferred it. That is the position of Mālik and his adherents.

It is related from Ibn al-Qāsim that if someone has more than what he needs for a day, he may not fast. Ibn al-Qāsim said in the book of Ibn Mazīn: 'If someone who breaks an oath has something left over after his food for the day, he should feed in expiation unless he fears hunger or is in a land where people will not give to him.' Abū Ḥanīfah said, 'If a person does not have the *niṣāb*, then he does not have the means.' Aḥmad and Isḥāq said, 'If he has food for a day and a night, he should feed with what is surplus to that.' Abū 'Ubayd said, 'When someone has food for a day and a night for himself and his dependants, and clothing sufficient for them, and after that still has the amount necessary for expiation, then he has the means.' Ibn al-Mundhir said, 'The position of Abū 'Ubayd is excellent.

should fast three days.

Ibn Mas'ūd's reading adds 'continuously', and that is the position of Abū Ḥanīfah and ath-Thawrī and one of the positions of ash-Shāfi'ī. Al-Muzanī preferred that, in that it is analogous to the fasting for the *ẓihār* divorce and is in harmony with the reading of Ibn Mas'ūd. Mālik and ash-Shāfi'ī in another view said that the requirement is satisfied if they are done separately because continuousness is a quality which is only obliged by a definitive text or analogy based on a text, and neither exists in this instance. If someone breaks one of the three days of fasting out of forgetfulness, Mālik said that he must make it up. Ash-Shāfi'ī says that he does not have to make it up as was explained in the commentary on fasting in *al-Baqarah* (2:187).

There is consensus that this *kaffārah* is prescribed by Allah in the case of free Muslims. There is disagreement about whether it is obliged for a slave who breaks an oath. Sufyān ath-Thawrī, ash-Shāfi'ī and the People of Opinion say that he only has to fast and nothing else satisfies it. The position of Mālik varies. Ibn Nāfi' related from him that a slave cannot expiate by emancipation because he has no *walā'*. He can expiate by *ṣadaqah* if his master allows him. That which is most correct is that he should fast. It is related that Ibn al-Qāsim said if a slave feeds or clothes with the permission of his master, it is all right, but I am unsure about it.

That is the expiation for breaking oaths when you have sworn them.

This is for covering over your oaths. To expiate a thing is to cover and conceal it as already mentioned (2:6). There is no disagreement that this expiation is for an oath sworn by Allah. Some of the *Tābi'ūn* believed that the expiation for an oath is to do the good he swore to abandon. In his *Sunan*, Ibn Mājah has a chapter on: 'Those who say that its expiation is to abandon it.' 'Alī ibn Muḥammad related from 'Abdullāh ibn Numayr from Ḥārithah ibn Abī ar-Rijāl from 'Amrah that 'Ā'ishah said that the Messenger of Allah ﷺ said, 'If someone swears to cut off kin or to do something incorrect, its fulfilment is not to do that.' It is reported from 'Amr ibn Shu'ayb from his father from his grandfather that the Prophet ﷺ said, 'If someone swears an oath and sees something else better than it, he should abandon it. Its abandonment is its expiation.'

This is supported by the story of Abū Bakr aṣ-Ṣiddīq that when he swore that he would not eat some food, his wife swore that she would not eat until he ate, and the guest or guests swore that they would not eat until he ate. Abū Bakr said, 'This is from Shayṭān.' He called for the food and ate and they ate as well. Al-Bukhārī transmitted it. Muslim added, 'In the morning he went to the Prophet ﷺ and said, "Messenger of Allah, they fulfilled their oaths and I broke mine." He told him the story and he said, "Rather you are the one who most fulfilled it and the best of them."' He said that he did not hear about any expiation.

There is disagreement about an oath sworn by other than Allah. Mālik said that if someone swears to give his wealth as *ṣadaqah*, he should give a third. Ash-Shāfi'ī says that he owes *kaffārah* for the oath. Isḥāq and Abū Thawr also said that, and it is related from 'Umar and 'A'ishah as well. Ash-Sha'bī, 'Aṭā' and Ṭāwūs said that he owes nothing.

As for the oath to walk to Makkah, it must be honoured according to Mālik and Abū Ḥanīfah, but according to ash-Shāfi'ī, Aḥmad ibn Ḥanbal and Abū Thawr, expiation of it is sufficient. Ibn al-Musayyab and al-Qāsim ibn Muḥammad said that he owes nothing. Ibn 'Abd al-Barr said, 'Most of the people of knowledge in Madīnah and others oblige expiation for an oath to walk to Makkah the same as the expiation for an oath sworn by Allah. That is the position of most of the Companions and *Tābi'ūn* and most of the Muslim *fuqahā'*.' Ibn al-Qāsim gave that *fatwā* to his son 'Abd aṣ-Ṣamad and he told him that it was the position of al-Layth ibn Sa'd. The famous position of Ibn al-Qāsim is that there is no expiation for an oath to walk to Makkah for a person who is able to do that other than walking there.

As for a person who swears to emancipate someone, according to Mālik, ash-Shāfi'ī and others he must emancipate the one he swore to emancipate. It is related from Ibn 'Umar, Ibn 'Abbās and 'Ā'ishah that he should make expiation for the oath and he is not obliged to emancipate. 'Aṭā' said that he should give something in *ṣadaqah*. Al-Mahdawī said, 'The consensus of reliable scholars is that divorce is obliged on someone who makes an oath to do it and breaks it.'

Keep your oaths.

It means: hasten to make the expiation you are obliged to make for breaking them. It is said that it means to avoid swearing oaths. If you do not make such oaths, there is no responsibility.

so that hopefully you will be thankful

The meaning of thankfulness and the adverb 'hopefully' were already discussed in *al-Baqarah* (2:21).

يَٰٓأَيُّهَا ٱلَّذِينَ ءَامَنُوٓاْ إِنَّمَا ٱلْخَمْرُ وَٱلْمَيْسِرُ وَٱلْأَنصَابُ وَٱلْأَزْلَٰمُ رِجْسٌ مِّنْ عَمَلِ
ٱلشَّيْطَٰنِ فَٱجْتَنِبُوهُ لَعَلَّكُمْ تُفْلِحُونَ ﴿٩٠﴾ إِنَّمَا يُرِيدُ ٱلشَّيْطَٰنُ أَن يُوقِعَ بَيْنَكُمُ ٱلْعَدَٰوَةَ
وَٱلْبَغْضَآءَ فِى ٱلْخَمْرِ وَٱلْمَيْسِرِ وَيَصُدَّكُمْ عَن ذِكْرِ ٱللَّهِ وَعَنِ ٱلصَّلَوٰةِ فَهَلْ أَنتُم
مُّنتَهُونَ ﴿٩١﴾ وَأَطِيعُواْ ٱللَّهَ وَأَطِيعُواْ ٱلرَّسُولَ وَٱحْذَرُواْ فَإِن تَوَلَّيْتُمْ فَٱعْلَمُوٓاْ أَنَّمَا
عَلَىٰ رَسُولِنَا ٱلْبَلَٰغُ ٱلْمُبِينُ ﴿٩٢﴾

90-92 You who believe! wine and gambling, stone altars and divining arrows are filth from the handiwork of Shayṭān. Avoid them completely so that hopefully you will be successful. Shayṭān wants to stir up enmity and hatred between you by means of wine and gambling, and to debar you from remembrance of Allah and from the prayer. Will you not then give them up? Obey Allah and obey the Messenger and beware! If you turn your backs, know that Our Messenger is only responsible for clear transmission.

You who believe!

All Muslims are told to abandon these things since they are habits and customs that were part of the Jāhiliyyah and they dominated people then. Some of them still remained in many of the believers. Ibn 'Aṭiyyah said, 'Those customs include the desire to be deterred by auguries and see omens in books and the like of such things which people still do today. As for wine, it had not yet been forbidden. Its prohibition was revealed in the year 3AH after Uḥud.' The Battle of Uḥud was in Shawwāl 3AH. Gambling was discussed in *al-Baqarah* (2:282). *Anṣāb* are idols. It is also said that this refers to backgammon and chess, and they will be dealt with in *Sūrat Yūnus* (10:32). Divining arrows have already been discussed (2:282). They were kept by the caretakers of the House and the custodians of the idols. When a man had a need, he would pick one of them. If the arrow said, 'My Lord commanded me', he would go to carry out his aim, whether he liked it or not.

The prohibition of wine happened gradually in stages. Many unfortunate events took place when people were inebriated. The first *āyah* to be revealed about it was: *'They will ask you about intoxicants and gambling. Say, "There is great wrong in both of them and also certain benefits for mankind"'* (2:219), referring to the trade in it. When this *āyah* was revealed, some people gave it up and said, 'We have no need of something with great harm in it.' Some people did not abandon it and said, 'We will take its benefits and leave its harm.' Then the *āyah* was revealed: *'Do not approach the prayer when you are drunk.'* (4:43) So more people abandoned it and said, 'We have no need of something that distracts us from the prayer.' Some people drank it outside the times of the prayers and then this *āyah* was revealed and so it became *ḥarām* for everyone. Some of them said, 'Allah has not forbidden anything more pernicious than wine.'

Abū Maysarah said, 'It was revealed because of 'Umar ibn al-Khaṭṭāb. He mentioned the detrimental effects of wine to the Prophet ﷺ and what happened to people because of it and asked Allah to forbid it. He said, "O Allah, clarify the matter of wine for us adequately!" and these *āyah*s were revealed. 'Umar said, "We will stop. We will stop."' It was mentioned in *al-Baqarah* (2:282) and *an-Nisā'* (4:43). In Abū Dāwūd Ibn 'Abbās reported that the *āyah*s in *an-Nisā'* and *al-Baqarah* were abrogated by this one.

In *Ṣaḥīḥ Muslim*, Sa'd ibn Abī Waqqāṣ said, 'Some of the *āyah*s of the Qur'ān were revealed about me. I came upon some of the Anṣār and they said, "Come and let us eat and drink wine." That was before wine was forbidden. I went to them in a garden and there was the head of a roasted camel with them and bottles of wine. I ate and drank with them. I mentioned the Muhājirūn and Anṣār to them and said, "The Muhājirūn are better than the Anṣār." A man grabbed the jawbone of the camel and hit me with it and injured (or split) my nose. I went to the Messenger of Allah ﷺ and told him and Allah revealed this *āyah*.' These *ḥadīth*s indicate that drinking wine was permitted and happened at that time and common among them so that there was no objection to it or effort to change it, and the Prophet ﷺ acknowledged it. There is no disagreement about that. That is indicated by 4:43.

Were they permitted to drink enough to make them intoxicated? There is the *ḥadīth* about Ḥamzah cutting the haunches of 'Alī's camels. 'Alī told the Prophet ﷺ about that and the Prophet ﷺ went to Ḥamzah who uttered disrespectful words to the Prophet ﷺ which indicated that he was not in control of himself since he was drunk. The transmitter said, 'The Messenger of Allah ﷺ recognised that he was intoxicated.' The Prophet ﷺ was not harsh to him while he was drunk or later on. He left him when Ḥamzah said, 'Are you anything but my father's slave?' and left.

This is contrary to what the *Uṣūlī*s say about intoxicants being forbidden in every *Sharī'ah* because all *Sharī'ah*s are in the best interests of people, not there to corrupt them. The fount of all good interests is the intellect as the fount of all corruption is lack of it. Therefore, it is obliged to forbid all that removes or muddles it. It is possible that Ḥamzah did not intend to drink until he was drunk, but was quickly overcome. Allah knows best.

Filth from the handiwork of Shayṭān

Ibn 'Abbās said that in this *āyah* the word '*rijs*' means anger. It is said that it means a foul smell, dirt and filth. *Rajz* means punishment and nothing else and *raks* means only filth. *Rijs* is used for both. The phrase '*from the handiwork of Shayṭān*' means that he encourages people to that and makes it seem attractive to them. It is said that he is the one who did these things in the beginning so that he would be imitated in them.

Avoid them completely

'Stay well away from these things.' Allah commands that these things be avoided. This is form of command which is coupled with the texts of *ḥadīth*s and the consensus of the Community. So 'avoidance' here entails a definitive prohibition. Thus wine is forbidden. There is no disagreement among Muslim scholars that *Sūrat al-Mā'idah* reveals the prohibition of wine. It is Madinan, coming near the end of the Revelation. The prohibition of carrion, blood and pork is found in Allah's words: '*Say: "I do not find..."*' (6:145) It is a stronger and more stressed prohibition. Ibn 'Abbās said, 'When wine was forbidden, the Companions of the Messenger of Allah ﷺ went to one another and said, "Wine is forbidden and made equivalent to *shirk*,"' meaning it is joined to sacrificing to idols, which is *shirk*. The phrase '*so that hopefully you will be successful*' connects success to the command, which strengthens the matter, and Allah knows best.

The majority understood it to entail the prohibition of wine and that the *Sharī'ah* judged wine to be foul and applied the word '*filth*' to it and commanded that it be avoided because it is an impurity (*najasah*). Rabī'a, al-Layth ibn Sa'd, al-Muzanī, the companion of ash-Shāfi'ī, and some later scholars of Baghdad and Qayrawān disagreed and said that it is pure but it is forbidden to drink it. Sa'īd ibn al-Ḥaddād al-Qarawī deduced that it is pure by the fact of its being poured out into the streets of Madīnah. He said, 'If it had been impure, the Companions would not have done that. The Prophet ﷺ would have forbidden it as he forbade relieving oneself in the street.' The response to this is that the Companions did that because they did not have drains or wells into which to pour it since they did not usually have lavatories in their houses. 'Ā'ishah said, 'They used to think that it was dirty to have lavatories in the houses and moving them outside Madīnah entailed hardship and difficulty and to do so would oblige delaying what was immediately needed.' It was also possible to protect oneself from it as the streets of Madīnah were wide. There was not so much wine that it would become a river and cover the whole road. It flowed in narrow streams so that it was possible to avoid it. That also had the benefit of making it known that it had been poured out onto the streets of Madīnah so that the practice of destroying it because of its unlawfulness would spread as well as the fact that there was no benefit in it. People corroborated it and agreed on it. Allah knows best.

If it is said that calling something impure is a legal ruling and that there is no definitive text regarding it and that the fact that a thing is forbidden does not render it impure, and many a thing forbidden in the *Sharī'ah* is not impure, our reply to this is that Allah uses the word 'filth' for it, which linguistically means impurity. If we were to judge that there can be no legal ruling unless we find a text substantiating it, then the *Sharī'ah* would become ineffective. The texts in in this respect are few. Where is the text that declares urine, faeces, blood, carrion and other things to be impure? There are clear facts, generalities and analogy. This matter will be explained in *Sūrat al-Ḥajj*, Allah willing.

The text demands complete avoidance so that none of it is used in any manner: not drinking, selling, making into vinegar, medicine or anything else. There are many *ḥadīth*s related on this. Muslim reports from Ibn 'Abbās: 'A man gave the Messenger of Allah ﷺ a small water-skin with wine in it. The Messenger of Allah ﷺ asked, "Do you not know that Allah has forbidden it?" "No," he replied. Then a man whispered to him and the Messenger of Allah ﷺ asked what he had whispered, and the man replied, "I told him to sell it." He said, "The One who made drinking it unlawful has also made selling it unlawful." The man then opened the water-skins and poured out what was in them.' If there had been any permitted use in it, the Messenger of Allah ﷺ would have made it clear, as he did with the carrion sheep whose skins he suggested should be tanned.

The Muslims are agreed that it is forbidden to sell wine and blood. That is an indication that it is also forbidden to sell dung and all impurities and what is not lawful to consume. Allah knows best, but that is why Mālik forbade selling manure, although Ibn al-Qāsim allowed it since there is benefit it. The analogy is based on what Mālik said and it is the position of ash-Shāfi'ī. This *ḥadīth* attests to the soundness of that.

A group of *fuqahā'* believe that it is not permitted for anyone to make wine into vinegar. If it had been permitted, the Messenger of Allah ﷺ would not have let the man open the skin to pour out its contents because vinegar is property and it is forbidden to waste property. No one says that a Muslim pouring out wine is destroying his property. 'Uthmān ibn Abī al-'Āṣ poured out the vinegar belonging to an orphan. The Prophet ﷺ was asked for permission to make it into vinegar and said, 'No.' This is the view of a group of scholars from the People of Ḥadīth and the People of Opinion. Saḥnūn ibn Sa'īd inclined to it. Others have said that there is nothing wrong with making wine into vinegar nor in consuming vinegar made from it by the intervention of a human being or otherwise. That is the position of ath-Thawrī, al-Awzā'ī, al-Layth ibn Sa'd and the Kufans.

Abū Ḥanīfah said, 'If someone puts musk or salt into it and it ferments and is changed from wine, then it is permitted.' Ash-Shaybānī disagreed with him about wine is made to change (through human intervention) and said, 'Wine should not be treated but may change to vinegar on its own.' Abū 'Umar said, 'The Iraqis cite Abū ad-Dardā' as evidence for making wine into vinegar since it is reported that he did that. 'Umar ibn al-Khaṭṭāb and 'Uthmān ibn Abī al-'Āṣ disagreed with him about changing wine into vinegar. There is nothing definitive about it in the *Sunnah*, and success is by Allah.' It is possible that the prohibition against making vinegar was at the beginning of Islam when the prohibition of wine was revealed so that it would not encourage drinking to continue when the prohibition was new, and out of a desire to break habits. If that happened, the prohibition against making it into vinegar and the command to pour it out does not preclude consuming it when it becomes lawful (by becoming vinegar).

Ashhab reported that Mālik said, 'When a Christian makes wine into vinegar, there is no harm in consuming it. The same applies if a Muslim makes it into vinegar, and I ask Allah's forgiveness.' This is mentioned by Ibn 'Abd al-Ḥakam in his book. The sound version is what Mālik said according to Ibn al-Qāsim and Ibn Wahb: 'It is not lawful for a Muslim to treat wine so that it turns into vinegar nor to sell it. He should pour it out.' There is no disagreement regarding the position of Mālik and his people that when wine becomes vinegar on its own, that vinegar is *ḥalāl.* That is the position of 'Umar ibn al-Khaṭṭāb, Qabīsah, Ibn Shihāb, Rabī'ah and one of the positions of ash-Shāfi'ī. It is his final position according to most of his people.

Ibn Khuwayzimandād mentioned that wine is something which can be owned. He inclines to that position since it is possible to prevent someone choking by the use of it and extinguish a fire with it. This transmission is not known from Mālik. It is derived from the position of those who think that it is pure. If it had been permitted to own it, then the Prophet ﷺ would not have commanded it to be poured out. Furthermore, ownership is a sort of benefit, which would be invalidated by pouring it out. Praise be to Allah.

This *āyah* indicates the prohibition of playing backgammon and chess for gambling purposes or otherwise, because when Allah forbade wine, He also makes clear the reason in the *āyah*, saying: 'Shayṭān wants to stir up enmity and hatred between you…' A little diversion leads to even more diversion, and enmity and hatred develop between those devoted to it. It prevents remembrance of Allah and the prayer and so it is like drinking wine and must be unlawful like it. If it is said that drinking wine brings about intoxication and the prayer is not possible in such a state, whereas this state does not exist in backgammon and chess, our reply is: Allah joined wine to gambling in the prohibition and described them as producing enmity and hatred between people and as being things that debar the remembrance of Allah and the prayer. It is known that that wine intoxicates and gambling does not, and so, in the sight of Allah, because of the things they have in common, this difference is not something which prevents them being equally prohibited. As a little wine does not intoxicate, nor does a little playing of backgammon or chess. Doing a little is forbidden, just as doing a lot is forbidden. Furthermore, beginning to play them brings about heedlessness and the way it takes over the heart is similar to intoxication. As wine is forbidden because it intoxicates and debars people from the prayer, so playing backgammon and chess brings about heedlessness and makes people forgetful of the prayer. Playing backgammon and chess are therefore forbidden because they are a distraction which may debar people from praying. Allah knows best.

The transmission indicates that the person concerned had not heard of the abrogation and that he was holding to the prior permissibility of those things. That is evidence that the ruling is not removed by the mere existence of the abrogating factor, as some *Uṣūlīs* say. It is only when that reaches someone, as this *ḥadīth* indicates. That is sound because the Prophet ﷺ did not censure him, but explained the ruling to him, and because the man had been instructed to act by the first ruling and if he had abandoned it, there is no disagreement that he would have acted wrongly, even though the abrogation already existed. That is like what happened with the people of Qubā' who were praying towards Jerusalem when someone came and told them of the abrogation and they then turned towards the Ka'bah. This was already discussed in *Sūrat al-Baqarah*, and wine and gambling were already discussed there (2:219). Altars and divining arrows were mentioned at the beginning of this *sūrah*.

Shayṭān wants to stir up enmity and hatred between you by means of wine and gambling

Allah informs His servants that Shayṭān desires to cause enmity and hatred between them by means of wine and other things and so He warns us about them and forbids them to us. It is reported that two tribes of the Anṣār drank wine and became drunk and started to fight one other. When they recovered, they saw the effect of what they had done on their faces. They had been brothers without rancour in their hearts and some then said, 'If my brother had truly cared for me, he would not have done this to me,' and rancour was engendered which is why Allah revealed this.

and to debar you from remembrance of Allah and from the prayer.

When you are drunk, you do not remember Allah and you do not pray. And if you did pray, you would be confused in your prayer as happened with 'Alī. It was also related about 'Abd ar-Raḥmān as mentioned in *an-Nisā'* (4:42).

'Ubaydullāh ibn 'Umar said that al-Qāsim ibn Muḥammad was asked about whether chess was gambling and whether backgammon was gambling. He replied, 'Anything that prevents you from remembering Allah and praying is gambling.' Abū 'Ubayd said that it is the interpretation of '*and to debar you from remembrance of Allah and from the prayer.*'

Will you not then give them up?

When 'Umar learned about this strong threat which goes beyond the meaning of just 'Stop', he said, 'We have stopped!' The Prophet ﷺ commanded that an announcement be made in the streets of Madīnah: 'Wine has been forbidden.' Jugs were broken and the wine flowed in the streets of Madīnah.

Obey Allah and obey the Messenger and beware!

This reinforces the prohibition and the threat and the encouragement to obey the command and refrain from what is forbidden. Beware of what is forbidden because there is a promise of a punishment in the Next World. The command '*Obey*' is repeated for emphasis and cautions against disobeying such commands and then threatens punishment in the Next World. The phrase '*If you turn your backs*' here means 'If you go against the prohibition.' '*The clear transmission*' is that of what is prohibited and the fact that there is punishment for disobedience and reward for obedience.

لَيْسَ عَلَى ٱلَّذِينَ ءَامَنُوا۟ وَعَمِلُوا۟ ٱلصَّٰلِحَٰتِ جُنَاحٌ فِيمَا طَعِمُوٓا۟ إِذَا مَا ٱتَّقَوا۟ وَّءَامَنُوا۟
وَعَمِلُوا۟ ٱلصَّٰلِحَٰتِ ثُمَّ ٱتَّقَوا۟ وَّءَامَنُوا۟ ثُمَّ ٱتَّقَوا۟ وَّأَحْسَنُوا۟ ۗ وَٱللَّهُ يُحِبُّ ٱلْمُحْسِنِينَ ٩٣

93 Those who believe and do right actions are not to blame for anything they have eaten provided they are godfearing and believe and do right actions, and then again are godfearing and believe, and then are godfearing and do good. Allah loves good-doers.

Ibn 'Abbās, al-Barā' ibn 'Āzib and Anas ibn Mālik said that when the prohibition of wine was revealed, some Companions said, 'What then will happen to those of us who died while still drinking wine and gambling?' and this *āyah* was revealed. Al-Bukhārī related that Anas said, 'I was serving wine to the people in the house of Abū Ṭālḥah when the prohibition of wine was revealed. A caller was commanded to announce it. Abū Ṭālḥah said, "Go and see what this shouting is!" I went out and then said, "This is a caller announcing that wine has been forbidden." He said, "Go out and spill it." So I went out and spilled it. The wine was made from dates. It flowed in the streets of Madīnah.' Some people said, People were killed while there was wine in their stomachs!' So Allah revealed, '*Those who believe and do right actions are not to blame for anything they have eaten.*'

This *āyah* and this *ḥadīth* are similar to their asking about those who died after only facing the first *qiblah* and Allah revealed about them: '*Allah would not let your prayer go to waste.*' (2:143) Anyone who did what was permitted until his death owes nothing and incurs no blame or censure or wrong action, nor reward or praise. What is permitted (*mubāḥ*) is neutral in the *Sharī'ah*. Therefore, one should not ask about the state of those who died with wine in their bellies at a time when it was allowed. Those who asked that were overcome by their fear of Allah and apprehension for their fellow Muslims thinking that they might be punished because of the prior consumption of wine. Allah dispelled that misconception in this *āyah*.

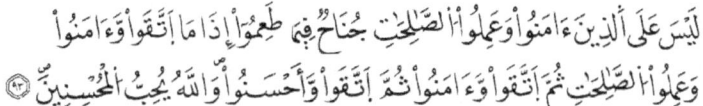

This *ḥadīth* about the revelation of the *āyah* is clear evidence that *nabīdh* made from dates is wine when it intoxicates. It is a definitive text and it is not permitted to ignore it because the Companions were people who knew the language and they understood that drinking that was tantamount to drinking wine, since they did not have actual grape wine in Madīnah at that time. [Abū Nūwas] al-Ḥakamī said:

We have wine which is not wine of grapes,
but from the fruit of lofty trees.
Noble in the sky, they are tall.
Its fruits are in the hands of harvesters.

Part of the clear evidence of that is what an-Nasā'ī reported from al-Qāsim ibn Zakariyyā from 'Ubaydullāh from Shaybān from al-A'mash from Muḥārib ibn Dithār Jābir that the Prophet ﷺ said, 'Raisins and dates are wine.' It is confirmed by sound transmission that 'Umar ibn al-Khaṭṭāb, who is enough for you in his knowledge of the *Sharī'ah* and language, addressed people from the minbar of the Prophet ﷺ and said, 'O people! the prohibition of wine was revealed on the day it was revealed. It is made from five things: grapes, dates, honey, wheat and barley. Wine is what befuddles the mind.'

This is the clearest thing which has been said about wine. 'Umar stated this in Madīnah on the minbar in the presence of a group of Companions, who knew the language, and they only understood wine to mean what we have mentioned. Since this is confirmed, it invalidates the view of Abū Ḥanīfah and the Kufans who say that wine is only made from grapes and nothing else, and that which is made from something else is not called 'wine', but *nabīdh*. A poet said:

I left *nabīdh* to the people of *nabīdh*
and became an ally of those who criticise it.
Drinking befouls the reputation of a young man
and opens the gates to evil.

Imam Abū 'Abdullāh al-Māzirī said, 'Most scholars from the early generations and others believe that everything that intoxicates is forbidden, whether a little or a lot, fresh or cooked. There is no difference between what is produced from grapes or anything else. If anyone drinks any of that, he receives the *ḥadd* punishment [for drinking wine.] As for what is produced from fresh grapes, there is consensus that it is unlawful, a little or a lot, even a single drop of it. As for other things, the great majority of people say that they are forbidden.

The Kufans, however, disagree about a little of other than what has been mentioned which does not lead to the state of intoxication, and about cooking with what is produced from grapes. Some of the people of Basra believe that the prohibition is confined to pressed grapes and the infusion of fresh raisins. They say that they are lawful when they are cooked or are fresh and that other things that are cooked which do not intoxicate are also lawful. Abū Ḥanīfah believed that the prohibition was confined to what was pressed from dates and grapes. So he thought that wine from grapes was unlawful, be it a little or a lot, unless it was cooked to the point that two-thirds of it had evaporated. As for what comes from raisins and dates, it becomes lawful by cooking even if the heat only effects it slightly and there is no definite amount. What is uncooked is unlawful, although no *ḥadd* is obliged for it. All of this is when there is no intoxication. If there is intoxication, then all are the same.'

The *faqīh*, Imām Abū al-'Abbās Aḥmad, said, 'The extraordinary thing about those who disagree regarding this matter is that they say, "A little pressed wine is *ḥarām* as is a lot of it, and there is consensus about that." When they are asked, "Why then is a little forbidden when it does not remove good sense?" the answer must be that it is because it leads to a lot. Then they are told, "All that you believe about a small amount of wine is the same in the case of a little *nabīdh*, and so it is also *ḥarām* since there is no difference between them except the name." This type of analogy is the most extreme form of analogy because the branch is the same as the fundamental in all its attributes. This is the same as making a slave-girl analogous to a male slave in respect of emancipation. It is truly extraordinary on the part of Abū Ḥanīfah and his people, may Allah have mercy on him! They go deeply into analogy and prefer it to single reports, but in spite of that, they abandon this clear analogy which is supported by the Book, *Sunnah* and consensus of the early community! No *ḥadīth*s are sound according to how *ḥadīth* scholars clarify their causes in their books. There is nothing of it in the *Ṣiḥāḥ* at all.' This question will be further dealt with in *Sūrat an-Naḥl*.

The root of '*ṭa'imū*' is eating. The *ṭa'ima* is used for eating food (*ṭa'ām*) and *shariba* is used for drinking. It can, however, be used for both, as when someone says, 'I have eaten (*aṭ'am*) bread, water or sleep.' A poet said:

Ostriches in a trap, with empty sides,
who only taste sleep while fasting.

This was adequately discussed in *al-Baqarah* (2:249)

Ibn Khuwayzimandād said, 'This *āyah* embraces consuming what is permissible, indulging appetites and making use of every pleasant food, drink and lawful marriage. This *āyah* is like: *"Do not make unlawful the good things Allah has made lawful for you"* (5:87) and: *"Say: 'Who has forbidden the fine clothing of Allah and the good kinds of provision He has produced for His slaves?'"* (7:32)'

provided they are godfearing and believe and do right actions

There are four things said about this.

The first is that there is no repetition in the mention of *taqwā*. The meaning is: 'They were fearful about drinking it and believed that it is forbidden, then they continued to fear and believe, and the third is being excellent in fearing.

The second view is: they were fearful before the prohibition about other things and then they were fearful afterwards about drinking it after its prohibition, and then they were fearful in their remaining actions and did good.

The third view is they feared *shirk* and believed in Allah and His Messenger, then they feared major wrong actions, and increased in faith, and then they feared minor wrong actions and did good, i.e. supererogatory actions.

Muḥammad ibn Jarīr said, 'The first fearing is fearing by learning the command of Allah and accepting it, affirming it and acting by it, the second fearing is being firm in affirmation, and the third is being firm in doing good and drawing near by voluntary actions.'

and then are godfearing and do good. Allah loves good-doers.

This is evidence that a godfearing good-doer (*muḥsin*) is better than a godfearing believer who does righteous actions because of the reward for doing good. This *āyah* was interpreted by Qudāmah ibn Maẓ'ūn al-Jumaḥī, one of the Companions. He was one of those who emigrated to Abyssinia with his brothers, 'Uthmān and 'Abdullāh. Then he emigrated to Madīnah and was present at Badr and Uḥud. He was related to 'Umar ibn al-Khaṭṭāb by marriage and was the maternal uncle of 'Abdullāh and Ḥafṣah. 'Umar appointed him governor of Baḥrayn and then dismissed him based on the testimony of al-Jarud, the chief of 'Abd al-Qays, that he drank wine.

It is related by ad-Dāraquṭnī from Abū al-Ḥasan 'Alī ibn Muḥammad al-Miṣrī from Yaḥyā ibn Ayyūb al-'Allāf from Sa'īd ibn 'Ufayr from Yaḥyā ibn Fulayj ibn Sulaymān from Thawr ibn Zayd from 'Ikrimah that Ibn 'Abbās said, 'In the time of the Messenger of Allah ﷺ those who drank were beaten with hands, sandals and sticks up until the time of the death of the Messenger of Allah ﷺ. There were more in the time of Abū Bakr than there had been in the time of the Messenger of Allah ﷺ. Abū Bakr gave them forty lashes until he died. Then 'Umar ibn al-Khaṭṭāb flogged them with forty lashes until one of the first Muhājirūn was brought to him and he commanded that he be flogged. He asked, "Why are you flogging me? The Book of Allah is between you and me!" 'Umar asked, "And where in the Book of Allah does it say that I should not flog you?" He replied, "Allah Almighty says in His Book: *'Those who believe and do right actions are not to blame for anything they have eaten…'* I am one of those who believed and then did right actions, then had *taqwā* and believed, and then had *taqwā* and did good. I was present with the Messenger of Allah ﷺ at Badr, Uḥud, the Ditch and all the battles." 'Umar said, "Will you not respond to what he says?" So Ibn 'Abbās said, "Those verses were revealed as a pardon for those who have passed. The argument is against the people because Allah says: *'O you who believe, wine and gambling…'* (5:90)" Then he recited until he finished the other verse: *"Those who believe…"* He concluded, "Allah forbade drinking wine." 'Umar said, "You spoke the truth. What do you think?" 'Alī stated, "When someone drinks, he becomes intoxicated. When he is intoxicated, he speaks nonsense. When he speaks nonsense, he slanders. There are eighty lashes for a slanderer." So 'Umar commanded that he receive eighty lashes.'

Al-Ḥumaydī reported from Abū Bakr ar-Barqānī that Ibn 'Abbās said, 'When al-Jārūd arrived from Baḥrayn, he said, "Amīr al-Mu'minīn, Qudāmah ibn Maz'ūn drank an intoxicant, and when I saw one of the rights of Allah contravened, I thought that I should present it to you." 'Umar asked, "Who will testify to what you say?" He replied, "Abū Hurayrah." He summoned Abū Hurayrah and said, "What is your testimony, Abū Hurayrah" He answered, "I did not see him drink, but I saw him drunk and vomiting." 'Umar said, "You have been extensive in testimony." Then 'Umar wrote to Qudāmah while he was in Baḥrayn, ordering him to come to him. When Qudāmah and al-Jārūd arrived in Madina, al-Jārūd spoke to 'Umar and said, "Will you carry out the Book of Allah on this one?" Then 'Umar said to al-Jārūd, "Are you a witness or a litigant?" Al-Jārūd replied, "I am a witness!" He said, "You have given testimony." He then said to 'Umar, "I ask you by Allah!" 'Umar said, "By Allah, control your tongue or I will cause you pain!" He retorted, "By Allah, what has that to do with the truth! Your nephew drank and so you will cause me pain!" 'Umar threatened him.

'Abū Hurayrah, who was sitting there, said, "Amīr al-Mu'minīn, if you doubt our testimony, then ask the daughter of al-Walīd, the wife of Ibn Maz'ūn." So 'Umar sent for Hind and asked her by Allah. Hind testified against her husband. 'Umar said, "Qudāmah, I will flog you." Qudāmah said, "By Allah, even if I drank as they said, you do not have the right to flog me, 'Umar!" "And why not, Qudāmah?" he asked. He replied, "Because Allah says: *'Those who believe and do right actions are not to blame for anything they have eaten…'*" 'Umar told him, "That is an erroneous interpretation, Qudāmah. When you fear Allah, you avoid what Allah has forbidden."

'Then 'Umar turned to the people and asked, "What do you think about flogging Qudāmah?" The people said, "We do not think you should flog him while he is ill." So 'Umar was silent about flogging him and then one day he asked his companions, "What do you think about flogging Qudāmah?" The people said, "We do not think you should flog him while he is ill." 'Umar said, "By Allah, I prefer that he meet Allah under the lash to my meeting Allah with the responsibility of punishing him still on my neck! By Allah, I will flog him! Bring me a whip!" His freedman Aslam brought him a small light whip. 'Umar took it and stroked it with his hand and then said to Aslam, "Have the bad habits of your family got you? Bring me a different whip!" So Aslam brought 'Umar a full whip and 'Umar commanded that Qudāmah be flogged. Qudāmah became angry and shunned 'Umar.

'They went on *ḥajj* while Qudāmah was still shunning 'Umar. When they returned from *ḥajj*, 'Umar stopped at Suqyā and slept there. When he woke up, he said, "Bring me Qudāmah immediately! Go and bring him to me! By Allah, I dreamt that someone came to me and said, 'Make peace with Qudāmah. He is your brother.'" When they went to Qudāmah, he refused to come to him. So 'Umar commanded that Qudāmah be dragged to him so that 'Umar could speak to him and ask forgiveness for him. It was the beginning of their reconciliation.' Ayyūb ibn Abī Tamīmah said, 'None of the people of Badr was flogged for wine except him.'

Ibn al-'Arabī said, 'This shows you the interpretation of the *āyah*. What is mentioned about it by Ibn 'Abbās in the *ḥadīth* found in ad-Dāraquṭnī, and 'Umar in the *ḥadīth* of al-Barqanī, is sound. Its explanation is that if someone who drank wine but feared Allah in other things did not receive the *hadd* for wine, then no one would receive the *ḥadd* for wine. This is a corrupt interpretation and Qudāmah was wrong.' He was informed of it by those to whom Allah had given success, like 'Umar and Ibn 'Abbās. The poet said:

Ḥarām. I do not think that time will weep
for the absence of someone as I weep for 'Umar.

It is reported from 'Alī that some people in Syria drank and said, 'It is lawful for us.' They used an interpretation of this *āyah*. 'Alī and 'Umar agreed to ask them to repent. If they did not repent, they would kill them. Aṭ-Ṭabarị mentioned it.

يَـٰٓأَيُّهَا ٱلَّذِينَ ءَامَنُوا۟ لَيَبْلُوَنَّكُمُ ٱللَّهُ بِشَىْءٍ مِّنَ ٱلصَّيْدِ تَنَالُهُۥٓ أَيْدِيكُمْ وَرِمَاحُكُمْ
لِيَعْلَمَ ٱللَّهُ مَن يَخَافُهُۥ بِٱلْغَيْبِ ۚ فَمَنِ ٱعْتَدَىٰ بَعْدَ ذَٰلِكَ فَلَهُۥ عَذَابٌ أَلِيمٌ ﴿٩٤﴾

94 You who believe! Allah will test you with game animals which come within the reach of your hands and spears, so that Allah will know those who fear Him in the Unseen. Anyone who oversteps the limits after this will have a painful punishment.

Allah will test you with game animals

Game is one of the forms of livelihood of the desert Arabs and common among all of them. So Allah tested them regarding that when they are in *iḥrām* and the *Ḥaram*, in the same way that He tested the tribe of Israel with regard to not violating the Sabbath. It is said that it was revealed in the year of al-Ḥudaybīyah. Some people went with the Messenger of Allah ﷺ, and some of them were not in *iḥrām*. When some game appeared, their states and actions varied and the rulings were unclear for them, and so Allah revealed this *āyah* to clarify their states and actions and what was forbidden with respect to *ḥajj* and *'umrah*.

Scholars disagree about whom this *āyah* addresses, and there are two positions. One is that those addressed are those out of *iḥrām*, and Mālik said that. The second is that it is addressed to those in *iḥrām*, and Ibn 'Abbās said that and connected it to the words, *'test you'*. The obligation of prohibition which is achieved by the test is for those in *iḥrām*. Ibn al-'Arabī said, 'This is not necessary. Responsibility is achieved in someone who is not in *iḥrām* by his observing the preconditions in hunting and what is prescribed for him about how to hunt. The sound view is that the *āyah* is addressed to all people, in *iḥrām* or out of *iḥrām*, because responsibility applies to all.' The words *'test you'* mean to make you responsible. All responsibility is a test, even if it varies in whether it is great or small, and distinct in weakness and strength. *'With game animals'* means with some game. It is not general to all that is caught because fishing is not included. Aṭ-Ṭabarī and others said that.

within the reach of your hands and spears

This refers to small and large game. Ibn Waththāb and an-Nakha'ī recite *'yanāluhu'*. Mujāhid says that hands take fledglings and eggs and what cannot flee. Spears take large game. Ibn Wahb said Mālik said that the words of Allah include anything that a human being takes with his hand, spear or any weapon and kills. That is *ṣayd*, as Allah says. Allah singles out the hands because they are what are mostly used in hunting. This includes hunting animals and snares and other traps that are prepared by hand. Spears are specifically mentioned because they were what was most used in hunting. That includes arrows and the like. Hunting animals were discussed at the beginning of the *sūrah*, Allah be praised.

What falls into snares or ropes belongs to their owner. When someone chases game and it runs into the trap and, if it had not been for the trap, the hunter would have taken it anyway, then the owner has a share. If bees join a beehive in the mountains, that is like a snare and trap. Pigeons from a dovecote belong to its owner if that is possible and the same applies to the bees in a hive. That is reported from Mālik. One of his people said that someone who obtains pigeons or bees in this way does not have to return them. If dogs force game to seek refuge and it enters someone's house or room, it belongs to the one who released the dogs rather than the owner of the house. If it enters a room without being forced by dogs, it belongs to the owner of the room.

Some people argue that, according to this *āyah,* game belongs to the one who takes it not the one who provoked it, because neither the hand nor the spear of the provoker obtained anything. This is the position of Abū Ḥanīfah.

Mālik disliked game caught by the People of the Book, but did not forbid it since the Almighty says: *'within the reach of your hands and spears'* meaning the people of faith since Allah says: '*You who believe.*' So the People of the Book are not included. Most of the people of knowledge disagree since Allah says: *'And the food of those given the Book is also lawful for you'* (5:5). They consider their game to be like their slaughtered animals. Our scholars reply that the *āyah* is about eating their food and that hunting is another topic which is not included in the generality of eating. The basis of this is that hunting is not prescribed for them and so it is not part of their food. If it had been prescribed for them in their *dīn*, then it would have been part of their food. Allah knows best.

يَٰٓأَيُّهَا ٱلَّذِينَ ءَامَنُوا۟ لَا تَقْتُلُوا۟ ٱلصَّيْدَ وَأَنتُمْ حُرُمٌ ۚ وَمَن قَتَلَهُۥ مِنكُم مُّتَعَمِّدًا فَجَزَآءٌ مِّثْلُ
مَا قَتَلَ مِنَ ٱلنَّعَمِ يَحْكُمُ بِهِۦ ذَوَا عَدْلٍ مِّنكُمْ هَدْيًۢا بَٰلِغَ ٱلْكَعْبَةِ أَوْ كَفَّٰرَةٌ طَعَامُ
مَسَٰكِينَ أَوْ عَدْلُ ذَٰلِكَ صِيَامًا لِّيَذُوقَ وَبَالَ أَمْرِهِۦ ۗ عَفَا ٱللَّهُ عَمَّا سَلَفَ ۚ وَمَنْ عَادَ
فَيَنتَقِمُ ٱللَّهُ مِنْهُ ۗ وَٱللَّهُ عَزِيزٌ ذُو ٱنتِقَامٍ ﴿٩٥﴾

95 You who believe! do not kill game while you are in *iḥrām*. If one of you kills any deliberately, the reprisal for it is a livestock animal equivalent to what he killed, as judged by two just men

among you, a sacrifice to reach the Ka'bah, or expiation by feeding the poor, or fasting commensurate with that, so that he may taste the evil consequences of what he did. Allah has pardoned all that took place in the past; but if anyone does it again Allah will take revenge on him. Allah is Almighty, Exactor of Revenge.

You who believe!

This is a general address to every Muslim, male and female. This prohibition is the test mentioned in the previous *āyah*. It is related that Abū al-Yusr 'Amr ibn Mālik al-Anṣārī was in *iḥrām* in the year of Ḥudaybīyah for *'umrah* and killed a wild ass and this was revealed.

do not kill game while you are in *iḥrām*.

'Killing' is any action which removes life: stabbing, slaughtering. choking, crushing and the like. Allah forbade any action towards the game which would cause its loss of life.

If one of you kills any deliberately, the reprisal for it is a livestock animal equivalent to what he killed, as judged by two just men among you,

Whoever kills game or slaughters it and then eats from it owes repayment for killing it rather than eating it. That is the position of ash-Shāfi'ī. Abū Ḥanīfah said, 'He owes repayment for what he eats,' i.e. its price. His two companions disagreed with him and said that he only need ask forgiveness because he took what was dead as he would have taken something else dead. This is why when another *muḥrim* eats it, he is only obliged to ask forgiveness. The argument of Abū Ḥanīfah is that he took something which was unlawful while he was in *iḥrām* because killing it was one of the things forbidden in *iḥrām*. It is known that the goal of killing is consumption. Whatever is used to obtain that goal is also unlawful and demands repayment.

We believe that it is not permitted for a *muḥrim* to slaughter game since Allah forbade that a *muḥrim* kill it. Abū Hanifah said that. Ash-Shāfi'ī said, 'A *muḥrim* can slaughter game. He is entitled to slaughter since he is a Muslim, as well as the fact that it is livestock. What is desired is to make eating lawful and its original basis is lawful.' We reply that a *muḥrim* is not entitled to slaughter game, because this capacity is not based on logic, but on the *Sharī'ah*, which is permission or lack of it, which is being forbidden to slaughter. A *muḥrim* is forbidden to slaughter game because Allah says: *'Do not kill game.'* We agree that when a *muḥrim* slaughters game, it is not lawful for him to eat it. According to you, others can eat it. Since the slaughter does not render it lawful for him, it is more likely that it will not make it lawful for others either because the branch follows the root in rulings. It is not sound that something be confirmed for him when its basis is not confirmed.

Ṣayd (game) is a verbal noun which is used as a noun and is used for hunted animals. The expression includes every sort of game, land or aquatic. Allah made an exception in 5:96 and allowed the catch of the sea for a *muḥrim* as we will mention in the next *āyah*. Scholars disagree about whether to exclude or include beasts of prey in the category of land game. Mālik said, 'Any beast of prey which does not attack, like cats, foxes, hyenas and the like, should not be killed by a *muḥrim*. If he does kills one of them, he owes *fidyah* for it.' He said, 'I do not think that a *muḥrim* should kill small wolves. If he does so, he owes *fidyah*.' It is the same for fledging crows.

There is no harm in killing animals which normally attack people, like lions, wolves, leopards, and panthers. There is also no harm in killing snakes, scorpions, mice, crows and kites. Ismā'īl said, 'That is based on the words of the Prophet ﷺ, "Five are vicious and can be killed, whether in *iḥrām* or out of it."' He called them vicious (*fāsiq*) and that describes their actions because the *fāsiq* does that which is vicious. The young have no such action. He described a dog as savage while its puppies are not savage and are not included in this description. Qāḍī Ismā'īl said, 'A vicious dog is something considered as being very harmful to people.' He said, 'Snakes and scorpions are included in that because they are feared. The same applies to kites and crows because they snatch meat from people's hands.' Ibn Bukayr said, 'There is permission to kill scorpions since they have venom, mice because they gnaw at water-skins and shoes, which sustain the traveller, and crows because they alight on the back and pierce the flesh.' It is related that Mālik said, 'Neither crows nor kites are killed unless they cause harm.'

Qāḍī Ismā'īl said, 'There is disagreement about hornets. Some consider them to be like snakes and scorpions. They say that once a hornet attacks, it is more ruthless to people than snakes and scorpions, but it is not in its nature to attack as is the case with snakes and scorpions. Hornets defend themselves when they are alarmed. When a hornet attacks someone and he defends himself against it, he owes nothing for killing it. It is confirmed that 'Umar ibn al-Khaṭṭāb permitted the killing of hornets. Mālik said that someone who kills one must feed (in expiation).' Mālik also said that about someone who kills fleas, flies, ants, and the like.

The people of opinion said that anyone who kills any of these things owes nothing. Abū Ḥanīfah said, 'A *muḥrim* may only kill savage dogs and wolves, whether or not they attack. If he kills another beast of prey, he owes *fidyah*.' He said, 'If another beast of prey attacks and he kills it, then he owes nothing.' He also said, 'There is nothing owed for killing snakes, scorpions, crows and kites.' This is the position of Abū Ḥanīfah and his people, except for Zufar, and it is the position of al-Awzā'ī, ath-Thawrī and al-Ḥasan. Their argument is that the Prophet ﷺ singled out specific creatures which he allowed a *muḥrim* to kill because of the harm they may cause. There is no reason to add to them unless there is consensus on something which is then included in the idea.

I say that it is extraordinary that Abū Ḥanīfah applied dirt to wheat when measuring, but did not make dogs aggressive beasts of prey on account of their viciousness and savageness as did Mālik and ash-Shāfi'ī, whether they attack or not. This is in contradiction to the *ḥadīth*. Zufar ibn al-Hudhayl said, 'Only wolves may be killed. If someone in *iḥrām* kills anything else, he owes *fidyah,* whether or not it initiated the hostility, because it is a dumb beast whose action is of no consequence.' This is contrary to the *ḥadīth* and opposes it.

Ash-Shāfi'ī said that a *muḥrim* may kill animals whose meat is not eaten, young or old, except for the kind of mongrel called *sim'*, which is a cross between a wolf and hyena. He said, 'There is nothing owed for vultures, bats, monkeys, ticks and what is not eaten because this is not game and it was game that Allah forbade in His words: *"Land game is unlawful for you while you are in iḥrām."* That indicates that the game which is forbidden is that which was lawful to kill before *iḥrām*.' Al-Muzanī and ar-Rabī' related this from him.

If it is asked why there is *fidyah* for killing lice when they cause harm and are not eaten, the answer is that there is only *fidyah* for the hair and nails and wearing what one cannot wear because getting rid of a louse is removing harm from oneself when it is in the hair and beard. So it is as if the person removed some of his hair. When it appears openly and is killed, there is no *fidyah* for it. The position of Abū Thawr regarding this topic is that same as that of ash-Shāfi'ī. Abū 'Umar said that.

The Imams related from Ibn 'Umar that the Messenger of Allah ﷺ said, 'There are five creatures which a *muḥrim* may kill without sin: crows, kites, scorpions, mice and savage dogs.' It is found in al-Bukhārī. Aḥmad and Isḥāq said that. We find in Muslim from Ā'ishah that the Prophet ﷺ said, 'Five vicious creatures can be killed whether one is in *iḥrām* or not: snakes, pied crows, mice, savage dogs and kites.' A group of the people of knowledge said that only pied crows may be killed because it refines the general category. We find in the book of Abū Dāwūd from

Abū Sa'īd al-Khudrī that the Prophet ﷺ said, 'Throw stones at crows, but do not kill them.' Mujāhid said that. One group of scholars take the position of the *ḥadīth* of Ibn 'Umar. Allah knows best. We find in Abū Dāwūd and at-Tirmidhī 'attacking beasts of prey.' This is clarification of the reason.

'While you are in iḥrām' is general to men and women, free people and slaves. The noun *ḥarām* is used for a man or a woman and the plural is *ḥurum*. The verb *aḥrama* is used for entering a *Ḥaram*. This expression includes the time, place and state of *iḥrām* as they share in it. It is not due to generality. A man may be described as *ḥarām* when he enters the Sacred months, enters the *Ḥaram*, or puts on *iḥrām* because making the time sacred is not considered by consensus. Thus responsibility remains for the sacredness of the place and the state of *iḥrām*. Ibn al-'Arabī said that.

Two places are *Ḥarams*: Madīnah and Makkah. Ash-Shāfi'ī adds Ṭā'if. It is not permitted to cut down their trees or hunt their game but if someone does that he owes no reparation. As for the *Ḥaram* of Madīnah, it is not permitted for anyone to hunt in it nor cut down trees just as is the case with the *Ḥaram* of Makkah. If someone does that, he sins, but he owes no reparation according to Mālik and ash-Shāfi'ī and their people. Ibn Abī Dhi'b says that he does owe reparation.

Abū Ḥanīfah said that the game found in Madīnah is not sacrosanct, and the same is true of its trees. Some of them use as evidence the *ḥadīth* reported by Sa'd ibn Abī Waqqāṣ in which the Prophet ﷺ said, 'If you find someone hunting within the confines of Madīnah or cutting down it trees, take their spoils.' Sa'd took the spoils of those who did that. He said, '*Fuqahā'* agree that one does not take spoils from someone who hunts in Madīnah. That indicates that the ruling is abrogated.' Aṭ-Ṭaḥāwī also uses the *ḥadīth* of Anas as evidence, 'What happened to the little sparrow?' when he did not object to him hunting and keeping it.

None of this, however, constitutes any proof. The first *ḥadīth* is not strong. If it had been sound, the abrogation of taking the spoils does not remove the soundness of Madīnah being a *Ḥaram*. Many a person who does what is forbidden is not punished in this world. As for the second report, it is possible that it was caught outside the *Ḥaram*. The same is true of the *ḥadīth* of 'Ā'ishah that the Messenger of Allah ﷺ had a wild pigeon. When he went out, it played and moved to and fro. When it sensed the Messenger of Allah ﷺ, it was still and did not move, not wanting to annoy him.

Our evidence is also what Mālik related from Ibn Shihāb from Sa'īd ibn al-Musayyab that Abū Hurayrah said, 'If I had seen a gazelle in Madīnah, I would have left it to graze and would not have frightened it. The Messenger of Allah

ﷺ said, "What is between the two lava-beds is a *Ḥarām*."' The statement of Abū Hurayrah about not frightening it is evidence that it is not permitted to alarm game inside the *Ḥaram* of Madīnah, as it is not permitted to alarm it in Makkah. That is also the case with Zayd ibn Thābit removing a hawk from the hands of Shuraḥbīl ibn Sa'd who had caught it in Madīnah. That is evidence that the Companions understood what the Messenger of Allah ﷺ meant in making game unlawful in Madīnah. They did not permit hunting in it nor owning what had been caught.

Ibn Abī Dhi'b explained the words of the Prophet ﷺ in the *Ṣaḥīḥ*: 'O Allah, Ibrāhīm made Makkah a *Ḥarām* and I make Madīnah a *Ḥarām* as he did Makkah. No one is allowed to uproot its plants, lop its trees or chase its game.' Because that forbids hunting in it, there is reparation for it as is the case with the *Ḥaram* of Makkah. Qāḍī 'Abd al-Wahhāb said, 'I consider this to be the most analogous with its roots, especially because the Companions considered Madīnah to be better than Makkah and because the prayer in it is better than prayer in the *Masjid al-Ḥarām*.'

Part of the argument of Mālik and ash-Shāfi'ī about there not being a ruling of reparation in it or taking booty, in the well-known position of ash-Shāfi'ī, is the general nature of the words of the Prophet ﷺ in the *Ṣaḥīḥ*: 'Madīnah is a *Ḥarām* between 'Ayr and Thawr. If someone innovates in it or gives refuge to an innovator, on him is the curse of Allah, His angels and all people. No recompense or ransom will be accepted from him.' So the Prophet ﷺ issued a severe threat and did not mention any expiation.

As for what was mentioned from Sa'd, that was his personal position based on the fact that it is related from him in the *Ṣaḥīḥ* that he rode to his fortress at al-'Aqīq and found a slave cutting a tree or knocking off its leaves and divested him of his possessions. When Sa'd returned, the slave's people went and asked him to return their slave to them or what he had taken from him. He said, 'I seek refuge from Allah from returning something that the Messenger of Allah ﷺ gave us as booty,' and refused to return anything. Allah knows best.

Allah mentions the one who kills deliberately and not the one who does so by mistake or forgetfully. What is relied on here is the one who intends to do the thing knowing that he is in *iḥrām*. The one who makes a mistake is the one who aims for something else and then inadvertently hits game. The one who forgets is the one who hunts deliberately not remembering that he is *iḥrām*. Scholars disagree about that, taking five positions about it.

The first is what ad-Dāraquṭnī related that Ibn 'Abbās said: 'Expiation is done for what is deliberate. They are harsh about the error so that people do not repeat it.'

The second view is that '*deliberately*' is what is usual, and the rare is connected to it as is the case with the fundamentals of the *Sharī'ah*.

The third view is that there is nothing owed by the one who errs and the one who forgets. Aṭ-Ṭabarī and Aḥmad ibn Ḥanbal in one transmission related it. It is related from Ibn 'Abbās and Sa'īd ibn Jubayr, and Ṭāwūs, and Abū Thawr stated it, and it is also the position of Dāwūd. Aḥmad said, 'Since Allah mentioned the deliberate, that indicates that other than that is different.' He added that the original basis is lack of responsibility, so someone who claims that it is deliberate must provide proof.

The fourth is that the ruling is the same for the deliberate, accidental and forgetful. Ibn 'Abbās said that, and it is related from 'Umar, Ṭāwūs al-Ḥasan, Ibrāhīm, and az-Zuhrī, and is stated by Mālik, ash-Shāfi'ī and Abū Ḥanīfah and their adherents. Az-Zuhrī said, 'Repayment is obliged for the deliberate by the Qur'ān, and the error and the forgetful by the *Sunnah*.' Ibn al-'Arabī said, 'By the *sunnah* he means the reports (*athār*) reported from Ibn 'Abbās and 'Umar. They are excellent and a good model.'

The fifth, which is the position of Mujāhid, is that when someone kills game deliberately, forgetting his *iḥrām*, this is connected to what Allah says afterwards: '*...but if anyone does it again Allah will take revenge on him.*' He said, 'If he remembers his *iḥrām*, the first penalty is obliged for him the first time. This indicates that Allah means someone who deliberately kills it, forgetting he is in *iḥrām*.' Mujahid said, 'If he remembers his *iḥrām*, then he is no longer in *iḥrām* and has no *ḥajj* since he has committed something forbidden while in *iḥrām*, and so his *ḥajj* is invalid for him, just as is the case if he speaks in the prayer or breaks *wuḍū'* in it. If someone errs, that is what is subject to repayment.'

Our evidence against Mujāhid is that Allah obliged repayment but did not mention invalidation. There is no difference between him remembering he is in *iḥrām* and forgetting that. It is not valid to judge the *ḥajj* by the prayer. They are different. It is also related from him that there is no ruling in it about killing game deliberately, and he should ask Allah's forgiveness and his *ḥajj* is complete. Ibn Zayd said that. Our evidence against Dāwūd is that the Prophet ﷺ was asked about hyenas and said, 'They are game.' He appointed a ram as *fidya* for a *muḥrim* when he shot it, and he did not mention whether it was deliberate or accidental.

Ibn Bukayr, one of our scholars, said, 'The word of Allah, "*deliberately*" does not convey overlooking the mistake. It is meant to clarify that it is not like the person who has no expiation for deliberately killing it and that there is expiation for killing game in his case, and that expiation is not cancelled for the one who does it accidentally.' Allah knows best.

If someone kills game time after time in his *iḥrām*, there is a judgment against him each time he kills it according to Mālik, ash-Shāfi'ī, Abū Ḥanīfah and others because of this *āyah*. So the prohibition is constant and continues for him as long as he is in *iḥrām*. When he kills it, then reparation is obliged for him because of that. It is related that Ibn 'Abbās said, 'There is no ruling against him twice in Islam, there is only one ruling against him. If he does it again, there is no judgment against him.' It was said to him, 'Allah will take revenge from you! He says: "...*if anyone does it again, Allah will take revenge on him.*"' That is the position of al-Ḥasan, Ibrāhīm, Mujāhid and Shurayḥ. Our evidence against them is what we mentioned about the prohibition continuing in *iḥrām* and that it is addressed in the *dīn* of Islam.

the reprisal for it is a livestock animal equivalent

There are four readings of this. One is *jazā'un mithlu* where the predicate is implied and that implies: he owes an equivalent repayment from livestock. This means that the '*equivalent*' is the reprisal or repayment itself. '*Jazā'u mithli*' where *mithl* is in *iḍāfah* means: he owes the reprisal of an equivalent for what he killed. *Mithl* is redundant, like 'I am nobler than your like' when you mean 'I am nobler than you. It is similar to the words of the Almighty in 6:122 where the implication is: 'like one in darkness' and in 42:11 where it means, 'He is not like anything.' This reading suggests that the reprisal is not really equivalent, since a thing is not ascribed to itself. Abū 'Alī said, 'He is obliged to make reprisal for what he killed, not to make reprisal of the like of what is killed. The *iḍāfah* demands reprisal of an equivalent, not the reprisal of what was killed.' This is the view of ash-Shāfi'ī. '*Livestock*' describes the reprisal in both readings. Al-Ḥasan read *na'am as na'm,* which is a dialect. Abū 'Abd ar-Raḥmān recited '*jazā'un*' and '*mithla*'. Abū'l-Fatḥ said, '*Mithl* is in the accusative by the reprisal itself. So he must repay the like of what he killed.' Ibn Mas'ūd and al-A'mash recited '*jazā'uhu mithlu*' with the *hā'*. It is possible that it refers to game, or to the hunter who did the killing.

Reprisal is demanded on account of killing game, not just for taking it, as Allah said. In the *Mudawwanah* we find: 'If someone catches a bird and cuts its feathers and then keeps it until its feathers grow and then it flies away, he owes no reprisal.' He said, 'It is the same if he cuts off a paw or foot or any of its limbs and it heals and the animal is sound. He owes nothing.' It is also said that he owes repayment for the amount he impaired of it. If it leaves without him knowing what he did, he owes reprisal for it. If the game is persistently ill and does not rejoin other game or he leaves it dying, he owes its full reprisal.

Two categories of game have equivalents: animals and birds. Animals are repaid by animals like them in form and physique. So there is a camel for an ostrich, a cow for a wild ass or wild cow, and a sheep for a gazelle. Ash-Shāfi'ī said that. Mālik says that the minimum which satisfies it is a feasible sacrifice of sacrificial animals. If an animal does not reach that, there is feeding or fasting in place of it. The price is owed for all doves, except the doves of Makkah. There is a sheep owed for each of them, following what the early generations did. Honey-birds, ring-doves and collared doves are all doves. Ibn 'Abd al-Ḥakam related from Mālik that there is a sheep for the doves and fledglings of Makkah. He also said that that is for the doves of the *Ḥaram*. There is arbitration for those not in the *Ḥaram*.

Abū Ḥanīfah said that value rather than physique is what is considered. The value of the game is assessed in dirhams in the place where he killed it, or the nearest place to it if he killed it in a place where game is not sold, and with that sum he can purchase a sacrificial camel or he can purchase food and feed the poor, each poor person receiving half a *ṣā'* of wheat or a *ṣā'* of barley or a *ṣā'* of dates. Ash-Shāfi'ī said that one looks for the equivalent in livestock and then estimates its value in livestock and takes the price of the equivalent as the price of the thing. The equivalent is the basis of the obligation. This is clear and derived from the reading of the *āyah* with *iḍāfah*.

The argument of Abū Ḥanīfah is that if the equivalence had been on the basis of similarity in physique, there would be a camel for an ostrich, a cow for a wild ass, and a sheep for a gazelle and the issue would not need to be submitted to two just men to give a ruling because the matter would be known and there would be no need for consideration and reflection. It requires just men and investigation of the circumstances. The manner of investigation is unclear.

Our evidence is the words: *'the reprisal of it is a livestock animal equivalent to what he killed.'* The term '*equivalent*' literally calls for physical likeness in form rather than meaning. Allah says: *'livestock animal'* and elucidates thereby the genus of the equivalent. Then He says: *'as judged by two just men among you.'* The pronoun '*bihi*' refers to the equivalence in livestock because nothing else has been mentioned to which the pronoun might refer. He then says: *'a sacrifice to reach the Ka'bah'* and the only thing conceivable in that respect are sacrificial animals of livestock similar to what was killed. As for the price, it is not conceivable with regard to a sacrificial animal. It was not mentioned in the *āyah* itself. Praise be to Allah. They say that if similarity was what was being considered, the ruling would not have been based on two just men. The response to that is that the consideration of two just men is necessary to investigate the state of the game and whether it is young or old and has a category and what does not and how to connect what does not have a text with what does have a text.

If someone who assumes *iḥrām* from Makkah closes the door of his house on the fledglings of a dove and they then die, there is a sheep due for each fledgling. Mālik said that what is owed for young game is the same as what is owed for adult game. That is the position of 'Aṭā'. According to Mālik there is no *fidyah* in the form of a year-old (*'anāq*) or half-year one (*jafrah*). Mālik said, 'That is the same as applies to blood-money. The young and adult are the same in that respect.' He believes that one should pay the value of lizards and jerboas in the form of food. Some of the people of Madīnah disagree about young game and taking account of age and take the position of Ibn 'Umar who says that there a year-old kid is owed for a rabbit and a half-yearling for a jerboa. Mālik related it *mawqūf.*

Abū az-Zubayr related from Jābir that the Prophet ﷺ said, 'If someone in *iḥrām* kills a lizard there a ram is owed. There is a sheep for a gazelle, a year-old for a rabbit, and a half-yearling for a jerboa.' A half-yearling (*jafrah*) is one that has been taken to pasture. We find in another report: 'I asked Abū az-Zubayr, "What is a *jafrah*?" He replied, "An animal that is weaned and gone to pasture."' Ad-Daraquṭnī transmitted it.

Ash-Shāfi'ī said, 'A camel is owed for an ostrich and a young camel for its young. A cow is owed for a wild ass and a calf for its young because Allah Almighty judged equivalence in respect of physique, and young and old differ in that respect and so one most consider young and old as one does with things that have been destroyed.' Ibn al-'Arabī said, 'This is sound and it is what is preferred by our scholars.' His words 'this is what is preferred by our scholars', give the impression that it is what is preferred and well known. This is not the case. It is the explicit school of ash-Shāfi'ī. They say, 'If the game is one-eyed, lame or broken, then the equivalent should be the same to realise equivalence. The one who destroys is not liable for more than he destroyed.' Our evidence is Allah's words: *'the reprisal for it is a livestock animal equivalent to what he killed,'* in which He does not distinguish between young and old. '*Hady*' means that which is covered by the term in general and demands a full sacrifice. Allah knows best.'

A tenth of the price of a camel is owed for an ostrich egg according to Mālik and he believes that a tenth of the price of a sheep is owed for a dove's egg. Ibn al-Qāsim said that it is the same whether or not there is a chick in it after it is broken. The person concerned owes the full penalty, the same as for an adult bird. Ibn al-Mawwāz said it is subject to the arbitration of two just men. Most scholars believe that a price is owed for the eggs of any bird. 'Ikrimah related from Ibn 'Abbās from Ka'b ibn 'Ujrah that the Prophet ﷺ gave a judgement of equivalence in price for the eggs of an ostrich which a *muḥrim* had hit. Ad-Daraquṭnī transmitted it. It is related that Abū Hurayrah said that the Messenger of Allah ﷺ said, 'For every ostrich egg, one owes fasting for a day or feeding a poor person.'

As for animals with no equivalents, such as sparrows and elephants, the price is based on their meat value or its equivalent in food rather than any idea of size equivalence because, in the case of pastured animals where there is an equivalent, the equivalent must be paid. If there is no equivalent, then the price takes its place, as is the case with misappropriation and other things. That is also because those who espouse the two schools say that one considers the price in all game and confines it to livestock that have no equivalent. That guarantees consensus about considering the price in the case of what has no equivalent.

In the case of elephants, it is said that a camel from the large species that has two humps is owed for it. They are white and Khorasanī. If none of these camels are available, one looks at its price in terms of food and the person owes that. The practice regarding it is to put an elephant in a boat and see how far it sinks in the water. Then the elephant is removed and food is put in the boat until it reaches the level that it did with the elephant in it. This is its equivalent in food. As for considering its price, it has an immense price because of its bones and tusks. So that would require a lot of food and would be excessively punitive.

as judged by two just men among you

Mālik related from 'Abd al-Malik ibn Qurayb that a man came to 'Umar ibn al-Khaṭṭāb and said, 'I was racing a friend on horseback towards a narrow mountain trail and we killed a gazelle accidentally while we were in *iḥrām*. What is your opinion?' 'Umar said to a man by his side, 'Come, so that you and I may make an assessment.' They decided on a female goat for him, and the man turned away saying, 'This Amīr al-Mu'minīn cannot even make an assessment in the case of a gazelle without calling on someone to help him decide.' 'Umar overheard the man's words and called him and asked him, 'Do you recite *Sūrat al-Mā'idah*?' and he answered, 'No.' He asked, 'Then do you recognise this man who has taken the decision with me?' and he answered, 'No.' He said, 'If you had told me that you did recite *Sūrat al-Mā'idah,* I would have dealt you a blow.' Then he said, 'Allah the Blessed and Exalted, says in His Book: "*...as shall be judged by two men of justice* *among you, a sacrificial animal to reach the Ka'bah"* (5:95), and this is 'Abd ar-Raḥmān ibn 'Awf.'

If the two judges agree, then the ruling is binding. That is what al-Ḥasan and ash-Shāfi'ī said. If they disagree, someone else looks into it. Muḥammad ibn al-Mawwāz said, 'He does not take the higher of their two views because that is acting without arbitration, nor does not move from the equivalent to feeding if the equivalent has been judged for feeding because that is binding.' Ibn Sha'bān said that. Ibn al-Qāsim said, 'If they are told to judge reprisal then they do it. If he is wants to move to feeding, that is permitted.' Ibn Wahb said in *al-'Utbiyyah,* 'Part of the *sunnah* is that the two judges give a choice to the one shoots game as Allah gives a choice in its payment: *"...expiation by feeding the poor, or fasting commensurate with that."* If he chooses sacrifice, they judge what they think is its equivalent in food. Then he can choose to give it as food or to fast a day in place of every *mudd.*' This is stated by Mālik in the *Mudawwanah.*

They make a new ruling on anything about which there has been no previous arbitration or on which it has not been carried out. If they apply the ruling of the Companions regarding what they judged to be the correct repayment for game, that is good. It is related from Mālik that there is arbitration regarding all animals except for the doves of Makkah, wild asses, gazelles and ostriches. The ruling of the early generations is applied in those four categories.

According to Abū Ḥanīfah it is not permitted for either of the arbiters to be a criminal. Ash-Shāfi'ī, in one of his views, said that it is permitted for one of the arbiters to be a criminal. This is a dispensation on his part, taking the literal meaning of the *āyah,* but it is not permitted for a person to judge for himself. If that had been permitted, he would only need himself because it is a ruling between him and Allah. The addition of a second is evidence that it is a new ruling with two men.

When a group of people who are in *iḥrām* participate in killing game, Mālik and Abū Ḥanīfah say that each of them owes full reparation. Ash-Shāfi'ī said that a single *kaffārah* covers all of them, based on the decision of 'Umar and 'Abd ar-Raḥmān. Ad-Dāraquṭnī related that some freedmen of Abū az-Zubayr were in *iḥrām* and a hyena passed by them. They threw their ropes at it and caught it. Then they were upset about it and went to Ibn 'Umar and mentioned it to him. He said, 'You all owe a ram.' They asked, 'Or do each of us owe a ram?' He answered, 'You helped one another and so you all owe a ram.' It is related from Ibn 'Abbās that some people killed a hyena and he said, 'You owe a ram between you.' Our evidence is found in the words of the Almighty: *'If one of you kills any deliberately, the reprisal for it is a livestock animal equivalent to what he killed'* which is addressed to each killer. Each of those who killed the game killed a living creature completely. That is evidenced by the fact that a group are killed for one person. If that were not the case, retaliation would be obliged on them. We said that it is obligatory by our and their consensus. So what we said is confirmed.

Abū Ḥanīfah said that if a group kill game in the *Ḥaram* when all of them are not in *iḥrām,* they owe one reprisal which is not the case when a group who are all in *iḥrām* participate in killing game in the *Ḥaram* or outside of it. There is no disagreement about that. Mālik says that each of them owes full reparation, based on the fact that a man is in *iḥrām* by entering the *Ḥaram* as he is in *iḥrām* by saying the *talbīyah* for *iḥrām*. Each of these two actions brings about the description which entails of the prohibition, and in both cases he violates it. The argument of Abū Ḥanīfah is what was mentioned by Abū Zayd ad-Dabūsī who said, 'The secret in it is that the crime in *iḥrām* is contrary to an act of worship. Each of them committed that which is forbidden by his *iḥrām,* but when those who are not in *iḥrām* kill game in the *Ḥaram*, they are destroying a sacrosanct creature. It is the same as a group killing an animal. Each of them kills the animal and they share in the price.' Ibn al-'Arabī said, 'Abū Ḥanīfah is more lenient. This is an argument which our scholars pay little attention to but it is difficult for us to set it aside.'

a sacrifice to reach the Ka'bah,

This means that when they judge what should be sacrificed, the person concerned does to it what is done to sacrificial animals with respect to marking or garlanding and it is taken from there to Makkah, slaughtered and given as *ṣadaqah* there because of these words. It does not mean the Ka'bah itself. It means the *Ḥaram*, and there is no disagreement about this. Ash-Shāfi'ī said that it is permitted to buy it in the *Ḥaram* based on the fact that a young sacrificial animal is obliged for young game. It can be purchased in the *Ḥaram* and given in it.

expiation by feeding the poor,

Kaffārah is on account of the game, not the sacrifice. Ibn Wahb mentioned that Mālik said, 'The best that I have heard about someone who kills game and is assessed for it is that the game which he has killed is assessed and its value in food is estimated and with that food he feeds poor men a *mudd* each, or fasts a day in place of each *mudd*.' Ibn al-Qāsim said, 'If the game is assessed in dirhams and then he spends it on food, that satisfies the requirement.' The first view is the correct one. 'Abdullāh ibn 'Abd al-Ḥakam said something similar. He said, 'There is a choice between these three.' If he does that, it satisfies the requirement whether he is wealthy or poor. That is the position of 'Aṭā' and the bulk of *fuqahā'* because 'or' implies choice. Mālik said, 'A person has a choice regarding everything in the Book of Allah about expiation which says "this or that". It means: he can do whichever he prefers to do.'

It is related that Ibn 'Abbās said, 'If a *muḥrim* kills a gazelle or its like, he owes a sheep to be slaughtered in Makkah. If he cannot find one, then he feeds six people. If he cannot do that, then he fasts for three days. If he kills a stag or its like, he owes a cow. If he cannot find one, then he feeds twenty poor people. If he cannot do that, then he fasts twenty days. If he kills an ostrich or ass, he owes a camel. If he cannot find one, then he feeds thirty poor people and if he cannot do that, he fasts thirty days. Feeding is a *mudd* each to satisfy them.' Ibrāhīm an-Nakha'ī and Ḥammād ibn Salamah said that 'or expiation' means if he does not find a sacrifice.

Aṭ-Ṭabarī related that Ibn 'Abbās said, 'When a *muḥrim* catches game, its reprisal is judged against him. If he finds its equivalent, he slaughters it and gives it as *ṣadaqah*. If he does not find its equivalent, then its value is estimated in dirhams and then the dirhams are estimated in terms of wheat. Then he can fast a day in place of every half *mudd*.' He said, 'By "feeding", Allah means to clarify the business of fasting. If he cannot find food, then he finds a reprisal.' It also has an *isnād* of as-Suddī. This statement is opposed by the literal text of the *āyah*. It is incompatible with it.

Scholars disagree about the time when the value of the killed animal should be assessed. Some people say that it should be on the day it is killed and others say that it should be on the day judgment is rendered. Others say that the greater of the two prices should be used. Ibn al-'Arabī said, 'Our scholars have the same disagreement. What is sound is that the price obliged for him is the one assessed on the day of its killing. The evidence for that is that existence is a right of the animal killed. When it no longer exists, the person concerned is obliged to bring its like into existence, and that is is judged by the day it ceased to exist.

As for sacrifices (*hady*), there is no disagreement that they must be in Makkah because of this *āyah*. In the view of Mālik there is disagreement about feeding people and whether that should be in Makkah or in the place where the game was killed. Ash-Shāfi'ī thinks that it should be in Makkah. 'Aṭā' said, 'If it is sacrifice or food, it is in Makkah, but the person may fast wherever he wishes.' That is the position of Mālik about fasting and there is no disagreement about it. Qāḍī Abū Muḥammad 'Abd al-Wahhāb said, 'It is not permitted to repay anything as recompense for game outside the *Ḥaram* except in the form of fasting.'

Ḥammād and Abū Ḥanīfah said that the expiation should be made where a person killed the game. Aṭ-Ṭabarī said that he may do the expiation wherever he wishes. The position of Abū Ḥanīfah has no logic or tradition behind it. The reason for fasting wherever he likes is because fasting is an act of worship particular to the faster and so it can occur in any place, as is the case with other expiations. The reason that feeding should be in Makkah is because it is like the sacrifice and the sacrifice is for the poor at Makkah. Those who say it can be done elsewhere consider it to be like every feeding and *fidyah*. Allah knows best.

or fasting commensurate with that,

The word for *'commensurate'* is read as *'adl* or *'idl*. They mean the same, as al-Kisā'ī says. Al-Farrā' said that *'idl* is the like of something of the same kind and *'adl* is its equivalent in another form. This view is also related from al-Kisā'ī. You say, 'I have the equivalent (*'idl*) of your dirhams in dirhams and 'I have the equivalent (*'adl*) of your dirhams in garments.' The sound position from al-Kisā'ī is that they are two dialectical forms which is the position of the Basrans. It is not valid to compare fasting to feeding in any direct numerical way.

Mālik said, 'He fasts a day for every *mudd* owed, even if that is more than two or three months.' Ash-Shāfi'ī also said that. Yaḥyā ibn 'Umar, among our people said, 'It is asked how many people would be fed by this game animal in order to calculate the number. Then it is decided how much food will satisfy that number. If someone wishes, he can pay that amount of food, and if he wishes, he can fast a number of days that are the same as the number of *mudds* it consists of.' This is an excellent statement which is comprehensive because the price of the game may be low. This view results in a lot of feeding. Some of the people of knowledge do not think that one should exceed two months in fasting for reparation. They said, 'It is the maximum in *kaffārah*.' Ibn al-'Arabī preferred that. Abū Ḥanīfah said, 'The person should fast a day for every two *mudds*, analogous to the *fidyah* on account of harm.'

so that he may taste the evil consequences of what he did.

'Tasting' here is metaphorical as in Allah's words: '*Taste that! You are the mighty one, the noble one!*' (44:49) and: '*…so Allah made it wear [lit. taste] the robes of hunger*' (16:112). The word is frequently used in such a way in Arabic. The reality of taste is experienced by the tongue, and it is used metaphorically in all these instances. An example of this usage is found in the following *ḥadīth*: 'The one who is pleased

with Allah as a Lord has tasted faith.' The noun *wabāl* means evil consequences. Pasture which is *wabīl* (unhealthy) is that which causes harm when eaten and food which is *wabīl* is heavy. It is used in the words:

The best wealth of an old man is like a staff (*wabīl*) as an argument.

His business refers to his entire state.

Allah has pardoned all that took place in the past;

This means any game you killed in the Jāhiliyyah. 'Aṭā' ibn Abī Rabāḥ and a group said that. It is also said that it means before *kaffārah* was revealed. In the words: *'But if anyone does it again'*, in other words does what has been forbidden here, *'Allah will take revenge on him'*, the *'revenge'* is by the imposition of *kaffārah*. It is also said that it is a reference to the Next World if the person considers what he did to be lawful.

Shurayḥ and Sa'īd ibn Jubayr said that the *kaffārah* is imposed on him the first time he does it. If he does it again, there is no imposition and he is told, 'Go, Allah will take revenge on you. Your wrong action is too great to be expiated.' This is also the case with false oaths: most of the people of knowledge say that there is no expiation for them because of the enormity of the wrong action involved. Those who are scrupulously aware protect themselves from this revenge by expiation. It is related that Ibn 'Abbās said, 'His back should be whipped until he dies.' It is related from Zayd ibn Abī al-Mu'allā that a man shot some game while he was in *iḥrām* and was excused. Then he did it again and Allah Almighty sent down a fire from heaven which burned him up. This was a lesson for the community and a deterrent against transgressors disobeying this ordinance.

"Allah is Almighty' and impregnable in His domain and none can prevent what He wills. *'He is the Exactor of Revenge'* on those who disobey Him, if He wills.

أُحِلَّ لَكُمْ صَيْدُ الْبَحْرِ وَطَعَامُهُ مَتَاعًا لَّكُمْ وَلِلسَّيَّارَةِ وَحُرِّمَ عَلَيْكُمْ صَيْدُ الْبَرِّ مَا دُمْتُمْ
حُرُمًا وَاتَّقُوا اللَّهَ الَّذِي إِلَيْهِ تُحْشَرُونَ ﴿٩٦﴾

96 Anything you catch in the sea is lawful for you, and all food from it, for your enjoyment and that of travellers, but land game is unlawful for you while you are in *iḥrām*. So have *taqwā* of Allah, Him to whom you will be gathered.

Anything you catch in the sea is lawful for you,

This is a ruling that the catch of the sea is lawful. It refers to all sorts of fish that are caught. *Ṣayd* means that which is caught. It is ascribed to the sea since it is the reason for it. The sea was already discussed in *al-Baqarah* (2:250).

and all food from it, for your enjoyment and that of travellers,

'Food' (*ṭa'ām*) applies to all that is eaten and it can be applied to any particular thing which is consumed, such as water on its own, wheat, dates, or milk. The word *ṭa'ām* can be applied to sleep as well as we already mentioned. (ref. 2:61) In this case it applies to what the sea casts up. It is reported that what is meant is dead fish which the sea throws up. Ad-Dāraquṭnī reported from Ibn 'Abbās about this *āyah* that its *'catch'* is what is caught from the sea and its *'food'* is what is thrown up by it. Something similar is related from Abū Hurayrah. That is the position of the majority of Companions and *Tābi'ūn*. It is related from Ibn 'Abbās that its *'food'* is its dead, and it has that meaning. It is also related from him that its *'food'* is what is salted and lasts. A group supported him in that. Some people said that its *'food'* is its salt which is procured from its water and all the rest of the plants and other things in it.

Abū Ḥanīfah said, 'Floating fish should not be eaten but other fish may be. None of the animals of the sea except fish are eaten.' That is the position of ath-Thawrī, according to Abū Isḥāq al-Fazarī. Al-Ḥasan also disliked eating floating fish. It is related from 'Alī ibn Abī Ṭālib that he too disliked that. It is also related that he disliked eating eels. It is related that he ate all those things, and that is sounder. 'Abd ar-Razzāq mentioned it from ath-Thawrī from Ja'far ibn Muḥammad from 'Alī. He said, 'Locusts and fish are slaughtered.' There is disagreement about 'Alī eating floating fish, but there is no disagreement that Jābir disliked it. That is the position of Ṭāwūs, Muḥammad ibn Sīrīn and Jābir ibn Zayd. They used the generality of the words of Allah: *'Forbidden to you is carrion'* (5:3) and what Abū Dāwūd and ad-Dāraquṭnī related from Jābir ibn 'Abdullāh that the Messenger of Allah ﷺ said, 'Eat what is taken from the sea and what it casts up. Do not eat what you find dead or floating on the water.' Ad-Dāraquṭnī said, 'Only 'Abd al-'Azīz ibn 'Ubaydullāh has it from Wahb ibn Kaysān from Jābir. 'Abd al-'Azīz is weak and not used as an authority.'

Sufyān ath-Thawrī related something similar from Abū az-Zubayr from Jābir from the Prophet ﷺ. Ad-Dāraquṭnī said, 'Only Abū Aḥmad az-Zubarī has it with an *isnād* from ath-Thawrī. Ad-Dāraquṭnī said, 'Only 'Abd al-'Azīz ibn 'Ubaydullāh has it from Wahb ibn Kaysān from Jābir. 'Abd al-'Azīz is weak and not used as an authority.' He is opposed by Wakī', the two 'Adanīs ['Abdullāh ibn al-Walīd and Yazīd ibn Abī Ḥakīm], 'Abd ar-Razzāq, Mu'ammal, Abū 'Āṣim and others. They related it *mawqūf* from ath-Thawrī, which is correct. That is how it is related by Ayyūb as-Sakhtiyānī, 'Ubaydullāh ibn 'Umar, Ibn Jurayj, Zuhayr, Ḥammād ibn Salamah and others from Abū az-Zubayr as *mawqūf.* Abū Dāwūd said, 'This *ḥadīth* has a path that is not weak from Ibn Abī Dhi'b from Abū az-Zubayr from Jābir from the Prophet ﷺ.' Ad-Dāraquṭnī said, 'It is related from Ismā'īl ibn Umayyah and Ibn Abī Dhi'b from Abū az-Zubayr as *marfū'*. It is not sound that it is *marfū'*. Yaḥyā ibn Sulaym has it *marfū'* from Ismā'īl ibn Umayyah. Others have it *mawqūf.*'

Mālik, ash-Shāfi'ī, Ibn Abī Laylā, al-Awzā'ī and ath-Thawrī, as transmitted by al-Ashjā'ī, said, 'All fish and animals in the sea of can be eaten, and all living creatures in the sea, whether they are caught or found dead.' Mālik's evidence and those who followed him is the words of the Prophet ﷺ about the sea, 'Its water is pure and its dead are lawful.' The soundest thing relating to this topic in respect of its *isnād* is the *ḥadīth* of Jābir about the fish called the sperm whale, and it is transmitted in the two *Ṣaḥīḥ* Collections: 'When we reached Madīnah, we mentioned that to the Prophet ﷺ and he said, "Eat, for it is provision which Allah has brought out. Feed us if there is any of it with you." So one of them brought part of it to the Messenger of Allah ﷺ and he ate it.'

Ad-Dāraquṭnī reported that Ibn 'Abbās said, 'I saw Abū Bakr say, "Floating fish are lawful for the one who wants to eat them."' He also said, 'I saw Abū Bakr eat fish which had been floating on the water.' It is related from Abū Ayyūb that he was on the sea with a group of his companions and they found a fish floating on the water and asked him about it. He asked, 'Is it good and not putrefied?' 'Yes.' they replied. He said, 'Eat it and save me my share of it.' He was fasting. It is related from Jabalah ibn 'Aṭiyyah that the companions of Abū Ṭalḥah got hold of a floating fish and asked Abū Ṭalḥah about it. He said, 'Give it to me.'

'Umar ibn al-Khaṭṭāb said, 'Fish are slaughtered and all locusts are slaughtered.' Ad-Dāraquṭnī related it from him. These traditions refute the position of those who dislike that and they refine the general meaning of the *āyah*. It is the argument of the majority, although Mālik dislikes porpoises because of their name ('sea pig'), but did not make them unlawful. He said, 'You said "pig"!' Ash-Shāfi'ī said that there is nothing wrong in eating porpoises. Al-Layth said that there is nothing wrong with the dead of the sea. He said, 'That is the same for sharks ("sea dogs") and hippopotamuses ("sea horses").' He said, 'One does not eat manatees (*insān al-baḥr* literally "sea-people") or "water pigs".'

Scholars disagree about amphibious animals and whether a *muḥrim* can hunt them or not. Mālik, Abū Miljaz, 'Aṭā', Sa'īd ibn Jubayr and others said, 'All that lives on land and spends time on it is considered land game. If a *muḥrim* kills it, he owes for it.' Abū Miljaz added, 'That includes frogs, turtles, and crabs.' According to Abū Ḥanīfah, frogs and their species are unlawful. There is no disagreement that ash-Shāfi'ī did not permit the eating of frogs. His position varies about things that have land equivalents which are not eaten such as pigs, dogs, and the like. The sound position is that all sea food may be eaten, because there is a text on 'sea pigs' being permitted, although they have a name similar to a land animal which may not be eaten. He says that one does not eat crocodiles, sharks or dolphins, and all that has fangs because the Prophet ﷺ forbade eating animals with fangs.

Ibn 'Aṭiyyah said, 'Some of these species which must have water to live in must be sea game. This is the basis of the reply of Mālik about frogs in the *Mudawwanah*. He said, "Frogs are water game."' 'Aṭā' ibn Abī Rabāḥ related something different and he took account of where the majority of the creature's life is spent and where it hatches. That is the position of Abū Ḥanīfah. What is correct about an animal born in the sea is that it is considered land game if it grazes and eats grain. Ibn al-'Arabī said, 'It is sound that he forbade animals that are amphibious because the two proofs contradict each other: one making it lawful and one making it unlawful. Out of cautiousness, the evidence of its being unlawful dominates. Allah knows best.'

There are two things said about the words: '*...and that of travellers*'. One is that it applies to residents and travellers, as comes in the *ḥadīth* of Abū 'Ubaydah, which says that they ate it when they were travelling. The Prophet ﷺ ate it while resident and so Allah made it clear that it is lawful for someone who is resident just as it is for travellers. The second is that travellers are those who are on the sea, as in the *ḥadīth* of Mālik and an-Nasā'ī: 'A man asked the Prophet ﷺ, "We travel by sea and we do not carry much fresh water with us so if we do *wuḍū'* with it we go thirsty. Can we perform *wuḍū'* with sea-water?" The Prophet ﷺ replied, "Its water is pure, and its dead creatures are lawful."' Ibn al-'Arabī said, 'Our scholars say that if the Prophet ﷺ had simply replied "Yes," then *wuḍū'* with it would only be permitted on account of fear of thirst because the answer is connected to the question. But the Prophet ﷺ gave the basis of the rule and clarified the *Sharī'ah* in his words: "Its water is pure, and its dead creatures are lawful."' So his answer would have been restricted to them rather than others were it not that the ruling of the *Sharī'ah* confirmed that the ruling for one is the ruling for all unless there is specification in the text, as when he ﷺ said to Abū Burdah about a young goat, 'Sacrifice it, but it will not be allowed for anyone other than you.'

but land game is unlawful for you while you are in *iḥrām*.

Making unlawful in this case does not describe the animals but is connected to the action involved, and so the *āyah* means that it is the action of hunting which is forbidden. It, however, also means that which is caught. The object often takes the name of the action. That is made clearer by the consensus of scholars that a *muḥrim* is forbidden to accept game as a gift and he is not permitted to buy it or hunt it or come to own it in any manner whatsoever. There is no disagreement among Muslim scholars about that since the expression here is general and the *ḥadīth* of aṣ-Ṣa'b ibn Jaththāmah supports it.

Scholars disagree about game a *muḥrim* may eat. Mālik, ash-Shāfi'ī and their people and Aḥmad said, and it is related from Isḥāq, and is confirmed from 'Uthmān ibn 'Affān, that there is nothing wrong in a *muḥrim* eating game which he did not hunt or which was not caught on his behalf, based on what at-Tirmidhi, an-Nasa'ī and ad-Dāraquṭnī related from Jābir that the Prophet ﷺ said, 'Land game is lawful for you as long as you did not hunt it or it was not caught on your behalf.' Abū 'Īsā says that this is the best *ḥadīth* on the subject. An-Nasā'ī said, "Amr ibn Abī 'Amr is not strong in *ḥadīth*, even though Mālik related from him.' If he eats game which was caught on his behalf, he pays reparation for it. That is what was said about al-Ḥasan ibn Ṣāliḥ and al-Awzā'ī.

Mālik's position varies about game which is caught for a *muḥrim*. The well-known position in his school among his people is that a *muḥrim* may not eat what is caught for any *muḥrim*, be it a specific person or not. He did not accept the words of 'Uthmān to his people when he was brought the meat of game while he was in *iḥrām*, 'Eat; you are not like me because it is game hunted for my sake.' That was the position of a group of the people of Madīnah and is also reported from Mālik.

Abū Ḥanīfah and his people said that it is permitted for a *muḥrim* to eat game in any case when someone not in *iḥrām* hunts it, whether or not it was for him, because of the literal sense of Allah's words: *'Do not kill game while you are in iḥrām.'* So He forbade those in *iḥrām* from hunting and killing, not from eating what others have caught. They take as evidence the *ḥadīth* of Zayd ibn Ka'b al-Bahzī about the Prophet ﷺ and the wild ass which he commanded Abū Bakr to divide among his company, as reported by Mālik (20.24.80) and others. There is also the *ḥadīth* reported by Qatādah in which the Prophet ﷺ said, 'Eat, it is food that Allah has fed you with.' That is the position of 'Umar ibn al-Khaṭṭāb, 'Uthmān ibn 'Affān in one transmission, Abū Hurayrah, az-Zubayr ibn al-'Awwām, Mujāhid, 'Aṭā' and Sa'īd ibn Jubayr.

It is related from 'Alī ibn Abī Ṭālib, Ibn 'Abbās and Ibn 'Umar that it is not permitted for a *muhrim* to consume game in any state, whether it was hunted for his sake or not, since it the *āyah* is general. Ibn 'Abbās said that it is unclear. That was stated by Ṭāwūs and Abū ash-Sha'thā' Jābir ibn Zayd. Mālik related it from ath-Thawrī and it is the position of Ishāq. They used as evidence the *ḥadīth* of aṣ-Ṣa'b ibn Jaththāmah al-Laythī who gave the Prophet ﷺ a wild ass at al-Abwā' or Waddān and the Messenger of Allah ﷺ gave it back to him. He said, 'When the Messenger of Allah ﷺ saw the expression on my face, he said, "We only gave it back to you because we are in *iḥrām*."' The Imāms report it, and this is the variant of Mālik.

Abū 'Umar said that Ibn 'Abbās related from Sa'īd ibn Jubayr, Miqsam, 'Aṭā' and Ṭāwūs that aṣ-Ṣa'b ibn Jaththāmah gave the Prophet ﷺ the meat of a wild ass. Sa'īd ibn Jubayr said, '...the rump of a wild ass. He returned it while it was dripping with blood as if it had been caught at that very moment.' Miqsām said that it was the leg of a wild ass. 'Aṭā' said, 'He gave him a front leg of game, but he did not accept it, saying, "I am in *iḥrām*."' Ṭāwūs said, 'a front leg of the meat of game.' Ismā'īl related it from 'Alī ibn al-Madīnī from Yaḥyā ibn Sa'īd from Ibn Jurayj from al-Ḥasan ibn Muslim from Ṭāwūs from Ibn 'Abbās, although some of them have it from Ibn 'Abbās from Zayd ibn Arqam.

Ismā'īl said, 'I heard Sulaymān ibn Ḥarb interpret this *ḥadīth* as meaning that it was because it was hunted for the Prophet ﷺ. If it were not for that, it would be permitted. Sulaymān said, "A factor indicating that it was hunted for the Prophet ﷺ is their words in the *ḥadīth*, 'He returned it while it was dripping with blood as if it had been caught at that very moment.'"' Ismā'īl said, 'Sulaymān interpreted this *ḥadīth* because it needed interpretation. As for the transmission of Mālik, it does not require interpretation because a *muḥrim* is not permitted to keep or slaughter live game.' Ismā'īl said, 'According to the interpretation of Sulaymān ibn Ḥarb, there is no disagreement about this in any of the *marfū'ah ḥadīth*s, Allah willing.'

If someone goes into *iḥrām* and has live game in his possession or in his house with his family, Mālik says: 'If it is in his personal possession, he should release it. If it is with his family, he does not have to release it.' That is the position of Abū Ḥanīfah and Aḥmad ibn Ḥanbal. In one of his two positions, ash-Shāfi'ī says that it is the same whether it is in his personal possession or in his house: he does not have to release it. That is the position of Abū Thawr. Something similar is related from Mujāhid and 'Abdullāh ibn al-Ḥārith, and it is related from Mālik. Ibn Abī

Laylā, ath-Thawrī and ash-Shāfi'ī, in another view, said that he must release it whether it is in his house or in his personal possession. If he does not release it, he is liable for reparation. The reason for his statement about releasing it is Allah's words: '*...land game is unlawful for you while you are in iḥrām*'. This is general to all types of possession and disposal. The reason for the statement that it may be kept is it does not prevent someone from beginning *iḥrām* and so it does not prevent him from continuing to own it. Its basis is similar to the ruling in respect of marriage.

If someone not in *ihrām* hunts outside of the *Ḥaram* and brings it to the *Ḥaram*, he is permitted to dispose of it in any manner: he can slaughter it and eat its meat. Abū Ḥanīfah says that it is not permitted. Our evidence is that it concerns what is done to the game and so it is permitted in the *Ḥaram* for someone not in *iḥrām*, like keeping and selling. There is no disagreement about that. If a *muḥrim* points out game to someone not *iḥrām* who kills it, there is disagreement. Mālik and ash-Shāfi'ī and Abū Thawr say that he owes nothing, and that is the position of Ibn al-Mājishūn. The Kufans, Aḥmad and Isḥāq and a group of Companions and *Tābi'ūn* say that he does owe reparation because a *muḥrim* is obliged by his *iḥrām* not to allude to something in that way, which includes game as well as pointing out something for a thief to steal.

They disagree about when a *muḥrim* points out game to another *muḥrim*. The Kufans and Ashhab among our people believe that each of them owes reparation. Mālik, ash-Shāfi'ī and Abū Thawr say that one who killed it owes reparation because Allah says: '*If any of you kills any deliberately.*' The obligation of reparation is connected to killing. That indicates that it is not owed by anyone other than the killer and does not incur any liability, as when someone not in *iḥrām* in the *Ḥaram* indicates game in the *Ḥaram*. The Kufans and Ashhab base their view on the words of the Prophet ﷺ in the *ḥadīth* of Abū Qatādah, 'Did you point or show?' This indicates the obligation of reparation. The first is sounder and Allah knows best.

When a tree grows outside of the *Ḥaram* but some of its branches are in it and someone catches game from the branch, reparation is owed because he took it in the *Ḥaram*. If its root is in the *Ḥaram* and the branch is outside of it, scholars disagree about what is taken from it: one considers the root and the other considers the branch.

So have *taqwā* of Allah, Him to whom you will be gathered."

This is intensification and information of the threat about the punishment after having been informed what is made lawful and unlawful. Then Allah mentions the Gathering and Rising to emphasise the warning. Allah knows best.

جَعَلَ ٱللَّهُ ٱلْكَعْبَةَ ٱلْبَيْتَ ٱلْحَرَامَ قِيَٰمًا لِّلنَّاسِ وَٱلشَّهْرَ ٱلْحَرَامَ وَٱلْهَدْىَ
وَٱلْقَلَٰٓئِدَ ذَٰلِكَ لِتَعْلَمُوٓا۟ أَنَّ ٱللَّهَ يَعْلَمُ مَا فِى ٱلسَّمَٰوَٰتِ وَمَا فِى ٱلْأَرْضِ وَأَنَّ ٱللَّهَ
بِكُلِّ شَىْءٍ عَلِيمٌ ﴿٩٧﴾

97 Allah has made the Ka'bah, the Sacred House, a special institution for mankind, and also the sacred months and the sacrificial animals and the ritual garlands. That is so you will know that Allah knows what is in the heavens and in the earth and that Allah has knowledge of all things.

Allah has made the Ka'bah

'*Ja'ala*' (*made*) here means 'created'. The name Ka'bah is given to it because it is cubic whereas most Arab houses were round. It is said that it is called that because of its growth and emergence. Anything that protrudes is called *ka'bah*, circular or not. It is used to describe the anklebone and a knob on a cane and for the breasts of a woman when they swell. A house is called that because it has a roof and walls and that is the reality of houseness, even if no one lives there. Allah appointed it as a *Ḥaram* as the Prophet ﷺ said, 'Allah made Makkah a *Ḥaram*. People did not do that.' This has already been adequately discussed (2:126).

a special institution for mankind

This refers to righteousness and livelihood since people are safe there and so the word (*qiyām*) means 'residing there' [and being safe]. It is also said that *qiyām* means establishing its laws. Ibn 'Āmir and 'Āṣim [al-Jaḥdarī] read it *qiyām*. *Qiwām* is also recited. Scholars say, 'The wisdom in Allah instituting these things for people is that Allah created humankind with the Adamic instincts of mutual envy, mutual rivalry, mutual severance, and disparity, pillage, attack, killing and revenge. So in the Divine Wisdom and original Divine Will there must be someone to curb and maintain things and to restrain and give hope.' Allah says: *'I am placing a caliph in the earth.'* (2:30) Allah commanded the caliphate and ordained people's affairs to be managed by one person to keep them from conflict and to impel them to mutual affection rather than cutting one another off, to defend the wronged from those who wrong them, and to confirm everyone in their ownership of their possessions. Ibn al-Qāsim related from Mālik that 'Uthmān ibn 'Affān used to say, 'A ruler may not control anything except what is controlled by the Qur'ān.' Abū 'Umar mentioned it.

A year's injustice on the part of a ruler is less harmful for people than chaos for a single instant, so Allah set up the caliph in order to confer this benefit: so that matters should proceed by his opinion and so that through him Allah might control the aggression of the masses. Similarly, Allah made the Sacred House immense in their hearts and put of awe of it in them. He made its *Ḥaram* esteemed by them. Whoever sought refuge there was protected. Whoever was oppressed was protected by being there. Allah says: *'Do they not see that We have established a safe haven while people all round them are violently dispossessed?'* (29:68) Scholars say, 'Since it is a special place which not everyone who is wronged knows about nor those in fear able to reach, Allah also instituted the sacred months as another refuge.'

and also the sacred months

'Months' (*shahr*) is a generic term and means, by the consensus of the Arabs, the four sacred months. Allah confirmed their sanctity in their hearts and they did not alarm anyone in them, seek blood in them nor take revenge in them, so that in them a man would meet the killer of his father, son and brother and not harm him. During them they stopped for a third of the time and made three months continuous, so that there was scope and the opportunity to travel in security and safety. And they sanctified one month on its own the middle of the year. That is the month of Rajab which is also called Muḍar. It is called Rajab al-Aṣamm (Rajab the Mute) because in it no sound of weapons was heard in it. It was also called Munṣil al-Asinnah, 'Downing the Spearheads', because they downed the points of spears in it. It is the month of Quraysh. 'Awf ibn al-Aḥwaṣ said:

The month of the Banū Umayyah and sacrifices.
When they are driven, the blood reddens them.

The Prophet ﷺ called it 'the Month of Allah,' i.e. 'the month of the people of Allah.' The people in the *Ḥaram* were called 'the people of Allah'. It may be 'the Month of Allah' because Allah reinforced and strengthened it since many Arabs did not think that. There will be more about the names of the months in *Sūrat at-Tawbah*, Allah willing.

and the sacrificial animals and the ritual garlands.

Then inspiration, or Divine Law, on the tongues of noble Messengers made the practice of sacrifices and garlands easy for them [to implement]. When they took a camel, they marked it with blood or hung sandals on it, or a man himself did the garlanding as we already mentioned earlier in the *sūrah*. Then no one would harass him when they met him. It separated him from those who sought him or wronged him. This was the situation until Allah brought Islam and clarified the truth by Muḥammad ﷺ. The *dīn* was put in order and the truth restored to its position. He was the leader and the obligation of leadership was established for people. That is the import of the words of the Almighty: *'Allah has promised those of you who believe and do right actions that He will make them successors in the land.'* (24:55) The rules for the leader were already discussed in *al-Baqarah* (2:30).

That is so you will know that Allah knows

The first *'that'* indicates that Allah instituted these matters. The meaning is: Allah did that so that you would know the details of the matters of the heavens and the earth and know your best interests in every instance and seek His kindness to His slaves in spite of their ingratitude.

إِعْلَمُوٓا۟ أَنَّ ٱللَّهَ شَدِيدُ ٱلْعِقَابِ وَأَنَّ ٱللَّهَ غَفُورٌ رَّحِيمٌ ﴿٩٨﴾

98 Know that Allah is fierce in retribution and that Allah is Ever-Forgiving, Most Merciful.

This is a reminder and a threat as well as a source of hope.

مَّا عَلَى ٱلرَّسُولِ إِلَّا ٱلْبَلَٰغُ ۗ وَٱللَّهُ يَعْلَمُ مَا تُبْدُونَ وَمَا تَكْتُمُونَ ﴿٩٩﴾

99 The Messenger is only responsible for transmission. Allah knows what you divulge and what you hide.

It is not the business of the Messenger to guide, grant success or give a reward. His job is simply to convey. This refutes the Qadariyyah as we already said (1:6 & 4:68). The root of *balāgh* (convey) is *bulūgh*, which is arrival. The verb *balagha* means to make something arrive. *Balāghah* (rhetoric) comes from the same root since it conveys the meaning to the soul in the best form of expression. *Balāgh* is sufficiency because it reaches the amount of need.

Allah knows what you divulge and what you hide.

Allah knows what you show outwardly and any disbelief or hypocrisy you conceal in your hearts.

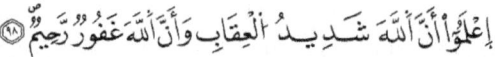

قُل لَّا يَسْتَوِي الْخَبِيثُ وَالطَّيِّبُ وَلَوْ أَعْجَبَكَ كَثْرَةُ الْخَبِيثِ فَاتَّقُوا اللَّهَ يَا أُولِي
الْأَلْبَابِ لَعَلَّكُمْ تُفْلِحُونَ ﴿١٠٠﴾

100 Say: 'Bad things and good things are not the same, even though the abundance of the bad things may seem attractive to you.' Have *taqwā* of Allah, people of intelligence, so that hopefully you will be successful.

Say: 'Bad things and good things are not the same,

Al-Ḥasan said that bad things are the unlawful and good things the lawful. As-Suddī said that it refers to believers and unbelievers. It is said that it is the obedient and disobedient. It is said that it is the vile and the excellent. These are metaphorical. The sound view is that the expression is general to all matters. It can be applied to earnings and actions, people, knowledge and other things. The bad things referred to are not successful or noble and do not have a good outcome, however many they are. Even if the good is little, it is beneficial and has a good outcome. Allah says: *'Good land gives forth its plants by the permission of its Lord, but that which is bad only gives forth meagrely.'* (7:58) Similar to this *āyah* are the words of Allah: *'Shall We make those who believe and do right actions like those who cause corruption on the earth? Shall We make the godfearing like the dissolute?'* (38:28) and: *'Or do those who perpetrate evil deeds suppose that We will make them like those who believe and do right actions.'* (45:21) The bad is not equal to the good in either quantity or output, nor in place or departure. The good takes the right hand and the bad the left. The good is in the Garden and the bad is in the Fire. This is clear. The reality of evenness is that it is on one level. The same is true of uprightness. Its opposite is crookedness.

Some of our scholars said that an invalid sale is nullified and may not be carried out either in a market transaction or by direct exchange so that it would be considered the same as carrying out a sound sale. Such a sale is always invalid and the price returned to the buyer if it has been paid. If the goods are destroyed while in his possession [the buyer], he is liable for them because he did not receive them as a trust. He received them by doubtful means. It is said that sale cannot be invalidated and returned after some time has passed because that would constitute harm and cheating of the seller. That might, for instance, result in a situation where goods worth a hundred would be returned to him worth only twenty. No punishment is imposed where property is concerned.

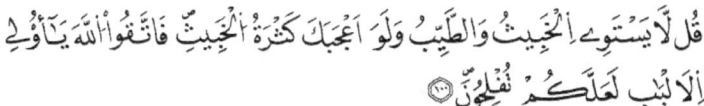

The first is sounder by the generality of the meaning of the *āyah* and because the Prophet ﷺ said, 'If anyone does something which is not part this affair of ours, it will be rejected.' Such instances are frequent in *fiqh*, as in the question of the person who misappropriates property. If someone builds on misappropriated land or plants in it, he is obliged to remove any building or planting because it is corrupt and rejected, which differs from Abū Ḥanīfah's words: 'It should not be destroyed and the owner should be paid its price.' This is rejected by the words of the Prophet ﷺ, 'The roots [of such planting by] of a wrongdoer have no right.' Hishām said, 'An unjust root results when a man plants in the land of another person to make himself entitled to it.' Mālik said, 'An unjust root is whatever is taken or planted without right.'

Mālik said, 'If someone misappropriates land and cultivates it or rents it out, or misappropriates a house in which he lives or lets out, then the owner can claim the rent for that from the misappropriator and that he returns what he took in rent.' His position varies if the owner does not live in it or cultivate the land and leaves it vacant. The well known position in his school is that the misappropriator then owes nothing for it. It is reported that he does owe rent in all such cases. Al-Waqqār chose that and it is the position of the school of ash-Shāfi'ī because the Prophet ﷺ said, 'An unjust root is whatever is taken or planted without right.'

Abū Dāwūd reported from Abū az-Zubayr that two men took a dispute to the Messenger of Allah ﷺ. One of them had planted palm trees in the land of the other man and the owner of the land took his land and ordered the owner of the trees to remove them. He said, 'I saw them with their trunks chopped by axes to remove them. They were thick.' This is a definitive text. Ibn Ḥabīb said, 'The ruling regarding it is that the owner of the land can choose in regard to the wrongdoer. If he wishes, he keeps that in his land for its price when uprooted. If he wishes, he has it uprooted from his land and the misappropriator has to pay the cost.'

Ad-Dāraquṭnī related that 'Ā'ishah said, 'The Messenger of Allah ﷺ said, "If someone builds on the land of a people with their permission, he is entitled to what it cost him. If someone builds without their permission, the loss is his."' Our scholars say that he has the price because he built in a place whose use he owns. That is like someone who builds or plants when his right is unclear. He has a right. If he wishes, the owner of the property can pay him the price of what he built. If the owner refuses, one who built or planted is told, 'Pay him the price of the land undeveloped.' If he then refuses, they become partners.

Ibn al-Mājishūn said, 'Their partnership is assessed in this manner: the undeveloped land is assessed and then assessed again after its development. The increase in its price by cultivation over its price when undeveloped is the extent to which the worker shares with the owner of the property. If they wish, they can divide it or keep it.' Ibn al-Jahm said, 'When the owner of the land pays the price of the development and takes the land, he is owed the rent for the past years.' Ibn al-Qāsim and others say that if a man builds something on someone else's land with his permission and then he obliges him to remove it, he pays him the cost of his structure when removed. The first is sounder because the Prophet ﷺ said, 'He has its price.' That is the position of most of the *fuqahā'*.

even though the abundance of the bad things may seem attractive to you.

This is apparently addressed to the Prophet ﷺ while it is his community which is meant. The Prophet ﷺ did not like bad things. It is said that the Prophet ﷺ himself is meant because of what he saw of the great amount of the unbelievers' unlawful wealth and the small amount of the believers' lawful wealth.

يَٰٓأَيُّهَا ٱلَّذِينَ ءَامَنُوا۟ لَا تَسْـَٔلُوا۟ عَنْ أَشْيَآءَ إِن تُبْدَ لَكُمْ تَسُؤْكُمْ وَإِن تَسْـَٔلُوا۟ عَنْهَا حِينَ
يُنَزَّلُ ٱلْقُرْءَانُ تُبْدَ لَكُمْ عَفَا ٱللَّهُ عَنْهَا ۗ وَٱللَّهُ غَفُورٌ حَلِيمٌ ﴿١٠١﴾ قَدْ سَأَلَهَا قَوْمٌ مِّن
قَبْلِكُمْ ثُمَّ أَصْبَحُوا۟ بِهَا كَٰفِرِينَ ﴿١٠٢﴾

101-2 You who believe! do not ask about matters which, if they were made known to you, would make things difficult for you. If you do ask about them when the Qur'ān is being sent down, they will be made known to you. Allah has ignored them. Allah is Ever-Forgiving, All-Forbearing. People before you asked about them and then later came to reject them.

Al-Bukhārī, Muslim and others related that Anas said, 'A man asked, "Who is my father?" and the Prophet ﷺ replied, "Your father is so-and-so." Then it was revealed: *"You who believe, do not ask about matters which, if they were made known to you, would make things difficult for you."*' It is also related from Anas that the Prophet ﷺ said, 'By Allah, you will not ask me about anything but that I will tell you as long as I am in this place.' A man stood up and asked, 'Where will I enter, Messenger of Allah?' 'The Fire,' he replied. 'Abdullāh ibn Ḥudhāfah rose and asked, 'Who is my father, Messenger of Allah?' He replied, 'Your father is Ḥudhāfah,' and mentioned the rest of the *ḥadīth*.

Ibn 'Abd al-Barr said, "Abdullāh ibn Ḥudhāfah became Muslim early on and emigrated to Abyssinia in the second Hijrah. He was present at Badr and sometimes joked. The Messenger of Allah ﷺ sent him to Khusrau with the letter from him ﷺ. When he asked, 'Who is my father, Messenger of Allah?' and he replied, 'Your father is Ḥudhāfah,' his mother said to him, 'I have not heard of a son more unfilial than you! Do you believe that your mother yielded to what the women of the Jāhiliyyah yielded to so as to disgrace me in front of people!' He said, 'By Allah, if he had attributed me to a black slave, I would have been attributed to him!'

At-Tirmidhī and ad-Dāraquṭnī reported from 'Alī, 'When the *āyah*: *"Ḥajj to the House is a duty owed to Allah by all mankind – those who can find a way to do it."* (3:97) was revealed, they said, "Messenger of Allah, is that every year?" He was silent. They asked, "Every year?" He said, "No, and if I had said yes, it would have been mandatory." Then Allah revealed: *"You who believe! do not ask about matters which, if they were made known to you, would make things difficult for you."*' The wording is that in ad-Dāraquṭnī. Al-Bukhārī was asked about this *ḥadīth* and said that it is a *ḥasan ḥadīth* although it is *mursal*. Abū al-Bakhtarī did not meet 'Alī. His name was Sa'īd.

Ad-Dāraquṭnī also transmitted it from Abū 'Iyāḍ from Abū Hurayrah who said that the Messenger of Allah ﷺ said, 'People! Ḥajj has been prescribed for you!' A man stood up and said, 'Every year, Messenger of Allah?' He turned away from him and the man repeated the question, 'Every year, Messenger of Allah?' He said, 'Who is the one who asks?' They said, 'So-and-so.' He said, 'By the One Who has my soul in His hand, if I had said yes, it would have been mandatory. If it had been mandatory, you would not be able to do it. If you were unable to do it, you would disbelieve.' Allah revealed: '*You who believe! do not ask about matters which, if they were made known to you, would make things difficult for you.*'

Al-Ḥasan al-Baṣrī said about this *āyah*, 'They asked the Prophet ﷺ about matters of the Jāhiliyyah which Allah had overlooked, and there is no way to ask about what Allah has overlooked.' Mujāhid reported from Ibn 'Abbās that it was revealed about some people who asked the Messenger of Allah ﷺ about the *baḥīrah, sā'iba, waṣīlah* and *ḥām* (superstitious practices connected with camels). That is the position of Sa'īd ibn Jubayr. He observed, 'Do you not see that afterwards Allah says: *"Allah did not institute any such thing as baḥīrah or sā'iba or waṣīlah or ḥām"*?' There is enough in the *Ṣaḥīḥ* and the *Musnad*. It could be that this *āyah* was revealed as an answer to all this and the questions are close to one another. Allah knows best.

The measure of *'ashyā'* (things) is *af'āl*. It is not inflected because it is like *ḥamrā'*. Al-Kisā'ī said that. It is also said that its measure is *af'ilā'*, like *hayn* and *ahwinā'*, as al-Farrā' and al-Akhfash said. The diminutive is *'ushayyā'*. Al-Māzinī said that its diminutive is *shuyayāt* like the diminutive of *aṣdiqā'* in the feminine: *ṣudayyiqāt* and in the masculine *ṣuddayyiqūn*.

Ibn 'Awn said, 'I asked Nāfi' about the words of Allah: *"Do not ask about matters which, if they were made known to you, would make things difficult for you."* He said, "People will continue to ask questions even when it will result in something disliked by them."' Muslim reported from al-Mughīrah ibn Shu'bah that the Messenger of Allah ﷺ said, 'Allah Almighty has forbidden you to disobey your mothers, to deny others what is rightfully theirs or demand what is not rightfully yours, and to bury your daughters alive and He dislikes you engaging in chit-chat, asking too many questions and wasting money.'

Many scholars said that 'a lot of questions' means asking a lot about *fiqh* questions due to obstinacy and affectation, captious questions and a desire to make things difficult. The early generations used to dislike that and thought that it was imposing a burden. They said, 'When an event has actually occurred, asking about it will have a successful outcome.' Mālik said, 'I know the people of this land and what knowledge they have of other than the Book and the *Sunnah*. When an event occurred, the ruler would gather those scholars who were present and carry out that on which they agreed. You ask a lot of questions whereas the Messenger of Allah ﷺ disliked people doing that.'

It is said that what is meant by a lot of questions is a lot of asking people insistently for money and needs and seeking a lot. Mālik also said that. It is said that what is meant by a lot of questions is asking about what does not concern a person about other people's circumstances so that that would lead to disclosing their faults and being aware of their bad qualities. This is like the *āyah*: *'And do not spy and do not backbite one another.'* (49:12) Ibn Khuwayzimandād said, 'It is why, when one of our companions was offered food, he did not ask, "Where is this from?" When he bought something he did not ask, "Where is this from?" People's affairs were assumed to be wholesome and good.' This *ḥadīth* can be taken in its general meaning and cover all aspects. Allah knows best.

Ibn al-'Arabī said, 'Some heedless people believe, based on this *āyah*, that it is unlawful to ask questions about cases before they actually occur. That, however, is not the case because this *āyah* explains that the sort of asking which is forbidden is that in which there is harm in the answer. There is no harm in answering about immediate events, and so there is a difference between the two.' It would be more fitting to say that some heedless people found it abhorrent to make questions about events unlawful, but in the normal way of things it inevitably continues to take place. We said that it is more fitting because some of the early generations disliked it. 'Umar ibn al-Khaṭṭāb used to curse those who asked about something which had not occurred. Ad-Dārimī mentioned that in his *Musnad*. He mentioned that az-Zuhrī said, 'We heard that when Zayd ibn Thābit al-Anṣārī was asked about a matter, he said, "Has it happened?" If they said, "Yes, someone who knows has reported it," [he answered.] If they said, "It has not," he said, "Leave it until it does."' It is reported that 'Ammār ibn Yāsir was asked about a question and said, 'Has it happened yet?' They replied, 'No,' and he said, 'Leave us until it does. When it does, we will take on its burden for you.'

Ad-Dārimī reported from 'Abdullāh ibn Muḥammad ibn Abī Shaybah from Ibn Fuḍayl from 'Aṭā' that Ibn 'Abbās said, 'I have not seen a people better than the Companions of the Messenger of Allah ﷺ. They only asked him about thirteen questions before he died. All of them are in the Qur'ān, including: *"They will ask you about the Sacred Month"* (2:217) and: *"They will ask you about menstruation"* (2:222), and the like of what they asked which was of real benefit to them.' Ibn 'Abd al-Barr said, 'It is not feared today that asking about something will bring about prohibition or making lawful. There is nothing wrong in seeking to understand, seeking knowledge, averting ignorance from oneself, or investigating the position one should take in respect of the *dīn*. The cure for error lies in asking. If someone asks out of obstinacy without seeking understanding or learning, then he is the one whose asking, whether a little or a lot, is not lawful.'

Ibn al-'Arabī said, 'What a scholar must occupy himself is explanation of evidence, clarifying the methods of investigation and obtaining the precedents in *ijtihād* and procuring the particular tool needed. When something occurs, go to it by its door and investigate its circumstances, and Allah will open the way to what is correct.'

If you do ask about them when the Qur'ān is being sent down, they will be made known to you.

Any ambiguity will be removed. The beginning of the *āyah* contained the prohibition against asking. Then this allows people to ask. It is said that the meaning is: 'when you ask about other things for which there is no need,' and the attribution is elided. It is not sound to apply it to other than the elision. Al-Jurjānī said, 'The allusion in "*about them*" refers to other things. It is a common usage in Arabic as can be seen in 23:12 where "*man*" refers to Ādam and in the following verse Allah refers to the children of Ādam because Ādam was not made "a drop in a secure receptacle", but when "*man*", who is Ādam, is mentioned, it indicates a man like him and that is known from the context.'

The meaning is: 'If you ask about things when the Qur'ān is being revealed which deal with making things *ḥalāl* or *ḥarām* or a ruling of *fiqh* or there is need of explanation, then it will be made clear to you.' This sort of asking is allowed. An example is that Allah made the *'iddah* of divorced women, widows and pregnant women clear but did not mention the *'iddah* of women without periods or pregnant women. They asked about it and 65:4 was revealed. The prohibition is against asking about things there is no need to ask about. Asking is allowed when there is need for it.

Allah has ignored them

This means the questioning they previously did. It is said it was the things they asked about regarding matters of the Jāhiliyyah and what happened during it. It is said that it means 'left them', i.e. left them without saying whether they are lawful or unlawful, and so they are overlooked and not investigated. Perhaps if it was made clear to them, the rulings would make it difficult for them. 'Ubayd ibn 'Umayr used to say, 'Allah made things lawful and unlawful. Accept as lawful what He makes lawful and avoid what He has made unlawful. Between that are things which He did not make *ḥalāl* or *ḥarām*. That is ignoring them on the part of Allah.' Then he recited this *āyah*.

Ad-Dāraquṭnī reported from Abū Tha'labah al-Khushānī that the Messenger of Allah ﷺ said, 'Allah Almighty has made some things obligatory so do not let them slip. He has made some things unlawful so do not violate them. He has set limits so do not exceed them. He has been silent about some things without forgetting them, so do not investigate them.' According to this there is a change in the word order and it means: 'Do not ask about things which Allah has ignored. If they were made known to you, they would cause you trouble.' This means that He refrained from mentioning them and so no ruling is obliged concerning them. It is said that there is no change in order, and the meaning is: Allah has overlooked your prior asking. The Prophet ﷺ dislikes it, so do not repeat the like of it. So 'them' refers to the questions, or the asking as we mentioned.

People before you asked about them and then later came to reject them.

Allah reports that some people before us asked, like us, for signs and then, when they were given them and made obligatory for them, they rejected them. They said, 'This is not from Allah.' Examples of that are the people of Ṣāliḥ who asked for the camel and the people of 'Īsā who asked for the Table. This is a warning against what occurred in earlier nations. Allah knows best.

If someone says, 'What you mentioned about the disliked kind of asking and its prohibition is contradicted by Allah's words: *"Ask the people of remembrance if you do not know"* (16:43), the answer is that this refers to Allah's confirmed and established commands to His servants which must be acted on. What it is is forbidden to ask about is things that are not connected with the worship of Allah and are not mentioned in His Book, and Allah knows best. Muslim reported from 'Āmir ibn Sa'd from his father that the Messenger of Allah ﷺ said, 'The Muslim who does the greatest wrong to other Muslims is the one who asks about something which has not been forbidden to the Muslims and then it becomes forbidden to them because of his asking.'

Abū Naṣr al-Qushayrī said, 'If the 'Ajlānī man had not asked about fornication, the *li'ān* divorce would not have been established.' Abū al-Faraj al-Jawzī said, 'This is applied to someone who asks about something to cause inconvenience or out of frivolity and is then punished because of his bad intention by having what he asked about made unlawful, and the prohibition is general and undefined (*'āmm*).' Our scholars said, 'The Qadariyyah cannot use this *ḥadīth* to say that Allah does something for the sake of something else which causes it to take place. Allah is exalted above this. Allah has power over all things and He has knowledge of all things. The cause is, in fact, one of His actions, since it was already decreed that He would forbid the thing asked about when the question occurred. It is not the case that the asking was the reason and cause for it. There are many examples of this. *"He will not be questioned about what He does, but they will be questioned."* (21:23)'

مَا جَعَلَ ٱللَّهُ مِنۢ بَحِيرَةٍ وَلَا سَآئِبَةٍ وَلَا وَصِيلَةٍ وَلَا حَامٍ وَلَٰكِنَّ ٱلَّذِينَ كَفَرُوا۟ يَفْتَرُونَ
عَلَى ٱللَّهِ ٱلْكَذِبَ وَأَكْثَرُهُمْ لَا يَعْقِلُونَ ١٠٣

103 Allah did not institute any such things as *baḥīrah* or *sā'ibah* or *waṣīlah* or *ḥām*. Those who disbelieved invented lies against Allah. Most of them do not use their intellect.

Allah did not institute any such things as *baḥīrah* or *sā'ibah* or *waṣīlah* or *ḥām*.

'Ja'ala' here means 'institute', as Allah says: *'We made it an Arabic Qur'ān'* (45:3). The meaning in this *āyah* is: 'Allah did not name or prescribe that as a ruling or act of worship in the *Sharī'ah* despite the fact that He knew it and brought it into existence by His power and will in creation.' Allah is the Creator of everything, good and evil, harm and benefit, obedience and disobedience.

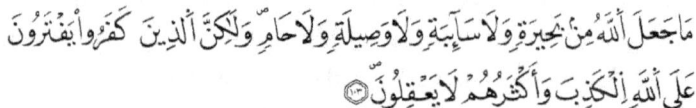

In *'as baḥīrah or sā'ibah'* the *'min'* is redundant. *Baḥīrah* is the form *fa'īlah* on the measure of *naṭīḥah* (gored) and *dhabīḥah* (slaughtered) with the passive meaning from *baḥara* which means 'to slit'. We find in the *Ṣaḥīḥ* that Sa'īd ibn al-Musayyab said, '*Baḥīrah* is an animal whose milk was set aside for the idols and which could not be milked by anyone. The *sā'ibah* is the one they used to set free for the sake of their gods.' It is said that *baḥīrah* is a dialect word for a she-camel with slit ears. Slitting the ear was a sign that it should be left alone. The verb *baḥara* is used for slitting the ear of a she-camel with a wide slit after which the camel is called *baḥīrah* or *mabḥūrah*. *Baḥr* is a sign of being left alone.

Ibn Sayyidah said, 'It is said that the *baḥīrah* was the camel left without a herdsman. It is also said that it is a she-camel with abundant milk.' Ibn Isḥāq said, 'The *baḥīrah* is the daughter of the *sā'ibah*, and the *sā'ibah* is a she-camel who produced ten successive females without a male between them. It was not ridden nor was its hair taken and its milk could only be drunk by a guest. Any females it produced after that had its ears slit and were left to go on their way with their mother. They were not ridden nor was their hair taken and their milk could only be drunk by a guest, like that of its mother. That is the *baḥīrah*, the daughter of the *sā'ibah*.'

Ash-Shāfi'ī said, 'When a she-camel bore five females, its ear was slit and it was made sacred.' He said:

Forbidden. People do not eat its meat.
We do not do anything. That is the case with *baḥīrah*s.

Ibn 'Uzayr said, 'A *baḥīrah* is a she-camel that has given birth five times. If the fifth is a male, they slaughter it and the men and women eat it. If the fifth is a female, they slit its ears and its meat and milk is forbidden to women. 'Ikrimah said that. If it dies, then it is lawful for women.

A *sā'ibah* is a camel set free by a vow that a man makes if Allah heals him of an illness or he reaches his home. It is not kept from pasture or water and no one may ride it. Abū 'Ubayd said that. A poet said:

The *sā'ibah* of Allah grows in gratitude.
Allah heals someone thriving or greedy.

Other animals can also be designated as *sā'ibah*. A slave could also me made a *sā'ibah* and would have no *walā'*. It is said that the *sā'ibah* is an animal that is released without any bindings or herdsman. The form of the active participle has a passive meaning like *rāḍiyyah* which means pleased. The verbs *sāba* and *insāba* are used for a snake entering its hole. A poet said:

You hamstrung the leg of the she-camel which belonged to my lord
and was a *sā'ibah*, so stand for the punishment!

As for the *waṣīlah* and *ḥām*, Ibn Wahb reported that Mālik said, 'The people of the Jāhiliyyah freed camels and sheep which they then let loose. The *ḥām* was a stallion camel. When its stud period was over, they put peacock feathers on it and let it loose. The *waṣīlah* was a sheep which has borne a female after a female. They released it unsupervised.' Ibn 'Uzayr said, 'The *waṣīlah* is in sheep.' He said, 'When a ewe had given birth seven times, they looked and if the seventh was a male, they slaughtered it and the men and women ate it. If it was female, they left it in the flock. If it was a male and a female, they said, "It is connected (*waṣalat*) to its brother," and did not slaughter it on account of its position [in being the seventh], and its flesh was forbidden to women and the milk of the female forbidden to women unless one of the pair died, and then men and women ate it. Ibn Isḥāq said, 'A *waṣīlah* is a sheep which has had ten successive females in five pregnancies with no male between them. They said, "It is connected (*waṣilat*)." Any young it produces after that is for their men and not women unless any of them dies and then men and women share in eating it.'

The *ḥām* is a camel stallion when it has fathered a number of camels.' He said:

Abū Qābūs protected (*ḥamā*) it in the might of his kingdom,
as the stallion guards (*ḥamā*) the children of its children.

It is said that it is ten camels. They said that its back is protected and it is not ridden, and it is not denied pasture or water.

Muslim reported from Abū Hurayrah that the Messenger of Allah ﷺ said, 'I saw 'Amr ibn 'Āmir dragging his intestines in the Fire, and he was the first person to establish the tradition of *sā'ibah*.' One variant has "Amr ibn Luḥayy ibn Qama'ah ibn Khindif, one of the Banū Ka'b, was dragging his intestines in the Fire.' Abū Hurayrah also said that he heard the Messenger of Allah ﷺ say to Aktham ibn al-Jūn, 'I saw 'Amr ibn Luḥayy ibn Qama'ah ibn Khindif dragging his intestines in the Fire. I have not seen a man who more resembles him than you nor you than him.' Aktham said, 'I fear that that resemblance may harm me, Messenger of Allah.' He said, 'No, you are a believer, and he was an unbeliever. He was the first to follow other than the religion of Ismā'īl, and he established the *baḥīrah*, *sā'ibah* and *ḥām*.' One variant has: 'I saw him as a short man with ample hair, dragging his intestines in the Fire.' We find in the transmission of Ibn al-Qāsim and others from Mālik from Zayd ibn Aslam from 'Aṭā' ibn Yasār that the Prophet ﷺ said, 'His stench harms the people of the Fire.' It is *mursal* and mentioned by Ibn al-'Arabī. It is said that the first to institute that was Junādah ibn Ibrāhīm. Allah knows best, and there is enough about it in the *Ṣaḥīḥ*.

Ibn Isḥāq said that the reason for the setting up of idols and altering the religion of Ibrāhīm was that 'Amr ibn Luḥayy went from Makkah to Syria. When he came to [the town of] Māb in the land of Balqā', the Amalekites were there at that time. They are the descendants of 'Imlīq or 'Imlāq ibn Lāwūdh ibn Sām ibn Nūḥ. He saw them worshipping idols. He asked them, 'What are these idols which I see you worshipping?' They replied, 'We ask these idols for rain and we have rain. We ask them for help and we have help.' He asked them, 'Will you give me one of them to take to the land of he Arabs so that they can worship it?' They gave him an idol called Hubal and he took it to Makkah and set it up. People began to worship and esteem it. When Allah sent Muhammad ﷺ this was revealed about it.

'Those who disbelieved' were Quraysh, Khuzā'ah and the Arab idolaters. *'They invented lies against Allah'* by saying that Allah made these animals sacred and claimed that they did that to please their Lord and obey Allah. Obedience to Allah is learned from His words and not from anything that they claim is from Allah. That is part of what they invented against Allah. They said, *'What is in the wombs of these animals is exclusively for our men'* (6:139), meaning offspring and milk, *'forbidden to our wives. But if it is stillborn,'* if it is born dead, then men and women share in it, *'they are partners in it. He will repay them for their false depiction,'* for denying the punishment in the Next World. *'He is All-Wise, All-Knowing'* with respect to making things lawful and unlawful. Allah revealed about it: *'Say: "What do you think about the things Allah has sent down to you as provision which you have then designated as lawful and unlawful?" Say: "Has Allah given you authority to do this or are you inventing lies against Allah?"'* (10:59) He revealed about it: *'Eight in pairs…'* (6:143) and: *'Animals over which they do not mention Allah's name, inventing falsehood against Him.'* (6:138)

Abū Ḥanīfah attached to it his prohibition of *ḥabūs* and his rejection of *waqfs* since Allah censured the Arabs for what they did in releasing the animals, making them sacred and keeping people from them. He made an analogy with the *baḥīrah* and *sā'ibah*, even though the difference is clear. If a man were to go to some property of his and say, 'This is a *ḥabūs* and its fruit will not be picked nor its land cultivated nor will any of it be used,' then that could be compared to the *baḥīrah* and *sā'ibah*. 'Alqamah said to those who asked him about these things, 'What do you want with something which the people of the *Jāhiliyyah* used to do?' and he left. Ibn Zayd said that. The majority of scholars took the position of allowing *ḥabūs* and *waqf*, except for Abū Ḥanīfah, Abū Yūsuf and Zufar. It was the position of Shurayḥ.

Abū Yūsuf withdrew from Abū Ḥanīfah's position regarding that since Ibn 'Ulayyah reported to him from Ibn 'Awn from Nāfi' that Ibn 'Umar asked the

Messenger of Allah ﷺ for permission to give his share of Khaybar as *ṣadaqah* and the Messenger of Allah ﷺ told him, 'Make a *ḥabūs* of the capital and the fruits as charity.' It is used as evidence by everyone who allows the *ḥabūs*. It is a sound *ḥadīth* as Abū 'Umar said. There is also the matter of the consensus of the Companions. That is because Abū Bakr, 'Umar, 'Uthmān, 'Alī, 'A'ishah, Fāṭimah, 'Amr ibn al-'Āṣ, Ibn az-Zubayr, and Jābir all established *waqf*s and their *waqf*s were well known in Makkah and Madīnah.

It is related that Abū Yūsuf said to Mālik in the presence of ar-Rashīd, 'The *ḥabūs* is not permitted.' Mālik said to him, 'These *ḥabūs* are the *ḥabūs* of the Messenger of Allah ﷺ at Khaybar, and Fadak. The Companions created *ḥabūs*. As for the argument of Abū Ḥanīfah based on the *āyah*, it is not evidence because Allah censured them for acting by their whims without any legislation being directed to them or responsibility imposed on them to cut off the path of use, to squander the blessing of Allah and to remove the benefit which people enjoy from those camels. It is by this that these *ḥabūs* and *waqfs* are distinct [from that].'

Among the things that Abū Ḥanīfah and Zufar used as evidence is what 'Aṭā' reported from Ibn al-Musayyab. He said, 'I asked Shurayḥ about a man who made his house a *ḥabūs* for the last of his children and he stated, "There is no *ḥabūs* where Allah's obligatory shares of inheritance are concerned."' They stated, 'This is Shurayḥ, the Qāḍī of 'Umar, and 'Uthmān and 'Alī, the Rightly-Guided caliphs, who gave that ruling.' He also used as evidence what Ibn Lahī'ah reported from his brother 'Īsā from 'Ikrimah from Ibn 'Abbās. He said, 'I heard the Prophet ﷺ say after *Sūrat an-Nisā'* was revealed and Allah revealed the shares of inheritance in it that he forbade the *ḥabūs*.'

Aṭ-Ṭabarī said, 'The *ṣadaqah* which is carried out is that which is set up while the person is alive according to what Allah made permissible on the tongue of His Prophet ﷺ and the action of the Rightly-Guided leaders. Allah's shares of inheritance are not part of any *ḥabūs*. There is no evidence in the statement of Shurayḥ nor in anyone who opposes the *Sunnah*. The action done by the Companions is the evidence against all other people. As for the *ḥadīth* of Ibn 'Abbās, Ibn Lahī'ah related it, and he is a man whose mind became confused at the end of his life, and his brother is not known and so it is not used as evidence. Ibn al-Qassār said that.'

If it is asked how it can be permissible to use a *waqf* to remove land from the possession of its owner to other than ownership by anyone, aṭ-Ṭaḥāwī said, 'They are told: "How can there be any objection to this when you and your opponents agree that its Owner made the land a place of prayer for the Muslims and let them have it? That is removing it from ownership to non-ownership, although it is in reality to Allah Almighty. That is also the case with waterwheels, stone bridges and wood bridges. That which necessarily opposes your argument also opposes you in all of this. Allah knows best.'

Those who allow the *waqf* disagree about what sort of control the donor can have over it. Ash-Shāfi'ī said that is forbidden for the donor of a *waqf* to own it in the same way that it is forbidden for him to own the liberty of a slave. He is permitted to manage his *ṣadaqah* and to distribute it by his own hand and to divide up what he spends of it because 'Umar ibn al-Khaṭṭāb continued to manage his *ṣadaqah*, as we have heard, until he died. He said, 'That is what 'Alī and Fāṭimah did. They managed their *ṣadaqah*.' Abū Yūsuf said that.

Mālik said, 'If someone makes a *ḥabūs* of land, palm trees or a house for the poor and it remains in his possession, with him managing it, renting it out and dividing it up among the poor until he dies with the *ḥabūs* still in his possession, then it is not a *ḥabūs*, unless he confirmed that it was to someone else, and it remains inheritance. A *ḥabūs* of any estates, gardens and land he has is not achieved or carried out completely until another person has control of it, which is not case with horses and weapons.' This is the position of his school among his adherents. It is the position of Ibn Abī Laylā as well.

It is not permitted for the donor of a *waqf* to benefit from his *waqf* because he has given it to Allah and removed it from his property. His using any of it is taking his *ṣadaqah* back. It is only permitted for him to use it if he stipulates that in the *waqf* deed or if the donor needs it. His heirs are permitted to eat from it. Ibn Ḥabīb mentioned that Mālik said, 'If someone establishes a *waqf* whose revenue goes to the poor, his children can be given from it if they are in need, whether they were poor or wealthy at the time of its establishment, but they are not given all of the revenue out of the fear that the *ḥabūs* will be wiped out. There must be a share for the poor so that it remains a *ḥabūs*. It can be prescribed that his children may be given to from it on the basis of poverty, but they have no right beyond that which the poor have.'

It is permitted to free a slave as *sā'ibah* (in which the owner has no *walā'*). That is when the master says, 'You are free' and intends emancipation, or says, 'I have freed you *sā'ibah*.' What is well known in the school of Mālik according to most of his people is that his *walā'* then belongs to the Muslim community and his emancipation is carried out. That is what is related from him by Ibn al-Qāsim, Ibn 'Abd al-Ḥakam, Ashhab and others. Ibn Wahb said that. Ibn Wahb related that Mālik said, 'No one may free someone as *sā'ibah* because the Messenger of Allah ﷺ forbade selling or giving away the *walā'*.' Ibn 'Abd al-Barr said, 'This is according to all who take his position. It is taken to imply only dislike for freeing someone as *sā'ibah*. If it happens, it is carried out and the ruling regarding it is what we mentioned.' Ibn Wahb and Ibn al-Qāsim related that Mālik said, 'I dislike *sā'ibah* emancipation and forbid it, but if it happens, it is carried out and the inheritance goes to the Muslim community and they are responsible for his blood money.'

Aṣbagh said, 'There is nothing wrong with *sā'ibah* emancipation.' He took the well known position of Mālik, and it is the argument of Qāḍī Ismā'īl ibn Isḥāq, and he is followed. Part of his argument respecting that is that the *sā'ibah* emancipation was well known in Madīnah and no scholar objected to it. 'Abdullāh ibn 'Umar and others from the early generations did *sā'ibah* emancipation. It is related from Ibn Shihāb, Rabī'ah and Abū az-Zinād. It is the position of 'Umar ibn 'Abd al-'Azīz, Abū al-'Ālīyah, 'Aṭā', 'Amr ibn Dīnār and others. Abū al-'Ālīyah ar-Riyāḥī al-Baṣrī at-Tamīmī was one of those who was the subject of *sā'ibah* emancipation. His female owner from the Banū Riyāḥ freed him as *sā'ibah* for the sake of Allah and took him around a circle in the mosque. His name was Rafī' ibn Mihrān.

Ibn Nāfi' said, 'There is no *sā'ibah* in Islam today. If someone frees someone in a *sā'ibah* emancipation, he has his *walā'*.' That is what was stated by ash-Shāfi'ī, Abū Ḥanīfah and Ibn al-Mājishūn. Ibn al-'Arabī inclined to it. They argued by the words of the Prophet ﷺ: 'If someone does a *sā'ibah* emancipation, he has his *walā*'' and 'The *walā'* belongs to the one who sets free.' So he said that the *walā'* does not go to anyone other than the emancipator. Their evidence is the words of the Almighty: *'Allah did not institute any such thing as baḥīrah or sā'ibah,'* the *ḥadīth*, 'There is no *sā'ibah* in Islam,' and what Abū Qays related that Huzayl ibn Shurḥbīl said, 'A man said to 'Abdullāh, "I have freed a slave of mine as *sā'ibah*. What do you think about it?" 'Abdullāh answered, "The people of Islam do not free people as *sā'ibah*. *Sā'ibah* was in the Jāhiliyyah. You are his heir and the guardian of his blessing."'

وَإِذَا قِيلَ لَهُمْ تَعَالَوْا إِلَىٰ مَا أَنزَلَ اللَّهُ وَإِلَى الرَّسُولِ قَالُوا حَسْبُنَا مَا وَجَدْنَا عَلَيْهِ آبَاءَنَا
أَوَلَوْ كَانَ آبَاؤُهُمْ لَا يَعْلَمُونَ شَيْئًا وَلَا يَهْتَدُونَ ﴿١٠٤﴾

104 When they are told, 'Come to what Allah has sent down and to the Messenger,' they say, 'What we found our fathers doing is enough for us.' What! Even if their fathers did not know anything and were not guided!

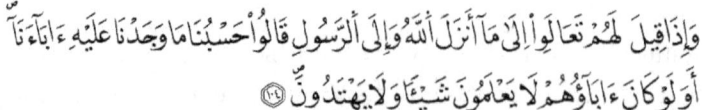

This was already discussed in *al-Baqarah*. (2:170)

يَٰٓأَيُّهَا ٱلَّذِينَ ءَامَنُواْ عَلَيۡكُمۡ أَنفُسَكُمۡۖ لَا يَضُرُّكُم مَّن ضَلَّ إِذَا ٱهۡتَدَيۡتُمۡۚ إِلَى ٱللَّهِ
مَرۡجِعُكُمۡ جَمِيعٗا فَيُنَبِّئُكُم بِمَا كُنتُمۡ تَعۡمَلُونَ ١٠٥

105 You who believe! you are only responsible for yourselves. The misguided cannot harm you as long as you are guided. All of you will return to Allah and He will inform you about what you were doing.

Our scholars said that what connects this *āyah* to the one before it is the warning of what one should be on guard against: the state of those already described who relied on blind imitation of their fathers and ancestors in their *dīn*.

The literal meaning would seem to indicate that commanding the right and forbidding the wrong is not an obligation when a man is upright, and no one is taken to task for the wrong action of another. If there had not been its explanation in the *Sunnah* and what the Companions and *Tābi'ūn* said, we would not have mentioned this.

You who believe! you are only responsible for yourselves.

This means: 'Guard yourselves against acts of disobedience.' You say, "*alayka Zaydan,*' meaning: 'Hold to Zayd.' It is not permitted to say, "*alayhi Zaydan*' in the third person. This is used in the address in the second person in three expressions: "*alayka Zaydan*' which means 'Take Zayd, "*indaka Zaydan*' which means 'Zayd is present with you [so take him],' and '*dūnaka Zaydan*' which means 'Zayd is near to you, [so take him].' [POEM]

Abū Dāwūd, at-Tirmidhī and others reported that Qays said, 'Abū Bakr aṣ-Ṣiddīq addressed us and said, "You recite this *āyah* and interpret it incorrectly. I heard the Messenger of Allah ﷺ say, 'When people see a wrongdoer and do not restrain his hands, Allah is on the point of enveloping them in a punishment from Him.'"' Abū 'Īsā said that it is a *ḥasan* sound ḥadith. Isḥāq ibn Ibrāhīm said that he heard 'Amr ibn 'Alī say that he heard Wakī' say, 'It is not sound to attribute it to Abū Bakr and it is not a single *ḥadīth*. Ismā'īl did not relate from Qays.' He said that Ismā'īl from Qays is *mawqūf*. An-Naqqāsh said, 'This is excess on the part of Wakī'. Shu'bah related it from Sufyān, and Isḥāq from Ismā'īl *marfū'*.'

Abū Dāwūd, at-Tirmidhī and others reported that Abū Umayyah ash-Sha'bānī said, 'I went to Abū Tha'labah al-Khashanī and asked him, "What do you say about this *āyah*?" "Which *āyah*?" he asked. I said: *"You who believe, you are only responsible for yourselves. The misguided cannot harm you as long as you are guided."* He replied, "By Allah, I asked someone with knowledge about it. I asked the Messenger of Allah ﷺ and he said, 'Command the right and forbid one another the wrong until the time when you see greed being indulged, passion being followed, this world being preferred and everyone admiring his own opinion. Then you must guard your own soul and leave what the masses are doing. Ahead of you are days requiring steadfastness, and steadfastness in those days will be like grasping live coals. The one who acts in those days will have the reward of fifty men who act as he does now.'"' One variant adds, 'Messenger of Allah, the reward of fifty of us or fifty of them?' He replied, 'The reward of fifty of you.' Abū 'Īsā said that it is a *ḥasan gharīb ḥadīth*. Ibn 'Abd al-Barr said some transmitters do not mention 'of you'.

At-Tirmidhī reported from Abū Hurayrah that the Prophet ﷺ said, 'You are living in a time in which one of you who abandons a tenth of what he has been commanded will be destroyed. Then a time will come in which whoever does a tenth of what he has been commanded will be saved.' This is a *gharīb ḥadīth*. It is reported that Ibn Mas'ūd said, 'This is not the time of this *āyah*. Speak the truth as long as it is accepted from you. When it is rejected from you, then you must see to yourselves.'

It was said to Ibn 'Umar during one of the times of *fitnah* (civil unrest), 'You should leave off speaking in these days, and not command or forbid.' He replied, 'The Messenger of Allah ﷺ said to us, "Let the one who is present convey to the one who is absent. We are present and so we must convey it you. There will come a time in which the truth will be spoken but not accepted."' In one variant, 'Let the one who is present convey to the one who is absent. We were present while you were absent, but this *āyah* is for people who will come after us. When they say it, it will not be accepted from them.'

Ibn al-Mubārak said that the words of Allah: *'You are only responsible for yourselves'* is addressed to all believers, i.e. 'you are responsible for the people of your *dīn*,' as when He says, 'Do not kill yourselves.' It is as if He said, 'You should command one another and forbid one another.' It is evidence of the obligation to command the right and forbid the wrong and then the misguidance of the idolaters, hypocrites and People of the Book will not harm you. This is because commanding the right is done by the Muslims towards people who disobey Allah as already stated. Something like this is related from Sa'īd ibn Jubayr. Sa'īd ibn al-Musayyab said, 'The meaning of the *āyah* is: "Those who are misguided will not harm you as long as you are guided after you command the right and forbid the wrong."'

Ibn Khuwayzimandād said, 'The *āyah* contains the fact that a human being should occupy himself with what concerns him and not turn to other people's faults and investigating their states. They will not be asked about his state and he will not be asked about their state. This is like Allah's words: *"Every self is held in pledge against what it earned,"* (74:38) and: *"No bearer of any burden can bear that of any other."* (6:164)' The Prophet ﷺ said, 'Sit in your room and be concerned with yourself.' It is possible that he is referring to a time in which it is difficult to command the right and forbid the wrong, and so a person should object to it in his heart and occupy himself with putting himself right.

There is a *gharīb* ḥadith from Ibn Lahī'ah from Bakr ibn Sawādah al-Judhāmī from 'Uqbah ibn 'Āmir that the Messenger of Allah ﷺ said, 'At the beginning of 200, you will not command the right nor forbid the wrong and then you must attend to yourself.' Our scholars said, 'That is due to the change of time and corruption of people's states and lack of those who are properly concerned with that.'

Jābir ibn Zayd said, 'The meaning of the *āyah* is: "O you who believe among the children of those who instituted the *baḥīrah* and *sā'ibah*, you are responsible for yourselves in going straight in the *dīn*. The misguidance of your ancestors will not harm you if you are guided."' He said, 'When someone became Muslim, the unbelievers said to him, "You have declared your ancestors foolish and misguided," and this and that. So Allah revealed the *āyah* because of that.'

It is said that the *āyah* is about the people of sects who do not benefit from being warned. When you know that a people will not accept what you say, but will openly make light of it, then be silent. It is said that it was revealed about the captives whom the idolaters tortured until some of them apostasised. It is said that it was for those who remained in Islam: 'You are responsible for yourselves. The apostasy of your companions will not harm you.' Sa'īd ibn Jubayr said that this is about the People of the Book when they pay the *jizyah*. It is said that it is abrogated by the instruction to command the right and forbid the wrong, as al-Mahdawī said. Ibn 'Aṭiyyah said that this is weak and the one who said it is not known. It is reported that Abū 'Ubayd al-Qāsim ibn Sallām said, 'There is no *āyah* in the Book of Allah which combines the abrogating and abrogated other than this *āyah*.' Another said, 'The abrogating element is *"if you are guided"* and guidance here is commanding the right and forbidding the wrong. Allah knows best.'

Commanding the right and forbidding the wrong is a specific duty when it is hoped that that will be accepted or it is hoped that the wrongdoer will be deterred by it, even if it takes force, as long as a person does not fear that doing that will result in harm to himself or *fitnah* for the Muslims, either by disrupting the unity of a group of Muslims or causing harm to them. If this is feared, then '*you are responsible for yourselves*' is the mandatory ruling and a person must stop with himself. As we already said, it is not a condition that the one who forbids be of upright character. This is the position of the people of knowledge as a whole. Know that.

يَٰٓأَيُّهَا ٱلَّذِينَ ءَامَنُواْ شَهَٰدَةُ بَيۡنِكُمۡ إِذَا حَضَرَ أَحَدَكُمُ ٱلۡمَوۡتُ حِينَ ٱلۡوَصِيَّةِ ٱثۡنَانِ
ذَوَا عَدۡلٖ مِّنكُمۡ أَوۡ ءَاخَرَانِ مِنۡ غَيۡرِكُمۡ إِنۡ أَنتُمۡ ضَرَبۡتُمۡ فِي ٱلۡأَرۡضِ فَأَصَٰبَتۡكُم مُّصِيبَةُ
ٱلۡمَوۡتِۚ تَحۡبِسُونَهُمَا مِنۢ بَعۡدِ ٱلصَّلَوٰةِ فَيُقۡسِمَانِ بِٱللَّهِ إِنِ ٱرۡتَبۡتُمۡ لَا نَشۡتَرِي بِهِۦ ثَمَنٗا
وَلَوۡ كَانَ ذَا قُرۡبَىٰ وَلَا نَكۡتُمُ شَهَٰدَةَ ٱللَّهِ إِنَّآ إِذٗا لَّمِنَ ٱلۡأٓثِمِينَ ١٠٦ فَإِنۡ عُثِرَ عَلَىٰٓ أَنَّهُمَا
ٱسۡتَحَقَّآ إِثۡمٗا فَـَٔاخَرَانِ يَقُومَانِ مَقَامَهُمَا مِنَ ٱلَّذِينَ ٱسۡتَحَقَّ عَلَيۡهِمُ ٱلۡأَوۡلَيَٰنِ فَيُقۡسِمَانِ
بِٱللَّهِ لَشَهَٰدَتُنَآ أَحَقُّ مِن شَهَٰدَتِهِمَا وَمَا ٱعۡتَدَيۡنَآ إِنَّآ إِذٗا لَّمِنَ ٱلظَّٰلِمِينَ ١٠٧ ذَٰلِكَ أَدۡنَىٰٓ أَن
يَأۡتُواْ بِٱلشَّهَٰدَةِ عَلَىٰ وَجۡهِهَآ أَوۡ يَخَافُوٓاْ أَن تُرَدَّ أَيۡمَٰنُۢ بَعۡدَ أَيۡمَٰنِهِمۡۗ وَٱتَّقُواْ ٱللَّهَ
وَٱسۡمَعُواْۗ وَٱللَّهُ لَا يَهۡدِي ٱلۡقَوۡمَ ٱلۡفَٰسِقِينَ ١٠٨

106-8 You who believe! when one of you is near to death and makes a will, two just men from among you should act as witnesses; or, if you are travelling when the misfortune of death occurs, two men who are strangers to you. You should detain them after the prayer and, if you are doubtful, they should swear by Allah: 'We will not sell it for any price, even to a near relative, and we will not conceal the testimony of Allah. If we did we would indeed be wrongdoers.' If it then comes to light that the two of them have merited the allegation of wrongdoing, two others who have the most right to do so should take their place and swear by Allah: 'Our testimony is truer than their testimony. We have not committed perjury. If we had we would indeed be wrongdoers.' That makes it more likely that they will give their evidence properly or be afraid that their oaths will be refuted by subsequent oaths. Have *taqwā* of Allah and listen carefully. Allah does not guide deviant people.

Makkī said, 'For the people of knowledge, these three *āyah*s are among the most problematic in the Qur'ān with respect to syntax, meaning and ruling.' Ibn

'Aṭiyyah said, 'This statement has no weight in terms of its *tafsīr*. That is clear in His Book. May Allah have mercy on him. We seek His help.' What Makkī said was said by an-Naḥḥās before him. I do not know of any disagreement that these *āyahs* were revealed because of Tamīm ad-Dārī and 'Adī ibn Baddā'. Al-Bukhārī, ad-Dāraquṭnī and others reported that Ibn 'Abbās said, 'Tamīm ad-Dārī and 'Adī ibn Baddā' used to go regularly to Makkah. A lad from the Banū Sahm went with them and died in a land where there were no Muslims. He made a verbal will instructing them and they gave what he left to his family but kept a silver goblet decorated with gold. The Messenger of Allah ﷺ made them take an oath, "We have not concealed nor are we aware." Then the goblet was found in Makkah. They said, "We bought it from 'Adī and Tamīm." Two of the heirs of the Sahmī came and swore that this goblet had belonged to him and that their testimony was truer than the testimony of the other two and that they had not transgressed. He said, "Take the goblet." It is about them that the *āyah* was revealed.' This is the version of ad-Dāraquṭnī.

At-Tirmidhī related from Tamīm ad-Dārī about the *āyah*: 'No one is to blame for it except for me and 'Adī ibn Baddā'.' They were two Christians who went to Syria before Islam, taking trade goods with them. A client of the Banū Sahm called Budayl ibn Abū Maryam came to them with a silver goblet meant for the king. It was the best thing he had. He fell ill and left a verbal will to them to convey his effects to his family. Tamīm said, 'When he died, we took that goblet and sold it for a thousand dirhams and 'Adī ibn Baddā' and I divided it between us. When we went to his family, we gave them what we had. They noticed that the goblet was missing and asked about it. We said, "He only left this and did not give us anything else."' Tamīm said, 'When I became Muslim after the arrival of the Messenger of Allah ﷺ in Madīnah, I felt guilty for doing that and went to his family and told them the story and gave them the five hundred dirhams. I told them that my companion had received the same. They took the case to the Messenger of Allah ﷺ and he asked them for evidence which they did not have. He told them to ask him to take an oath which was binding for the people of his *dīn*. He did so and Allah revealed this.' Then 'Amr ibn al-'Āṣ rose with another man and they swore an oath and took the five hundred from 'Adī ibn Baddā'. Abū 'Īsā said that this is a *gharīb ḥadīth* whose *isnād* is not sound.

Al-Wāqidī said that the three *āyahs* were revealed about Tamīm and his brother 'Adī who were Christians and used to trade with Makkah. When the Prophet ﷺ emigrated to Madīnah, Ibn Abī Maryam, the client of 'Amr ibn al-'Āṣ, came to Madīnah intending to trade in Syria. He left with Tamīm and his brother

'Adī, and the *ḥadīth* continues. An-Naqqāsh mentioned that it was revealed about Budayl ibn Abī Maryam who went to trade in Abyssinia with two Christian men, one of whom was Tamīm, who was from Lakhm, and 'Adī ibn Baddā'. Budayl died on the ship and was buried at sea. He wrote his will and put it in his baggage. It said: 'Convey these goods to my family.' When Budayl died, they took the property and took what they liked. Among those things was a silver vessel three hundred *mithqals* in weight, engraved with gold. Sunayd mentioned it and said, 'When they reached Syria, Budayl fell ill. He was a Muslim.'

You who believe! when one of you is near to death and makes a will, two just men from among you should act as witnesses;

The verb *shahada* in the Book of Allah has various meanings. One is found in Allah's words: *'Two men among you should act as witnesses'* (2:282) meaning they are summoned as witnesses. Another is in the meaning 'to inform' as in: *'Allah bears witness that there is no god but Him.'* (3:18). It is used with the meaning of 'affirm' as in: *'The angels bear witness.'* (4:166). Another meaning is 'to judge' as Allah says: *'A witness from her people then declared.'* (12:26) It can mean swear as in the *li'ān* divorce. It can mean 'to order', as in this case. It is said that here it means attend the will.

Aṭ-Ṭabarī believed that *shahādah* referred to an oath and so the meaning is: 'the oath between you is that two swear.' That is used as evidence from other than the witnesses because it is not known that Allah obliged witnesses to take an oath. Al-Qaffāl took this position. An oath is called *shahādah* because a judgment is affirmed by the witnessing of it. Ibn 'Aṭiyyah preferred here that it is the witnessing which is preserved and conveyed and considered the meaning of presence and oath weak in this instance.

It is said that *'one of you'* means 'in what is between you' and *mā* is elided. '*Shahādah'* is ascribed to the adverb and '*bayn'* is used as a noun. Grammarians call it a passive based on expanding [the adverbial usage] as is said:

A day [in which] we witnessed Sulaym and 'Āmir.

Allah says: *'It was your scheming [in the] night and day.'* (34:33) [ANOTHER POEM&AYAT] *'Near to death'* means when someone is close to death because, of course, a dead person cannot make a will. It is like the usage in Allah's words: *'Whenever you recite the Qur'ān, seek refuge from the accursed Shayṭān'* (16:98) and: *'When you divorce women, divorce them…'* (65:1) This sort of usage is frequent in Arabic. The regent in 'when' us the verbal noun which is the verbal noun 'act as witnesses'.

In the expression *'and makes a will'* the word *'ḥīna'* is an adverb of time whose regent is *ḥaḍara*. *'Two'* demands two individuals, and it is probable that it is two men because after that Allah says, *'just men'*. So it is clear that He means two men because the word '*dhawā*' is only used for males as *dhawātā* (55:48) is only for females. The word '*two*' is in the nominative as the predicate of the inchoative, which is '*shahādah*'. Abū 'Alī said that '*shahādah*' is in the nominative by the inceptive and the predicate is in the word '*two*'. It implies: the witnessing between you in your wills is the witnessing of two' and the *muḍāf* is elided and replaced by the *muḍāf ilayh* as in Allah's words: '*his wives are their mothers*' (33:60), which in fact means 'like their mothers'. It is also possible that the word '*two*' is in the nominative by '*shahādah*' and implies: 'in what has been revealed to you' or 'so that among it should be' that two act as witnesses or two should undertake the witnessing. '*Just men*' describes '*two*' and '*among you*' and it is an adjective after an adjective.

or two men who are strangers to you

'*Two men who are strangers to you*' means the testimony of two men other than yourselves. 'Other than you' describes the other two men. The distinction in this *āyah* is problematic. Scholars disagree about it and have three positions regarding it. The first is that the pronoun '*kum*' (you) refers to the Muslims, and the other two men are unbelievers. According to this, on a journey the testimony of the People of the Book against Muslims is permitted where wills are concerned. This is the most likely meaning from the context and what is affirmed by *ḥadīth*s and it is the position of three Companions who were present at its revelation: Abū Mūsā al-Ash'arī, 'Abdullāh ibn Qays, and 'Abdullāh ibn 'Abbās. The meaning of the *āyah* from beginning to end confirms this understanding. Allah Almighty informs us that His judgment regarding the witnessing of someone making a will when he is close to death is that it should be by two just men. If the person is on a journey and there are no believers with him, then two witnesses from the people of the unbelievers who are present should act as witnesses. When they come and give testimony about the will, they swear after the prayer that they have not lied or altered anything, that their testimony is true and that they have not concealed anything they bore witness to. Judgment is then given based their testimony. If it is discovered afterwards that they lied or were deceitful or anything else constituting wrong action, two of the relatives of the testator, who was travelling, then swear an oath and the two witnesses are liable for anything disclosed against them.

This is the meaning according to Abū Mūsā al-Ash'arī, Sa'īd ibn al-Musayyab, Yaḥyā ibn Ya'mar, Sa'īd ibn Jubayr, Abū Miljaz, Ibrāhīm, Shurayḥ, 'Abīdah as-

Salmanī, Ibn Sīrīn, Mujāhid, Qatādah, as-Suddī, Ibn 'Abbās and others, and it is the view of *fuqahā'* like Sufyān ath-Thawrī. Abū 'Ubayd al-Qāsim ibn Sallām inclined to it in much of what he said. Aḥmad ibn Ḥanbal preferred it and said, 'The people of the *dhimmah* can testify against the Muslims on a journey when there are no Muslims present. All of them say that "*among you*" refers to believers and the "*strangers to you*" to unbelievers.' Some people say that the *āyah* was revealed when there were no believers except in Madīnah. They used to trade in the company of the People of the Book, idolaters and other unbelievers. According to Abū Mūsā, Shurayḥ and others, the *āyah* is one of judgment.

The second view is that *'two men who are strangers to you'* is abrogated. This is the position of Zayd ibn Aslam, an-Nakha'ī, Mālik, ash-Shāfi'ī, Abū Ḥanīfah and other *fuqahā'*, although Abū Ḥanīfah differed and said, 'The testimony of unbelievers against one another is permitted, but not permitted against the Muslims.' Their evidence is the words of Allah: *'...with whom you are satisfied as witnesses'* (2:282) and: *'Call two upright men from among yourselves as witnesses'* (65:2). They state that the *Āyah* of the Debt was the last part of the revelation and it says: *'...with whom you are satisfied as witnesses'* and abrogates this *āyah*. Islam at that time was only in Madīnah so that the testimony of the People of the Book was permitted. Today Islam has spread throughout the land and so the testimony of unbelievers is no longer valid. Muslims agree that the testimony of the impious (*fussāq*) is not permitted. The unbelievers are impious and so their testimony is not permitted.

This is sound, but it is necessary that on journeys there must be permission for the people of the *dhimmah* to testify against the Muslims in respect of wills when there is no Muslim present, but not when there are Muslims present. So there is no abrogation, as they claim, reported by any who were present at the revelation. Three Companions held the first view and [the second] is not stated by anyone else. The people of knowledge dislike opposing the Companions in favour of anyone else. This is reinforced by the fact that *Sūrat al-Mā'idah* was among the last parts of the Qur'ān to be revealed so that Ibn 'Abbās, al-Ḥasan and others said that nothing in it is abrogated. The claim of abrogation is, therefore, not sound. Abrogation must necessarily be based on an aspect of the abrogating *āyah,* which makes it impossible to combine it with the one abrogated, and the abrogating *āyah* must have been revealed later than the one it abrogates. So what they have said cannot validly entail abrogation. [What they said about abrogation] refers to other than the aforementioned story of that will, [and it is possible that the will is a specific case] arising from need and necessity, and it is not forbidden for there to be a difference in rulings in cases of necessity. It is possible that a Muslim will consider an unbeliever to be trustworthy and be satisfied with him cases of necessity and so there is nothing abrogating in what they have said.

The third view is that there is no abrogation in the *āyah*. Az-Zuhrī, al-Ḥasan and 'Ikrimah said that: His words, *'to you'* means from your tribe and relatives because they are more knowledgeable and less likely to forget. So the meaning of '*strangers to you*' is, in fact, 'other than your tribe and relatives'. An-Naḥḥās said, 'This is based on a profound knowledge of Arabic. That is that the meaning of 'other' (*ākhar*) in Arabic must be of the same genus as the first thing referred to. You say, "I passed by a generous man and another generous man." "Other" indicates that he is of the same genus as the first. It is not permitted to say in Arabic, "I passed by a generous man and another base man," or "I passed by a man and another donkey". So the other two here must be two upright men and unbelievers are not considered upright. Therefore, this must mean "Muslims who are from other than your tribe."' This is linguistically speaking an excellent meaning. It is used as evidence by Mālik and those who take his position, because they consider that the '*strangers to you*' are people from other than your tribe. This is despite the fact that this view is contradicted by the beginning of the *āyah*, *'You who believe,'* which is addressed to the entire community of believers.

Abū Ḥanīfah used the *āyah* as evidence for the permission for unbelievers to testify against the people of the *dhimmah* in matters occurring between them. He said that the words in the *āyah* mean 'from other than the people of your *dīn*.' So it is permitted for them to testify against one another. The response to him is: 'Your words do not accord with what the *āyah* demands, because it was revealed about accepting the testimony of the people of the *dhimmah* against the Muslims. You are saying something other than that and so the use of it in your argument is not sound.'

Some have said that this *āyah* indicates that it is permitted to accept the verbal testimony of the people of the *dhimmah* against the Muslims and that it indicates that testimony of the people of the *dhimmah* is accepted against other people of the *dhimmah* in terms of providing information. That is because if their testimony is accepted against Muslims, it is even more fitting for it to be accepted against their own people, the people of the *dhimmah*. But then the evidence indicates that their testimony against the Muslims is invalid and so all that remains is their testimony against their own people according to what it is.

This has no weight because accepting the testimony of the people of the *dhimmah* against the people of the *dhimmah* is a sub-branch of accepting their testimony against the Muslims. If their testimony against the Muslims, which is the basis, is invalid, then it is more likely that their testimony against the people of the *dhimmah*, which is the secondary branch, is also invalid. Allah knows best.

or, if you are travelling when the misfortune of death occurs,

If you are travelling at that time, then make your will with two men you think are upright and hand over to them what property you have. Then if you die they must take it to your heirs. If they are suspected and it is claimed that they have been unfaithful to the trust, then the ruling is that they are detained after the prayer, in other words kept in custody. Allah calls death a misfortune here. Our scholars said, 'Even if death is a great misfortune and major loss, worse than it is heedlessness of death, avoiding remembering it, and not thinking about it or acting for it. It on its own is a lesson for the one who contemplates and reflection for the one who reflects.' It is reported that the Prophet ﷺ said, 'If animals knew what you know about death, you would not have a plump animal.'

It is reported that a bedouin was travelling on a camel of his when the camel dropped dead. The bedouin dismounted and began to go around it and reflect on it. He said, 'Why don't you get up? Why don't you move? These limbs are whole and parts are sound? What is wrong with you? What supported you? What will resurrect you? What has struck you down? What stops you from moving?' Then he left reflecting and marvelling about it.

You should detain them after the prayer

This *āyah* is a basis for detaining those who owe something. Rights are of two types: some can be paid in full immediately and some cannot be paid immediately. If the one who has a debt is let go, he may disappear, and conceal himself and so the right will be lost. Therefore one must be sure of his whereabouts. As for a substitute for the right, there can be a pledge or a person who represents him in respect of the demand and liability and takes responsibility for it. The latter is less reliable than a pledge since he may also be abscond and it may be as difficult for him to appear as it is for the actual debtor. More than this is not possible. If there is no other security, all that remains is to detain the debtor himself until he pays in full or it is clear that he is in constricted circumstances.

If what is owed is physical, no substitute can be accepted, as in the case of the *ḥudūd* or retaliation. It must be satisfied immediately and so he can only be secured by imprisonment. This is why imprisonment is prescribed. Abū Dāwūd, at-Tirmidhī and others related from Bahz ibn Ḥakīm from his father from his grandfather that the Prophet ﷺ imprisoned a man on suspicion. Abū Dāwūd related from 'Amr ibn ash-Sharīd from his father that the Messenger of Allah ﷺ said, 'If someone who has the wherewithal delays payment, his honour and punishment are lawful.' Ibn al-Mubārak said, 'His honour is lawful and one is harsh to him and his punishment is being detained.'

Al-Khaṭṭābī said, 'There are two types of imprisonment: one is as a punishment and one is as a precaution. Punishment is only for something mandatory. When it is for suspicion, then it is used as a precaution until the true facts are known. It is related that he ﷺ imprisoned a man out of suspicion for part of a day and then released him.' Ma'mar related from Ayyūb that Ibn Sīrīn said, 'When Shurayḥ judged that a man owed something, he would order him to be detained in the mosque until he finished his sitting. If the person did not deliver what he owed, he ordered him to be taken to prison.'

after the prayer

This is after the *'Aṣr* prayer according to most scholars because godfearing people esteem that time and avoid lying and false oaths then. Al-Ḥasan said that it is *Ẓuhr* and it is also said that it can be any prayer. It is said that it is after their prayer if they are unbelievers. As-Suddī said that. It is said that that the point of its connection to being 'after the prayer' is because of respect for that moment, the angels being present at that time. In the *Ṣaḥīḥ* we find: 'Anyone who swears a false oath after *'Aṣr* will meet Allah with anger against him.'

This *āyah* is the basis for making things difficult in oaths. Making things difficult occurs in four ways. The first is the time, as we have mentioned. The second is the place, like making it in the mosque and at the minbar, which differs from Abū Ḥanīfah and his people who say that it is not mandatory for anyone to take an oath by the minbar of the Prophet ﷺ, nor between the Corner and the Maqām, except in respect of a few matters. This is the position to which al-Bukhārī inclines as he has 'The Chapter on the Person Against whom a claim is made being made to make an oath, and he does not have to move from his place to another place [to make it].' Mālik and ash-Shāfi'ī said that for the oaths in the *qasāmah* people are summoned to Makkah from its provinces and the oaths are sworn between the Corner and the Maqām. In the case of the provinces of Madīnah, they are forced to come to Madīnah to swear at the minbar.

The third is the circumstances. Muṭarrif, Ibn al-Mājishūn and some of the people of ash-Shāfi'ī say that oaths should be sworn standing facing the *qiblah* because that makes it more of a deterrent. Ibn Kinānah says that the swearers should be sitting. Ibn al-'Arabī said, 'I think that people should swear in the position in which judgment will be delivered on them. If that is standing, then they swear standing; if sitting, then they swear sitting. Some scholars, however, take the statement of 'Alqamah ibn Wā'il from his father, 'Go and swear,' to mean standing when giving an oath. Muslim transmitted it, and Allah knows best. The fourth is stressing its seriousness by means of the expression used. One group believe that swearing may only be by Allah and nothing else since Allah says: *'They swear by Allah'*, *'Say, "By my Lord"'* (10:53) and *'By Allah, I will devise some scheme against your idols'* (21:53) and the words of the Prophet ﷺ: 'Whoever swears should swear by Allah or be silent.' A man says, 'By Allah, I will not give them more.'

Mālik said, 'The oath should be: "I swear by Allah, and there is no god but Him, I do not owe him anything and what he claims against me is false."' His evidence is what Abū Dāwūd related from Musaddad from Abū al-Aḥwaṣ from 'Aṭā' ibn as-Sā'ib from Abū Yahyā from Ibn 'Abbās that the Prophet ﷺ said, 'It means that a man swears: "I swear by Allah, and there is no god but Him, that I do not have anything he is entitled to."' The Kufans say that someone may only swear by Allah, and if the Qāḍī suspects him, he must make the oath stronger and swear: 'By Allah, there is no god but Him, the Knower of the Unseen and Visible, the All-Merciful, Most Merciful, who knows what He knows of the secret and what He knows of the public, who knows what is hidden from the eyes and what the hearts conceal.'

The people of ash-Shāfi'ī intensify the oath by swearing by a copy of the Qur'ān. Ibn al-'Arabī says this is an innovation, not mentioned by any of the Companions. Ash-Shāfi'ī stated that he saw Ibn Māzin, the Qāḍī of Sana'a, swear by a copy of the Qur'ān and he commanded his people to do that and reported it from Ibn 'Abbās. It is not sound. In the book, *al-Muhadhdhab,* it states that people should swear by a copy of the Qur'ān and what it contains. Ash-Shāfi'ī related from Muṭarrif that Ibn az-Zubayr used to swear on a copy of the Qur'ān. He said, 'I saw Muṭarrif in San'a' swearing on a copy of the Qur'ān.' Ash-Shāfi'ī said that it is good. Ibn al-Mundhir said, 'There is consensus that a judge cannot make someone take an oath to divorce, to free a slave or by a copy of the Qur'ān.' This has already been discussed in connection with oaths (5:89). Qatādah used to swear by a copy of the Qur'ān. Aḥmad and Isḥāq said that it is not disliked to do so. Ibn al-Mundhir related that from them both.

Mālik and ash-Shāfi'ī disagree regarding the amount of property for which an oath concerning property should be made. Mālik said, 'There is no oath for any amount less than three dirhams, based on analogy with cutting off the hand.

Any property for which the hand can be amputated, and the sanctity of the limb cancelled, is great.' Ash-Shāfi'ī said, 'There is no oath for less than twenty dinars by analogy with *zakāt*.' The oath may be made by the minbar of any mosque.

they should swear by Allah

The *fā'* denotes adding one sentence to another or it is the apodosis of the protasis because 'you should detain them' means to detain them for the oath and so it is the apodosis of the command which is indicated by the words. It is as if Allah were saying, 'when you detain them, they should swear.' [POEM]

There is disagreement about what this means. It is said that it about the two executors when their word is doubted. It is said that it refers to the two witnesses if they are not upright and the judge has suspicions about what they saw and so he makes them swear an oath. Ibn al-'Arabī said in invalidation of this, 'What I heard – and it is an innovation – from Ibn Abī Laylā is that the claimant swears with his two witnesses that what he says is true and then the judgment is given in his favour. I think that that the context of this is when the judge suspects that someone has taken possession of the property and he swears that he has not. One does not pay attention to anything else. How can a claimant be imprisoned or be made to swear?'

We have already mentioned the position of aṭ-Ṭabarī that one does not assign a reason to Allah for ordaining the ruling that a witness must make an oath. It is said that the witnesses are made to take an oath because there is a claim against them when the heirs claim that they have been treacherous with property.

if you are doubtful

This is a necessary condition for the witnesses being made to take an oath. If there is no doubt or disagreement, there is no oath. Ibn 'Aṭiyyah said, 'As for the apparent ruling of Abū Mūsā about making *dhimmīs* make an oath to complete their testimony and then carrying out the bequest to the beneficiaries, Abū Dāwūd related from ash-Sha'bī that a Muslim in Daqūqā' [in eastern Syria] was dying and could not find any Muslim to witness his will. So he asked two of the People of the Book to act as witnesses. They went to Kufa to Abū Mūsā al-Ash'arī and informed him about that and presented what he had left and his will. Al-Ash'arī stated, "This business has not happened since what occurred in the time of the Messenger of Allah ﷺ." So he made them take an oath after the *'Aṣr* prayer which was, "By Allah, we have not betrayed, altered, concealed or changed. It is the will of the man and what he left." Then he carried it out.'

Ibn 'Aṭiyyah said, 'This doubt, for those who do not think that the *āyah* is abrogated, lies in the possibility of treachery and suspicion of bias in favour of one of the beneficiaries rather than another. That may occur even with an oath in their view. As for those who think that the making of an oath has been abrogated, there is no oath unless there is suspicion of treachery or of some kind of transgression. They consider that an oath need only be made when there is a claim of impropriety, not to simply complete the testimony.' Ibn al-'Arabī said, 'There are two categories of oaths made because of doubt and suspicion: one is when there is doubt after the right is confirmed and the claim delivered, in which case there is no disagreement that an oath must be made. The second is when there is a general suspicion about rights and *ḥudūd*, as is made clear in the books of secondary rulings. Here the claim should be verified and strengthened as is mentioned in transmissions.'

We will not sell it for any price, even to a near relative,

They say in their oath: 'We will not sell our oath for goods which we take instead of following what was actually stated in the will and we will not give them to anyone, even if the one to whom they are is allotted is our relative.' There is a lot of implication in the words as we also see in 13:23-24. 'Selling' here is not literally selling, but means to cause someone to obtain something.

The *lām* in *'lā tashtarī'* is the apodosis of 'they should swear' because the use of the verb *'aqsama'* has the same weight as swearing an articulated oath. It is *'lā'* and *'mā'* in the negative. The pronoun in *'bihi'* refers to the Name of Allah which was the last to be mentioned. It means: 'We will not sell our portion with Allah Almighty for these goods.' It is also possible that it refers to the testimony which was mentioned with the meaning of a statement, as when the Prophet ﷺ said, 'Fear the supplication of the wronged. There is no veil between it and Allah.' So the pronoun refers to the idea of the supplication. This was already mentioned in *Sūrat an-Nisā'* (4:8).

The Kufans say that *'price'* means 'with a price', in other words 'goods with a price', and this is elided. In our view and that of many scholars, the word *thaman* can refer to either the price or the goods. In our view, the price is paid and so both of them constitute a price and sale whether the sale is based on goods and cash, barter, or exchange of two forms of cash. Based on this principle, when the buyer is bankrupt and a seller finds the goods he sold him, has he the right to reclaim them? Abū Ḥanīfah said that he does not and he bases that on this principle. He said, 'Their owner is the same as the other creditors.' Mālik said that he has that right in the case of bankruptcy but not of death. Ash-Shāfi'ī said that the owner has that right in cases of both bankruptcy and death.

Abū Ḥanīfah held to what we mentioned and the universal basis is that the debt is the liability of both the bankrupt and the deceased and what is in their possession is used to repay it and so all the creditors share in it according to the amount they are owed and there is no difference regarding that whether the individual items still exist or not since they are no longer owned by the seller who is simply owed what they cost. Therefore, there are only prices or what remains of them. Mālik and ash-Shāfi'ī make this rule more specific by reports related in this area by Abū Dāwūd and others.

we will not conceal the testimony of Allah.

The testimony Allah has informed us of. There are seven readings of this. You can find them in *at-Taḥṣīl* and elsewhere.

If it then comes to light that the two of them have merited the allegation of wrongdoing.

'Umar said, 'This *āyah* is the most difficult in this sūrah with regard to rulings.' Az-Zajjāj said, 'The most difficult case of syntax in the Qur'ān is *"who have the most right to do so."*' (see below) *'Comes to light'* (*'uthira*) means 'to become aware of'. One says, 'I became aware (*'athartu*) of treachery and 'made someone else aware (*a'thartu*) of it.' Another example of that is: *'We made them chance upon (a'tharnā) them'* (18:21), because they had been looking for them while their location was concealed from them. The root of *'uthūr* is to stumble and fall over something. The verb is used when someone's toe hits something which blocks it and he trips. It is used for a horse that stumbles (*'ithār*). [POEM] *'Ithīr* is fine dust which arises because it falls on the face. *'Athyar* is the hidden track which one falls upon.

'The two of them' refers to the executors mentioned before according to Sa'īd ibn Jubayr. Ibn 'Abbās says that it refers to the two witnesses. *'Wrongdoing'* is lack of faithfulness and taking what is not theirs, or a false oath or false testimony. Abū 'Alī said that here *'ithm'* (wrongdoing) is the name of the thing taken because by taking it, the one who took it did wrong. So it is called *'ithm'* in the same way that something taken without any right is called 'injustice'.

Two others who have the most right to do so should take their place should take their place

Two others take their place in making the oaths or giving the testimony. Allah says *'two others'* since it is agreed that there are two relatives. 'Others' is in the accusative by the action of an implied verb. 'Their place' (*maqām*) is a verbal noun and it implies: they should stand as the other two stood.' Ibn as-Sārī said, 'The meaning is that they are more entitled than the others to act as executors.' An-Naḥḥās said, 'This is part of the best of what is said about it because one does not make a particle (*ḥarf*) an appositive for another particle. Ibn al-'Arabī preferred that. It is the explanation of it because the meaning according to those who know *tafsīr* is: "those who are more entitled to the bequest."'

'Two who have the most right' is an appositive for *'two others'* as Ibn as-Sārī said. An-Naḥḥās preferred that. It is replacing the indefinite with the definite, which is permitted. It is said that when the indefinite is mentioned earlier and then repeated, it becomes definite. An example of this can be seen in 24:35 with the mention of *'glass'*. It is also said that it is an appositive for the pronoun in *'the two of them take their place'*, or it is a predicate whose subject is elided, implying: 'Two others take their place who have more right.' Ibn 'Īsā said that *'two others who have the most right'* is the object of 'entitled' based on the elision of the *muḍāf*, meaning that they are more entitled because of the wrong action of the first two. So *''alayhim'* means *'fīhim'* as we see used in 2:103 in reference to the kingdom of Sulaymān. [POEM]

The readings of Yaḥyā ibn Waththāb, al-A'mash and Ḥamzah have *'al-awwalinā'* instead of *'al-awlayanā'*, which is the plural of *'awwal'* as an appositive for *'those'* or the joined pronoun *'hum'*. Rather than the more general reading of *istuhiqqa*, Ḥafṣ has *istaḥaqqa*. It is related from Ubayy ibn Ka'b and the subject is *'al-awlayāni'* and the object is elided. It implies: 'Two who have more right to the deceased and his will which he made.' It is said that it means: 'Two who have the right to refute the oaths.' *'Al-awlāni'* is related from al-Ḥasan and Ibn Sīrīn has *'al-awlayni'*. An-Naḥḥās said that both meanings are grammatically incorrect. One does not say *'mathnān'* for *'mathnā'* other than what is related from al-Ḥasan: *'al-awwalāni'*.

and swear by Allah:

The other two who take the place of the witnesses make an oath affirming that what the person said in his will is true and 'the wealth which was left to us was more than we have been given and this vessel was part of the goods which the person left and formed part of he wrote in his will and you two have been unfaithful.' This is the import of the words: *'Our testimony is truer than their testimony,'* meaning our oath is truer than their oath. *'Testimony'* can validly have the meaning of 'oath'. An example of that usage is found in Allah's words: *'such people should testify four times'* (25:6). Ma'mar related from Ayyūb from Ibn Sīrin that 'Abīdah said, 'Two of the relatives of the deceased rose and said, "Our testimony is truer."' 'We have not committed perjury' means we have not exceeded the truth in our oath. *'If we had we would indeed be wrongdoers'* if our oath were false and we were to take what was not ours.

That makes it more likely that they will give their evidence properly

'An' is in the position of the accusative and *'give'* is in the accusative by *'an'* and *'be afraid'* is added to it. It is said that the pronoun in *'give'* and *'be afraid'* refers to the one who gives them the bequest. That is more in keeping with the course of the *āyah*. It is said that it it makes it more likely that people will beware of treachery and testify to the truth out of fear of disgrace when the oaths are rejected. Allah knows best.

Have *taqwā* of Allah and listen carefully.

This is a command: listen to what you are told and accept it and follow the command of Allah in respect of it. *'Allah does not guide deviant people.' Fisq* is when someone leaves obedience for disobedience, which was already discussed (2:26), and Allah knows best.

يَوۡمَ يَجۡمَعُ ٱللَّهُ ٱلرُّسُلَ فَيَقُولُ مَاذَآ أُجِبۡتُمۡۖ قَالُواْ لَا عِلۡمَ لَنَآۖ إِنَّكَ أَنتَ
عَلَّٰمُ ٱلۡغُيُوبِ ١٠٩

109 On the day Allah gathers the Messengers together and says, 'What response did you receive?' they will say, 'We do not know. You are the Knower of unseen things.'

On the day Allah gathers the Messengers together

If it is asked what the connection between this *āyah* and the one before it is, the reply is that it is connected to the curbing any tendency to make a public statement which differs from what is actually there in the case of wills or other things, since the Ultimate Repayer has knowledge of them. It is said that it implies: 'Fear the day when Allah will gather the Messengers together,' as az-Zajjāj states. It is said that it implies: 'Remember or beware of the Day of Rising when Allah will gather the Messengers together.' The meanings are similar. What is meant is to threaten and alarm people.

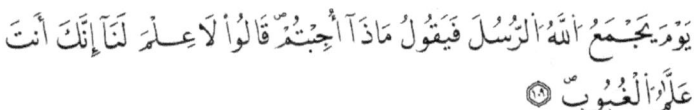

and says, 'What response did you receive?'

'What answer did your nations give you? How did your people answer you when you called them to My *tawḥīd*?'

they will say, 'We do not know. You are the Knower of unseen things.'

The people of interpretation disagree about the meaning of 'We do not know.' It is said that it means, 'We have no knowledge of the inward response of our nations because that is what their repayment from You will depend on.' This is related from the Prophet ﷺ. It is said that it means: 'We have no knowledge other than what You taught us,' and there is elision. Ibn 'Abbās and Mujāhid said that. Ibn 'Abbās said, 'It means that we have no knowledge except what You know better than us.' It is said that they will be dumbfounded by the terror of that Day and too alarmed to answer. Then they will give this answer after their senses return to them. Al-Ḥasan, Mujāhid and as-Suddī said that. An-Naḥḥās said: 'This is not sound because the Messengers have no fear and feel no sorrow.'

This is the case in most situations on the Day of Rising. We find in tradition, 'When Hell is brought, it will heave a sigh and there is no Prophet or truthful person who will not fall to their knees.' The Messenger of Allah ﷺ said, 'Jibrīl alarmed me about the Day of Rising until he made me weep. I said, "Jibrīl, have I not been forgiven any past wrong actions and any future ones?" He told me, "Muḥammad, you will witness the terror of that Day which will make you forget forgiveness."' If this question is posed when Hell sighs, as some say, then what Mujāhid and al-Ḥasan said is sound, and Allah knows best. An-Naḥḥās said, 'The sound view regarding this is that the meaning is: "What answer did you receive secretly and publicly?" and is meant as a rebuke to the unbelievers. So they will say, "We have no knowledge." This is to deny those who turned the Messiah into a god.'

Ibn Jurayj said, 'The meaning of "What response did you receive?" is "What did they do after you left them?" They will reply, "We do not know. You are the Knower of unseen things."' Abū 'Ubayd said, 'Something similar to this is the *ḥadīth* of the Prophet ﷺ: "Some people will be come to me at the Basin and will be driven away. I will say, 'My Community!' and he will be told, 'You do not know what they did after you.'"' Most read *ghuyūb* for 'unseen things', but Ḥamzah, al-Kisā'ī and Abū Bakr read *ghiyūb*.

Al-Māwardī said, 'If it is asked, "Why did Allah ask them about what He knows better than them?" there are two answers. One is that He asked them so that He could inform them about what they did not know regarding the disbelief and hypocrisy of their people and their denial of them after they died. The second is that He means he will disgrace those people by that in front of witnesses so that it is a form of punishment.'

إِذْ قَالَ ٱللَّهُ يَٰعِيسَى ٱبْنَ مَرْيَمَ ٱذْكُرْ نِعْمَتِى عَلَيْكَ وَعَلَىٰ وَٰلِدَتِكَ إِذْ أَيَّدتُّكَ
بِرُوحِ ٱلْقُدُسِ تُكَلِّمُ ٱلنَّاسَ فِى ٱلْمَهْدِ وَكَهْلًا ۖ وَإِذْ عَلَّمْتُكَ ٱلْكِتَٰبَ
وَٱلْحِكْمَةَ وَٱلتَّوْرَىٰةَ وَٱلْإِنجِيلَ ۖ وَإِذْ تَخْلُقُ مِنَ ٱلطِّينِ كَهَيْـَٔةِ ٱلطَّيْرِ
بِإِذْنِى فَتَنفُخُ فِيهَا فَتَكُونُ طَيْرًۢا بِإِذْنِى ۖ وَتُبْرِئُ ٱلْأَكْمَهَ وَٱلْأَبْرَصَ
بِإِذْنِى ۖ وَإِذْ تُخْرِجُ ٱلْمَوْتَىٰ بِإِذْنِى ۖ وَإِذْ كَفَفْتُ بَنِىٓ إِسْرَٰٓءِيلَ عَنكَ إِذْ
جِئْتَهُم بِٱلْبَيِّنَٰتِ فَقَالَ ٱلَّذِينَ كَفَرُوا۟ مِنْهُمْ إِنْ هَٰذَآ إِلَّا سِحْرٌ مُّبِينٌ ﴿١١٠﴾

110 Remember when Allah said, "Īsā, son of Maryam, remember My blessing to you and to your mother when I reinforced you with the Purest *Rūḥ* so that you could speak to people in the cradle and when you were fully grown; and when I taught you the Book and Wisdom, and the Torah and the Gospel; and when you created a bird-shape out of clay by My permission, and then breathed into it and it became a bird by My permission; and healed the blind and the leper by My permission; and when you brought forth the dead by My permission; and when I held back the tribe of Israel from you, when you brought them the Clear Signs and those of them who disbelieved said, "This is nothing but downright magic";

Remember when Allah said, "Īsā, son of Maryam, remember My blessing to you

This is part of the description of the Day of Rising, as if Allah is saying: 'Remember the Day when Allah gathers the Messengers and when He says to 'Īsā …' That is what al-Mahdawī said. "Īsā' can be in the nominative if 'son of Maryam' is a second vocative, or in the accusative because the vocative is accusative. [POEM]

Allah reminds 'Īsā of His blessing to him and his mother. He mentions them both for two reasons. One is so that the honour which they alone had, and their being singled out for that position, will be proclaimed to the world. The second is to support His evidence and refute the one who denies him. Then He begins to enumerate the blessings He gave him.

when I reinforced you with the Purest *Rūḥ*

'When I reinforced you' means 'strengthened you', taken from *aydi* (hands) which is strength. There are two points about *'Purest Rūḥ'*. One is that it is the pure *Rūḥ* which Allah singled him out for, as mentioned in *Sūrat an-Nisā'* (4:171). The second is that it refers to Jibrīl, and this is the soundest, as was pointed out in *al-Baqarah* (2:87).

so that you could speak to people in the cradle and when you were fully grown;

This means that he spoke to people both while he was a babe in the cradle and as a Prophet when he was mature. This was mentioned in *Sūrat Āli 'Imrān* (3:45-46).

and when I held back the tribe of Israel from you, when you brought them the Clear Signs

'I held back' means 'I defended you and kept the tribe of Israel from you when they wanted to kill you.' *'The Clear Signs'* are proofs and miracles, which are mentioned here. Those who disbelieved are those who did not believe in him and denied his Prophethood. They claimed that the miracles were nothing but magic. Ḥamzah and al-Kisā'ī read *sāḥir* instead of *siḥr*, meaning 'This is nothing but a powerful magician.'

وَإِذْ أَوْحَيْتُ إِلَى الْحَوَارِيِّـۧنَ أَنْ ءَامِنُوا بِي وَبِرَسُولِي قَالُوٓا ءَامَنَّا
وَاشْهَدْ بِأَنَّنَا مُسْلِمُونَ ١١١

111 and when I inspired the Disciples to believe in Me and in My Messenger, they said, "We believe. Bear witness that we are Muslims."'

The meanings of this *āyah* were already discussed. (3:52) In Arabic, the word 'revelation' (*waḥy*) means inspiration. It is of two types: revelation in the sense of Jibrīl being sent to the Messengers; and revelation in the sense of inspiration as in this *āyah* when it means 'I inspired them and made them feel in their hearts.' Other examples of that are the *āyahs*: *'Your Lord inspired the bee'* (16:68) and: *'We inspired the mother of Mūsā.'* (28:7) Revelation can mean information while awake or asleep. Abū 'Ubaydah said that it can also mean 'commanded' and *'ilā'* is connective. *Awḥā* and *waḥā* both mean the same. Allah says: *'...because your Lord has inspired (awḥā) it.'* (99:5) Al-'Ajjāj said:

He commanded (*awḥā*) her to remain and she remained.

It can also mean 'made clear to them'.

Bear witness that we are Muslims.'

'We' (*annanā*) is based on the linguistic root. Some people elide one of the *nūns*. It means, 'Lord, witness!' It is said that it means, 'O 'Īsā, that we are Muslims, submitted to Allah.'

إِذْ قَالَ ٱلْحَوَارِيُّونَ يَٰعِيسَى ٱبْنَ مَرْيَمَ هَلْ يَسْتَطِيعُ رَبُّكَ أَن يُنَزِّلَ عَلَيْنَا
مَآئِدَةً مِّنَ ٱلسَّمَآءِ ۖ قَالَ ٱتَّقُوا۟ ٱللَّهَ إِن كُنتُم مُّؤْمِنِينَ ﴿١١٢﴾

112 And when the Disciples said, "Īsā son of Maryam! Can your Lord send down a table to us out of heaven?' He said, 'Have *taqwā* of Allah if you are believers!'

Can your Lord send down a table to us out of heaven?'

Al-Kisā'ī, 'Alī, Ibn 'Abbās, Sa'id ibn Jubayr and Mujāhid read 'can' with a *tā'* and with 'your Lord' in the accusative. Al-Kisā'ī elides the *lām* of '*hal*' into the *tā'*. The rest recite it with *yā'* and '*your Lord*' in the nominative. This is a more problematic reading than the first reading. As-Suddī said that the *āyah* means 'Will your Lord obey you if you ask him to "*send down...*"' with the word *yastatī'u* – 'can' – meaning *yutī'u* – 'obey'. Similarly, *istajāba* can mean *ajāba* (answer). It is said that it means: 'Can your Lord?' This question was asked at the beginning of their path before they had firm knowledge of Allah. Because of the lack of respect in their request, 'Īsā was severe in the response: *'Have taqwā of Allah if you are believers!'* meaning 'Do not doubt the power of Allah.' This is debatable because the Disciples were the loyal followers of the Prophets and their Helpers as we find in Allah's words: *'"Who will be my helpers to Allah?" The Disciples said, "We will be the helpers of Allah."'* (61:14) The Prophet ﷺ said, 'Every Prophet has a disciple and my disciple is az-Zubayr.'

It is known that all the Prophets brought knowledge of Allah, comprising knowledge of what is necessary for Him, what is permissible for Him, and what is impossible for Him, and that they conveyed that knowledge to their nations. How could that knowledge be hidden from those who were close to them, and devoted to them, so that they would be ignorant of the power of Allah? It is, however, possible to say that such things were voiced by people who met them, in the way that an ignorant bedouin once said to the Prophet ﷺ, 'Give us tamarisks as they have tamarisks.' Another example is what the people of Mūsā said: *'Appoint a god for us as they have a god'* (3:138) as will be clarified in *al-A'rāf*, Allah willing.

It is said that these people did not in fact doubt the ability of the Creator because they were believers who possessed knowledge. It is as one says, 'Can so-and-so come?' It is known that he can and so it really means: 'Will he do that? Will he respond or not?' They knew about Allah's ability to do that and other things logically, by report and theoretically, but they desired the direct knowledge that comes from actually seeing it, in the way that Ibrāhīm said: *'Lord, show me how You bring the dead to life.'* (2:260) Ibrāhīm knew by report and theoretically that He could, but he wanted to see it in a manner which left no room for doubt or uncertainty because theoretical knowledge and second-hand report may be affected by doubt and demurral, but eye witnessing is subject to none of that. That is why the Disciples said: *'So that our hearts will be at peace'* in the same way that Ibrāhīm said: *'So my heart may be at peace.'* (2:260) This is an excellent interpretation, but better than it is that the words were spoken by someone who was with the Disciples as will be explained.

Ibn al-'Arabī includes *'al-Mustatī''* among the Names of Allah. He said, 'Neither the Book nor the *Sunnah* reports it as a Name, but the action is reported.' He mentioned the words of the Disciples: '*Can your Lord*?' Ibn al-Ḥaṣṣār replies to that in the *Sharḥ as-Sunnah* and elsewhere: 'Allah's words speak about the Disciples and what they said to 'Īsā. There is no doubt about His ability. It is polite way of asking and showing proper manners with Allah Almighty since it is known that not everything that is possible will actually occur. The Disciples were the best of those who believed in 'Īsā. How could it be supposed that they would be ignorant of Allah's power to do every possible thing?'

As for the reading with *tā'*, it is said that it means: 'Can you ask your Lord?' This is the position of 'Ā'ishah and Mujāhid. 'Ā'ishah said, 'Those people had too much knowledge of Allah to say, "Can your Lord?"' It is related that she said, 'The Disciples did not doubt that Allah had the power to make a Table descend, but they said, "Can you ask your Lord?"' Mu'ādh ibn Jabal said, 'The Prophet ﷺ recited to us, "Can you [ask] your Lord."' Mu'ādh said, 'I heard the Prophet ﷺ say several times, "Can you [ask] your Lord."' Az-Zajjāj said, 'The meaning is: "Can you verify the claim that your Lord will do anything you ask Him to?" It is also said to mean, "Can you call on or ask your Lord?"' The meaning is similar. If it is read with *tā'*, something must be elided. If it is read with *yā'*, then that is not the case.

'Have taqwā of Allah,' in other words fear disobeying Him and asking too many questions since you have no idea what the consequences will be of your asking Him for signs, because Allah always does what is in the best interests of His slaves. The words: '... *if you are believers'* means 'if you believe in Him and what I have brought.' Enough has been said about this.

قَالُوا۟ نُرِيدُ أَن نَّأْكُلَ مِنْهَا وَتَطْمَئِنَّ قُلُوبُنَا وَنَعْلَمَ أَن قَدْ صَدَقْتَنَا
وَنَكُونَ عَلَيْهَا مِنَ ٱلشَّٰهِدِينَ ﴿١١٣﴾

113 They said, 'We want to eat from it and for our hearts to be at peace and to know that you have told us the truth and to be among those who witness it.'

This explains the reason for their request when they had been forbidden to ask for it. There are two aspects to the words: *'We want to eat from it'*. One is that they wanted to eat from it out of need. That was because when 'Īsā went out, five thousand or more would follow him. Some were his Companions and some were hoping for him to supplicate for them because of their illness or disability if they were chronically ill or blind. Others were simply looking on and mocking. One day he went to a place in the desert and they had no provisions with them and they became hungry. They said to the Disciples, 'Tell 'Īsā when he prays to ask for a table to descend on us from the sky.' Sham'ūn came to him at the head of the Disciples and told him that the people were asking for him to pray for a table to descend on them from the sky, 'Īsā said to Sham'ūn to tell them: *"Have taqwā of Allah if you are believers."'* So Sham'ūn told the people and they told him, 'Tell him, "*We want to eat from it.*"' The second aspect is they wanted to eat from as a means of gaining blessing, not out of need. Al-Māwardī said, 'This is more likely because if they had needed it, they would not have been forbidden to ask for it.'

and for our hearts to be at peace

There are three points here. One is for their hearts to be at peace with the belief that Allah has sent a Prophet to them. The second is for their hearts to be at peace with the fact that Allah has chosen them for His call. The third is for their hearts to be at peace through Allah's granting of what they have asked for. Al-Māwardī mentioned that. Al-Mahdawī said, 'Our hearts are at peace because Allah has accepted our fasting and other actions.' Ath-Tha'labī said, 'We will have certainty of His power and our hearts will be at peace.'

'…and to know that you have told us the truth' that you are truly the Messenger of Allah, *'and to be among those who witness it,'* who attest to the Oneness of Allah and to your Message and Prophethood. It is said that it means, 'We will bear witness about you to those who did not see it when we return to them.'

قَالَ عِيسَى ٱبْنُ مَرْيَمَ ٱللَّهُمَّ رَبَّنَآ أَنزِلْ عَلَيْنَا مَآئِدَةً مِّنَ ٱلسَّمَآءِ تَكُونُ لَنَا عِيدًا لِّأَوَّلِنَا وَءَاخِرِنَا وَءَايَةً مِّنكَ وَٱرْزُقْنَا وَأَنتَ خَيْرُ ٱلرَّٰزِقِينَ ﴿١١٤﴾

114 'Īsā son of Maryam said, 'Allah, our Lord, send down a table to us out of heaven to be a feast for us, for the first and last of us, and as a Sign from You. Provide for us! You are the Best of Providers!'

According to Sībawayh, the root of *'Allahumma'* is 'O Allah" and the two *mīms* are in place of the *yā'*. The word used for table (*mā'idah*) here is a table which has food on it. Quṭrub said, 'It is not called a *mā'idah* until it has food on it. Otherwise it called *khuwān* or *khiwān*. The verb *māda* means "to provide with food, to give food." Al-Akhfash cites Ru'bah:

We guide the leaders of the wealthy peers
to the Amīr al-Mu'minīn, asking for a gift (*mumtād*).'

The *mā'idah* is the means of providing the food. Food is also called *mā'idah* metaphorically because it is eaten off the table, as the sky is called 'rain'. The people of Kufa say that it is called *mā'idah* because it and what is on it can be moved, as the verb *māda* also means 'to lean and be moved'. A poet said:

Perhaps you weep when a dove sings,
The branches of trees bending, moving (*tamīdu*) with it.

Someone else said:

The death of al-Kisā'ī unsettled me,
and the the vast earth moved (*tamīdu*) with me.

An example of this is the words of Allah: *'He cast firmly embedded mountains on the earth so that it would not move (tamīda) under you.'* (16:15) Abū 'Ubaydah said said that *mā'idah* is an active participle with the meaning of the passive as seen in *rāḍiyah* (69:21) meaning 'pleased' and *dāfiq* (86:6) meaning 'spurted'.

to be a feast for us

The verb '*to be*' refers back to '*a table*'. It is not an apodosis. Al-A'mash recited '*takun*' as an apodosis. It means: the day of its descent is for the beginning and end of our Community. It is said that table descended on them at on a Sunday for their midday and evening meals. That is why they make Sunday a festival (*'īd*). *'Īd* is the singular of *a'yād*. It has a *yā'* although its root is *wāw*. It is said that that is because of the difference between it and *a'wād* (branches). They celebrated (*'ayyada*) the *'īd*. Al-Jawharī said that. It is said that the root of the verb is *'āda, ya'ūdu*, 'to return', and it is *'iwd* and the *wāw* has been changed to a *yā'* because of the *kasrah* before it, as in *mīzān*, *mīqāt*, and *mī'ād*. That is the reason for applying the word to the days of *Fiṭr* and *al-Aḍḥā*. They are called that because they recur every year.

Al-Khalīl said, 'The *'īd* is every day on which people gathered as if they were returning to it.' Ibn al-Anbārī said that it is called *'īd* because of the intensity (*'awd*) of joy and happiness on it. It is the day when everyone is happy. Do you not see that on that day those in prison are not sought after or punished? Animals and birds are not hunted and children do not go to schools.

It is said that it is called *'īd* because everyone reverts to his station. Do you not see the difference in people's dress, appearance and food? Some give hospitality and some receive hospitality. Some show mercy and some are shown mercy. It is said that it is called that because it is a noble day. It is a noble stallion among the Arabs and ascription is made to it. Excellent camels are called '*'īdīyah*'. [POEM]

Zayd ibn Thābit recited *'li-ūlānā wa ukhrānā'* in the plural. Ibn 'Abbās said, 'On it the last of the people eat as well as the first of the people. The phrase *'and as a Sign from You...'* means a proof and an indication. *'Provide for us!'* means 'give us.' *'You are the Best of Providers!'*, in other words the Best of those who give and provide, since You are the Rich beyond need, the Praiseworthy.

قَالَ ٱللَّهُ إِنِّي مُنَزِّلُهَا عَلَيْكُمْ فَمَن يَكْفُرْ بَعْدُ مِنكُمْ فَإِنِّيٓ أُعَذِّبُهُۥ عَذَابًا لَّآ أُعَذِّبُهُۥٓ
أَحَدًا مِّنَ ٱلْعَٰلَمِينَ ۝١١٥

115 Allah said, 'I will send it down to you but if anyone among you disbelieves after that, I will punish him with a punishment the like of which I will not inflict on anyone else in all the worlds!'

Allah said, 'I will send it down to you

This is a promise from Allah in response to the request of 'Īsā as 'Īsā responded to the request of the Disciples. This confirms that He sent it down as His promise is true. The people denied it and disbelieved after it was sent down and so they were transformed into monkeys and pigs. Ibn 'Amr said, 'The people with the worst punishment on the Day of Rising will be the hypocrites and those who rejected among the people of the Table and the people of Pharaoh as Allah says here.'

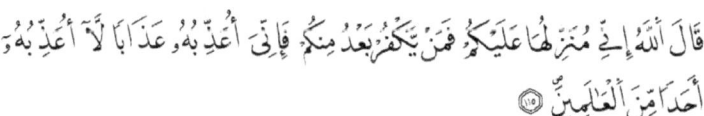

Scholars disagree about whether or not the table was sent down. The position of the majority, which is the truth, is that it was sent down because of these words. Mujāhid said, 'It was not sent down but was made an example for Allah's creatures. He forbade them to ask His Prophets for signs.' It is said that He promised them the answer. When Allah said to them: *'If anyone among you disbelieves after that,'* they absolved themselves from it and asked for Allah's forgiveness, saying, 'We do not want this.' Al-Ḥasan said that. This position and the one before it are wrong. The truth is that it was actually sent down.

Ibn 'Abbās said, "Īsā ibn Maryam said to the tribe of Israel. "Fast for thirty days. Then ask Allah for whatever you wish and He will give it to you." So they fasted thirty days and said, "'Īsā, if we work for someone, when we finish the work he feeds us. We fasted and are hungry, so ask Allah to send down to us a table from heaven. The angels brought a table, which they carried, on which were seven loaves and seven fish and placed it before them. So everyone, from the first to the last person ate from it.'"

Abū 'Abdullāh Muḥammad ibn 'Alī at-Tirmidhī al-Ḥakīm mentioned in *Nawādir al-Uṣūl* from 'Umar ibn Abī 'Umar from 'Ammās ibn Hārūn ath-Thaqafī from Zakariyyā ibn Ḥakīm al-Ḥanẓalī from 'Alī ibn Zayd ibn Jud'ān from Abū 'Uthmān an-Nahdī that Salmān al-Fārisī said, 'When the Disciples asked 'Īsā ibn Maryam, may Allah's blessings and peace be upon him, for the Table, he rose and removed his wool garments and put on smooth garments: trousers made of smooth black material and a black cloak. He stood with his feet together, heel to heel and toe to toe, and placed his right hand on his left hand and then bowed his head in humility before Allah. Then he began to weep until the tears ran down his beard and began to drop on his chest. He said: *"'Allah, our Lord, send down a table to us out of heaven to be a feast for us, for the first and last of us, and as a Sign from You. Provide for us! You are the Best of Providers!' Allah said, 'I will send it down you.'"* So a red table descended between two clouds: one above it and one below it, while the people were looking at it. 'Īsā said "O Allah, make it a mercy and not do not make it a trial! My God, I ask You for marvels and You grant them!" It descended in front of 'Īsā covered with a cloth. 'Īsā prostrated as did the Disciples. They experienced a delicious aroma whose like they had never smelt before. 'Īsā said, "Whoever of you worships Allah the most, is bold towards Allah and has the greatest reliance on Allah should uncover this table so we can eat from it and mention the Name of Allah over it and praise Allah for it."

'The Disciples said, "Spirit of Allah. You are the most entitled to do that!" So 'Īsā rose and did *wuḍū'* very thoroughly and prayed excellently and made a lot of supplication. Then he sat at the table and uncovered it. On it was grilled fish without spines which was like smooth fat. Around it was every sort of vegetable except leeks. At the head was salt and vinegar and at its other end there were five loaves, on each of which was a pomegranate. At one end of it were dates and at the other end olives.' Ath-Tha'labī said, 'On one of them were olives, on the second honey, on the third eggs, on the fourth cheese and on the fifth jerky.'

He continued, 'When the Jews heard about that, they came in sorrow and grief, looking at it and seeing a wondrous occurrence. Sham'ūn, the leader of the Disciples said, "Spirit of Allah, is this the food of this world or the food of the Garden?" 'Īsā answered, "If you split up regarding such matters I fear that you will be punished." Sham'ūn said, "By the God of the tribe of Israel, I did not intend evil by asking that!" They said, "Spirit of Allah, if only there could be another sign along with this sign?" 'Īsā said, "Fish! Come to life by the permission of Allah," and the fish moved again with its eyes all white. The Disciples were frightened and 'Īsā said, "Why do I see you asking about something and then when you are given it disliking it? I very much fear you will be punished."'

He continued, 'It descended from the sky and what was on it was not from the food of this world or the food of the Garden, but was something Allah created by His extensive power. He said to it, "Be!" and it was.'

He continued, "Īsā said, "Fish! Return to how you were!" It reverted to being a grilled fish as it had been. The Disciples said, "Spirit of Allah! Be the first to eat from it!" 'Īsā said, "I seek refuge with Allah! Those who sought it and asked for it will eat from it." The Disciples refused to eat from it out of the fear that it might be an example and trial. When 'Īsā saw that, he invited the poor, wretched, sick, and chronically ill, and the lepers, crippled, blind, and ill to it and said, "Eat of the provision of your Lord and the supplication of your Prophet. Praise Allah for it." He added, "It will be enjoyment for you and punishment for others." So they ate of it until it had satisfied seven thousand and three hundred people. Anyone who was ill and ate from it was cured and it was enough for every poor person who ate from it until his death.

'When the people saw that, they crowded to it, and there was no one, young or old, rich or poor, who did not come to eat from it, pressing against one another. When 'Īsā saw that, he made them take it in turns. It would descend one day and not descend another like the She-Camel of Thamūd that would graze one day and drink one day. It descended for forty days at mid-morning and remained until the afternoon.'

Ath-Tha'labī said, 'It remained set up, with people eating from it, until afternoon and then flew upwards. So the people ate from it and then it returned to heaven with the people looking at its shadow until it covered them. At the end of forty days, Allah Almighty revealed to 'Īsā: "'Īsā! Dedicate this table of Mine to the poor rather than the wealthy." So the wealthy objected to that and were hostile towards the poor. They objected and made others object. Allah said, "'Īsā! I will seize them by My Sign." In the morning thirty-three of them had turned into pigs, eating filth and searching out garbage when they were used to eating good food and sleeping on soft beds. When the people saw that, they gathered to 'Īsā, weeping, and the pigs came and knelt at 'Īsā's feet, weeping, their eyes overflowing with tears. 'Īsā recognised them and said, "Are you not so-and-so?" It would indicate with its head, unable to speak. They remained like that for seven days, and some say four days. Then Allah called 'Īsā to take their souls and no one knew where they went. Did the earth swallow them or what happened to them?"

There is some question about this *ḥadīth* and its *isnād* is not sound. Ibn 'Abbās and Abū 'Abd ar-Raḥmān as-Sulamī said that the food on the table was bread and fish. 'Aṭiyyah said, 'They used to consider fish the best of any food.' At-Tha'labī mentioned it. 'Ammār ibn Yāsir and Qatādah said, 'The Table descended from heaven with the fruit of the Garden on it.' Wahb ibn Munabbih said, 'Allah sent down plates of barley and fish.'

At-Tirmidhī mentions in his chapters of *tafsīr* that 'Ammār ibn Yāsir reported that the Messenger of Allah ﷺ said, 'The Table descended from heaven with bread and meat and they were commanded not to act treacherously or store up for the next day, but they acted treacherously and stored up and removed some for the next day and so they were transformed into apes and pigs.' Abū 'Īsā said, 'This *ḥadīth* was related from Abū 'Āṣim and more than one person from Qatādah from Khillās from 'Ammār ibn Yāsir *mawqūf*. We only know it as *marfū'* from al-Ḥasan ibn Qaza'ah. Ḥumayd ibn Mas'adah related something similar from Sufyān ibn Ḥabīb from Sa'īd ibn Abī 'Arūbah and did not make it *marfū'*. This is sounder than the *ḥadīth* of al-Ḥasan ibn Qaza'ah. We do not know of any *marfū' ḥadīth*.

Sa'īd ibn Jubayr said, 'Everything except meat and bread was sent down on the table.' 'Aṭā' said, 'Everything except meat and fish was sent down on it.' Ka'b said, 'The table was sent down from heaven, carried by angels between heaven and earth. On it were all foods except meat.' These three statements differ from the *ḥadīth* of at-Tirmidhī. It is better than them because, even if it is not sound that it is *marfū'*, it is sound that it is *mawqūf* from a great Companion. Allah knows best.

What is definite is that it was sent down and there was edible food on it. Allah has the best knowledge of its specifics.

Abū Nu'aym mentioned from Ka'b that it was sent down a second time to some of the worshippers of the tribe of Israel. Ka'b said, 'Three of the worshippers of the tribe of Israel gathered and met in the wilderness. Each of the men had knowledge of one of the Names of Allah Almighty. One of them said, "Ask me and I will pray to Allah for what you wish." They said, "We ask you to pray to Allah to show us a flowing spring in this place as well as a green meadow and a carpet." He prayed to Allah and there was a running spring, green meadow and a carpet. Then one of them said, "Ask me and I will pray to Allah for what you wish." They said, "We ask you to pray to Allah to feed us some of the fruits of the Garden." He prayed to Allah and dates descended and they ate from them. Whenever they ate one type of them, it was taken up. Then one of them said, "Ask me and I will pray to Allah for what you wish." They said, "We ask you to pray to Allah to send down to us the table that He sent down to 'Īsā." He prayed and it descended and they ate what they needed from it and it ascended.

Point. The table is explained in the *ḥadīth* of Salmān that we mentioned. It was a table-mat (*sufrah*), not a table with legs. A *sufrah* was the kind of table used by the Prophet ﷺ and the Arabs. Abū 'Abdullāh al-Ḥakīm transmitted from Muḥammad ibn Bassār from Mu'ādh ibn Hishām from his father from Yūnus from Qatādah that Anas said, 'The Messenger of Allah ﷺ never ate from a table (*khiwān*) or used saucers nor did he have refined bread.' He said, 'I asked Anas, "What did they eat from?" "Table-mats," was his answer.' Muḥammad ibn Bashshār said that this Yūnus was Abū al-Furāt al-Iskāf. This is a sound firm *ḥadīth* about whose men al-Bukhārī and Muslim agree. At-Tirmidhī transmitted it from Muḥammad ibn Bashshār from Mu'ādh ibn Hishām. He mentioned it and said that it is *gharīb ḥasan*.

Abū 'Abdullāh at-Tirmidhī said that a table (*khiwān*) is something new made by the Persians. The Arabs did not use it but used to eat from table-mats, *sufar*, the singular of which is *sufrah*. They are made from animal skins which can be opened out and folded up. When it is opened out, it is called *sufrah* because when its ties are undone, it opens out and what is on it is disclosed and so it is called *sufrah*. A journey is called *safar* because one takes himself beyond the houses (*safara*) and habitation. Saucers (*sukurrujah*) are dyed vessels, the colours of which are different from their natural coloring. They used to eat *tharīd* (bread and broth) on which pieces of meat were laid. He said, 'Bite meat. It is more delicious and healthy.'

It may be remarked that the word *mā'idah* is mentioned in *ḥadīths*, as in the *ḥadīth* of Ibn 'Abbās who said, 'If lizard meat had been unlawful, it would not have been eaten on the table of the Prophet ﷺ.' Muslim and others transmitted it. 'Ā'ishah said that the Messenger of Allah ﷺ said, 'The angels pray on a man as long as his table is set in place.' Reliable men transmitted it. The response to this is that a *mā'idah* is anything that is stretched out and expanded, like a handkerchief and cloth. It should actually be *māddah* with a double *dāl* but one of the *dāl*s has been made into a *yā'* and so *mā'idah* is said. The verb uses it and so it should be *mamdūdah [in the passive form]*, but it is used in language like an active participle. Similarly they say '*sirr kātim*' (a sealed secret) when it should be *maktūm*, and 'a pleasing life (*rāḍiyyah*)' which should be *marḍiyyah*. It is a linguistic usage when an active participle is used like a passive one. Other examples of this are: an unlucky man where he is *mash'ūm* or *shā'im*, and a covering veil which is *mastūr* or *sātir*.

A *khiwān* is raised above the earth by its legs, a *mā'idah* is what is stretched out and expanded, and a *sufrah* is what is opened out from the inside. That is because it is tied together. Al-Ḥasan said, 'Kings eat from a *khiwān*, Persians eat from a *mandīl* (tablecloth), and Arabs eat from a *sufrah*, and it is the *Sunnah*.' Allah knows best.

وَإِذْ قَالَ ٱللَّهُ يَٰعِيسَى ٱبْنَ مَرْيَمَ ءَأَنتَ قُلْتَ لِلنَّاسِ ٱتَّخِذُونِي وَأُمِّيَ إِلَٰهَيْنِ مِن
دُونِ ٱللَّهِ قَالَ سُبْحَٰنَكَ مَا يَكُونُ لِيٓ أَنْ أَقُولَ مَا لَيْسَ لِي بِحَقٍّ إِن كُنتُ قُلْتُهُۥ فَقَدْ
عَلِمْتَهُۥ تَعْلَمُ مَا فِي نَفْسِي وَلَآ أَعْلَمُ مَا فِي نَفْسِكَ إِنَّكَ أَنتَ عَلَّٰمُ ٱلْغُيُوبِ ١١٦

116 And when Allah says, "Īsā son of Maryam! Did you say to people, "Take me and my mother as gods besides Allah?"' he will say, 'Glory be to You! It is not for me to say what I have no right to say! If I had said it, then You would have known it. You know what is in my self, but I do not know what is in Your Self. You are the Knower of all unseen things.

And when Allah says, "Īsā son of Maryam!

There is disagreement about the time when this is said. Qatādah, Ibn Jurayj and most commentators say that it is said on the Day of Rising. As-Suddī and Quṭrub said that it was said to him when Allah raised him to heaven and the Christians said what they said about him. Their evidence is His words: *'If You punish them, they are Your slaves.'* (5:118) *'Idh'* (when) in Arabic is used for the past.

The first view is sounder and it is indicated by what precedes it: *'On the day Allah gathers the Messengers together'* (5:109) and what comes after it: *'This is the Day when the truthfulness of the truthful will benefit them ...'* (5:119) So *'idh'* can be *'idhā'* as we see in 34:51. [POEMS WITH USAGE] The past tense can refer to the future because it is for the completion of the matter and the manifestation of its proof and so it is as if it had actually occurred. We see this, for example, in 7:44, where *nādā* (call), which is in the past tense, refers to the future. There are numerous examples of that,

The people of interpretation disagree about the meaning of this question, which is not a question asking for information, even if it is in the form of a question, and take two positions regarding it. The first is that Allah asks him about that as a rebuke to those who claimed that about him so that his denial following the question would be even stronger would and make the rebuke and deterrence more severe. The second is that by it Allah meant to inform him that his people had changed things after him and made claims about him that he did not make. If it is asked how that can be said about them since the Christians did not take Maryam as a god, the reply is that since it is integral to their position that she did not bear a mortal, but rather a god, they must say that she must share in the position of her son due to her participation, and that is the logical consequence of what they say.

He will say, 'Glory be to You! It is not for me to say what I have no right to say!

At-Tirmidhī transmitted from Abū Hurayrah, "'Īsā learned his argument and Allah taught it to him in His words: *"And when Allah says, "'Īsā son of Maryam!..."""* Abū Hurayrah reported that the Prophet ﷺ said, 'Allah taught him,' and quoted the entire *āyah*. Abū 'Īsā said that this is a *ḥasan* sound *ḥadīth*.

There are two reasons for glorification preceding the statement. One is that by it 'Īsā frees himself from what was ascribed to him. The second is humbleness before Allah's Might and fear of His Power. It is said that when Allah Almighty says to 'Īsā: *'Did you say to people, "Take me and my mother as gods besides Allah?"'* he will tremble at those words until he hears the sound of his own bones shaking. He will say: *'Glory be to You! It is not for me to say what I have no right to say!'* meaning 'I would not claim anything I am not entitled to, since I am a vassal and not a Lord, a worshipper and not worshipped.' Then he said: *'If I had said it, then You would have known it,'* referring that back to Allah's knowledge. Allah knows that he did not say it but He asked him about it to rebuke those who took 'Īsā as a god.

Then he said, *'You know what is in my self but I do not know what is in Your Self,'* in other words, 'You know what is hidden in me but I do not know what is in Your

Unseen.' It is said that the meaning is: 'You know what I know and I do not know what You know.' It is said that it means: 'You know what I conceal and I do not know what You conceal.' It is also said to mean, 'You know what I want and I do not know what You want.' And: 'You know my secret and I do not know Your secret' because the locus of the secret is the self. It is said that it means: 'You know what I did in this world and I do not know what You will do in the Next Abode.'

The sense of these statements is similar, meaning: 'You know my secret and what is inside my consciousness which You created, but I do not know what You alone possess of Your Unseen and knowledge.' *'You are the Knower of all unseen things'* of what was and what will be and what will not be and what is.

مَا قُلْتُ لَهُمْ إِلَّا مَا أَمَرْتَنِي بِهِۦٓ أَنِ ٱعْبُدُوا۟ ٱللَّهَ رَبِّى وَرَبَّكُمْ ۚ وَكُنتُ عَلَيْهِمْ
شَهِيدًا مَّا دُمْتُ فِيهِمْ ۖ فَلَمَّا تَوَفَّيْتَنِى كُنتَ أَنتَ ٱلرَّقِيبَ عَلَيْهِمْ ۚ وَأَنتَ عَلَىٰ
كُلِّ شَىْءٍ شَهِيدٌ ﴿١١٧﴾

117 I said to them nothing but what You ordered me to say: "Worship Allah, my Lord and your Lord." I was a witness against them as long as I remained among them, but when You took me back to You, You were the One watching over them. You are Witness of all things.

'I said to them nothing but what You ordered me to say' in this world regarding *tawḥīd.* The particle *'an'* [before 'Worship'] has no place in syntax, but is explanatory, as we also see in 38:6. It can also be in the accusative, meaning: 'I only told them to worship Allah.' It can be in the position of the genitive, meaning 'that they should worship Allah,' and it is better to have a *ḍammah* on the *nūn* because is it considered heavy to have a *kasrah* followed by a *ḍammah* although a *kasrah* is permitted on the basis of two silent letters meeting.

'I was a witness against them', I acted upon what I instructed them to do, and *mā* is in the position of the accusative, meaning 'during the time I remained among them.'

but when You took me back to You, You were the One watching over them.

It is said that this indicates that Allah Almighty made him die before He took him up, but that has no basis because the reports support one another that He raised him up and that he is alive in heaven and will descend and kill the Dajjāl, as will be explained. The meaning is: 'When You raised me to heaven.'

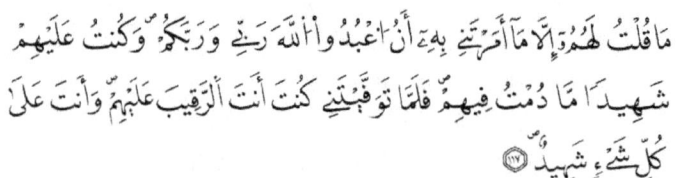

Al-Ḥasan said, "'*Wafā* (demise)" is used in three ways in the Qur'ān: there is the demise of actual death, as when Allah says: *'Allah takes back people's selves when their death arrives'* (39:42), in other words when their lifespan comes to end. There is also the demise of sleep. Allah says: *'It is He who takes you back to Himself at night'* (6:60), meaning when He makes you sleep. The third is the demise of raising up. Allah says: "Īsā, *I will take you back to myself.'* (3:55).

Here the repetition in *'You were'* (*kunta anta*) is for emphasis. *Ar-Raqīb* is the Watcher. It means 'the Protector of them, Knower of them, and the one who witnesses their actions.' Its root is *muraqābah* (supervision). *Marqābah* (watchtower) comes from the same root because it is the place for a watcher from a high place.

You are Witness of all things.

'You witnessed my words and their words.' It is said, 'those who obeyed and disobeyed.' Muslim transmitted from Ibn 'Abbās: 'The Messenger of Allah stood among us admonishing us and said, "O people! You will be gathered to Allah Almighty barefoot, naked and uncircumcised. *'As We originated the first creation, so We will regenerate it. It a promise binding on Us. That is what We will do.'* (21:103) The first of creatures to be clothed on the Day of Rising will be Ibrāhīm. Men of my community will come and will be taken to the left. I will say, 'O Lord, my Companions!' and it will be said, 'You do not know what innovations they introduced after you.' I will say the same as the righteous slave ('Īsā) said: *'I was a witness against them as long as I remained among them, but when You took me back to You, You were the One watching over them. You are Witness of all things. If You punish them, they are Your slaves. If you forgive them, You are the Almighty, the All-Wise.'* I will be told, 'They never stopped turning back on their heels from the time you left them.'"'

إِن تُعَذِّبْهُمْ فَإِنَّهُمْ عِبَادُكَ وَإِن تَغْفِرْ لَهُمْ فَإِنَّكَ أَنتَ الْعَزِيزُ الْحَكِيمُ ﴿١١٨﴾

118 If You punish them, they are Your slaves. If you forgive them, You are the Almighty, the All-Wise.'

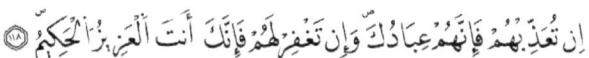

An-Nasā'ī related that Abū Dharr said, 'The Messenger of Allah stood reciting a certain *āyah* all through the night until morning. The *āyah* was: "*If You punish them, they are Your slaves. If you forgive them…*"' There is disagreement about the interpretation of this *āyah*. It is said that it expresses compassion and kindness to them as a master is kind to his slave. That is why he did not say, 'If they disobey You.' It is said that it indicates submission to His command and seeking refuge from His punishment when he knows that Allah will not forgive unbelievers. It is said that the pronoun '*them*' in '*punish them*' refers to those of them who die as unbelievers and the '*them*' in '*forgive them*' refers to those who of them who repent before death. This is good.

As for those who say that 'Īsā did not know that unbelievers would not be forgiven, that is an audacious statement against the Book of Allah Almighty because statements from Allah cannot be abrogated. It is said that 'Īsā knew that they had introduced disobedience and had done after him things that Allah had not commanded them to do, although they remained on the basic substance of his *dīn* and so he said, 'If You forgive the disobedience they introduced after me...'

You are the Almighty, the All-Wise.

He said this and did not say, 'You are the Ever-Forgiving, the Most Merciful', as the story demands acceptance of Allah's command and entrusting oneself to His judgment. If he had said, 'You are the Ever-Forgiving, Most Merciful,' it might make one think that it is a supplication for forgiveness for those who died while committing *shirk*, and that is impossible. It implies: 'If you make them remain in their disbelief until they die and punish them, they are Your slaves. If You guide them to Your *tawḥīd* and obedience, and forgive them, You are the Almighty and none can prevent what You will, and the Wise in what You do. You misguide whomever You wish and guide whomever You wish.'

One group read 'You are the Ever-Forgiving, Most Merciful,' but that is not part of the Qur'anic text. Qāḍī 'Iyāḍ mentioned that in *ash-Shifā'*. Abū Bakr al-Anbari said, 'It is an attack on the Qur'ān to say that: "*You are the Almighty, the All-Wise*" is not in keeping with His words: "*If You forgive them*" because that which is in keeping with forgiveness is "You are the Ever-Forgiving, Most Merciful."' The response to those people is that only what Allah revealed is conceivable. If it is taken in the context of what is being referred to, the meaning is weakened. If one restricts 'the Ever-Forgiving, Most Merciful' to the second conditional phrase ['If You forgive them'] mentioned in the *āyah*, then there is no connection to the first conditional phrase ['If You punish them]. It can only be as Allah revealed it, and the recitation on which the Muslims agree makes it clear that it is connected to both of the two conditional phrases, first and second. It can be summarised as: 'If you punish them, then You are Almighty, All-Wise. If You forgive them, You are Almighty, All-Wise in respect of both punishment and forgiveness.' So the Almighty, All-Wise is connected to both as it is non-specific. It combines both conditions. That is not the case with 'the Ever-Forgiving, Most Merciful' because it does not bear the general meaning which 'Almighty, All-Wise' bears, which attests to the greatness and justice of Allah and His praise throughout the entire *āyah*. These two Divine Names are more suitable and firmer in meaning in the *āyah* than other Names.

Muslim transmitted from 'Abdullāh ibn 'Amr ibn al-'Āṣ that the Prophet ﷺ recited Allah's words in *Sura Ibrāhīm*: *'My Lord! They have misguided many of mankind. If anyone follows me, he is with me but if anyone disobeys me, You are Ever-Forgiving, Most Merciful'* (14:36). 'Īsā said: *'If you punish them, they are Your slaves. If You forgive them, You are the Almighty, All-Wise.'* He raised his hands and said, 'O Allah, my community!' and wept. Allah said, 'Jibrīl, go to Muḥammad – and your Lord knows better – and ask him, "What has made you weep?"' So Jibrīl went to him and the Messenger of Allah ﷺ told him what he had said – and Allah knows better. Allah said, 'Jibrīl, go to Muḥammad and tell him, "We will please you regarding your Community and not upset you."'

Some say that there is a change in the normal order here, and the meaning is: 'If you punish them, You are the Almighty, All-Wise, and if You forgive them, they are Your slaves.' Success is by Allah.

قَالَ ٱللَّهُ هَٰذَا يَوْمُ يَنفَعُ ٱلصَّٰدِقِينَ صِدْقُهُمْ لَهُمْ جَنَّٰتٌ تَجْرِى مِن تَحْتِهَا ٱلْأَنْهَٰرُ
خَٰلِدِينَ فِيهَآ أَبَدًا رَّضِىَ ٱللَّهُ عَنْهُمْ وَرَضُوا۟ عَنْهُ ذَٰلِكَ ٱلْفَوْزُ ٱلْعَظِيمُ ١١٩

119 Allah will say, 'This is the Day when the sincerity of the sincere will benefit them. They will have Gardens with rivers flowing under them, remaining in them timelessly, for ever and ever. Allah is pleased with them and they are pleased with Him. That is the Great Victory.'

'Allah will say, "This is the Day when the sincerity of the sincere will benefit them,"' referring to their sincerity in this world. As for the Next World, sincerity will not be of any benefit in it. Their sincerity in this world can mean their sincerity in acting for Allah. It is possible that it is their not lying about Him and His Messengers. Sincerity will benefit them on that particular Day, even if it is of benefit on every other day, because of the reward for it. It is said that what is meant is their sincerity in the Next World. That is about the testimony that their Prophets have conveyed the Message and about their bearing witness against themselves regarding their actions. It can be that the aspect of benefit on it is that they are protected from punishment by not concealing testimony, and so they

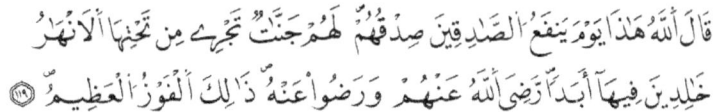

are forgiven because of their affirmation of their Prophets and admission against themselves, and Allah knows best.

Nāfi' and Ibn Muḥayṣin recite the noun '*Day*' in the accusative (*yawma*) while the rest have it in the nominative (*yawmu*), which is the clear reading based on subject and predicate. As for the reading of Nāfi' and Ibn Muḥayṣin in the accusative, Ibrāhīm ibn Ḥumayd related from Muḥammad ibn Yazīd that this reading is not permitted grammatically. Ibrāhīm ibn as-Sārī said, 'It is permitted with the meaning that Allah said this to 'Īsā the son of Maryam on the Day when the sincerity of the sincere will benefit them.' It is said that it implies that Allah said that these things will be of benefit on the Day of Rising. Al-Kisā'ī and al-Farrā' said that the noun '*Day*' here is based on the accusative because it is ascribed to other than a noun as you might say, 'It passed on that day.' Al-Kisā'ī quoted:

At a time when I criticised gray hair for youthful passion
I said, 'Is it then sounder when gray hair curbs it.

Az-Zajjāj said, 'The Basrans do not permit what the two of them said about ascribing an adverb to a verb in the present tense. If it is ascribed to the past tense, it is good as we saw in the above verse. It is permitted to ascribe verbs to adverbs of time because the verb has the meaning of a verbal noun.' It is said that it is permitted for it to be an accusative adverb and for it to be the predicate of an inceptive which is '*This*' because it indicates something temporal, and adverbs of time report about events. You say, 'The fighting of today' and 'the emerging of the Hour', and the sentence is in the position of the accusative as has been said.

It is said that it is permitted for the word '*This*' to be in the nominative by the inceptive, with '*Day*' as the predicate of the inceptive with the regent elided. It can imply: 'Allah said that what we related will occur on the Day when the sincerity of the sincere will benefit them.' There is a third reading which has '*yawmun*' with *tanwīn* making it indefinite. There is an elision in the words which implies 'in it' as we see in 2:48 and 2:123. This is the reading of al-A'mash.

They will have Gardens with rivers flowing under them,

Rivers will flow under their rooms and the trees as already mentioned (2:25). Then Allah makes their reward clear and that He is pleased with them with such pleasure that it will never be followed by anger ever again. *'They are pleased with Him'* and with the reward which He bestowed on them. *'That is the Great Victory."* Its good is abundant and copious and the position of the one who gains it is exalted and his honour great.

لِلَّهِ مُلْكُ السَّمَاوَاتِ وَالْأَرْضِ وَمَا فِيهِنَّ وَهُوَ عَلَىٰ كُلِّ شَيْءٍ قَدِيرٌ ١٢٠

120 The kingdom of the heavens and the earth and everything in them belongs to Allah. He has power over all things.

This *āyah* puts paid to the claim that the Christians made that 'Īsā is a god. Allah states that the kingdom of the heavens and the earth is His alone and does not belong to 'Īsā to the exclusion of other creatures. It is possible that it means: 'the One who has the kingdom of the heavens and the earth will give the Gardens already mentioned to those of His slaves who obey Him.' May Allah make us among them by His grace and generosity!

This is the end of *Sūrat al-Mā'idah.*

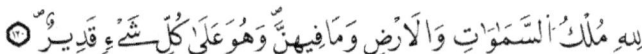

Table of Contents for *Āyats*

1 You who believe, fulfil your contracts... 2
2 You who believe! do not profane the sacred rites of Allah... 7
3 Unlawful for you are carrion, blood and pork, and ... 18
4 They will ask you what is lawful for them. Say: 'All good things... 34
5 Today all good things have been made lawful for you... 44
6 You who believe, when you get up to pray, wash your faces... 48
7 Remember Allah's blessing to you and the covenant He made with you... 75
8-10 You who believe, show integrity for the sake of Allah... 76
11 You who believe! remember Allah's blessing to you ... 77
12 Allah made a covenant with the tribe of Israel... 78
13 But because of their breaking of their covenant, We have cursed them... 81
14-16 We also made a covenant with those who say, 'We are Christians'... 84
17 Those who say, 'Allah is the Messiah, son of Maryam,' have rejected... 86
18 The Jews and Christians say, 'We are Allah's children and... 87
19 People of the Book! Our Messenger has come to you... 89
20-26 Remember when Mūsā said to his people, 'My people! remember... 91
27 Recite to them the true report of Ādam's two sons... 101
28-29 'Even if you do raise your hand against me to kill me, I am not... 104
30 So his lower self persuaded him to kill his brother, and he killed him... 106
31 Then Allah sent a crow which scratched at the earth to show him... 109
32 on account of that. So We decreed for the tribe of Israel... 112
33-34 The reprisal against those who wage war on Allah and... 114
35-36 You who believe! have *taqwā* of Allah... 124
37 They will want to get out of the Fire but they will not be able to... 125
38-39 As for thieves, both male and female, cut off their hands... 126
40 Do you not know that the kingdom of the heavens and earth belongs... 141
41 O Messenger! do not be grieved by those who rush headlong... 141
42 They are people who listen to lies and consume ill-gotten gains... 148
43 How can they make you their judge when they have the Torah... 153
44 We sent down the Torah containing guidance and light... 154
45 We prescribed for them in it: a life for a life, an eye for an eye... 157
46-47 And We sent 'Īsā son of Maryam following in their footsteps... 173

48 And We have sent down the Book to you with truth… 174
49 Judge between them by what Allah has sent down and do not follow… 176
50 Do they then seek the judgment of the Time of Ignorance?… 178
51 You who believe! do not take the Jews and Christians as your friends… 180
52-53 Yet you see those with sickness in their hearts rushing to them… 181
54 You who believe! if any of you renounce your *dīn*, Allah will bring… 183
55 Your friend is only Allah and His Messenger and those who believe… 184
56 As for those who make Allah their friend, and His Messenger… 186
57 You who believe! do not take as friends any of those given the Book… 186
58 When you call to the prayer they make a mockery and a game of it… 187
59-60 Say: 'People of the Book! do you resent us for any other reason… 195
61-63 When they come to you, they say, 'We believe.' But… 198
64 The Jews say, 'Allah's hand is chained.' Their hands are chained… 199
65-66 If only the People of the Book had believed and been godfearing… 203
67 O Messenger! transmit what has been sent down to you… 204
68 Say: 'People of the Book! you have nothing to stand on until… 206
69 Those who believe and those who are Jews and the Sabaeans… 207
70 We made a covenant with the tribe of Israel… 208
71 They thought there would be no *fitnah*. They were blind and deaf… 209
72 Those who say that the Messiah, son of Maryam, is Allah… 210
73-74 Those who say that Allah is the third of three are unbelievers… 210
75 The Messiah, the son of Maryam, was only a Messenger… 211
76 Say: 'Do you worship, besides Allah, something which has no power… 212
77 Say: 'People of the Book! do not go to extremes in your *dīn*… 213
78 Those among the tribe of Israel who disbelieved were cursed… 213
79 They would not restrain one another from any of the wrong things… 214
80 You see many of them taking those who disbelieve as their friends… 215
81 If they had believed in Allah and the Prophet… 215
82 You will find that the people most hostile to those who believe… 216
83 When they listen to what has been sent down to the Messenger… 219
84 How could we not believe in Allah, and the truth that has come to us… 220
85-86 Allah will reward them for what they say with Gardens… 220
87 You who believe! do not make unlawful the good things… 221
88 Eat the lawful and good things Allah has provided for you… 224
89 Allah does not take you to task for your inadvertent oaths… 225
90-92 You who believe! wine and gambling, stone altars and… 244
93 Those who believe and do right actions are not to blame… 251
94 You who believe! Allah will test you with game animals… 257
95 You who believe! do not kill game while you are in *iḥrām*… 258

96 Anything you catch in the sea is lawful for you, and all food from it… 273
97 Allah has made the Ka‘bah, the Sacred House, a special institution… 280
98 Know that Allah is fierce in retribution and… 282
99 The Messenger is only responsible for transmission… 282
100 Say: ‘Bad things and good things are not the same… 283
101-2 You who believe! do not ask about matters… 285
103 Allah did not institute any such things as *baḥīrah* or *sā’ibah*… 290
104 When they are told, ‘Come to what Allah has sent down… 296
105 You who believe! you are only responsible for yourselves… 297
106-8 You who believe! when one of you is near to death… 300
109 On the day Allah gathers the Messengers together… 313
110 Remember when Allah said, “Īsā, son of Maryam, remember… 315
111 and when I inspired the Disciples to believe in Me and… 316
112 And when the Disciples said, “Īsā son of Maryam!… 317
113 They said, ‘We want to eat from it and for our hearts to be at peace… 319
114 ‘Īsā son of Maryam said, ‘Allah, our Lord, send down a table… 320
115 Allah said, ‘I will send it down to you but if anyone among you… 321
116 And when Allah says, “Īsā son of Maryam! Did you say to people… 326
117 I said to them nothing but what You ordered me to say… 328
118 If You punish them, they are Your slaves. If you forgive them… 329
119 Allah will say, ‘This is the Day when the sincerity of the sincere… 331
120 The kingdom of the heavens and the earth… 333

Glossary

Abū al-'Abbās: Muḥammad ibn Yazīd al-Mubarrad, a leading philologist and grammarian of the school of Basra. He died in Baghdad in 285/898. He wrote many books, including *al-Kāmil* and *al-Kitāb*.
Abū Ḥātim: Sahl ibn Muḥammad al-Jushanī as-Sijistānī, d. 255/869, a prominent Basran philologist.
Abū Ḥaywah: Shurayḥ ibn Yazīd al-Ḥaḍramī, the Qur'an reciter of Syria from Homs. He has a *shādhdh* reading, and died in 203/818.
Abū Isḥāq: Ibrāhīm ibn as-Sarī az-Zajjāj, author of *I'rab al-Qur'ān*.
Abū Ja'far: aṭ-Ṭabarī, historian.
Abū 'Ubayd: al-Qāsim ibn Sallām al-Harawī or al-Baghdādī, d. 224/838.
Abū 'Ubaydah: Ma'mar ibn al-Muthanna at-Taymī, d. 209/824, author of *Majāz al-Qur'ān*, the first book on the linguistic analysis of the Qur'an.
Al-Aḍbā': a very fast camel belonging to the Prophet ﷺ.
'Ād: an ancient people in southern Arabia to whom the Prophet Hūd was sent.
adhān: the call to prayer.
Al-Akhfash: Abū al-Khaṭṭāb 'Abd al-Ḥamīd ibn 'Abd al-Majīd al-Akhfash al-Kabīr, a grammarian in Basra, one of the first to study Arabic poetry as well as contributing to philology and lexicography and recording Bedouin vocabulary. He revised *al-Kitāb*, the first book on Arabic grammar, written by his student Sībawayh. He was a client of the Qays tribe and died in 177/793.
Amīr al-Mu'minīn: 'the Commander of the Believers', the caliph.
Anṣār: the "Helpers", the people of Madīnah who welcomed and aided the Prophet ﷺ.
'Aqabah: lit. the steep slope, a pass to the north of Makkah, just off the caravan route to Madīnah, where the Prophet ﷺ met with the first Muslims from Yathrīb (Madīnah) in two successive years. On the first occasion, they pledged to follow the Messenger ﷺ, and in the second or Great Pledge of 'Aqabah, to defend him and his Companions as they would their own wives and children.

'Arafah: a plain 15 miles to the east of Makkah. One of the essential rites of the *ḥajj* is to stand on 'Arafah on the 9th of Dhu-l-Ḥijjah.
'arīf: an overseer, a particular office of authority.
Ash'arites: from a South Arabian tribe descended from al-Ash'ar.
Ashja': a sub-tribe of Ghaṭafān.
Al-Aṣma'ī: Abū Sa'īd ibn 'Abd al-Malik ibn Qurayb, 122/740-213/820, an early philologist and grammarian of Basra. He also wrote on genealogy, natural science and zoology and was a scholar of Arabic poetry in the court of Hārūn ar-Rashīd. He spent a great deal of time recording the language of desert Bedouins.
'Aṣr: the mid-afternoon prayer.
āyah: a verse of the Qur'an.
Ayyūb: the Prophet Job.
bādi'ah: an injury that penetrates the skin.
Badr: a place near the coast, about 95 miles to the south of Madīnah where, in 2 AH in the first battle fought by the newly established Muslim community, the 313 outnumbered Muslims led by the Messenger of Allah overwhelmingly defeated 1000 Makkan idolaters.
Baghlī dirham: a dirham minted by the assay-master, Ra's Baghl at the command of 'Umar ibn al-Khaṭṭāb based on the Persian drahm. It weighed twenty *qirāṭ*s. (There are other theories of the source of the name as well.)
baḥīrah: in the Jāhiliyyah period, a female camel which had given birth five times, the last being a male. Its ears were slit and it was let free to graze.
Bajīlah: a South Arabian tribe.
Banū: lit. sons, meaning a tribe or clan.
basmalah: the expression 'In the name of Allah, the All-Merciful, the Most Merciful'.
dāmighah: a head wound which penetrates the skull and penetrates the membrane of the brain.
dāmiyyah: a wound which bleeds.
ḍammah: the Arabic vowel 'u'.
Dāwūd: the Prophet David.
Dāwūdiyya: another name for the Ẓāhiriyyah school of fiqh, taken from the name of its founder, Dāwūd ibn Khalaf.
Dhāt ar-Riqā': an expedition to Najd led by the Prophet ﷺ. They had to bandage their feet with rags (*riqā'*).
dhimmah: obligation or contract, in particular a treaty of protection for non-Muslims living under Muslim governance.
dhimmī: a non-Muslim living under the protection of Muslim rule.

Dhu-l-Ḥijjah: the twelfth month of the Muslim calendar, the month of the *ḥajj*.

Dhu-l-Qa'dah: the eleventh month of the Muslim calendar.

dīn: the life-transaction, lit. the debt between two parties, in this usage between the Creator and created.

Fadak: a small, rich oasis in the north of the Hijaz near Khaybar.

Fajr: the dawn prayer.

faqīh: pl. *fuqahā'*, a man learned in knowledge of *fiqh* who by virtue of his knowledge can give a legal judgment.

farḍ: an obligatory act of worship or practice of the *dīn* as defined by the Sharī'ah.

Al-Farrā': Abū Zakariyyā Yaḥyā ibn Ziyād, ca. 144/761- 207/882, a noted grammarian of Kufa. Al-Farrā' means 'he who skins/scrutinises language'. He wrote *Majāz al-Qur'an*.

fāsiq: someone not meeting the legal requirements of righteousness. The evidence of such a person is inadmissible in the court.

fatḥah: the Arabic vowel 'a'.

Fātiḥah: "the Opener", the first *sūrah* of the Qur'an.

fatwā: an authoritative statement on a point of law.

fitnah: civil strife, sedition, schism, trial, temptation, also *shirk*.

Fuḍūl alliance: an alliance formed by various Makkans before Islam to establish fair commercial dealing. The Prophet Muḥammad ﷺ took part in it.

fuqahā': plural of *faqīh*.

Furqān: discrimination, that which separates truth from falsehood, one of the names of the Qur'an.

ghusl: major ablution of the whole body with water. It is required to regain purity after menstruation, lochia and sexual intercourse.

Hābīl: Abel.

ḥadd: Allah's boundary limits for the lawful and unlawful. The *ḥadd* punishments are specific fixed penalties laid down by Allah for specified crimes.

hadīth: reported speech of the Prophet ﷺ.

ḥāfiẓ: pl. *ḥuffāẓ*, someone who has memorised the Qur'an.

ḥajj: the annual pilgrimage to Makkah which is one of the five pillars of Islam.

ḥāl: In Arabic grammar, a circumstantial adverb in the accusative case which describes something happening at the same time as the action or event mentioned in the main clause.

ḥalāl: lawful in the Sharī'ah.
ḥām: a male camel which had fathered ten females in succession and was then freed from working.
hamzah: the character in Arabic which designates a glottal stop.
Ḥanīfiyyah: the religion of the Prophet Ibrāhīm, the primordial religion of *tawḥīd* and sincerity to Allah.
harām: unlawful in the Sharī'ah.
Ḥaram: Sacred Precinct, a protected area in which certain behaviour is forbidden and other behaviour necessary. The area around the Ka'bah in Makkah is a Ḥaram, and the area around the Prophet's Mosque in Madīnah is a Ḥaram. They are referred to together as al-Ḥaramayn, 'the two Ḥarams'.
ḥarbī: a belligerent.
ḥārishah: a head wound that scratches the skin slightly.
al-Ḥarrah: a stony tract of black volcanic rock east of Madīnah where a terrible battle took place in 63 AH (26 August 683) between the forces of Yazīd I and 'Abdullāh ibn az-Zubayr which ended in Madīnah being sacked and plundered.
Hārūn: the Prophet Aaron, the brother of Mūsā.
ḥasan: good, excellent, often used to describe a *ḥadīth* which is reliable, but which is not as well authenticated as one which is *ṣaḥīḥ*.
Hāshim: the Banu Hāshim is a clan of the Quraysh tribe of which the Prophet ﷺ was a member, the name coming from his great-grandfather, Hāshim ibn 'Abd Manāf.
Ḥashwiyyah: a sect who took the verses of the Qur'an literally and hence became anthropomorphists. They also espoused other innovations.
hāshimah: a blow to the head that fractures the skull.
Hawāzin: one of the large Arab tribes in the Hijaz who were part of the Qays tribal grouping.
Ḥawwā': Eve, the first woman.
Hijaz: the region along the western seaboard of Arabia in which Makkah, Madīnah, Jidda and Ta'if are situated.
al-Ḥijr: the unroofed portion of the Ka'bah which at present is in the form of a semi-circular compound towards the north of the Ka'bah.
Hijrah: emigration in the way of Allah. Islamic dating begins with the Hijrah of the Prophet Muḥammad ﷺ from Makkah to Madīnah in 622 AD.
Hubal: pre-Islamic idol worshipped by Quraysh at the Ka'bah.
Hūd: the Prophet sent to the people of 'Ād.

Ḥudaybīyah: a well-known place ten miles from Makkah on the way to Jiddah where the Homage of ar-Riḍwān took place.
ḥudūd: plural of *ḥadd.*
Iblīs: the personal name of the Devil. He is also called Shayṭān or the 'enemy of Allah'.
Ibrāhīm: the Prophet Abraham.
'Īd: a festival, either the festival at the end of Ramadan or at the time of the Hajj.
iḍāfah: a possessive construction in Arabic in which the first noun is indefinite and the second usually definite. It is used to indicate possession. The first word is called '*muḍāf*' and the second is '*muḍāf ilayhi*'.
idghām: In Qur'an recitation, to assimilate one letter into another. Thus *an-ya'bud* becomes *ay-ya'bud*, *qad tabayyan* becomes *qattabayyan*, etc.
Idrīs: a Prophet, possibly Enoch.
iḥrām: the conditions of clothing and behaviour adopted by someone on *ḥajj* or *'umrah.*
ijtihād: to exercise personal judgment in legal matters.
Ilyās: also Ilyāsīn, the Prophet Elijah or Elias.
imālah: a vowel shift in Arabic where an open vowel rises, *ā* towards *ī*, and short *a* towards *i*.
imam: Muslim religious or political leader; leader of Muslim congregational worship.
īmān: belief, faith.
iqāmah: the call which announces that the obligatory prayer is about to begin.
'Īsā: the Prophet Jesus.
'Ishā': the obligatory evening prayer.
Isḥāq: the Prophet Isaac.
Ismā'īl: the Prophet Ishmael.
Isrāfīl: the archangel who will blow the Trumpet which announces the end of the world.
isnād: a *hadīth*'s chain of transmission from individual to individual.
i'tikāf: seclusion, while fasting, in a mosque, particularly in the last ten days of Ramadan.
Jacobites: in Arabic, the Ya'qūbiyyah, the Monophysite Syrian Christian church founded by Jacob Baradeus. They rejected the Council of Chalcedon and espoused the doctrine of miaphysitism, the belief that Christ is a union of divine and human without separation or mixture.
Jadhīmah: an Arab tribe that was a sub-tribe of the 'Abd al-Qays tribe.

Jahannam: Hell.
Jāhiliyyah: the Time of Ignorance before the coming of Islam.
jā'ifah: a penetrative wound.
janābah: major ritual impurity requiring a *ghusl*: brought about by sexual intercourse, sexual discharge, menstruation, childbirth.
Jawāthā: a mosque in al-Kilabiya, north east of Hofuf, believed to be the first mosque built in eastern Arabia in 7 AH by the Banū 'Abd al-Qays.
Jibrīl: the angel Gabriel.
jihād: struggle, particularly fighting in the way of Allah to establish Islam.
jinn: inhabitants of the heavens and the earth made of smokeless fire who are usually invisible.
jizyah: a protection tax payable by non-Muslims living under Muslim rule as a tribute to the Muslim ruler.
Jumāda-l-Ākhir: the sixth month of the Muslim calendar.
Jumāda-l-Ulā: the fifth month of the Muslim calendar.
Jumu'ah: the day of gathering, Friday, and particularly the Jumu'ah prayer which is performed instead of *Ẓuhr* by those who attend it.
Ka'bah: the cube-shaped building at the centre of the Ḥaram in Makkah, originally built by the Prophet Ibrāhīm. Also known as the House of Allah.
kasrah: the Arabic vowel *i*.
Al-Khalīl: Abū 'Abd ar-Raḥmān ibn 'Amt al-Farāhidī, 110/718-170/786, born in Oman, a leading grammarian, philologist and lexicographer of Basra. He compiled the first Arabic dictionary: *Kitāb al-'Ayn*, and was the first to codify the metres of Arabic poetry. His students included Sībawayh and al-Aṣma'ī.
Khārijites: the earliest sect, who separated themselves from the body of the Muslims and declared war on all those who disagreed with them, stating that a wrong action turns a Muslim into an unbeliever.
Khaybar: Jewish colony to the north of Madina which was laid siege to and captured by the Muslims in the seventh year after the Hijra because of the Jews' continual treachery.
khums: the fifth taken from the booty which is given to the ruler for distribution.
khuṭbah: a speech, and in particular a standing speech given by the imam before the Jumu'ah prayer and after the two 'Īd prayers.
Kindah: a tribal group of southern Arabs that originated from the area west of Hadramawt, and spread into central and northern Arabia at the end of the 5th century CE as a kingdom that consisted of a loose confederacy.

After a devastating defeat by the Lakhmid al-Harith, the kingdom split into Asad, Taghlib, Qays and Kinānah.

Kitābī: Someone who is one of the People of the Book, i.e. a Jew or Christian.

kufr: disbelief, to cover up the truth, to reject Allah and refuse to believe that Muhammad ﷺ is His Messenger.

kunyah: a respectful but intimate way of addressing someone as "the father of so-and-so" or "the mother of so-and-so."

lahd: a form of grave in which a niche is dug on the side of the grave facing qiblah into which the deceased is placed.

lāhūt: Godhood, divine nature.

Lūṭ: the Prophet Lot.

maddah: prolongation. There are three letters which are subject to prolongation in recitation of the Qur'an: *alif*, *wāw* and *yā'*.

Madyan: Midian, the people to whom the Prophet Shu'ayb was sent.

Maghrib: the sunset prayer; also the western part of Muslim lands. Today it means Morocco.

ma'mūnah: a head wound exposing the cerebral membrane.

marfū': 'elevated' , a narration from the Prophet ﷺ mentioned by a Companion, e.g. 'The Messenger of Allah ﷺ said...'

Maryam: Mary, the mother of 'Īsā.

Masjid al-Ḥarām: the great mosque in Makkah.

mawla: a person with whom a tie of *walā'* has been established, usually by having been a slave and then set free.

mawqūf: 'stopped', a narration from a Companion without mentioning the Prophet ﷺ.

Melkites: or Melchites, an early Christian church that accepted the Council of Chalcedon.

Mīkā'īl: the archangel Michael.

mithqāl (plural *mathāqīl*): '*miskal*', the weight of one dinar, the equivalent of 72 grains of barley (equals 4.4 grams).

Monophysites: a branch of Christians who rejected the Council of Chalcedon. They held that Christ had only a single inseparable nature that was either divine or a synthesis of the divine and human in which the human was subordinate to the divine. It was the antithesis of Nestorianism.

mu'adhdhin: someone who calls the *adhan* or call to prayer.

mudd: a measure of volume, approximately a double-handed scoop.

mūḍiḥah: a wound which exposes the bone.

Muhājirūn: Companions of the Messenger of Allah ﷺ who accepted Islam in Makkah and made hijrah to Madīnah.
muḥārib: a brigand, someone involved in *ḥirābah*.
Muḥarram: the first month of the Muslim lunar year.
muḥṣan (or *muḥṣin*): a person who is or has been previously legally married.
munaqqilah: a head wound in which the bone is displaced and causes part of the bone to be removed.
munkar: "denounced", a narration reported by a weak reporter which goes against another authentic *hadīth*.
Al-Muraysī': a battle between the Prophet and the Banu al-Muṣṭaliq in 6/627.
mursal: a *hadīth* where a man in the generation after the Companions quotes directly from the Prophet ﷺ without mentioning the Companion from whom he got it.
Mūsā: the Prophet Moses.
muṣḥaf: a physical copy of the Qur'an.
musnad: a collection of *hadīths* arranged according to the first authority in its *isnād*; also a *hadīth* which can be traced back through an unbroken *isnād* to the Prophet ﷺ.
mutalāḥimah: a wound which penetrates the skin but does not go as deep as a *samḥāq*.
Mu'tazilite: someone who adheres to the school of the Mu'tazilah which is rationalist in its approach to existence. Originally they held that anyone who commits a sin is neither a believer nor an unbeliever. They also held the Qur'an to be created.
An-Naḍīr: a Jewish tribe in Madīnah.
An-Naḥḥās: Abū Ja'far Aḥmad ibn Muḥammad an-Naḥḥās, d. 338/949, an Egyptian scholar of grammar and *tafsīr* in the Abbasid period.
Najd: the region around Riyadh in Arabia.
nafs: the lower self.
Najrān: a region in the southern Arabian peninsula which borders Yemen.
nāsūt: human nature.
Nestorian: a branch of Christianity which is the antithesis of Monophysitism and holds that Jesus existed as two persons: a divine one and a human one. It was developed by Nestorius.
Nūḥ: the Prophet Noah.
People of the Book: principally the Jews and Christians whose religions are based on the Divine Books revealed to Mūsā and 'Īsā; a term also used

to refer to any other group who claim to be following Divine Revelation revealed prior to the Qur'an.

People of Hadith: 'the adherents of Hadith', the movement who considered only the Qur'an and *hadīth* to be valid sources of *fiqh*.

People of Opinion (*ra'y*)**:** a term used to describe those who use personal opinion to deduce judgment. It was a term used particularly to describe the early Ḥanafīs.

Qābīl: Cain.

Qadariyyah: a sect who said that people have power (*qadar*) over their actions and hence free will.

qāḍī: a judge, qualified to judge all matters in accordance with the Sharī'ah and to dispense and enforce legal punishments.

qarḍ: a loan of money or something else.

qiblah: the direction faced in the prayer, which is towards the Ka'bah in Makkah.

qinṭār: plural *qanāṭīr*, a relatively large measure for food grains, approx. 45 kgs.

qirāṭ: plural *qarārīṭ*, a measure of weight with various meanings, either a twelfth of a dirham or a huge weight like that of Mount Uḥud.

Quraysh: one of the great tribes of Arabia. The Prophet Muḥammad ﷺ belonged to this tribe, which had great powers spiritually and financially both before and after Islam came. Someone from this tribe is called a Qurashī.

Qurayẓah: one of the Jewish tribes of Madīnah.

qurbah: an act by which one seeks to draw near to Allah.

Rabī'i-l-Awwal: the third month of the Muslim calendar.

Rabī'i-l-Ākhir: the fourth month of the Muslim calendar.

Rāfiḍites: the *Rawāfiḍ*, a group of the Shi'ah known for rejecting Abū Bakr and 'Umar as well as 'Uthmān. It is a nickname, meaning "deserters".

Rajab: the seventh month of the Muslim calendar.

rak'ah: a unit of the prayer consisting of a series of standings, bowing, prostrations and sittings.

Ramadan: the month of fasting, the ninth month in the Muslim lunar calendar.

Rāshidūn: 'Rightly Guided', the title given to the first four caliphs in Islam: Abū Bakr, 'Umar, 'Uthmān and 'Alī.

ra'y: opinion, personal discretion. (see also People of Opinion.)

Riddah: the defection of various Arab tribes after the death of the Prophet ﷺ which brought about the Riddah War.

Riḍwān: the Homage of Riḍwān was a pledge which the Muslims took at Ḥudaybīyah to avenge 'Uthmān when they thought that Quraysh had murdered him in 6/628.
rūḥ: (plural *arwāḥ*) the soul, vital spirit.
rukū': the bowing position in the prayer.
ṣā': a measure of volume equal to four *mudd*s.
Sabaeans: a group of believers. It is not entirely clear who they were. Possibly they were Gnostics or Mandaeans.
ṣadaqah: charitable giving in the Cause of Allah.
Ṣafā and Marwah: two hills close to the Ka'bah. Going between them is one of the rites of Hajj and 'Umra.
Ṣafar: the second month of the Muslim lunar calendar.
ṣaḥīḥ: healthy and sound with no defects, used to describe an authentic *hadīth.*
Ṣaḥīḥ: "the Sound", the title of the *hadīth* collections of al-Bukhārī and Muslim.
sā'ibah: in the Jāhiliyyah, a she-camel let loose to graze, usually as a result of a vow to idols.
sajdah: prostration.
Salaf: the early generations of the Muslims.
Ṣāliḥ: the Prophet sent to the people of Thamūd.
samḥāq: a wound which reaches the fine membrane between the flesh and the bone.
Sha'bān: the eighth month in the Muslim calendar.
shahādah: bearing witness, particularly bearing witness that there is no god but Allah and that Muhammad is the Messenger of Allah. It is one of the pillars of Islam. It is also used to describe legal testimony in a court of law.
shaqq: a grave with a narrower trench dug at the bottom in the centre for the deceased.
Sharī'ah: The legal modality of a people based on the revelation of their Prophet. The final Sharī'ah is that of Islam.
Shawwāl: the tenth month of the Muslim calendar.
Shayṭān: devil, particularly Iblīs, one of the jinn.
Aṣ-Ṣiḥāḥ: the famous dictionary *Tāj al-'Arūs wa-ṣ-Ṣiḥāh al-'Arabīyah*, by Ismā'īl ibn Ḥammād al-Jawharī.
shirk: the unforgivable wrong action of worshipping something or someone other than Allah or associating something or someone as a partner with Him.

Shu'ayb: the Prophet Jethro.
Sīrah: biography, particularly biography of the Prophet ﷺ.
siwāk: a small stick, usually from the arak tree, whose tip is softened and used for cleaning the teeth.
Ṣubḥ: the dawn prayer
sujūd: prostration.
sukūn: a diacritic mark that means that there is no sound after a consonant.
Sulaymān: the Prophet Solomon.
sunan: plural of sunnah.
Sunnah: the customary practice of a person or group of people. It has come to refer almost exclusively to the practice of the Messenger of Allah ﷺ.
sūrah: a chapter of the Qur'an.
Tābi'ūn: the second generation of the early Muslims who did not meet the Prophet Muhammad ﷺ but learned the *dīn* of Islam from his Companions.
Tabūk: a town in northern Arabia close to Jordan.
tafsīr: commentary or explanation of the meanings of the Qur'an.
Taghlib: an Arab tribe who were Christians.
Ṭā'if: a walled town south of Makkah known for its fertility. It was the home of the tribe of Thaqīf.
takbīr: saying '*Allāhu Akbar* – Allah is greater'.
talbīyah: saying '*Labbayk* – At Your service' during the *ḥajj*.
Tamīm: one of the largest of the Arab tribes, located in Najd.
tanwīn: nunnation.
taqiyyah: concealment of one's views to escape persecution.
taqwā: awe or fear of Allah, which inspires a person to be on guard against wrong action and eager for actions which please Him.
tarjī': making the voice quaver.
tathwīb: a repetition, the expression 'Prayer is better than sleep' pronounced twice in the *adhan* for Fajr.
ṭawāf: circumambulation of the Ka'bah, done in sets of seven circuits.
tawḥīd: the doctrine of Divine Unity.
tayammum: purification for the prayer with clean dust, earth, or stone, when water for *ghusl* or *wuḍū'* is unavailable or would be detrimental to health.
Thawr: a mountain near Makkah where the cave of Ḥirā' is located.
Uḥud: a mountain just outside of Madīnah where five years after the Hijrah, the Muslims lost a battle against the Makkan idolaters. Many great Companions, and in particular Ḥamzah, the uncle of the Prophet ﷺ, were killed in this battle.

Umm al-Kitāb: literally 'Mother of the Book'. It has a number of meanings, one of which is the celestial prototype of the Qur'an. It is also used for the Fātiḥah.
Umm al-Mu'minīn: literally 'Mother of the Believers', an honorary title given to the wives of the Prophet ﷺ.
Umm al-Qur'ān: literally 'the Mother of the Qur'an', the opening *sūrah* of the Qur'an, al-Fātiḥah.
Ummah: the body of Muslims as one distinct Community.
'umra: the lesser pilgrimage to the Ka'bah in Makkah performed at any time of the year.
ūqiyyah: unit of measurement equal to a 12th of a raṭl.
'Uzayr: Ezra.
walī: (plural *awliyā'*) someone who is a 'friend' of Allah, thus possessing the quality of *wilāyah.* Also a relative who acts as a guardian.
wasīlah: intermediary, the means by which something is approached or a goal obtained.
waṣīlah: in the *Jāhiliyyah*, a she-camel that has given birth to two females with no male in between them. It was set loose to graze.
wasq: a measure of volume equal to sixty *ṣā*'s.
wuḍū': ritual washing to be pure for the prayer.
Yaḥyā: the Prophet John the Baptist, the son of Zakariyyā.
Yamāmah, Battle of: also known as the Battle of 'Aqraba, the major battle of the Riddah War in which the Muslims defeated the forces of the false Prophet Musaylimah in 12/633.
Yahūdhā: Judah.
Ya'qūb: the Prophet Jacob, also called Isrā'īl (Israel).
Yūnus: the Prophet Jonah.
Yūsuf: the Prophet Joseph.
Zabūr: the Psalms of Dāwūd.
Ẓāhiriyya: a school of fiqh which derived its judgments from the literal text of the Qur'an and Sunnah, and rejected the use of other legal principles such as analogy.
Zakariyyā: the Prophet Zachariah, the father of Yaḥyā, John the Baptist, and guardian of Maryam.
zakat: a wealth tax, one of the five pillars of Islam.
Ẓuhr: the midday prayer.

www.ingramcontent.com/pod-product-compliance
Lightning Source LLC
Chambersburg PA
CBHW082026300426
44117CB00015B/2369
* 9 7 8 1 9 1 4 3 9 7 0 0 4 *